The Case Against the Global Economy

And for a Turn Towards Localization

Edited by

Edward Goldsmith and Jerry Mander

Earthscan London

First published in the UK in 2001 by
Earthscan Publications Ltd

A catalogue record for this book is available from the British Library

ISBN: 1 85383 742 3 paperback
       1 85383 741 5 hardback

Typesetting by JS Typesetting, Wellingborough, Northants
Printed and bound by Creative Print and Design (Wales), Ebbw Vale
Cover design by Yvonne Booth

For a full list of publications please contact:

Earthscan Publications Ltd
120 Pentonville Road
London, N1 9JN, UK
Tel: +44 (0)20 7278 0433
Fax: +44 (0)20 7278 1142
Email: earthinfo@earthscan.co.uk
http://www.earthscan.co.uk

Earthscan is an editorially independent subsidiary of Kogan Page Ltd and publishes in
association with WWF-UK and the International Institute for Environment and
Development

This book is printed on elemental chlorine-free paper

Contents

PART 3 STEPS TOWARDS RELOCALIZATION

Acknowledgements

We would like to thank Alexander Goldsmith and Simon Retallack for the important editing work that they have done; Rita Kasai and Rebecca Blech for their invaluable assistance in Richmond; and Akan Leander of Earthscan and Andrea Service, who copy-edited the book, for their skilful help in preparing the book for publication. We would also like to thank Barbara Ras of Sierra Club Books, without whom the original version of this book would not have been published.

Edward Goldsmith and Jerry Mander
April 2001

Acronyms and Abbreviations

ACEA	European Automobile Manufacturers' Association
ADB	Asian Development Bank
ADM	Archer Daniels Midland
AID	Agency for International Development (US)
AMS	aggregate measure of support
AOA	Agreement on Agriculture (WTO)
ATM	automated teller machine
BGH	bovine growth hormone
BP	British Petroleum
BSE	bovine spongiform encephalopathy
BTU	British thermal unit
CAFE	Corporate Average Fuel Economy (US)
CD	compact disc
CEO	chief executive officer
CES	Centre for Environment and Society (UK)
CFC	chlorofluorocarbon
CHIPS	New York Clearing House Interbank Payment System
CITES	Convention on International Trade in Endangered Species
CO_2	carbon dioxide
CSA	community-supported agriculture
CSI	Coalition of Service Industries (US)
CWS	Cooperative Wholesale Society (UK)
DDT	dichlorodiphenyltrichloroethane
DETR	Department of the Environment, Transport and the Regions (UK)
ECA	US export-credit agency
EEC	European Economic Community
EGAT	Thailand State Electricity Corporation
EPA	Environmental Protection Agency (US)
ERBD	European Bank for Reconstruction and Development
ESAF	extended structural adjustment facility
ESN	European Services Network
EU	European Union
Ex-Im	Export-Import Bank
FABBL	Farm Assured British Beef and Lamb

FABPIG	Farm Assured British Pigs
FAO	Food and Agriculture Organization (UN)
FDA	Food and Drug Administration (US)
FDI	foreign direct investment
FDIC	Federal Deposit Insurance Corporation (US)
FTZ	free-trade zone
FIFRA	Federal Insecticide, Fungicide and Rodenticide Act
FoE	Friends of the Earth
GAO	General Accounting Office (US Congress)
GAST	General Agreement for Sustainable Trade
GATS	General Agreement on Trade in Services
GATT	General Agreement on Tariffs and Trade
GDP	gross domestic product
GM	General Motors
GM	genetically modified
GMO	genetically modified organism
GNP	gross national product
GPI	genuine progress indicator
IAFS	Integrated Arable Farming System
ICM	Integrated crop management
IFCT	Thailand Industrial Finance Corporation
IFG	International Forum on Globalization
ILSR	Institute for Local Self-Reliance (US)
IMF	International Monetary Fund
IPCC	Intergovernmental Panel on Climate Change
IPR	intellectual property rights
IPS	Institute for Policy Studies
IRS	Internal Revenue Service (US)
LEAF	linking environment and farming
LETS	local exchange trading system
MAI	multilateral agreement on investment
MEA	multilateral environmental agreement
MJ	megajoule
MMPA	Marine Mammal Protection Act (US)
NAFTA	North American Free Trade Agreement
NESDB	Thailand National Economic and Social Development Board
NFU	National Farmers' Union (US)
NIC	newly industrialized country
NGA	National Gardeners' Association (US)
NGO	non-governmental organization
NLC	National Labour Committee (US)
ODA	Overseas Development Agency (UK)
OECD	Organization for Economic Cooperation and Development

OPEC	Organization of Petroleum Exporting Countries
OPIC	Overseas Private Investment Corporation
PC	personal computer
PCB	polychlorinated biphenyl
PER	public expenditure review
PPM	process and production method
PR	public relations
PYO	pick your own
R&D	research and development
rBGH	recombinant bovine growth hormone
RCRA	Resources Conservation and Recovery Act
RRS	'Roundup Ready' soybean
RTK	revenue ton-kilometre
S&L	savings and loans
SAL	structural adjustment loan
SAP	structural adjustment programme
SPS	sanitary and phytosanitary measures
TABD	Transatlantic Business Dialogue
TBAG	Times Beach Action Group (US)
TBT	technical barriers to trade
TED	turtle exclusion device
TNC	transnational corporation
TOES	the other economic summit
TRIP	Trade-Related Intellectual Property Right
UK	United Kingdom
UN	United Nations
UNDP	United Nations Development Programme
US	United States
USDA	US Department of Agriculture
USAID	United States Agency for International Development
VCR	video cassette recorder
WHO	World Health Organization
WI	Women's Institute (UK)
WLO	World Localization Organization
WTO	World Trade Organization

Introduction: Facing the Rising Tide

Jerry Mander

The first goal of this book is to help clarify the form of what is being called the *global economy* and to show how the rush toward globalization is likely to affect our lives. The second goal is to suggest that the process must be brought to a halt as soon as possible and reversed.

. . .

Economic globalization involves arguably the most fundamental redesign of the planet's political and economic arrangements since at least the Industrial Revolution. Yet despite the scale of the global reordering, neither our elected officials nor our educational institutions nor the mass media have made a credible effort to describe what is being formulated or to explain its root philosophies.

Descriptions and predictions about the global economy that *are* found in the media usually come from leading advocates and beneficiaries of this new order: corporate leaders, their allies in government and a newly powerful centralized global trade bureaucracy. The visions they have offered us are unfailingly positive, even utopian: globalization will be a panacea for our ills.

Shockingly enough, the euphoria they express is based on their freedom to deploy, at a global level – through global free trade rules and through the deregulating and restructuring regimes – large-scale versions of the economic theories, strategies and policies that have proven spectacularly unsuccessful over the past several decades wherever they've been applied. In fact, these are the very ideas that have brought us to the grim situation of the moment: the spreading disintegration of the social order and the increase of poverty, landlessness, homelessness, violence, alienation and, deep within the hearts of many people, extreme anxiety about the future. Equally important, these are the practices that have led us to the near breakdown of the natural world, as evidenced by such symptoms as global climate change, ozone depletion, massive species loss, and near maximum levels of air, soil and water pollution.

We have been asked to believe that the development processes that have further impoverished people and devastated the planet will lead to diametrically different and highly beneficial outcomes, if only they can be accelerated and applied everywhere, freely, without restriction – that is, when they are *globalized*.

That's the bad news. The good news is that it is not too late to change course.

THE 'RISING TIDE'

The passage in 1995 of the Uruguay Round of GATT (the General Agreement on Tariffs and Trade), with its associated WTO (World Trade Organization), was celebrated by the world's political leadership and transnational corporations (TNCs) as a sort of global messianic birth. They claimed that these new arrangements would bring on a global economic order that would produce a US$250 billion expansion of world economic activity in a very short time, with the benefits 'trickling down' to us all. The dominant political–economic homily has become 'the new rising tide will lift all boats'.

Indeed, the global economy is new, but less so in form than in scale: the new global rules by which it now operates; the technologically enhanced speedup of global development and commerce that it facilitates; and the abrupt shift in global political power that it introduces. Surely, it is also new that the world's democratic countries voted to suppress their own democratically enacted laws in order to conform to the rules of the new central global bureaucracy. Also new is the elimination of most regulatory control over global corporate activity and the liberation of currency from national controls, which lead, in turn, to what Richard Barnet and John Cavanagh describe as the *casino economy*, ruled by currency speculators. It also helped bring on the terrible 1998 global economic crisis.

But the deep ideological principles underlying the global economy are not so new. They are the very principles that have brought us to the social, economic and environmental impasse we are in. They include the primacy of economic growth; the need for free trade to stimulate the growth; the unrestricted 'free market'; the absence of government regulation; and voracious consumerism combined with an aggressive advocacy of a uniform worldwide development model that faithfully reflects the Western corporate vision and serves corporate interests. The principles also include the idea that all countries – even those whose cultures have been as diverse as, say, Indonesia, Japan, Kenya, Sweden and Brazil – must sign on to the same global economic model and row their (rising) boats in unison. The net result is *monoculture* – the global homogenization of culture, lifestyle and level of technological immersion, with the corresponding dismantling of local traditions and economies. Soon, every place will look and feel like every place else, with the same restaurants and hotels, the same clothes, the same malls and superstores and the same streets crowded with cars. There'll be scarcely a reason ever to leave home.

. . .

Many elements of this formula have been at work for a long while, with devastating effect, as several of the chapter authors report. And my coeditor, Edward Goldsmith, argues that all of these ideological principles amount to little more than rationalizations for a new kind of corporate colonialism, visited upon poor countries and the poor in rich countries.

But does this system work? Will the promised economic expansion actually happen? If so, can it sustain itself? Where will the resources – the energy, the wood, the minerals, the water – come from to feed the increased growth? Where will the effluents of the process – the solids and the toxics – be dumped? Who benefits from this? Who will benefit most? Will it be working people who, in the US at least, seem mainly to be losing jobs to machines and corporate flight? Will it be farmers who, thus far, whether in Asia, Africa or North America, are being manoeuvred off their lands to make way for huge corporate monocultural farming – no longer producing diverse food products for local consumption but coffee and beef for export markets with their declining prices? Will it be city dwellers, now faced with the immigrant waves of the newly landless peoples desperate to find, someplace, the rare and poorly paid job? And what of the ecological results? Can ever-increasing consumption be sustained forever? When will the forests be gone? How many cars can be built and bought? How many roads can cover the land? What will become of the animals and the birds. Does anyone care about that? Is this a better life? Is all the destruction worth the result? Are we – as individuals, as families and as communities and nations – made more secure, less anxious, more in control of our destinies? Can we possibly benefit from a system that destroys local and regional governments while handing real power to faceless corporate bureaucracies in Geneva, Tokyo and Brussels? Will people's needs be better served from this? Is it a good idea or a bad one? Do we want it? If not, how do we reverse the process?

The German economic philosopher Wolfgang Sachs argues in his book *The Development Dictionary* that the only thing worse than the failure of this massive global development experiment would be its success. For even at its optimum performance level, the long-term benefits go only to a tiny minority of people who sit at the hub of the process and to a slightly larger minority that can retain an economic connection to it, while the rest of humanity is left groping for fewer jobs and less land, living in violent societies on a ravaged planet. The only boats that will be lifted are those of the owners and managers of the process; the rest of us will be on the beach, facing the rising tide.

THE FAILURE OF THE MEDIA

The authors who contributed to this book comment on all the issues raised above: the impacts of globalism, the theories underlying it, and the 'engines' that drive it. They also explore alternatives. But it's worth mentioning first of all that it's a failure of our media that a book such as this is even necessary. Our society has been methodically launched onto a path to we know not where, and the people who are supposed to shed light on events that affect us have neglected to do so.

From time to time, the mass media do report on some major problem of globalization, but the reporting rarely conveys the connections between the specific crises they describe and the root causes in globalization itself. In the area of environment, for example, we read of changes in global climate and occasionally of their long-term consequences, such as the melting polar ice caps (the *real* rising tide), the expected staggering impacts on agriculture and food supply or the destruction of habitat. We read, too, of the ozone layer depletion, the pollution of the oceans or the wars over resources such as oil and, perhaps soon, water. But few of these matters are linked directly to the imperatives of global economic expansion, the increase of global transport, the overuse of raw materials or the commodity-intensive lifestyle that corporations are selling worldwide via the culturally homogenizing technology of television and its parent: advertising. Obfuscation is the net result.

I personally have had some harsh direct experience of this obfuscation. While working with Public Media Center in the runup to the vote on GATT and the WTO, my colleagues and I were preparing educational ads about the environmental consequences of this vote, particularly its 'sabotaging' effect on existing major environmental laws. We collaborated on the project with 25 environmental groups who signed the ad, among them the Sierra Club, Public Citizen, Friends of the Earth (FoE) and Rainforest Action Network. The groups felt the campaign was important precisely because the media had carried so few stories about environmental opposition to globalization. Instead, news stories tended to lump all opponents together under the single dismissive label of *protectionist*.

One week after our first ad finally appeared in the *New York Times*, a report in *Newsweek* magazine advised its readers that the advertisement was not really from the environmental community at all; it was secretly funded by labour union 'protectionists'. In outrage, Public Media Centre's executive director, Herb Chao Gunther, immediately responded to *Newsweek* and finally got the magazine to run a small corrective notice. But the damage was done. A good opportunity to broaden the public's thinking about economic globalization was undermined. In this book we attempt to counter this appalling failure of the media to cover the environmental consequences of globalization. We offer two articles by Simon Retallack on these themes, and further details from Lori Wallach, Alexander Goldsmith and Vandana Shiva.

Other examples of serious media misunderstanding include the coverage of the Barings Bank debacle of 1995, the Mexican financial crises of 1994–95 or the global financial crisis of 1998. Rarely has any medium made clear the role that the new global computer networks play in creating the capability for *instantaneous* transfer anywhere on the planet of astounding amounts of money.

Nor do the media describe the consequences of deregulating financial speculation or the role that the World Bank and the International Monetary Fund (IMF) play in creating the conditions that encouraged such speculation. For example, the Mexican story was carried in the US press as if the US' 'bailout of Mexico' was some kind of do-gooder act on the part of the US; good neighbours coming to the aid of our Mexican friends. In fact, the main people bailed out were Wall Street investors who, with the direct complicity of the World Bank and the IMF, largely brought on the crises in the first place. For middle-class and working-class Mexicans, the bailout was devastating, and that story has yet to be told by the mass media.

Most media continue to characterize *all* opposition to free trade as being virtually in the same category as those who still believe in a flat earth. And just as the tens of thousands of environmentalists who oppose GATT and the WTO are dismissed as 'protectionists', to be ignored, the press has also ignored the important fact that opposition to globalization cuts across all parties, including human rights advocates, small farmers, small businesspeople, groups concerned with immigrant rights or indigenous rights, advocates of democracy, as well as labour and many other categories of people who believe in an equitable, environmentally sustainable society.

The media have also passively accepted the cynical statements of the heads of the WTO, the World Bank and the IMF that they are mainly in business to help the world's poor. A notable example of this came during April 2000, while protestors were attempting to shut down the meetings of the World Bank and IMF in Washington, DC. The institutions issued daily statements about how protestors were actually the *enemies* of the poor, which the major media of the world dutifully passed on to their readers. And yet, simultaneous to the Washington bank meetings, the world's less developed countries, the G-77 nations, were meeting in Havana and issued a unanimous statement in praise of the protestors and against the Bank and the IMF. The *International Herald Tribune* carried the opposing statements side by side on its front page, but no American papers carried the Havana statement at all, and few European publications did, leaving the distorted official view intact.

As for reporting on the concrete social and environmental impacts of the rules of the WTO, little has been done. (In this book, however, we present several detailed descriptions of the effects of the WTO rules, especially in chapters on the WTO by Lori Wallach and Agnes Bertrand.)

Some publications have stories about 'corporate greed' as expressed by the firing of thousands of workers while corporate profits soar and top executive salaries are being raised to unheard-of levels. Even these stories, however, rarely mention the crucial point that the new corporate restructuring is essential for assuring competitiveness within the context of the global economy, and that it is happening all over the world. Obfuscation yet again.

In the autumn of 1995, the international press carried reports on the paralysing strike by hundreds of thousands of French railway and other public service workers. Most reports described the workers as trying to protect their privileges, benefits and jobs against government cutbacks. True enough. But the stories left out that the cutbacks were mandated by the rules of Europe's Maastricht 'single currency' agreement, itself part of the corporatizing, homogenizing and globalizing of Europe's economic system to make it compatible and competitive globally.

The media also report daily about the immigration crises, about masses of people trying to cross borders in search of jobs, only to be greeted by xenophobia, violence and demagoguery in high places. But the role that international trade agreements play in making life impossible for people in their countries of origin is not mentioned in such reports. The North American Free Trade Agreement (NAFTA), for example, was a virtual knockout blow to the largely self-sufficient, small corn-farming economy of Mexico's indigenous peoples – as the Zapatista rebels pointed out only too convincingly in 1994 – making indigenous lands vulnerable to corporate buyouts and foreign competition from the US. Meanwhile, in India, Africa, South-East Asia and South America, similar World Bank development schemes over the past few decades have deliberately displaced whole populations of relatively well-off peoples, including small-scale self-sufficient farmers, to make way for giant dams and other megadevelopment schemes. The result of such 'development' is that millions of small farmers are turned into landless refugees seeking non-existent urban jobs.

Now and then we see media reports on food shortages, yet rarely is the connection drawn between hunger and the increased control of the world's food supply by a small number of giant (subsidized) corporations, notably Cargill, which effectively determines where food will grow, under what conditions it will grow and what ultimate price consumers will pay. The food, rather than being eaten by local people who grow it, is now typically shipped thousands of miles (at great environmental cost) to be eaten by the already well fed.

Horrible new disease outbreaks are very thoroughly reported with ghoulish relish in the Western press. The part that is omitted, however, is the connection between these outbreaks and the destruction of the rainforest and other habitats. As economic expansionism proceeds, previously uncontacted organisms hitch rides on new vectors for new territory.

We also read stories about the 'last indigenous tribes' in the Amazon, Borneo, Africa or the Philippines – stories that lament the inevitability that native people, even against their clearly articulated wishes, even against the resistance of arrows and spears, must be drawn into the Western economic model to benefit from our development plans. Insufficiently reported are the root causes of this: the demands of economic growth for more water or forest resources; the desperate need for new lands for beef cattle, coffee or timber plantations; the equally desperate need to convert previously self-sufficient people into consumer clones;

the belief in an almost God-given right to expand and colonize. This, too, is part of the globalization project, the homogenization of our conceptual frameworks, the monoculturalization of people and lands which Helena Norberg-Hodge so artfully describes in the case of Ladakh. The point is further amplified by Martin Kohr's eloquent recitation of the effects of economic globalization in the developing world and in the industrial world.

As for the role of technology, the powers-that-be continue to speak of each new generation of technological innovation in the same utopian terms they used to describe each preceding generation, going back to the private automobile, plastics and 'clean nuclear energy', each introduced as panaceas for society. Now we have global computer networks that are said to 'empower' communities and individuals, when the exact opposite is the case. The global computer–satellite linkup, besides offering a spectacular new tool for financial speculation, empowers the global corporation's ability to keep its thousand-armed global enterprise in constant touch, making instantaneous adjustments at the striking of a key. As we will see later, computer technology may actually be the most centralizing technology ever invented, at least in terms of economic and political power. This much is certain: the global corporations of today could not exist without the electronic computer web. This technology makes globalization possible by conferring a degree of control beyond anything ever seen before.

Meanwhile, new technologies such as biotechnology bring the development framework to entirely new terrain by enabling the enclosure and commercialization of the internal wilderness of the gene structure, the building blocks of life itself. The invention and patenting of new life forms, from cells to insects to animals to humans, will have profound effects on developing world agriculture, ecology and human rights, as Vandana Shiva describes in Chapter 18.

As for reportage about the corporate conglomerates and transnationals that have become the centres of global power, the determinants of political process and the unifiers of global consciousness, the media tend to treat corporate figures mainly as subjects of gossip, like glamorous movie stars, athletes or politicians. The media speaks respectfully of the new language of corporate consolidation – 'structural engineering', 'downsizing' and 'efficiency' – without attempting to present such activities within their wider economic, social and ecological context. Yet such terms are today euphemistic. *Efficiency* today really means replacing workers with machines; *competitiveness* means lowering wages to match low-wage foreign competitors; *flattening of the corporate structure* means eliminating middle managers' jobs and effectively spreading well-justified social anxiety from the inner cities to the heart of the suburbs.

The point is this: all of the subjects are treated by the media, government officials and corporations alike as if they were totally unrelated. This is not helpful to an insecure public that is trying to grasp what's happening and what might be done about it. The media do not help us to understand that each of these issues

– overcrowded cities, unusual new weather patterns, the growth of global poverty, the lowering of wages while stock prices soar, the elimination of local social services, the destruction of wilderness, even the disappearance of songbirds – is the product of the same global policies. They are all of one piece, a fabric of connections that are ecological, social and political in nature. They are reactions to the world's economic–political restructuring in the name of accelerated global development. This restructuring has been designed by economists and corporations and encouraged by subservient governments; soon it may be made mandatory by international bureaucrats, who are beyond democratic control. All claim that society will benefit from what they are doing. But we don't think so.

. . .

We are trained to believe that our economic system operates on a rational basis on our behalf and that the people in charge have benevolent motives and know what they are doing. I have doubted that for a while, and on this point the newspapers, inadvertently perhaps, do expose the conflicting realities that come at us like Orwellian econometric doublespeak.

One basic thing is certain. During the past few decades, the gap between rich and poor just about everywhere has been increasing rather than decreasing.

The United Nations *Human Development Report 1999* confirmed the growing inequality *between* countries and *within* countries and directly blamed economic globalization for the trend.

What is also increasing, however, is the power of the largest corporations and the wealthiest people. Such is the degree of concentration of wealth that right now the world's 475 billionaires are collectively worth the combined incomes of the bottom 50 per cent of humanity. And of the largest one hundred economies in the world, 52 are now corporations. Mitsubishi is the 22nd largest economy in the world, General Motors the 26th, Ford the 31st. Each is larger than the economies of Denmark, Thailand, Turkey, South Africa, Saudi Arabia, Norway, Finland, Malaysia, Chile and New Zealand, to name only a few.

Even in the US, which has benefited disproportionately from globalization, the same trends are apparent. A *New York Times* report on 17 April 1995 explained that the period of most rapid economic growth in the US (the 1960s to the 1990s), which also ushered in the period of rapid corporate and economic deregulation and the most aggressive promotion of 'free' trade, also saw a widening gap between rich and poor.

The *Times* quotes the Federal Reserve: 'Figures from 1989, the most recent available, show that the wealthiest 1 per cent of US households, with a net worth of at least US$2.3 million each, own nearly 40 per cent of the nation's wealth. Further down the scale, the top 20 per cent of American households, worth US$180,000 or more, have more than 80 per cent of the country's wealth, a higher figure than in other industrial nations. Income statistics are similarly skewed.'

If this is a rational process, it rationalizes a staggering inequality of benefit. To make matters worse, for most people, social services for the poor and the middle class have been assaulted as never before under the same ideological banner of 'free market' or 'free trade', which produced the skewed figures just mentioned. This dismantling of services within the US amounts to an internal *structural adjustment* comparable to the infamous IMF and World Bank structural adjustment programmes that have been imposed on developing world countries ever since the 1980s' debt crises and have produced horrifying social and ecological results. Walden Bello tells us more about those in Chapter 10. In addition, Alexander Goldsmith points out that the whole world is now being redesigned into a single 'free trade zone'. England is already advertising globally how its wage levels are decreasing in an effort to encourage foreign investors. The elimination of tariffs, minimum wage laws and local social services are all symptoms of the same scheme. The goal everywhere is the same: free all economic resources to serve the needs of corporations, not people or the environment.

FLAWED PARADIGMS

All of these problems must be seen as *systemic* since many of the principal paradigms by which this system explains its choices and its behaviour are fatally flawed. For example, it is clearly a preposterous idea that an economic system based on limitless growth can be supported on a finite Earth. A system that feeds on itself cannot keep eating forever.

As for free trade itself, David Morris shows how the only thing 'free' about it is the freedom it provides corporate players to deprive everyone else of their freedoms, including the freedom previously enjoyed by democratic nations to defend their domestic economies, their communities, their culture and their natural environment.

. . .

Economic philosopher and activist Susan George, together with Fabrizio Sabelli, have argued against the idea popular in some circles that a global conspiracy is at the root of the disastrous direction in which global economic policy is taking us in their recent book *Faith and Credit* (1994). At least insofar as the pathetic performance of global institutions such as the World Bank and the IMF is concerned, George and Sabelli put the blame more on incompetence, ideology and a virtually religious belief in the dogmas of Western development. Like religious zealots, as each new development project fails to achieve its highly advertised benefits and causes social and environmental chaos, the global economists simply move on to preparing the ground for yet another disaster, applying the same sad formulas. In their book, George and Sabelli catalogue the World Bank's predictions regarding the outcome of its policies against their real performance, one that has left poor people poorer and destroyed traditional, viable economic arrangements in the name of a fictional development utopia.

Of course, we are left to wonder how any bona fide economist, even if trained personally by Milton Friedman and even if blinded by economic zealotry, could believe that benefits would come from the World Bank's structural adjustment programme loans (SAPs). These loans are granted only to countries that agree to dismantle their economic and social structures and redesign them according to an imposed free market–free trade ideology.

Walden Bello reports in his chapter on SAPs about some of the conditions that countries typically have to accept:

1   the removal of protective tariffs, which directly endangers local industry;
2   the removal of rules controlling foreign investment, which ushers in the foreign domination of local industry;
3   the conversion of self-sufficient, small-scale diverse agriculture to corporate export-oriented monocultures, which make it more difficult for local populations to feed themselves;
4   the elimination of price controls together with the imposition of wage controls;
5   the drastic reduction in social health services;
6   the aggressive privatization of government agencies, which renders social services inaccessible to the poor; and
7   the ending of popular 'import substitution' programmes that encouraged local people to make themselves self-sufficient in food and other essential products.

Ordinary logic suggests that such formulas would only cripple a country's ability to survive, and indeed that has been the result. Many countries who accepted these interventions and who have now also accepted entry into the WTO (which has similar rules) have seen their own economies crumble and have watched as foreign transnational corporations take control over both their economies and their governments.

Why did these countries accept? In many cases, it was less a matter of faith than of force.

The roots of the trend go back to the infamous Bretton Woods conference after World War II, as David Korten points out in Chapter 2. But a more recent key moment came in 1968, when Robert McNamara became president of the World Bank. Flush from his horrendous performance in running the Vietnam War and (according to his apologetic book *In Retrospect: The Tragedy and Lessons of Vietnam*, 1995) apparently not feeling so good about himself, McNamara decided he could save his soul by saving the poor via the World Bank. He approached this task with the economist-manager's quantified viewpoint – which ignores what people really require in order to be 'saved' – and with the true believer's arrogance. 'To this day,' he wrote in his book, 'I see quantification as a language to add precision to reasoning about the world. I have always believed that the more important the issue the fewer people should be involved in the decision.' Confident of his numbers, McNamara pressed developing world countries to accept World Bank conditionalities for loans and to transform their traditional economies to maximize economic specialization and global trade. Countries that did not sign on to the globalization programme would simply be left behind.

McNamara pushed hard, and most countries felt they had little choice but to sign on. No longer 'destroying villages to save them', McNamara was destroying whole economies. Today, the countries that went along with him are saddled with silted-up megadams, useless crumbling roads to nowhere, empty high-rise office buildings, ravaged forests and fields, and the overwhelming, unpayable debt to Western bankers that makes up much of the legacy of World Bank policy from McNamara to now. Whatever destruction this man caused in Vietnam, he did more during his tenure at the World Bank. Perhaps soon we will see him apologize for that role, as well.

MECHANISMS OF SELF-DELUSION

In a London *Times* article (5 March 1994), the late James Goldsmith was quoted as saying, 'What an astounding thing it is to watch a civilization destroy itself because it is unable to re-examine the validity, under totally new circumstances, of an economic ideology'. Perhaps it is simply that economists, like other true believers, cannot see outside the framework of their own thinking. This much, at least, is definite: economists have devised the perfect measurements for gauging their own success and confirming their self-delusions.

Most important among these self-serving illusory measurements are the primary tools now used to judge economic progress: the gross national product (GNP) or gross domestic product (GDP). These measure total economic activity – that is, every monetary transaction within a nation state. By this standard, more economic activity means a healthier economy.

Negative events such as, say, the depletion of natural resources, the construction of more prisons and the manufacture of bombs are all measures of 'health' by current economic theories. Meanwhile, other incomparably more desirable activities, such as unpaid household work, child care, community service, or the production of food to be eaten and artifacts to be used rather than sold via the formal economy are, absurdly, not registered in the statistics at all. They are simply not regarded as indicators of economic health.

To illustrate the point, Edward Goldsmith likes to tell the apocryphal story of two friends who each inherit 10,000-acre tracts of adjoining forestland. Friend number one decides to do nothing with the forest, leaving it in its pristine state. Friend number two sells the trees to McMillan Bloedel Corporation, which cuts them down. He then sells the topsoil and the subsurface mining rights for minerals and coal. When that activity is exhausted, he permits the holes to be filled in with low-level toxic waste from a computer chip manufacturer and paves over the place. After that he constructs an industrial complex with a megamall and theme park, multiplex theatres, indoor swimming pools and wave machines.

Friend number one is considered odd by the community for permitting such an economic opportunity to go to waste on behalf of trees and birds. He is called idealistic and impractical.

Friend number two is considered a pillar of the community for developing the land, employing people and adding to the GNP. Exceedingly wealthy by now, he puts millions into high-tech equipment manufacture on the Mexican border and runs for public office. His slogan: 'The rising tide will lift all boats.'

The moral of the tale is clear: in the dominant view, GNP is all that matters. Development is the way. People who act to save nature are mistrusted and marginalized. Such behaviour is not beneficial by current economic standards.

American economists Ted Halstead and Clifford Cobb propose an answer for this. They have devised a new set of measurements called the genuine progress indicator (GPI), which pulls in all the social and environmental dimensions of economic activity that are left out of GNP measurements and gives real value to previously unvalued activity that benefits households, community and the natural world.

. . .

Economic globalization, of course, brings benefit to certain institutions. Tony Clarke identifies them in Chapter 5. The unprecedented scale of global corporations and the degree to which they can now consolidate their economic power is instantly apparent in Clarke's opening sentences. He writes that, '70 per cent of global trade is controlled by just 500 corporations; and a mere 1 per cent of the TNCs on this planet own half the stock of foreign direct investment'. What is more, the new trade agreements can only greatly accelerate corporate concentration and increase corporate power in relation to nation-states. Indeed, that is one of 'free' trade's main purposes.

Among the factors that make this concentration possible are the new technologies of communication: satellite television and global computer capability. The computer–satellite linkup has effectively become the global corporation's nervous system, enabling the diasporous corporate paths to work in synch. Meanwhile, the globalization of television and advertising enables corporations to expand their ideological reach and deliver idealized images of happy Western commodity-intensive lifestyles even to places where, until recently, there may not have been roads. Richard Barnet and John Cavanagh offer two chapters on these themes (Chapters 4 and 15), honing in on the homogenization of global culture and the globalization of money.

We also offer two concrete examples of corporate behaviour: one by Brian Tokar about Monsanto (Chapter 7), and one by Andrew Rowell about the 'global retailer' WalMart, which is bringing panic to local downtowns and small businesses everywhere (Chapter 8).

THE EBBING TIDE: RELOCALIZATION

The last part of this book addresses what is invariably the most difficult question regarding these issues: 'If we don't do things this way, what do we do?' The answer may be quite simple. Since the direction in which we're heading is sure to fail, we must stop in our tracks and then change direction. If your car is headed for the cliff, first you stop it and back up, then you look at the next road map to follow.

It is critically important to recognize that the course we are on is not something that 'we' as citizens have actually chosen. The democratic process was openly circumvented to create the instruments of globalization. In this anti-democratic rush, the Western 'democracies' behaved no better than anyone else; in fact, we were far worse. Since it was our scheme to begin with, we used our economic and military stature to intimidate smaller, more resistant countries into acceptance. The movement toward economic globalization is no expression of democracy, nor is it the inevitable 'evolutionary' process that its advocates claim it is, like a force of nature. It is simply a scheme people thought up, an economic experiment designed to favour the institutions that promote it. It's been sold to businesses as an answer to the growing problems of the corporate and political elite. But it's the wrong answer, and it's not in the people's or the planet's interest to continue. Although it is still difficult for most people in industrial countries to accept, a better answer than economic globalization is a shift in the direction of revitalized, local, diversified and at least partially self-sufficient smaller economies.

It's also relevant to remember that not too long ago, most of the world was not on the globalization path, nor did it want to be. At this moment, in fact, most people in the world still maintain relatively traditional economies, many are not 'poor', and a high percentage of those who *are* poor have been made so by the very policies of free trade that are decried in these pages.

Many of the non-industrial countries have never really bought the idea that destroying their local economies would somehow improve their lives. In this vein, I am reminded of some comments I heard from Martin Khor, president of Third World Network, speaking at a PREPCOM Conference in New York before the 1992 United Nations Conference on Environment and Development in Rio.

Khor was asked how he could so strongly argue against the big trade agreements. Was he not worried that without an expanded production and consumption base, developing world peoples would be deprived of Western standards of living? His answer, which I am paraphrasing, was something like this:

> *'I think you have it backward. Those who most depend on an expanding economy are not Malaysians nor other Third Worlders, but you in the First World. In your world, you no longer have contact with the land, and you don't know how to get along without luxuries. For us, if the whole global trade system collapsed, we might be better off. We have never lost touch with the land: we know how to grow food for our communities, how to make our own clothes, how to develop the fairly simple technologies we need. This is how most of us lived until recently. We wouldn't mind having some of the new technologies you offer, and some kinds of trade are very useful, but if the Western colonial powers and transnational corporations would simply leave us alone, stop exploiting our resources and our land so we could again retain their use, we could probably survive quite well. But what would you do?'*

In any case, there will ultimately not be much choice. The globalized economy cannot be made to work for the general benefit. It cannot be sustained. No one can really argue that its fundamental bases – exponential economic growth, economies built for the export trade rather than for satisfying local needs, the continued emphasis on commodity accumulation – can be sustained beyond a very short time.

But how do we turn in another direction? In the end, of course, this is the task of the hundreds of activist organizations – environmentalists, human rights groups, workers' unions, small businesses, consumer groups, small farmers and the new economic thinkers, some of whom are featured in this book. We cannot articulate, on their behalf, the campaigns and ideas that they are and will be generating. We are instead going to advance some ideas about the viability of smaller-scale, localized, diversified economies hooked into but not dominated by outside forces. Helena Norberg-Hodge leads off this discussion by offering an interesting and extensive list of concrete ideas and proposals for a transitional period away from global economic structures.

Meanwhile, Colin Hines and Tim Lang go head-on against the globalizers' argument that to favour localization is a kind of 'protectionism', which is a term that's been given a very pejorative cast in the age of free trade (Chapter 25). Hines and Lang argue for a *new* protectionism that proclaims the intrinsic right of citizens of all communities and nations to work toward local solutions, local development and the protection of local resources, workers and nature. Global trade should be an economic option primarily when local conditions inadequately satisfy local needs; that is the far more socially and ecologically sustainable approach.

Philosopher and farmer Wendell Berry identifies a unique political opportunity of this moment, a natural and clear division between those who favour globalization with its accompanying social, economic and political arrangements and those who work to promote and protect community and place (Chapter 22).

And Perry Walker and Edward Goldsmith report on the extraordinary emergence of new local currencies that enable people to separate themselves more easily from the larger economic grid (Chapter 23). This may prove a useful means of surviving if, in the future, the global economy takes the nosedive that some expect.

The chapters in the last part of this book may not yet provide a clear road map from here to there, but what is certainly clear, as Edward Goldsmith writes in the final chapter, is that the shift in a more local direction is mandatory. It is the only strategy that makes sustainability possible. The present path we are on is, in fact, impossible; it can only lead to disaster. Despite this, to speak of changing directions is for many people little more than utopian. But it seems clear to me, and to my coeditor in this project, that the charge of utopianism is unjustified. What is truly utopian, and perhaps obsessive, is to insist that the totally aberrant global economy that we are creating today, an economy that defies natural limits and ignores economic and social equity, can possibly survive for long.

Part 1

Engines of Globalization

Chapter 1

Development as Colonialism

Edward Goldsmith

The massive effort to industrialize the developing world in the years since World War II was not motivated by purely philanthropic considerations, but by the need to bring the developing world into the orbit of the Western trading system in order to create an ever-expanding market for the West's goods and services and to gain a source of cheap labour and raw materials for its industries. This was also the goal of colonialism, especially during its last phase which started in the 1870s. For that reason, there is a striking continuity between the colonial era and the era of development, both in the methods used to achieve their common goal and in the social and ecological consequences of applying them. With the development of the global economy, we are entering a new era of corporate colonialism that could be more ruthless than the colonialism that preceded it.

Edward Goldsmith is the founder of The Ecologist *magazine (founded in 1969) and is author and coauthor of a number of books including* A Blueprint for Survival *(with Robert Allen, Tom Stacy Ltd, 1972),* A Stable Society *(Wadebridge Ecological Centre, 1978),* The Social and Environmental Effects of Large Dams *(with Nicholas Hildyard, Sierra Club Books, 1985) and* The Way: An Ecological Worldview *(Rider Books, 1992). He has taught courses at Michigan University at Ann Arbor and at what is now the University of Illinois at Springfields. He received the Honorary Right Livelihood Award in Stockholm in 1984 and is a member of the board of the International Forum on Globalization.*

It is customary to trace the origin of the idea of development to a statement made by US President Harry Truman in 1949, who, in his inauguration speech before Congress, drew the attention of his audience to conditions in poorer countries and defined them for the first time as 'underdeveloped areas'. Truman may have formulated the idea of development in a new way, but it is an old idea, and the path along which it is leading the countries of the developing world is a well-trodden one.

As François Partant, the French banker-turned-archcritic of development, has put it:

> *'The developed nations have discovered for themselves a new mission*
> *– to help the Third World advance along the road to development . . .*
> *which is nothing more than the road on which the West has guided*
> *the rest of humanity for several centuries.'* (Partant, 1982)

The thesis of this article is that Partant was right. *Development* is just a new word for what Marxists call *imperialism* and what we can loosely refer to as *colonialism* – a more familiar and less loaded term.

A quick look at the situation in the developing world today undoubtedly reveals the disquieting continuity between the colonial era and the era of development. There has been no attempt by the governments of the newly independent countries to re-draw their frontiers. No attempt has been made to restore precolonial cultural patterns. With regards to the key issues of land use, the colonial pattern has also been maintained. As Randall Baker notes, 'Essentially the story is one of continuity' (Baker, 1984), while the peasants, who as Erich Jacoby writes, 'identified the struggle for national independence with the fight for land' never recovered their land. 'National independence simply led to its take-over by a new brand of colonialists' (Jacoby, 1961).

SAME GOALS

If development and colonialism (at least, in its last phase from the 1870s onwards) are the same process under a different name, it is largely that they share the same goal. This goal was explicitly stated by its main promoters. For instance, Cecil Rhodes – Britain's most famous promoter of colonialism in the 1890s – declared that:

> *'We must find new lands from which we can easily obtain raw materials*
> *and at the same time exploit the cheap slave labour that is available*
> *from the natives of the colonies. The colonies would also provide a*
> *dumping ground for the surplus goods produced in our factories.'*

Similar sentiments were expressed openly during the late 1800s by Lord Lugard, the English governor of Nigeria, and by former French president Jules Ferry.

But many countries in Asia and elsewhere were simply not willing to allow Western powers access to their markets or to the cheap labour and raw materials required. Nor were they willing to allow corporations to operate on their territory and undertake large-scale development projects such as road building and mining.

In Asia a small number of states were eventually bullied into complying with Western demands. Thus, in 1855, Siam signed a treaty with Britain, as did Annam with France in 1862. However, China was not interested, and two wars had to be fought before it could be persuaded to open its ports to British and French trade. Japan also refused, and only the threat of an American naval bombardment persuaded its government to open its ports to Western trade.

By 1880, European powers had obtained access to the markets of most of Asia's coastal regions, having negotiated special conditions for expatriate residents, such as greater freedom of activity within the countries concerned and the right to build railways and set up enterprises inland.

However, just as is the case today, commercial interests continued to demand and often obtained ever more comprehensive concessions, creating ever more favourable conditions for European corporations. Eventually, in China, Western commercial activities, as Harry Magdoff notes, largely 'escaped China's laws and tax collections. Foreign settlements had their own police forces and tax systems, and ran their own affairs independently of nominally sovereign China' – a situation reminiscent of what goes on today in the developing world's free trade zones.

> *'At the same time, the opium trade which had been forced on the Chinese government militarily was legalized, customs duties reduced, foreign gunboats patrolled China's rivers and foreigners were placed on customs-collection staffs to ensure that China would pay the indemnities imposed by various treaties.'* (Magdoff, 1978)

In Egypt, Britain and France managed to obtain even more favourable conditions for their commercial enterprises by imposing the famous 'capitulations' on the Ottoman sultan which provided all sorts of concessions to foreigners operating within his empire. In Egypt, they could import goods at the price they saw fit, they were largely exempt from taxes and constituted a powerful pressure group well capable of defending its commercial interests and of ensuring that the interest on the Egyptian bonds of which they were the principal holders was regularly paid. Throughout the non-industrial world, it was only if such conditions could no longer be enforced, usually when a new nationalist or populist government came to power, that formal annexation was resorted to. As D K Fieldhouse puts it, 'colonialism was not a preference but a last resort' (Fieldhouse, 1984).

D C Platt, another contemporary student of 19th century colonialism, adds that colonialism was necessary 'to establish a legal framework in which capitalist relations could operate'. If no new colonies were created in Latin America in the late 19th century, it is largely because a legal system 'which was sufficiently stable for trade to continue was already in existence'. This was not so in Africa, where the only way to create the requisite conditions was by establishing colonial control (Platt, 1976).

Slowly, as traditional society disintegrated under the impact of colonialism and the spread of Western values, and as the subsistence economy was replaced by the market economy on which the exploding urban population grew increasingly dependent, the task of maintaining the optimum conditions for Western trade and penetration became correspondingly easier. As a result, says Fieldhouse, by the mid-20th century:

> *'European merchants and investors could operate satisfactorily within the political framework provided by most reconstructed indigenous states as their predecessors would have preferred to operate a century earlier but without facing those problems which had once made formal empire a necessary expedient.'* (Fieldhouse, 1984)

In other words, formal colonialism came to an end not because the colonial powers had decided to forgo the economic advantages it provided, but because, in the new conditions, these could now largely be obtained by more politically acceptable and more effective methods.

THE 'LEVEL' PLAYING FIELD

This was probably clear to the foreign policy professionals and heads of large corporations that began meeting in Washington, DC, in 1939, under the aegis of the US Council on Foreign Relations, to discuss how the postwar, post-colonialist world economy could best be shaped in order to satisfy US commercial interests.

In 1941, the council formulated the concept of 'the Grand Area' – that area of the world that the US would have 'to dominate economically and militarily' to achieve its purposes, and which would have to include most of the Western hemisphere, what remained of the British Empire, the Dutch East Indies, China and Japan – and which could be expanded as circumstances allowed.

The US Department of State was also thinking along these lines and created its own Advisory Committee on Post War Foreign Policy. Like the council, with which it was in close contact, it was committed to the idea of creating a vast economic empire that would provide US corporations with the export markets they required and the necessary sources of cheap raw materials. Economic development was the means for achieving this goal and it was by promoting free trade that this could be maximized.

Free trade is said to involve competition on 'a level playing field', and nothing could seem fairer. However, when the strong confront the weak on a level playing field, the result is a foregone conclusion, as it was at the Bretton Woods conference in 1944 when the Allies set up the World Bank and the IMF. (The GATT was set up four years later.) At the time of that conference, in the twilight of World

War II, the US totally dominated the world politico-economic scene; the European industrial powers had been ruined by the war, their economies lying in tatters, and Japan had been conquered and humiliated.

We must not forget that a century earlier, it was Britain that was preaching free trade to the rest of the world, and for the same reasons. At that time, Britain effectively dominated the world economy. Not only was a quarter of the world's terrestrial surface under Britain's direct imperial control, and not only did its navy control the seas, but the City of London was the world's financial centre and was capable of financing the industrial expansion that free trade would make possible. Besides, according to Hobsbawm (1986), Britain already produced about two-thirds of the world's coal, perhaps about half its iron, five-sevenths of its steel, half of its factory-produced cotton cloth, 40 per cent (in value) of its hardware and a little less than one-third of its manufactures. Labour in Britain was also cheap and plentiful, for the population had more than trebled since the beginning of the industrial revolution and had accumulated in the cities, while there was little social regulation to protect the rights of the workers.

In such conditions, Britain was incomparably more 'competitive' than its rivals and free trade was clearly the right vehicle for achieving its commercial goals. As George Lichtheim, another well-known student of imperialism, puts it:

> *'A country whose industries could undersell those of its competitors was favourably placed to preach the universal adoption of free trade, and so it did – to the detriment of those among its rivals who lacked the wit or the power to set up protective barriers behind which they could themselves industrialize at a pace that suited them.'*
> (Lichtheim, 1971)

As a result, between 1860 and 1873, Britain succeeded in creating something not too far removed from what Hobsbawm refers to as 'an all embracing world system of virtually unrestricted flows of capital, labour and goods', though clearly on nothing like the scale that this is being achieved today after the signature of the GATT Uruguay Round Agreement. Only the US remained systematically protectionist, though it reduced its duties in 1832 to 1860 and again between 1861 and 1865 after the Civil War.

By the 1870s, Britain had lost its competitive edge over its rivals. Partly as a result, British exports declined considerably between 1873 and 1890, and again towards the end of the century. At the same time, between the 1870s and 1890s, there were prolonged economic depressions, which also weakened the belief in free trade. Tariffs were raised in most European countries, especially in the 1890s, though not in Belgium, The Netherlands or Britain. Companies now found their existing markets reduced by these factors and started looking abroad towards the markets of Africa, Asia, Latin America and the Pacific, which, with the development of faster and more spacious steamships, had become much more accessible. As Fieldhouse notes, if free trade did not work, the answer was to take over those countries where goods could be sold at a profit without having to worry about competition from more efficient European countries (Fieldhouse, 1984). There followed a veritable scramble for colonies. In 1878, 67 per cent of the world's terrestrial area had been colonized by Europeans. By 1914, the figure had risen to 84.4 per cent.

SETTING UP INDIGENOUS ELITES

The most effective means of colonizing developing world countries is undoubtedly to set up a Westernized elite hooked on economic development, a process which this elite is willing to promote regardless of its adverse effects on the vast majority of its fellow citizens. This has now been very effectively achieved, and, as a result, the interests of developing world governments today, as Francois Partant says, are 'largely antagonistic to those of the bulk of their countrymen'. The developing world elites are, in fact, the West's representatives in the countries they dominate, probably to the same extent as were the colonial administrators that they have supplanted.

The need to create such elites was, of course, well known to the Western powers during the colonial era. During the debate in British political circles after the 1857 Indian Mutiny, the main question at issue was whether an anglicized elite favourable to British commercial interests could be created in time to prevent further uprisings. If not, it was generally conceded, formal occupation would have to be maintained indefinitely (Danaher et al, 1988).

Of course, the elite must be suitably armed if it is to impose economic development on the population, since it must necessarily lead to the expropriation and impoverishment of a very large number of people. Today, this is one of the main objects of our so-called aid programmes, some two-thirds of US aid taking the form of 'security assistance'. This includes military training, arms and cash transfers to governments that are regarded as defending US interests.

Even food aid provided by the US is security related. US politicians have openly stated that food is a political weapon, Vice President Hubert Humphrey once declaring:

> 'If you are looking for a way to get people to lean on you and to be dependent on you, in terms of their cooperating with you, it seems to me that food-dependence would be terrific.'

Most of the governments that have received security aid are military dictatorships such as those in Nicaragua, Chile, Argentina, Uruguay and Peru in the 1960s and 1970s. These faced no external threats. It was not to defend themselves against a potential foreign invader that all this security aid was required, but to impose economic development on people who had already become impoverished by it and whom it could only still further impoverish.

Engineering Coups d'État

Of course, when a government unfavourable to Western commercial interests somehow succeeds in coming to power, Western governments will go to any ends to remove it from office. Thus in 1954, the US organized the military overthrow of the government of Guatemala that had nationalized US-owned banana plantations, and it did the same to the government of Jose Goulart in Brazil in the 1960s. Goulart had sought to impose a limit to the amount of money foreign corporations could take out of the country. Worse still, he initiated a land reform programme which, among other things, meant taking back control of the country's mineral resources from Western transnational corporations. He also gave workers a pay rise, thereby increasing the cost of labour to the transnationals, in defiance of IMF instructions.

During the colonial era, the colonial powers constantly sent in troops to protect compliant regimes against popular revolts. Both France and Britain, for instance, participated in the suppression of the populist Tai Ping Rebellion in China and later the xenophobic Boxer Rebellion. Britain also sent troops to help the Khedive Ismail put down a nationalist revolt in Egypt.

The Western powers still do not hesitate to do this if there is no other way of achieving their goals. Thus, when President M'ba, the dictator of Gabon, was threatened by a military coup in 1964, French paratroopers immediately flew in to restore him to power, while the coup leaders were imprisoned in spite of widespread popular demonstrations. Significantly, the paratroopers remained to protect M'ba's successor, President Bongo, whom Pierre Pean regards as 'the choice of a powerful group of Frenchmen whose influence in Gabon continued after independence', against any further threats to him and hence to French commercial interests. Neither the UK nor the US has been any less scrupulous in this respect (Colchester, 1993).

Killing the Domestic Economy

If the role of the colonies was to provide a market for the produce of the colonial countries and a source of cheap labour and raw materials for their industries, then it could not at the same time provide a market for local produce and a source of labour and raw materials for its own productive enterprises.

In effect, the colonial powers were committed to destroying the domestic economy of the countries whom they had colonized. This was explicitly noted by a delegate to the French Association of Industry and Agriculture in March 1899. For him, the aim of the colonial power must be:

> *'To discourage in advance any signs of industrial development in our colonies, to oblige our overseas possessions to look exclusively to the mother country for manufactured products and to fulfil, by force if necessary, their natural function, that of a market reserved by right to the mother country's industry.'* (quoted in Dumont, 1988)

The favourite method was to tax whatever the colonials particularly liked to consume. In Vietnam, it was salt, opium and alcohol, and a minimum level of consumption was set for each region, village leaders being rewarded for exceeding the quota. In the Sudan, it was crops, animals, houses and households that were singled out for taxation. Of course, there is no way in which local people could meet their tax obligations save by agreeing to work in the mines and plantations or growing cash crops for sale to their colonial masters.

At the same time, every effort was made to destroy indigenous crafts, particularly in the production of textiles. In this way, the British destroyed the textile industry in India, which had been the very lifeblood of the village economy throughout the country. In French West Africa in 1905, special levies were imposed on all goods which did not come from France or a region under French control; this forced up the price of local products and ruined local artisans and traders.

Economic development after World War II, on the other hand, was theoretically supposed to help the ex-colonial countries build up their own domestic economies, but such development, by its very nature, could not occur. At the very start, the colonies were forced to reorientate their production towards exports – what is more, towards an exceedingly small range of exports.

A typical example is sugar. Under World Bank influence, vast areas of the developing world were converted to sugarcane cultivation for export, without any consideration for whether a market for sugar existed abroad. In fact, the US has continued to apply very strict quotas on sugar imports while continuing to countenance the production of corn syrup and the increasing use of artificial sweeteners, while the European Union (EU) has persisted in subsidizing sugar beet production among its member states. However, none of these considerations has prevented the World Bank from encouraging the production of ever more sugar for export. Cynics might maintain that this was the object of the operation in the first place since, after all, it was implicitly at least part of the World Bank's original brief to encourage the production of cheap resources for the Western market.

At the same time, developing world countries who have sought to diversify their production have immediately been accused of practising 'import substitution' – a heinous crime in the eyes of today's economists, in particular those who are influential within the Bretton Woods institutions. Indeed, import substitution is precisely what developing world countries must promise not to undertake if they hope to obtain a structural adjustment loan. Not surprisingly, as Walden Bello and Shea Cunningham note in their book *Dark Victory*, when a country is subjected to such a programme, its exports clearly tend to rise, but not necessarily its GNP, because of the inevitable contraction of its domestic economy (Bello et al, 1994).

When developing world countries have nevertheless succeeded in creating a modest domestic economy, the World Bank and IMF, in league with US government officials and transnational corporations, have set out systematically to destroy it, a process that could not be better documented, in the case of the Philippines, than by Walden Bello, David Kinley and Elaine Elinson in their book *Development Debacle: The World Bank in the Philippines* (1990). The book, based on 800 leaked World Bank documents, shows how that institution, in league with the CIA and other US agencies, set out purposefully to destroy the domestic economy of the Philippines so as to create those conditions that best favoured TNC interests. Achieving this goal first meant sacrificing the peasantry and transforming it into a rural proletariat. The standard of living of the working class had to be reduced, since, as a World Bank spokesman said at the time, 'wage restraint' is required to encourage 'the growth of employment and investment'. Meanwhile, the local middle class who depended for its very existence on the domestic economy had to be destroyed to make way for a new cosmopolitan middle class dependent on the TNCs and the global economy.

Clearly, such a drastic social and economic transformation of an already partly developed country could not be achieved by a democratic government. This explains why it was decided to provide dictator Ferdinand Marcos with the funding he required to build up an army capable of imposing such a programme by force. As Marcos put it at the time, 'Only an authoritarian system will be able to carry forth the mass consent and to exercise the authority necessary to implement new values, measures and sacrifices' (Fieldhouse, 1984). In essence, this is what he did. Martial law was declared by Marcos, and the people were bludgeoned into accepting the transformation of their society, economy and natural environment.

LENDING MONEY

Lending large sums of money to the compliant elite of a non-industrial country is by far the most effective method of controlling it and thereby of obtaining access to its market and its natural resources. However, if the government is to be capable of repaying the money borrowed or of paying interest on it, the money must be invested in enterprises that are competitive on the international market, since interest payments must be paid in foreign exchange, usually US dollars.

Unfortunately, this is extremely unlikely to occur. To begin with, anything up to 20 per cent of the money, and sometimes very much more, will be skimmed off in the form of kickbacks to various politicians and officials. Some of the money will be spent on useless consumer products, mainly luxury goods for the elite; much will be spent on infrastructural projects which will not generate a direct return for a very long time, if at all; and more will go on armaments to enable the government to put down uprisings by the victims of the development process. So the countries who borrow large sums of money must necessarily fall into unrepayable debt. Once in debt, rather than cutting down on expenditure, they inevitably become hooked on further and further borrowing and thus fall under the power of the lending countries. At this point the latter, through the IMF, can institutionalize their control over a debtor country through structural adjustment programmes (SAPs) that, in effect, take over its economy to ensure that interest payments are regularly met. This arrangement leaves the borrowing country as a *de facto* colony.

This technique of informal colonialist control is by no means new. It was resorted to during the colonial era, as in Tunisia and Egypt in the mid-1800s. In the case of Tunisia, a lot of money was lent to the Bey of Tunis to build up an army in order to loosen his ties with Turkey, not a particularly profitable investment – and, of course, it did not take long before the Bey was unable to pay interest on the loan. Much of the money was borrowed in the form of bonds and most of the bondholders were French. The latter viewed the situation with considerable alarm and appealed to the French foreign office for help, which was granted. The Bey's economy was subjected to financial supervision, 'a technique frequently used by the British and French governments in Latin America' just as it still is today.

A joint Franco–Tunisian commission was set up in 1869 for such supervision and the conditions it imposed were draconian, to say the least. It had the right to collect and distribute the state's revenues in order to ensure that the shareholders had precedence over any other debtors. (Significantly, in 1994 President Clinton imposed a similar deal on the Mexican government as a condition for lending it the billions of dollars required to bail out its Wall Street creditors.)

From 1869 onwards, Tunisian 'public finance and therefore effectively the government were now under alien control' (Fieldhouse, 1984). Tunisia had been reduced to the status of an informal colony. To pay interest on the loans, the Bey had to increase taxes, which gave rise to a popular movement. In order to secure and protect its interests, France finally annexed Tunisia in 1881.

The course of events in Egypt was similar though more complex. Egypt involved itself in trade with Europe as early as the 1830s. During the 1850s, European banks were set up in Alexandria. The government spent a lot of money on modernizing the army and the bureaucracy and also on public works, including the Suez Canal. Inevitably, expenditure soon outstripped receipts and the Khedive was forced to borrow heavily from foreign bankers and eventually to issue treasury bonds. In 1862, as Roger Owen notes, Egypt first began to issue foreign loans and by 1875 the country was heavily in debt to European banks (Owen and Sutcliffe, 1976). Like developing world governments today, the Egyptian government was forced to increase production for export – in this case, cotton and sugar – in order to earn the foreign currency with which to pay interest on its debts. This meant creating bigger and bigger plantations and, as usual, expropriating the peasants. The government's efforts, as usual too, were thwarted by foreign competition, in this case by subsidized sugar exports from Russia and Germany.

Egypt's debts rose massively from 3 to 68 million Egyptian pounds. In the 1870s, more than two-thirds of the government's income had to be sent abroad as interest, which is more than most developing world countries have to pay to service their present debts. In 1877, only about 10 percent of the country's revenue was left for domestic expenditure. The Khedive had to resort to heavy short-term borrowing and was forced to sell his shares in the Suez Canal Company. In 1876, he suspended payments on treasury bills. Egypt was bankrupt, just as Tunisia had been in 1869. The bondholders then appealed to the British and French governments for support and got it. It took the form of the financial supervision of Egypt along Tunisian lines – very much as debtor countries are supervised by the IMF and the World Bank today.

This failed and more direct intervention was necessary. A commission of inquiry into Egypt's financial affairs was set up, forcing the Khedive to accept two European ministers in his cabinet to implement the recommendations of the report. This failed too. All sorts of hopeless solutions were proposed until the country was formally annexed by Britain in 1882. For Owen, 'the loss of economic independence not only preceded the loss of political independence, it also prepared the way for it' (Owen and Sutcliffe, 1976). Magdoff sums up the Egyptian experience very neatly:

> *'Egypt's loss of sovereignty resembled somewhat the same process in Tunisia: easy credit extended by Europeans, bankruptcy, increasing control by foreign-debt commissioners, [milking] the peasants to raise revenue for servicing the debt, growing independence movements, and finally military conquest by a foreign power.'* (Magdoff, 1978)

During the era of development, we have perfected the technique of lending money to developing world countries as a means of controlling them. Much of it now goes euphemistically under the name of development 'aid'. To justify aid, 'poverty' in the developing world is made out to be but a symptom of the latter's 'underdevelopment', development thereby being taken to provide an automatic cure. However, developing world countries are also seen to be seriously hampered in their development efforts because they have lacked the requisite capital and technical knowledge – precisely, as Cheryl Payer notes, 'what the Western corporative system is capable of providing' (1991). She quotes Galbraith, who puts it, 'Having the vaccine, we have invented smallpox.'

There is, of course, no reason to believe that borrowing money from abroad, even at concessionary rates, is a means of achieving economic success, let alone of eliminating poverty. Nor should we believe that the money borrowed can then be paid off by increasing exports. The countries that are held up as a model for developing world countries to emulate are the so called 'Tigers' – the newly industrialized countries (NICs) – which include South Korea, Taiwan, Singapore and Hong Kong. Neither Singapore nor Hong Kong, as Payer notes, borrowed any significant amount of money for their development. Taiwan borrowed a little in the early days, but managed to resist US pressure to overspend and borrow more extensively. South Korea is the only one of them to have borrowed fairly extensively. Payer argues that if South Korea succeeded in exporting its way out of what debts it had where others failed, it is largely because it resisted World Bank and IMF pressures to open up its markets. Imports and capital controls were maintained, as they previously had been by Japan. Clearly, some capital is required for development, but, as Payer notes, 'the truly scarce commodity in the world today is not capital, it is markets'.

Aid is a particularly good instrument for opening up markets, because much of it is officially tied to purchasing goods from donor countries. In the same way that colonies were once forced to buy their manufactured goods from the country who had colonized them, aid recipients must spend much of the money that is supposed to relieve their poverty and malnutrition on irrelevant manufactured goods that are produced by the donor countries. If they dare refuse, they are immediately brought to heel by the simple expedient of threatening to cut off the aid on which they tend to become highly dependent.

Thus, a few years ago the British government threatened to cut off aid to the government of India if it did not go ahead with its plan to buy 21 large helicopters, costing UK£60 million, from a British corporation called Westland – an effort, it is encouraging to note, that was bitterly opposed by responsible elements within Britain's Overseas Development Agency (ODA). This is but a more sophisticated method of achieving what Britain achieved in the previous century when it went to war with China in order to force that country to buy opium from British merchants in India.

In general terms, aid cannot be of use to the poor of the developing world because they necessarily depend on the local economy for their sustenance, and the local economy does not require the vast highways, the big dams or, for that matter, the hybrid seeds, fertilizers and pesticides of the Green Revolution any more than it does the fleet of helicopters that the British government imposed on India. These are only of use to the global economy, which can only expand at the expense of the local economy, whose environment it degrades, whose communities it destroys and whose resources (land, forests, water and labour) it systematically appropriates for its own use.

WORLD BANK AND COLONIALISM

Significantly, at the beginning of the era of development in the 1940s and early 1950s, developing world countries showed practically no interest in borrowing money from the foremost aid agency, the World Bank. This was interpreted as demonstrating that they lacked the necessary technical and planning skills to draw up suitable projects. The answer was to provide them with these skills and thereby create a demand for World Bank loans. Bruce Rich, in his book *Mortgaging the Earth*, states how in the 1950s a primary focus of World Bank policy was 'institution building' (Rich, 1994a; see also Rich, 1994b). This usually took the form of creating largely autonomous World Bank-dominated agencies within developing world governments, responsible for undertaking large-scale projects for which World Bank funding would be continually solicited. Over the years, such agencies have been set up in most developing world countries. For instance, in Thailand, they include the State Electricity Corporation (EGAT), the Industrial Finance Corporation (IFCT) and the National Economic and Social Development Board (NESDB). Between them, these institutions have so far obtained 199 World Bank loans of a total of some US$4374 billion. The World Bank also trains their officials at its Economic Development Institute (EDI) in World Bank techniques for project appraisal and long-term country lending strategies. Many of this institution's ex-alumni have achieved positions of great power in their respective countries. Some have become prime ministers or ministers for planning and finance. Rich sees these agencies as vast 'patronage networks'. They have provided the World Bank 'with critical power bases through which it has been able to transform national economies, indeed whole societies, without the bothersome procedures of democratic review and discussion of alternatives', and have thereby given the World Bank 'some of the powers of a surrogate government'.

These conclusions are consistent with those of a study undertaken by the International Legal Centre in New York on the World Bank's involvement in Colombia between 1949 and 1972. It concluded that the autonomous agencies set up in that country by the bank had a profound impact on the political structure and social evolution of the entire country, weakening 'the political party system and minimizing the roles of the legislature and of the judiciary'. Colombia had, in effect, become a World Bank colony or rather a colony of the US and the other industrial countries that control the bank.

The IMF, like the World Bank, has done everything it can to persuade countries who still have low debt burdens to borrow more and more money. Payer goes so far as to say that 'such countries were wooed by the Fund with what might be called "special introductory offers"' – loans with only light conditionality attached. Thus, Tanzania since its independence refused to allow TNCs to operate within its borders. However, in 1974, it received an IMF loan with light conditionality to help it over a temporary crisis. By 1977, the crisis was over and Tanzania had built up 'a comfortable "cushion" of foreign exchange reserves'. At this point, the IMF and the World Bank advised the Tanzanian government 'that its reserves were embarrassingly large and might lead the country's aid donors to reduce their contributions'. A poor country should not 'hoard its reserves but spend them in order to develop more rapidly'. The government was induced to abolish its foreign exchange budgeting system, called 'confinement', and lift controls on imports. The Tanzanian officials were convinced that the IMF and the bank were 'virtually creating the crisis which gave them power over the Tanzanian government' (Payer, 1991). They were probably right.

Cheryl Payer notes that even after the oil price rise in 1973, instead of making it clear to debtor countries that their chances of exporting their way out of their growing debts were now dimmer than they had ever been, they went on encouraging them to borrow still more money.

When President Mobuto of Zaire failed to service his country's debts in the 1970s, the IMF installed a representative, Erwin Blumenthal, in a key position in his Central Bank. Two years later, in 1980, Blumenthal resigned on the grounds that corruption in Zaire was so 'sordid and pernicious' that there was 'no chance, I repeat no chance' that its numerous creditors would recover their loans, the money lent merely serving to swell Mobuto's personal fortune abroad and to import luxuries for his cronies. However, even this did not prevent the IMF, only a few months after Blumenthal's report, from granting Zaire the largest loan ever given to an African country.

Michel Chossudovsky notes just how drastic is the control exerted by the World Bank and the IMF over the economic policies of debtor countries. He explains that countries wishing to borrow money under a structural adjustment programme have to start off by providing evidence to the IMF that it is 'seriously committed to economic reform'. Before it does this, no actual loan negotiation can be held.

Once a loan has actually been granted the country's performance is monitored four times a year by the IMF and the World Bank and if the reforms are not considered to be 'on track', disbursements are immediately cut off, the country is put on a blacklist and runs the risk of reprisals in trade and capital flows. Many debtor countries are forced to write 'policy framework papers' under the close supervision of the IMF and the World Bank. The latter is closely involved with the implementation of the programme through its country representative office and its many technical missions. In addition, it has representatives in the country's key ministries such as health, education, industry and agriculture, transportation and the environment, whose policies fall increasingly under its jurisdiction. The bank also closely monitors public expenditure in each of the government departments under its supervision via its public expenditure review (PER).

Significantly, the World Bank's job will be greatly facilitated by the fact that many of the key positions in the government of the debtor countries are likely to be ex-World Bank executives, who have been imbued with that institution's economic philosophy and trained to implement its policies. In India, during the recent government of Narasimha Rao, no fewer than 21 key positions in India's ministries of trade and finance were occupied by ex-World Bank executives. Today, under the aegis of the WTO which is, in effect, a world government with its own legislation, its own executive and its own judiciary, control is indeed incomparably more sophisticated than that exerted by the colonial powers of old.

THE NEW CORPORATE COLONIALISM

Furthermore, as a result of the GATT Uruguay Round, developing world countries are under obligation to accept all investments from abroad; give 'national treatment' to any foreign corporation who establishes itself within their borders, whether it is involved in agriculture, mining, manufacturing or the service industries; eliminate tariffs and import quotas on all goods, including agricultural produce; and abolish non-tariff barriers, such as regulations to protect labour, health or the environment that might conceivably increase corporate costs.

Conditions more favourable to the immediate interests of TNCs could scarcely be imagined. Many of these conditions were imposed during GATT negotiations by the US delegation and by the delegations of the EU and Japan who presumably believed the vast bulk of the TNCs were and always would be located in such countries.

However, it seems more and more that this may change. Even strong national governments are no longer able to exert any sort of control over TNCs. If a country passes a law that TNCs regard as a hindrance to their further expansion, they merely threaten to leave and establish themselves elsewhere, which, under the new conditions, they can do at the drop of a hat. Indeed, TNCs are now free to scour the globe and establish themselves wherever labour is the cheapest, environmental laws are the laxest, fiscal regimes are the least onerous and subsidies are the most generous. They need no longer be swayed by sentimental attachments to any nation state.

Today, as a few giant TNCs consolidate their respective control in the worldwide sale of a particular commodity, so it is likely to become ever less advantageous for them to compete with each other. Competition mainly reduces profit margins; cooperation, on the other hand, enables them to increase their hold over governments and to deal with the inevitable opposition from populist and nationalist movements and others who might seek to restrict corporate power and influence.

Already, TNCs are resorting to more and more vertical integration, thereby controlling virtually every step in the economic process in their respective fields, from the mining of minerals, to the construction of the factories, the production of goods, their storage, their shipping to subsidiaries in other countries and their wholesaling and retailing to local consumers. In this way, TNCs are effectively insulating themselves from market forces and ensuring that it is they themselves, rather than competition from their rivals, who determine, at each step, the prices that are to be charged (Hultgren, 1995).

Already, between 20 per cent and 30 per cent of world trade is between TNCs and their subsidiaries. Rather than being real trade, this is but a facet of corporate central planning on a global scale. For Paul Ekins, the British ecological economist, TNCs are becoming 'giant areas of bureaucratic planning in an otherwise market economy'. He sees a 'fundamental similarity between giant corporations and state enterprises. Both use hierarchical command structures to allocate resources within their organizational boundaries rather than the competitive market'. What, we might ask, is to prevent 50 per cent, 60 per cent or even 80 per cent of world trade from eventually occurring within such 'organizational boundaries'? At present, very little, and as we move relentlessly in this direction, so may we be entering a new era of global corporate central planning, one that will be geared to a new type of colonialism: global corporate colonialism.

The new colonial powers have neither responsibility for, nor accountability to, anybody but their shareholders. They are little more than machines geared to the single goal of increasing their immediate profitability. What is more, TNCs will now have the power to force national governments to defend corporate interests whenever such interests are in conflict with those of the people whose interests the governments have been elected to protect. The new corporate colonialism is thus likely to be more cynical and more ruthless than anything that we have seen so far. It is likely to dispossess, impoverish and marginalize more people, destroy more cultures and cause more environmental devastation than either the colonialism of old or the development of the last 50 years. The only question is: how long can it last? In my opinion, a few years perhaps, or a decade at most, for a global economy that will create misery on such a scale is both aberrant and necessarily short-lived.

Chapter 2

The Failure of Bretton Woods

David Korten

This chapter is adapted from David C Korten's keynote address at the 1994 convention of the Environmental Grantmakers Association of America, held at the Mt Washington Hotel, Bretton Woods, New Hampshire, on the 50th anniversary of the famous Bretton Woods conference that created the World Bank, the International Monetary Fund (IMF) and, soon after, the General Agreement on Tariffs and Trade (GATT).

Korten has emerged as one of the world's clearest critics of the economic philosophies and practices that drive our system. He formerly worked in Asia for the US Agency for International Development (USAID) and the Ford Foundation's development programmes. He holds a PhD from Stanford University's Business School and served on the faculty of Harvard University's Business School. He is president of the People-Centred Development Forum in New York, and author of When Corporations Rule the World *(1995).*

The fame of Bretton Woods and of this hotel dates from July 1944, when the UN Monetary and Financial Conference was held here. The world was in the throes of World War II. Mussolini had been overthrown. The Allies had landed at Normandy, but Hitler would last another 10 months. War also continued to rage in the Far East, and Japan would not surrender for another 13 months. The UN charter was still a year away. In that context, the economic leaders who quietly gathered at this hotel were looking beyond the end of the war with hopes for a world united in peace through prosperity. Their specific goal was to create the institutions that would promote that vision.

The Bretton Woods meeting did create new institutions that have shaped and controlled the world's economic activity since that time, but some theorists will say that the plans for these institutions go back still further, to the 1930s and to the US Council on Foreign Relations. A meeting ground for powerful members of the US corporate and foreign policy establishments, the council styled itself as a forum for the airing of opposing views, an incubator of leaders and ideas unified in their vision of a global economy dominated by US corporate interests.

Members of this group assessed early on that, at a minimum, the US national interest required free access to the markets and raw materials of the Western Hemisphere, the Far East and the British Empire. On 24 July 1941, a council memorandum outlined the concept of a *grand area:* the part of the world that the US would need to dominate economically and militarily to ensure materials for its industries. The council also called for the creation of worldwide financial institutions for 'stabilizing currencies and facilitating programmes of capital investment for constructive undertakings in backward and underdeveloped regions' (Sklar, 1980). President Franklin D Roosevelt was duly apprised of the council's views.

Three years later, at the opening session at Bretton Woods, Henry Morgenthau, then US secretary of the treasury and president of the conference, read a welcoming message from Roosevelt and gave his own opening speech, which set the tone and spirit of the gathering. Morgenthau envisaged 'the creation of a dynamic world economy in which the peoples of every nation will be able to realize their potentialities in peace and enjoy increasingly the fruits of material progress on an Earth infinitely blessed with natural riches'. He called on participants to embrace the 'elementary economic axiom . . . that prosperity has no fixed limits. It is not a finite substance to be diminished by division'.

Thus Morgenthau set forth one of several underlying assumptions of the economic paradigm that guided the work of the architects of the Bretton Woods system. Many of these assumptions were reasonably valid, but two of the most important were deeply flawed. The first erroneous assumption is that economic growth and enhanced world trade would benefit everyone. The second is that economic growth would not be constrained by the limits of the planet.

By the end of this historic meeting, the World Bank and the IMF had been founded, and the groundwork had been laid for what later became the GATT. In the intervening years, these institutions have held faithfully to their mandate to promote economic growth and globalization. Through SAPs, the World Bank and the IMF have pressured countries of the South to open their borders and change their economies from self-sufficiency to export production. Trade agreements negotiated through GATT have reinforced these actions and opened economies in both North and South to the increasingly free importation of goods and money.

As we look back 50 years later, we can see that the Bretton Woods institutions have indeed met their goals. Economic growth has expanded fivefold. International trade has expanded by roughly 12 times, and foreign direct investment has been expanding at two to three times the rate of trade expansion. Yet, tragically, while these institutions have met their goals, they have failed in their purpose. The world has more poor people today than ever before. We have an accelerating gap between the rich and the poor. Widespread violence is tearing families and communities apart nearly everywhere. And the planet's ecosystems are deteriorating at an alarming rate.

Yet, the prevailing wisdom continues to maintain that economic growth offers the answer to poverty, environmental security and a strong social fabric, and that economic globalization – erasing economic borders to allow free flow of goods and money – is the key to such growth. Indeed, the more severe the economic, environmental and social crises, the stronger the policy commitment to these same prescriptions, even as evidence mounts that they are not working. In fact, there is a growing consensus outside of official circles that they cannot work, for reasons I will explain.

ECOLOGICAL LIMIT TO GROWTH

As the founder of ecological economics, Herman Daly, regularly reminds us, the human economy is embedded in and dependent on the natural ecosystems of our planet. Until the present moment in human history, however, the scale of our economic activity relative to the scale of the ecosystems has been small enough so that, in both economic theory and practice, we could, up to a point, afford to ignore this fundamental fact.

Now, however, we have crossed a monumental historical threshold. Because of the fivefold economic expansion since 1950, the environmental demands of our economic system have filled up the available environmental space of the planet. In other words, we live in a 'full world'.

The first environmental limits that we have confronted and possibly exceeded are not the limits to non-renewable resource exploitation, as many once anticipated, but rather the limits to renewable resources and to the environment's sink functions – its ability to absorb our wastes. These are limits related to the loss of soils, fisheries, forests and water; to the absorption of carbon dioxide (CO_2) emissions; and to destruction of the ozone layer. We could argue whether a particular limit was hit at noon yesterday or will be passed at midnight tomorrow, but the details are far less important than the basic truth that we have no real option other than to adapt our economic institutions to the reality of a 'full world'.

The structure and ideology of the existing Bretton Woods system is geared to an ever-continuing expansion of economic output – economic growth – and to the integration of national economies within a seamless global economy. The consequence is to intensify competition for already overstressed environmental space. In a 'full world', this intensified competition accelerates destruction of the regenerative capacities of the ecosystem on which we and future generations depend; it crowds out all forms of life not needed for immediate human consumption purposes; and it increases competition between rich and poor for control of ecological resources. In a free market – which responds only to money, not needs – the rich win this competition every time. We see it happening all over the world: hundreds of millions of the financially disenfranchised are displaced as their lands, waters and fisheries are converted to uses serving the wants of the more affluent. As long as their resources remain, the demands of the rich can be met – which may explain why so many of the rich see no problem. The poor experience a very different reality, but in a market economy their experience doesn't count.

The market cannot deal with questions relating to the appropriate scale of economic activity. There are no price signals indicating that the poor are going hungry because they have been forced off their lands; nor is there any price signal to tell polluters that too much CO_2 is being released into the air, or that toxins should not be dumped into soils or waters. Steeped in market ideology and highly responsive to corporate interests, the Bretton Woods institutions have demonstrated little capacity to give more than lip service either to environmental concerns or to the needs of the poor. Rather, their efforts have *de facto* centred on ensuring that people with money have full access to whatever resources remain – with little regard for the broader consequences.

A new Bretton Woods meeting to update the international system would serve a significant and visionary need – if its participants were to accept that economic growth is no longer a valid public policy priority. Indeed, whether the global economy grows or shrinks is largely irrelevant. Having crossed the threshold to a full world, the appropriate concern is whether the available planetary resources are being used in ways that:

1   meet the basic needs of all people;
2   maintain biodiversity; and
3   ensure the sustained availability of comparable resource flows to future generations.

Our present economic system fails on all three counts.

ECONOMIC INJUSTICE

In *How Much Is Enough?* (1992), Alan Durning divided the world into three consumption classes: overconsumers, sustainers and marginals. The overconsumers are the 20 per cent of the world's people who consume roughly 80 per cent of the world's resources – that is, those of us whose lives are organized around automobiles, airplanes, meat-based diets and wastefully packaged disposable products. The marginals, also 20 per cent of the world's people, live in absolute deprivation.

If we turn to measurements of *income* rather than *consumption*, the figures are even more stark. The United Nations Development Programme (UNDP) *Human Development Report 1992* introduces the champagne glass as a graphic metaphor for a world of extreme economic injustice. The bowl of the champagne glass represents the abundance enjoyed by the 20 per cent of people who live in the world's richest countries and receive 82.7 per cent of the world's income. At the bottom of the stem, where the sediment settles, we find the poorest 20 per cent of the world's people, who barely survive on 1.4 per cent of the total income. The combined incomes of the top 20 per cent are nearly 60 times larger than those of the bottom 20 per cent. Furthermore, this gap has doubled since 1950, when the top 20 per cent enjoyed only 30 times the income of the bottom 20 per cent. And the gap continues to grow.

These figures actually understate the true inequality in the world, because they are based on national averages rather than actual individual incomes. If we take into account the very rich people who live in poor countries and the very poor people who live in rich countries, the incomes of the richest 20 per cent of the world's people are approximately 150 times those of the poorest 20 per cent. That gap is growing as well.

Robert Reich, the US secretary of labour in the Clinton administration, explained in his book *The Work of Nations* (1991) that the economic globalization the Bretton Woods institutions have advanced so successfully has served to separate the interests of the wealthy classes from a sense of national interest and thereby from a sense of concern for and obligation to their less fortunate neighbours. A thin segment of the super rich at the very lip of the champagne glass has formed a stateless alliance that defines *global interest* as synonymous with the personal and corporate financial interests of its members.

This separation has been occurring in nearly every country in the world to such an extent that it is no longer meaningful to speak of a world divided into Northern and Southern nations. The meaningful divide is not geography – it is class.

Whether intended or not, the policies so successfully advanced by the Bretton Woods institutions have inexorably empowered the super rich to lay claim to the world's wealth at the expense of other people, other species and the viability of the planet's ecosystem.

FREEING CORPORATIONS FROM CONTROL

The issue is not the market *per se*. Trying to run an economy without markets is disastrous, as the experience of the Soviet Union demonstrated. However, there is a fundamentally important distinction between markets and free markets.

The struggle between two extremist ideologies has been a central feature of the 20th century. Communism called for all power to the state. Market capitalism calls for all power to the market – a euphemism for giant corporations. Both ideologies lead to their own distinctive form of tyranny. The secret of Western success in World War II and the early postwar period was not a free market economy; it was the practice of democratic pluralism built on institutional arrangements that sought to maintain balance between the state and the market and to protect the right of an active citizenry to hold both accountable to the public interest.

Contrary to the claims of ideologues who preach a form of corporate libertarianism, markets need governments to function efficiently. It is well established in economic theory and practice that markets allocate resources efficiently only when markets are competitive and when firms pay for the social and environmental impact of their activity – that is, when they *internalize* the costs of their production. This requires that governments set and enforce the rules that make cost internalization happen, and, since successful firms invariably grow larger and more monopolistic, that governments regularly step in to break them up and restore competition.

For governments to play the necessary role of balancing market and community interests, governmental power must be equal to market power. If markets are national, then there must be a strong national government. By expanding the boundaries of the market beyond the boundaries of the nation state through economic globalization, the concentration of market power moves inevitably beyond the reach of government. This has been a most important consequence of both the SAPs of the World Bank and IMF and the trade agreements negotiated under GATT. As a result, governance decisions are transferred from governments, which at least in theory represent the interests of all citizens, to TNCs, which by their nature serve the interests only of their dominant shareholders. Consequently, societies everywhere on the planet are no longer able to address environmental and other needs.

Enormous economic power is being concentrated in the hands of a very few global corporations relieved of constraints to their own growth. Anti-trust action to restore market competition by breaking up the concentrations is one of the many casualties of globilization. Indeed, current policy encourages firms to merge into ever more powerful concentrations to strengthen their position in global markets.

The rapid rate at which large corporations are shedding employees has created an impression in some quarters that the firms are losing their power. It is a misleading impression. The Fortune 500 firms shed 4.4 million jobs between 1980 and 1993. During this same period, their sales increased 1.4 times, assets increased 2.3 times, and chief executive officer (CEO) compensation increased 6.1 times. Of the world's 100 largest economies, 50 are now corporations, not including banking and financial institutions.

Any industry in which five firms control 50 per cent or more of the market is considered by economists to be highly monopolistic. The *Economist* recently reported that five firms control more than 50 per cent of the global market in the following industries: consumer durables, automotive, airlines, aerospace, electronic components, electricity and electronics, and steel. Five firms control over 40 per cent of the global market in oil, personal computers and – especially alarming in its consequences for public debate on these very issues – media.

FORUMS FOR ELITE DOMINATION

It is worth adding here that the forums within which corporate and government elites shape the global policies of the Western world were not limited to Bretton Woods. In May 1954, a powerful group of North American and European leaders also began meeting as an unofficial, low-profile group with no acknowledged membership. Known simply as Bilderberg, the group played a significant role in advancing the EU and shaping a consensus among leaders of the Atlantic nations on key issues facing Western-dominated transnational systems. Participants included heads of state, other key politicians, key industrialists and financiers, and an assortment of intellectuals, trade unionists, diplomats, and influential representatives of the press with demonstrated sympathy for establishment views. One Bilderberg insider had observed that 'today there are very few figures among governments on both sides of the Atlantic who have not attended at least one of these meetings'.

As Japan assumed an increasingly powerful and independent role in the global economy, the need became evident for a forum that included the Japanese and that had a more formal structure than Bilderberg.

In response, the Trilateral Commission was formed in 1973 by David Rockefeller, chair of Chase Manhattan Bank, and Zbigniew Brzezinski, who served as the commission's director–coordinator until 1977 when he became national security advisor to President Jimmy Carter.

The members of the Trilateral Commission include the heads of four of the world's five largest non-banking TNCs; top officials of five of the world's six largest international banks; and heads of major media organizations. US presidents Jimmy Carter, George Bush, and Bill Clinton were all members of the Trilateral Commission, as was Thomas Foley, former speaker of the US House of Representatives. Many key members of the Carter administration were both Bilderberg and Trilateral Commission members. Many of President Clinton's cabinet and other appointments are former members of the Trilateral Commission.

Both Bilderberg and the Trilateral Commission have provided forums in which top executives from the world's leading corporations meet regularly, informally and privately with top national political figures and opinion leaders to seek consensus on immediate and longer-range problems facing the most powerful members of the Western Alliance.

To some extent, the meetings help maintain 'stability' in global policies, but they also deprive the public of meaningful participation and choice – as some participants explicitly intend. Particularly significant about these groups is their bipartisan political membership. Certainly, the participation of both George Bush and Bill Clinton in the Trilateral Commission makes it easier to understand the seamless transition from the Republican Bush administration to the Democratic Clinton administration with regard to US commitment to pass GATT and NAFTA. Clinton's leadership in advancing what many progressives saw as a Bush agenda won him high marks from his colleagues on the Trilateral Commission.

INSTRUMENTS OF CONTROL

Corporations have enormous political power, and they are actively using it to reshape the rules of the market in their own favour. The GATT has now become one of the corporations' most powerful tools for reshaping the market. Under the new GATT agreement, a World Trade Organization (WTO), has been created with far-reaching powers to provide corporations the legal protection they feel they need to continue expanding their far-flung operations without the responsibility to serve any interest other than their own bottom line.

The WTO will hear disputes brought against the national or local laws of any country that another member country considers to be a trade barrier. Secret panels made up of three unelected trade experts will hear the disputes, and their rulings can be overturned only by a unanimous vote of the member countries. In general, any health, safety or environmental standard that exceeds international standards set by industry representatives is likely to be considered a trade barrier, unless the offending government can prove that the standard has a valid scientific basis.

As powerful as the large corporations are, they themselves function increasingly as agents of a global financial system that has become the world's most powerful governance institution. The power in this system lies within a small group of private financial institutions that have only one objective: to make money in massive quantities. A seamless electronic web allows anyone with proper access codes and a personal computer to conduct instantaneous trade involving billions of dollars on any of the world's financial markets. The world of finance itself has become a gigantic computer game. In this game the smart money does not waste itself on long-term, high-quality commitments to productive enterprises engaged in producing real wealth to meet the real needs of real people. Rather, it seeks short-term returns from speculation in erratic markets and from simultaneous trades in multiple markets to profit from minute price variations. In this game, the short-term is measured in microseconds, the long-term in days. The environmental, social and even economic consequences of financial decisions involving more than US$1 trillion a day are invisible to those who make them.

Joel Kurtzman, former business editor of the *New York Times* and currently editor of the *Harvard Business Review,* estimates that for every US$1 circulating in the productive economy today, US$20 to US$50 circulates in the world of pure finance. Since these transactions take place through unmonitored international computer networks, no one knows how much is really involved. The US$1 trillion that changes hands each day in the world's international currency markets is itself 20 to 30 times the amount required to cover daily trade in actual goods and services. If the world's most powerful governments act in concert to stabilize exchange rates in these same markets, the best they can manage is a measly US$14 billion a day – little more than pocket change compared to the amounts mobilized by speculators and arbitrageurs (see Chapter 4 on electronic money).

The corporations who invest in real assets (as opposed to ephemeral financial assets) are forced by the resulting pressures to restructure their operations in order to maximize immediate short-term returns to shareholders. One way to do this is by downsizing, streamlining and automating their operations, using the most advanced technologies to eliminate hundreds of thousands of jobs. The result is jobless economic growth. Contemporary economies simply cannot create jobs faster than technology and dysfunctional economic systems can shed them. In nearly every country in the world there is now a labour surplus, and those lucky enough to have jobs are increasingly members of a contingent work force without either security or benefits. The resulting fear and insecurity make the jobs-versus-environment issue a crippling barrier to essential environmental action.

Another way to increase corporate profits is to externalize the cost of the firm's operations on the community, pitting localities against one another in a standards-lowering competition to offer subsidies, tax holidays, and freedom from environmental and employment standards. Similarly, workers are pitted against one another in a struggle for survival that pushes wages down to the lowest common denominator. This is the true meaning of global competitiveness – competition among localities. Large corporations, by contrast, minimize their competition through mergers and strategic alliances.

Any corporation who does not play this game to its limit is likely to become a take-over target by a corporate raider who will buy out the company and profit by taking the actions that the previous management – perhaps in a fit of social conscience and loyalty to workers and community – failed to take. The reconstruction of the global economic system makes it almost impossible for even highly socially conscious and committed managers to operate a corporation responsibly in the public interest.

. . .

We are caught in a terrible dilemma. We have reached a point in history where we must rethink the very nature and meaning of human progress. Yet the vision and decisions that emerged some 50 years ago catalysed events that have transformed the governance processes of societies everywhere such that the necessary changes in thought and structure seem very difficult to achieve. It has happened so quickly that few among us even realize what has happened. The real issues are seldom discussed in a media dependent on corporate advertising.

Nonetheless, the fact is that sustainability in a growth-dependent globalized economy is what Herman Daly calls an impossibility theorem. What is the alternative? Among those of us who are devoting significant attention to this question, the answer is the opposite of globalization. It lies in promoting greater economic localization – breaking economic activities down into smaller, more manageable pieces that link the people who make decisions in ways both positive and negative. It means rooting capital to a place and distributing its control among as many people as possible.

Powerful interests stand resolutely in the way of achieving such a reversal of current trends. The biggest barrier, however, is the limited extent of public discussion on the subject. The starting point must be to get the issues on the table and bring them into the mainstream policy debates in a way that books such as this may help to achieve.

Chapter 3

Technologies of Globalization

Jerry Mander

Chapters elsewhere in this book present evidence of the multiple harms caused by biotechnology, robotics, global computer networks, global television, the production and dumping of toxics, and industrial expansion. All of these technologies and processes are intrinsic aspects of a globalized economy. Given the evidence, however, we still hesitate to draw conclusions about the political drift of modern technologies. We cling to the idea that technologies are 'neutral', just as we like to think of science as 'value free' – that it is only a matter of access. This chapter argues that the very idea that technology is neutral is itself not neutral, as it leads to passivity regarding technology's onrush and unconsciousness about its role in the globalization process.

Jerry Mander is the president of the International Forum on Globalization (IFG), which is an alliance of 60 organizations in 20 countries providing public education and campaigns on global economic issues. He is also the programme director for the Foundation for Deep Ecology and a senior fellow at the Public Media Centre, a non-profit advertising company working only for environmental and social causes. In the 1960s Mander was president of a major San Francisco advertising company before turning his talents to environmental campaigns throughout that decade. In 1971 Mander formed the United States' first non-profit advertising agency, Public Interest Communications, for environmental, community and social action groups. He was also director of the Elmwood Institute, an ecological think-tank. His books include Four Arguments for the Elimination of Television *(1977) and* In the Absence of the Sacred *(1991). He holds a graduate degree (MS) from Columbia University's Business School in international economics.*

It is commonplace nowadays to hear new technologies described as 'revolutionary', but rarely do we learn whether the revolution is right-wing or left. This is especially true of the most dominant technologies and those with the greatest impact. Automobiles, television and computers, for example, have so enveloped society that we scarcely remember a world before they existed. Society accepts the onrush of these technologies with alarming passivity, and without any systematic consideration of the social and political changes they bring with them. Indeed, despite calling the technologies revolutionary, we rarely acknowledge that they have any political implications, such as the way they accelerate the globalization process. The great technology critic Langdon Winner has written that 'all artifacts have politics', meaning that each technology has predictable social, political, and environmental outcomes. He says: 'The most interesting puzzle of our times is that we so willingly sleepwalk through the process for reconstituting the conditions of human existence. . . In the technical realm we repeatedly enter into a series of social contracts, the terms of which are revealed only after the signing' (Winner, 1986).

Two decades earlier, Marshall McLuhan made surely one of the most important and importantly misunderstood comments of the century when he said 'the medium is the message' (1964). He meant that the most significant aspects of technology lie not in their apparent content (the transportation that a car provides or the news programme that the television supplies) but in the systemic changes that they catalyse. The questions we need to learn to ask include the following. How does the technology change work, family life, leisure, art? How does it alter our experience of everyday life? How does it change our concepts of self, community, politics, nature, time, distance? How does it influence how we learn, what we know, and what we are capable of knowing? What are its implications for human health and disease, and the environment? How does it reorganize power arrangements in society? For instance, does it centralize power or decentralize it? Does it serve to homogenize cultures or, on the contrary, to maintain diversity? Who gains and who loses?

Why hasn't our society developed a process of articulating and evaluating the totality of the effects caused by technology and then voting upon them before they become so pervasive that they become extremely difficult to dislodge? Indeed, certain technological inventions change society far more dramatically than do any of the political figures we vote for. Our total immersion in computers, for example, has and will continue to revolutionize our experience of life far more than whether our president is Republican or Democrat. But there is no congressional vote on this; there are no popular referenda. Even in this most democratic of societies, we have no process for decision-making about technology and little practice in evaluating it. We have only the market to make our decisions for us, and that process is profoundly skewed, as we will see.

How did things get this way? There are dozens of possible explanations, but I will only cite three main points.

The first has to do with the information climate about technology. It is a melancholy fact that in our society the first waves of descriptions about new technologies invariably come from the corporations and scientists who invent and market these technologies and who have much to gain by our accepting a positive view. Their descriptions are invariably optimistic, even utopian, and are supported by hundreds of millions of dollars in advertising and public relations. The 'Green Revolution' will solve global hunger. Nuclear power will solve the world's energy problems and provide clean, safe, cheap, inexhaustible energy. Television will unify global consciousness and bring peace and understanding everywhere. The microcomputer revolution will bring all the information in the world to every person merely by the striking of a key.

One could find similarly optimistic statements for every new technology that comes along. Those who emit such statements have nothing to gain from our learning the possible negative consequences of these new commodities, so we are left with a constant stream of best-case scenarios and virtually no counter-vailing voice. As we have discovered, however, many manufacturers and industries – including nuclear, chemical, auto, cigarette and tobacco – are aware of the serious negative outcomes of their technologies, but choose not to share these with the public and often hide them even from investigative inquiry.

Over the century since the Industrial Revolution, wave after wave of techno-utopian visions have so immersed us in positive expectations that the development of new technologies has become virtually synonymous with the general advance-ment of society. It is only long after a technology has entered into general production and has gained an important role in everyday life that we begin to perceive its adverse effects on humans or nature. Even then, the proposed solutions usually consist of creating new generations of technology designed to fix the problems of the old. Thus the wave rolls on to the next technical generation.

A second factor explaining our utter passivity to technology is that, when we do attempt to analyse the virtues of a particular technology, we do so in personal terms. The car drives us where we need to go in relative comfort and convenience. The television is often entertaining and informative. The airplane shrinks the globe; we can be anywhere on Earth in hours. The computer edits, stores data, hooks us to other like-minded people, speeds up our work, and permits us to 'publish' our viewpoints to a potentially vast audience. All technology is useful or entertaining, or else we'd have no interest in it in the first place. But to base our ultimate conclusions about technology mainly on our personal experience leaves out the social, political and ecological dimensions; in other words, it overlooks the effects on everything but ourselves. What are the other consequences of high-speed travel? Is a smaller world better? Who else benefits from global computer networks?

In our individualistic society, we are not practised in making judgements beyond our personal experience, but it is just that practice – seeking the systemic or holistic effects – that will help us evaluate the positive and negative aspects of specific technologies. The question then is not how or whether technology benefits us but who benefits most and what outcomes are involved.

This brings us to the third and, I think, most important reason for our passivity about technology – the blinding notion that technologies are neutral, that the only thing that matters about them is who is in control, that they have no intrinsic qualities which inevitably produce certain ecological or political outcomes. It may be one of the most important survival skills of our times to break with this idea. Every technology has a predetermined political drift, and it is critical that we perceive that and make our judgements and adjustments accordingly.

To help clarify this point, I'll use two familiar examples of energy technologies: nuclear power and solar power. Both of these technologies will light the lamps in your house and run the refrigerator, the television and the computer. But there the similarities end.

Intrinsic Bias in Energy Technologies

When a society decides to use nuclear power, it commits itself to many additional outcomes besides the delivery of the energy itself. To build and operate nuclear power plants requires a large, highly technical, and very well-financed infrastructure. It's not something that people in your neighbourhood can get together and decide to do. It can only be done by huge, centralized institutions. Without such institutions, nuclear power could not exist.

Nuclear power also depends upon substantial military protection against possible terrorist attacks, or thefts of dangerous ingredients. And nuclear energy produces a terrifying waste product, some of which needs to be stored safely someplace for as long as 250,000 years – a technical task that is still not solved – requiring techno-scientific–military care and protection for all that time, something no society could guarantee. This also preempts many choices that might otherwise be available for future generations. For example, what if, a few centuries down the road, a society wishes to re-establish agrarianism and low-impact technology as its primary *modi operandi*? It would still have to monitor the dangerous wastes from centuries earlier and maintain a technical capability for doing it. So, nuclear power today predetermines much about the form of future society.

Solar power, on the other hand, has entirely different intrinsic characteristics. The technology is so simple and inexpensive that my sons and I and a few friends could probably install solar units on most of the houses in our neighbourhood, without backing from any centralized financial interests. We would require no military to protect the units; there would be very negligible dangerous waste product; and the technology would not predetermine the shape of any future society.

So it would be fair to say that nuclear power is an appropriate technology for an industrialized, mass society such as ours, organized around large central military and financial systems. Solar power is more appropriate for societies made up of small communities, catering to local markets, with very low environmental impact.

What is important to note is that the significant features of each of these rival technologies are *intrinsic* to them. If the authors in this book were somehow put in charge of the world's nuclear power plants, we would surely have to operate them in more or less the same way as they are presently being run, albeit perhaps with a higher degree of caution. But all of the major implications of nuclear power – financial, military and environmental – would remain, because they are determined by the technology itself. So it is truly preposterous to argue that either of these technologies is neutral, when both are intrinsically predisposed to produce dramatically divergent outcomes.

That kind of comparative *systemic* technological analysis should have occurred long before our society made any of its choices about which energy technologies to employ. Other energy sources such as coal, gas, oil, and biomass should also have been included in a comprehensive comparison, long before corporate marketing interests were able to exert their persuasive influence. In the end, the question becomes: what kind of technology relates to what kind of society?

Consider the case of the automobile.

REFERENDUM ON THE AUTO

What would have happened if a systemic analysis of the automobile had been offered to the public at the time of its invention? It's not as if most of the negative effects were not known ahead of time, for businesses spend enormous sums researching both the market potential of their product and the possible downside disasters. Businesses don't like surprises. Indeed, an excellent study of the level of awareness of certain technologies' impacts at the time of their invention can be found in the *Retrospective Technology Assessment* reports financed by the National Science Foundation and managed by the Massachusetts Institute of Technology.

When Henry Ford and others first promoted the automobile before the turn of the 20th century, the technology was described, as usual, solely in 'best-case' terms. Automobiles would bring a 'revolutionary' new era of personal freedom and democracy in the form of private transportation that was fast, clean (no mud or horse manure) and independent. But what if people had been told that the car would bring with it the modern concrete city? Or that the car would contribute to cancer-causing air pollution, to noise, to global warming, to solid waste problems and to the rapid depletion of the world's resources? What if it had been reported that for production efficiency the private car would eventually be manufactured by a small number of giant corporations that would acquire tremendous economic and political power? That these corporations would create a new mode of mass production – the assembly line – which in turn would cause worker alienation, physical injury, drug abuse and alcoholism? That these corporations might conspire to eliminate other means of popular transportation, including trains? That the automobile would facilitate suburban growth with its intolerable impact on landscapes? What if we had known that 30,000 people would die annually in car accidents? What if the public had been forewarned of the unprecedented need for oil that the private car would create, and that horrible wars would be fought over oil supplies? What if the public had realized that automobiles and roads would redesign even the most exotic societies into forms and behaviour very much like ours? That cities such as Bangkok and Kathmandu would increasingly feel like Manhattan at rush hour?

Would a public informed of such outcomes have decided to proceed with developing the private automobile? Would the public have still thought it a good thing?

I really cannot guess whether a public so well informed and given the chance to vote would have voted against cars. Perhaps not. But the public was not so informed.

If such a debate about the automobile had occurred in the public realm, there surely would have been more support for public transport, and we surely would not have seen quite the proliferation of private cars and public roads. Some countries and locales might have prohibited private cars completely and thereby retained their indigenous social, cultural, biological and geographical characteristics.

TV: The Cloning of Cultures

Several contributors to this book have described aspects of the globalization and homogenization of values, culture, and consciousness that cultural exports of Western films, fashion, music, and television have introduced (see Chapters 14 and 15). With the new trade agreements effectively suppressing the remaining ability of individual nations to resist such cultural invasions, the process of cultural cloning is accelerating, but it has been advancing for some while.

Because of the advent of satellite television in the 1970s and 1980s, more than 75 per cent of the global population now has access to daily television reception. People living in remote parts of Borneo or in the Himalayas or in the tundras of Siberia are watching nearly identical programmes, mostly produced by Western corporate interests, all of it expressing Western values and imagery, instigating enormous cultural change.

I had the chance to observe this process up close during a visit to the Mackenzie River Valley of the Northwest Territories of Canada in the mid 1980s. I was invited there by the Native Women's Association, which expressed deep concern about the sudden changes caused by the recent introduction of satellite television into their communities.

The Mackenzie Valley stretches south from the Arctic Circle and runs 2400 kilometres to the Great Slave Lake. If you're not familiar with the area, let me remind you of the Russian nuclear satellite that fell from orbit some years ago. It was feared it would fall on Paris or New York or Tokyo, so there was a great relief when it fell on what was described in the press as 'an icy unpopulated wasteland'.

To call this area unpopulated only confirms how invisible native people are to the mass media because it is actually populated by 26 communities of Dene Indians and Inuit (Eskimo) peoples – about 20,000 people in all – who have lived there successfully for 4000 years. To this day they speak 22 native tongues, mostly as a first language. In many of these places, the traditional economy of hunting, ice fishing and dog sled travel has survived, largely because the Canadian government had little interest in the area. But when oil was discovered in the 1960s, oil workers were needed, and the government decided it was time that the natives be turned into Canadians.

Television is the normal instrument of choice for such cultural conversion. The government offered each of the 26 communities free satellite dishes and television sets; most communities accepted, but not all.

When I arrived in Yellowknife, the capital city of the Northwest Territories (population then 9000; the only town with paved streets and cars), the weather was 40 degrees Celsius below zero. The women who greeted me told me they were at first pleased about television. Dene and Inuit communities are often hundreds of kilometres from each other, without any connecting roads. Communication between these places was difficult: dog team, radio and airplane. 'Until recently it didn't matter,' I was told by the Dene Nation communications director, Cindy Gilday. 'Most of the communities have been self-sufficient for centuries, but now the government is changing things so fast, it's important for people to know what's going on.'

Television had seemed a logical advance in communications, but it had not lived up to its potential. As with most indigenous and developing world locales where television is just arriving, the programmes are not produced locally, but come mostly from the US or other Western countries. Sixty per cent of the programmes in the Northwest Territories were from the US, including *Dallas*, *Edge of Night*, *Happy Days*, and *The Six Million Dollar Man* (and, lately, CNN). Gilday said:

> *'There's only one hour per week of local shows, and rarely does that have anything to do with native people, though we're the majority population here. . . We can already see that TV has had a devastating effect, especially in the villages out in the bush. The effect has been to glamorize behaviours and values that are poisonous to life up here. Our traditions have a lot to do with survival. Community cooperation, sharing, and non-materialism are the only ways that people can live here. But TV always presents values opposite to those.'*

Many of the women I met were schoolteachers, and they said that when television came to the villages they saw an immediate change. The children immediately lost interest in the native language; they wanted only to learn Canadian English. Now the children want all kinds of new things like cars; yet most of the communities have no roads. They don't want to learn how to fish on the ice or go hunting anymore. 'But worst of all is what it's doing to the relations between the young and the old,' I was told by the women. 'TV makes it seem like the young people are all that's important, and the old have nothing to say. And yet in our cultures, the old people are the ones who tell the stories and teach the kids how to be Indians.'

Most important of all, the women said, was that TV had put a stop to storytelling. It used to be that the old people would sit each evening in the corner of the house, telling the children ancient stories about life in the North. Through that process, the elders had been the windows through which the younger generation could see their own past and traditions; it was how the children could sense their own Indian roots. It was also an educational system teaching how to survive in such a harsh place. The women were horrified that the process was being interrupted by television. They saw it as the death of their culture. Gilday told me:

> 'You have to realize that most people still live in one- or two-room houses. The TV is going all the time, and the little kids and the old people are all sitting around together watching it. They're watching something totally alien, and they're not hearing the stories anymore; they don't want to be Indians now. They hate being Indians.
>
> They want to be Canadians and Americans. . . It's so crazy and so awful. Nobody ever told us that all this would be coming in with TV. It's like some kind of invasion from outer space or something. First it was the government coming in here, then those oil companies and now it's TV.'

With satellite television now bringing *Dallas*, *The Edge of Night*, and *The Oprah Winfrey Show* to 75 per cent of the world population, the process just described in the Mackenzie Valley is happening globally. Television technology is clearly the most efficient instrument ever invented for global cultural cloning, and it is the pathbreaker for what follows: cars; paved roads; Western franchise foods; economies converted from self-sufficiency to corporate export; frantic and stressful lifestyles; loss of traditional skills; immersion in computers, walkmans, and CD ROMs; and so on.

One can certainly argue that the benefits of modernization are well worth the sacrifice, even when the sacrifice is not apparent at the time of the change and comes as a shocking surprise. In fact, it is the ultimate rationalization for the entire Western development ethic that the sacrifice of cultural and biological diversity is worth what is gained, even if every place on Earth begins to look like Bakersfield, California. That viewpoint notwithstanding, we should become exquisitely aware of the nature of the bargain and give ourselves the freedom and the opportunity to conclude that, on balance, it may be a losing proposition for everyone.

Television is one technology that does live up to the promises proposed by its inventors: it produces a unified global consciousness. But is that good?

THE COMPUTER REVOLUTION

The computer revolution is an odd kind of revolution, because every corner of society, including those that normally disagree fiercely with each other on most issues, is in agreement on this one: they all think it's good. The engineers and the artists; the Al Gores and the Newt Gingriches; corporations and their anti-corporate counterparts; conservatives and liberals – all are dazzled by images of computer-driven utopias, though it's possible they have slightly different utopias in mind.

Most of my own friends and colleagues share this utopian expectation. My writer friends wonder how it is even possible to write books without a computer, though several writers in history – from Shakespeare to Hemingway to Atwood to Illich – are known to have done it. Even now, there are those who write books by longhand (Edward Goldsmith and Wendell Berry, among them). And there is the impressive fact that 400,000 generations of human beings got through their days without computers. It has been done.

'That is not the point,' my friends say. They argue that I fail to appreciate how 'empowering' computers can be (a popular way of describing them these days) and how they can help us organize against the corporate juggernaut. Computers bring real power back to the individual, and the cybernet helps us build new alliances with like-minded radicals sitting at their terminals, using e-mail and web pages to spread news and mobilize battles. By such analyses, computers seem clearly to be in service of 'progressive', democratizing, decentraliz-ing tendencies.

The more esoteric among my colleagues like to invoke the views of influential *Wired* magazine editor Kevin Kelly, who has described a new 'revolutionary' political structure that he feels microcomputation has wrought. 'The correct symbol of today is no longer the atom,' he says, 'it's the net.' The political centre has been wiped out, and a revolutionary structure has replaced it. This is leading to a new decentralized worldview that 'elevates the power of the small player' and promotes heterogeneity. It also leads to a new kind of pure democracy and an 'incipient technospiritualism' (Kelly, 1994).

Kelly is right on the 'technospiritualism' point, though frankly I prefer the old kind of spiritualism that requires no mediation through machines. As for the main idea that the old political centre has been eliminated and that our new net or web politics brings us computer-enhanced democracy run through cyberspace, let me ask: should we call it *virtual democracy*? As Richard Barnet and John Cavanagh point out in Chapter 4 on the casino economy, the giant financial institutions of today could not exist on their present scale if there were no computers. Computers are their global nervous systems; their way of keeping track of billions of moving parts, keeping them synchronized and moving in the same direction for central purposes. Richard Sclove of the Loka Institute put it this way:

> *'For all the hype in the media about how the new technologies will enhance democracy, what we are getting is not individual empowerment but a new empowerment for multinational corporations and banks, with respect to workers, consumers, and political systems.'*
> (Sclove, 1994).

In fact, it is my opinion that computer technology may be the single most important instrument ever invented for the acceleration of centralized power. While we sit at our PCs editing our copy, sending our e-mail and expressing our cyberfreedoms, the TNCs are using their global networks, fed by far greater resources. They are able to achieve not only information exchange but concrete results that express themselves in downed forests, massive infrastructural development, destruction of rural and farming societies, displacement of millions of people and domination of governments. In a symbiotic embrace with other technologies of rapid economic development, they operate on a scale and at a speed that make our own level of cyberempowerment pathetic by comparison. Speaking in traditional political terms, the new telecommunications technologies assist the corporate, centralized, industrialized enterprise (the 'right'?) far more efficiently than the decentralized, local, community-based interests (the 'left'?), which suffer a net loss.

So much for elevating 'the power of the small player'.

. . .

I have been describing a few macro effects of computers. It is relevant to mention a few other dimensions: the role computer production plays in creating the toxic crises of the industrial and developing worlds; the role of computer-based surveillance technologies in corporations to measure and objectify worker performance; and the manner in which microcomputation has sped up and amplified the power of the military technologies of the advanced industrialized nations. This was already obvious in the infamous 'launch-on-warning' phenomenon of the old Cold War and the 'smart bombs' of the hotter and more recent US–Iraq war, where mass killing by automated bombs left human beings (save for those at the receiving end) free of dirty-handed engagement in the killing process.

Then there is the simple dimension of speed. E F Schumacher told us that small is beautiful, but one could also make the case that *slow* is beautiful, especially in preserving the natural world. Computers speed up communications exchanges over long distance, a quality that is most advantageous to the large centralized institutions we have been describing in this book. Of course, it also offers a speedup for resistance movements, but that speedup is mainly to keep pace with the high-speed activity of corporations.

Has there been a net gain? In political terms, I think not. In environmental terms, surely not. To ensure the survival of nature, everything, especially development and especially people, must slow down and synchronize with the more subtle and slower rhythms of the natural world. In our cyber-walkman-airplane-fax-phone-satellite world, we are so enclosed within a high-speed technical reality that the values and concerns of nature tend to become opaque to our consciousness.

THE COMPUTER AS IT AFFECTS EDUCATION AND SOCIETY

Portland State University Professor of Education C A Bowers has been focusing on the way computer usage affects the basic ecological and political values of the people who use them. Bowers makes the case that the advance of computers is contributing to a loss of ecological sensitivity and understanding, since the very process of using computers, particularly educating through computers, effectively excludes an entire set of ideas and experiences that earlier had been the building blocks for a developing connection with the Earth. Bowers opposes the use of computers in primary and secondary education, saying that they change the way children's minds process information and affect not only what they know but what they are capable of knowing – that is, computers alter the pathways of children's cognition. Newly immersed in data-based forms of knowledge and limited to information transmissible in digital form, our culture is sacrificing the subtle, contextual, and memory-based knowledge gleaned from living in a nature-based culture, meaningful interactive learning with other humans, and an ecologically based value system (Bowers, 1993).

So, by accepting computers so completely for schools, says Bowers, our society also accepts a massive cultural transformation, leaving human beings altered in predictable ways. McLuhan said that we turn into the technologies that we use. And so, says Bowers, the more we use the computer and the more it is used globally, the stronger its culturally homogenizing effects and the greater likelihood that our new globalized digital culture will be less concerned about the disappearance of nature.

Richard Sclove adds this final political point:

> *'People are using telecommunications to establish [virtual] social bonds that are completely unrelated to territorial relations or face-to-face acquaintance. I might now have a lively social life with people in Amsterdam but not a clue about what's going on with my neighbour next door. Spending one's life on-line, with little direct experience of the natural world – without sensuous knowing – debases our willingness to act with responsibility toward the environment. . . The ultimate political risk comes down to this: to the extent that virtual community takes over for face-to-face community, we get a mismatch between bonds of social affiliation, which are non-territorial, and political systems, which are territorial. How do political jurisdictions govern when the citizens within those boundaries have nothing to do with each other or with the realities of the place?'*

MEGATECHNOLOGY

It is not only individual technologies which need systemic ideological consideration, but what they combine to achieve. For example, as recently as two decades ago it was possible to speak about two different parts of the planet as distinct places with distinct cultures, living habits, conceptual frameworks, behaviours and power arrangements. It was also possible to speak of distinctly different geographies. And one could sensibly speak about individual technologies as if they were distinct from one another: television as opposed to computers; lasers as opposed to satellites.

However, technological evolution has brought us to the point where such distinctions among cultures, places, systems of organization and technological forms are being wiped out under the homogenization drives of a much larger technical juggernaut. Telecommunications, highspeed computer technology, satellite systems, robotics, lasers and other new technologies have made possible, practical and inevitable an interlocked worldwide communication system that enables corporate actors to perform globally with unprecedented speed and efficiency. In such a system corporations themselves are an intrinsic part of the technical machine. In fact, they are technical forms, too, inventing the machines that operate on this global scale and in turn being spawned by them in an accelerating symbiotic cycle.

Finally, there is one more technical form to complete the picture: the recently restructured global economic system itself, which is specifically designed to overcome resistance to the megatechnological homogenization drive.

The big trade agreements are an intrinsic part of the global technical structure; in fact, they are the 'consciousness' of the megadevelopment, megatechnological, monocultural model that encircles the globe and permeates our lives.

In such a context, democracy has a difficult future. In fact, democracy is already suffering its greatest setback, as a direct result of this *de facto* conspiracy of technical structures, technologies themselves and corporate purposes, all within the Western development paradigm. Understanding of that entire set of forces – *megatechnology* – must be grasped quickly. Otherwise we will be led blind and powerless through a destruction of nature, culture and diversity beyond anything that has preceded it.

Individual technologies have defined roles to play. Television serves as the worldwide agent of imagery for the new global corporate vision; computers are the nervous system that facilitates the setup of new global organizations; trade agreements wipe out resistance; telecommunications provide instant capital and resource transfer; genetics and space technologies expand the world market into the new wilderness areas – the internal cell structure of living creatures and the far reaches of untrammelled space. Together, these and other technologies combine to form the new technosphere that is anathema to democracy and diversity.

The answer to the trend is, of course, to work to reverse it, and to bring real power back to the local community, while supporting communities, cultures and nations who attempt to stand in the way of the juggernaut.

Chapter 4

Electronic Money and the Casino Economy

Richard Barnet and John Cavanagh

Deregulation of banking and financial markets, combined with the new rules of free trade and the new technologies that offer instantaneous worldwide money transfers, have combined to profoundly transform the modes of financial activity all over the planet. Incomprehensibly large amounts of money are shifting from market to market and then back again in the time it takes to make a keystroke. Governments are left nearly helpless to ensure the stability of markets or currency values in the face of the tremendous acceleration of speculation. The role of the global financial gamblers in creating many of the current money crises has been seriously underreported in the media. In this chapter a condensed history of these enormous changes and their consequences is presented.

Richard J Barnet is a former arms control expert in the Kennedy administration. He has written 14 books, most recently (with Ann Barnet) The Youngest Minds, *and (with John Cavanagh)* Imperial Corporations and the New World Order. *Barnet cofounded the Institute for Policy Studies in 1963 and is currently a Distinguished Fellow at the institute. He has published hundreds of articles on foreign policy, globalization and domestic policy in the* New Yorker, Harpers Magazine, *the* New York Review of Books, *the* Nation *and other publications.*

    John Cavanagh is director of the Institute for Policy Studies and vice president of the board of the International Forum on Globalization, where he chairs the Alternatives Working Group. He has coauthored ten books on the global economy, most recently (with Sarah Anderson and Thea Lee) A Field Guide to the Global Economy. *His articles appear in the* Washington Post, *the* New York Times, Foreign Policy *and other publications. Cavanagh has degrees from Dartmouth College and Princeton University and has authored studies on transnational corporations for the United Nations Conference on Trade and Development and the World Health Organization.*

On 30 January 1995, 24 hours before President Bill Clinton orchestrated a US$50 billion bailout of the Mexican economy, the world financial system came perilously close to meltdown. As news spread around global financial markets that Mexico was on the verge of defaulting on government bond payments, capital fled stock markets from Brazil and Argentina and even from countries as far away as Poland and the Czech Republic. On that day, Asian markets were spared only because stock markets were closed in observance of Chinese New Year.

Just two and half years later, in mid 1997, a similar financial panic spread across the world. This time, the crisis began in Thailand but quickly moved to the Philippines, South Korea, Indonesia, Russia and Brazil. As international investors panicked in country after country, their 'hot money' left much faster than it had arrived. Big-time currency speculators such as George Soros deepened the crisis by betting against the currencies of the crisis nations. International Monetary Fund (IMF) policy advice only quickened the exodus. Currencies and stock markets from South Korea to Brazil nosedived, spreading pain, dislocation, death and environmental ruin. This sort of crisis is more than likely to recur in the coming years, and next time it might have even more devastating effects worldwide.

The root causes of these crises are twofold:

1　the total deregulation of the global financial systems that leaves banks and other financial institutions without controls; and
2　the corresponding revolution in communications technology that has brought radical change in the scale, speed and manner of financial activity.

This combination of factors has enabled currency speculators to run wild, moving their immense resources electronically, instantaneously, from country to country, beyond the abilities of any government to control the process. In this cybertech globalized world, money has become free of its place and, as we will see, from most connections to its former sources of value: commodities and services. Money itself is the product that money buys and sells.

Because of the tremendous financial requirements for playing in this global money game, banks and finance houses are quickly diminishing in number but increasing in size; as a result, they are becoming still more difficult to control. The net effect is that the world financial system has become exquisitely vulnerable to technological breakdown, the high-risk consequences of short-term speculation and freelance decision-making. If anything goes wrong in this fragile arrangement, which is increasingly likely in the context of a wired-up economy based on free trade, then the following scenario is likely. When a crisis in one place directly affects financial flows everywhere else, speculators panic, speculative funds will be moved without warning (as happened in Mexico, Asia, Russia and Brazil), and we will be quickly threatened by a rapid domino effect among the world's interdependent stock markets. Global economic collapse is possible.

The following are some elements in this larger story.

THE NATURE OF ELECTRONIC MONEY

Most business and personal financial transactions still involve cash, that is, the exchange of coins and bank notes issued by treasuries and central banks. According to the Federal Reserve, about 85 per cent of dollar transactions are in cash at banks, supermarkets, petrol stations, restaurants and the like. But the trillions sloshing back and forth between countries, within and between corporations, and between large investors and entrepreneurs, are transferred from one account to another through an electronic network. Unlike withdrawals at automated teller machines (ATMs), these large transactions do not take place in public view. The number of electronic transfers amounts to only 2 per cent of the total transfers; yet these transactions involve US$5 out of every US$6 that move in the world economy.

Traders still shout at one another at exchanges around the world, buying and selling money in one form or another, but more and more dollars, yen, or lire move from one account to another hundreds or thousands of kilometres away because someone in a quiet room has hooked into a global electronic network and punched a key. Well over US$2 trillion a day travels across the street or across the world at unimaginable speed as bits of electronic information. A treasury bill, as James Grant, the editor of *Grant's Interest Rate Observer,* puts it, 'no longer exists except as an entry on a computer tape' (Passell, 1992).

Information technology has transformed global banking more than any other economic activity. The software that guides electronic networks now permits 24-hour trading in a wide variety of money products – securities, options, futures and so on – all across the planet, and it has changed the human relations of banking. As Felix Rohatyn of Lazard Freres puts it: 'People buy and sell blips on an electronic screen. They deal with people they never see, they talk to people on the phone in rooms that have no windows. They sit and look at screens. It's almost like modern warfare, where people sit in bunkers and look at screens and push buttons and things happen' (Sampson, 1989).

The sheer size of global financial operations is reducing costs substantially. Any multimillion dollar transfer across the globe can be accomplished for just 18 US cents. By developing the most advanced foreign-exchange software, Bankers Trust was able to achieve a ten-second advantage over other traders – enough time, according to a 1987 Office of Technology Assessment study, to execute four or five trades. The opportunity to react to new information a few seconds ahead of the market can be worth billions (O'Brien, 1992).

The introduction of state-of-the-art information technology has changed what banks are and what banks do. Computers and electronic communications networks have expanded the markets for money products and reduced the costs of making transfers, in large measure by eliminating thousands of jobs for clerks, tellers, messengers and the like. But the installation of the automated systems has required huge capital investments. In 1990, commercial banks in the United

States spent US$15 billion on information technology. The need to amass large investment funds for such purposes has encouraged the consolidation of investment and banking corporations. Firms merge to save costs by sharing expensive data systems. These systems facilitate the speedy settlement of money trading; even a few seconds of exposure before a transfer is settled can spell disaster if millions of dollars are involved.

In other words, global banking has become highly dependent on a few centralized information operations to accomplish and monitor the transfers. CHIPS is the New York Clearing House Interbank Payment System. Inside a reinforced concrete-and-glass office building on a run-down block on Manhattan's West Side, two Unisys A-15 J mainframe computers about the size of refrigerators dispatch funds across the Earth. Requests for payment stream in through 134 telephone lines, and, after the requests are screened for possible fraud by 22 electronic black boxes, the mainframes move the money, as *New York Times* writer Peter Passell (1992) puts it, in the form of 'weightless photons through the electromagnetic ether'.

As bankers contemplate this electronic money web, the nightmare – which most dismiss – is that a massive fraud, a flash of lightning or a diabolical computer virus could trigger power failure, scrambled money messages, gridlock, and breakdown in the global banking system, and lead to the world's first computer-driven worldwide financial panic. CHIPS takes all this seriously enough to adopt elaborate security arrangements, to put in auxiliary power and water systems, and to replicate the entire Manhattan operation just across the river in New Jersey, down to a maze of white-walled rooms, a network of telephone lines, a Halon fire-protection system and water-resistant ceilings.

According to Peter Passell, a US$20 million theft did occur in 1989, a fraudulent transfer from a Zurich bank to the State Bank of New South Wales via its New York branch. A Malaysian con man secured the cooperation of two employees of the Swiss Bank and conjured up a fictitious bank in Cameroon to work the scheme. The thieves were caught and convicted. The US$20 million had been transferred in a fraction of a second, but recovering it took longer. Three years later, US$12 million of it was still missing. Despite all the technological precautions and hurdles, even more imaginative inside jobs on an even larger scale are possible.

John Lee, president of the New York Clearing House Association, estimates that 99 per cent of CHIPS transactions are legitimate. That may well be true, given the huge volume of daily transactions. Nevertheless, the speed and anonymity of the global money-transfer system presents an opportunity for large-scale criminal operations and tax fraud.

Electronic transfers are secret. Anyone with funds in the bank who prefers to hide them from regulators, creditors, wives or husbands can communicate with the bank by fax or modem and order wire transfers across the globe without ever speaking to a bank officer. Tax havens are nesting grounds for criminal gains or untaxed profits. Indeed, most of the deposits sitting in these out-of-the-way places are there to avoid scrutiny by regulatory and taxing authorities. Typically, tax havens are tiny – Cayman Islands, Bahamas, Bermuda, Cape Verde, Hong Kong, Bahrain – mostly islands featuring warm weather, good flight connections and plenty of faxes. Grand Cayman's financial district is reputed to have the highest concentration of fax machines in the world to serve its 548 banking outposts, which hold assets of about US$400 billion.

The volume and reach afforded by instantaneous banking transactions across the world make global banking highly profitable, but some economists fear that these same characteristics could also be its undoing. On a typical day, well over 100 banks are sending and receiving pay orders via CHIPS at the rate of US$2 billion a minute. Unlike payments in currency, which are final, electronic orders to pay are not settled until the close of the business day, and then the accounts are cleared multilaterally. Passell (1992) likens the process to a poker game: 'Each institution that is in arrears makes payments into the kitty much the way the "bank" settles accounts for a half-dozen players' when the game breaks up. Should a bank lack the funds to settle accounts at the end of its business day, the electronic entries would be reversed – *unwound* in global-banking lingo – and every bank engaged in a transfer to or from the defaulting bank would feel its effects. The gridlock caused by the hundreds of corrections, especially if multiple bank defaults are involved or a stock market crash is also occurring, could trigger a chain reaction of bank failures. The system could be shut down for weeks, during which time corporations would be starved of working capital. Bankers profess great confidence that such scenarios are highly improbable, but they acknowledge that the complexity, speed, and dynamism of global banking arrangements expose the system to hazards we cannot even imagine. That, they say, is always the risk of technological advance. And as with other technological catastrophes – from Chernobyl to Bhopal – a financial markets computer breakdown would ultimately injure innocent workers and civilians just as it has in Mexico, Asia and elsewhere.

GLOBALIZATION AND THE PRESSURE TO DEREGULATE

The technology of money lending and the explosion in money packaging have outpaced banking regulations designed for a simpler and slower age. The pressures of globalization have been used to remove regulations of all sorts from the financial services industry; US banks are subject to more regulations than their German or Japanese competitors and therefore, it is argued, the global playing field is not level. Bigger German and Japanese banks with broader powers are outcompeting global banks that fly the US flag.

Changes in Japanese banking regulations are also putting Tokyo-based banks in a stronger competitive position. On 18 October, two weeks before the 1992 presidential election, Secretary of the Treasury Nicholas Brady gave a speech to the American Bankers Association in which he said that increasing the competitiveness of the US financial services industry was critical to stimulating growth in the US economy. The key, he said, was to eliminate 'the old arbitrary legal framework that governs the banking system, especially outdated restrictions on products and geography'. In other words, banks should be free to leave their original neighbourhoods – where they may have helped local business and the public – and go to Asia or Europe, or wherever the action is, to serve themselves.

The argument that globalization requires deregulation is at least a quarter-century old. Deregulation of the US financial services industry has actually been underway for years, as part of a global shift in the relationship between governments and banks all over the world. To a great extent the US financial services industry deregulated itself. By resorting to creative corporation rearrangements, such as holding companies and mergers, the banking, brokerage and insurance industries slipped out of the legislative restraints intended to limit their geographical reach and their permissible activities long before Congress acted to loosen them. Through its parent corporation, Citicorp, which is not a bank under the law, Citibank could operate as a credit-card banker in all 50 states, rendering irrelevant and unenforceable the New Deal legislation that was supposed to keep banks serving their own communities. To get around legal requirements that banks lend only a certain percentage of their cash reserves, Citibank could sell its loans to Citicorp, which is not subject to these requirements. (In 1998, a giant financial conglomerate, Travelers Group, acquired Citicorp for US$72.6 billion; the new merged firm is called Citigroup.)

Congress had not anticipated that the nation's largest bank would make such effective use of the one-bank holding company to escape regulation, and friends of the banking industry in the US Senate effectively blocked efforts to plug the loophole. By the 1980s, banks were not only operating across state lines but had become sellers of insurance as well. Brokerage houses and automobile manufacturers were now deeply involved in the real estate market. All had, one way or another, jumped over the fences Congress had put up to separate investment banks from commercial banks and to keep brokerage firms, insurance companies and thrifts concentrated on the businesses for which they were chartered. Thanks to information technology and the ingenuity of lawyers, money now travelled faster, farther and in ways never envisioned by banking legislation and regulatory authorities. As Clive Crook in the *Economist* puts it, deregulation 'is often no more than an acknowledgement that the rules are no longer working' (Crook, 1992).

But deregulation, whether by circumvention of official policy or by law, had unanticipated and extremely unpleasant consequences. Like war plans, bank regulations are written with the catastrophes of the previous generation in mind.

After the Great Depression, when the national banking system collapsed because of risky loans, the Federal Reserve was given authority to set interest-rate ceilings on deposits. Regulation Q, as this grant of regulatory authority was known, was designed to stop banks from offering higher interest rates as a way of competing for deposits. The theory was that if banks were paying high interest, they would have to earn more on their loans and would be under pressure to take big risks with depositors' money. Since the deposits were now insured by the Federal Deposit Insurance Corporation (FDIC), the risk would eventually fall on the taxpayers if the economy turned sour. In normal times, the fees all the member banks paid into the FDIC are sufficient to cover the deposits of banks in trouble; but if failures were to reach a certain point, FDIC reserves would be exhausted, and Congress would have to come up with the money to pay off depositors. This is, of course, exactly what happened in the late 1980s in the infamous savings and loan industry debacle. But the roots of the problem were planted decades earlier.

EVOLUTION OF HOMELESS MONEY

All through the Cold War years, US savers were sending more of their money abroad to take advantage of higher returns. In 1966, under pressure from lobbies representing elderly and retired persons, the Federal Reserve Board agreed to let financial institutions such as brokerage houses and insurance companies pay market rates on consumer savings accounts. These new accounts offering higher returns for consumers were known as *money market funds*. As nominal interest rates soared in the 1970s, money market funds accumulated hundreds of billions of dollars. By 1979, savings banks, savings and loan associations (S&Ls) and credit unions, which had their deposits tied up in long-term, low-interest home mortgages arranged before inflation became rampant, tottered on the edge of bankruptcy.

Congress came to the rescue with two pieces of legislation: one known as the Deregulation and Monetary Control Act of 1980 and the other the Garn–St Germain Act of 1982. Essentially, these laws phased out regulatory limits on interest rates for savings institutions, allowed them to offer interest-paying checking accounts, and granted authority to make all sorts of loans. Previously, thrifts had survived by lending most of the home-mortgage money in the nation, but now they were permitted to make consumer loans and commercial real-estate loans. At the same time, companies such as Sears, GM, and Prudential, along with the commercial banks, could expand further into the commercial mortgage market. By tradition and by law, commercial banks were in business to supply working capital and investment funds to industry. But now they rushed into the real estate market. Citibank increased its mortgage portfolio from US$100 million to US$14.8 billion in just ten years. All this competitive zeal to finance unneeded office buildings spelled disaster for the S&Ls. Half of them disappeared. Our children and millions more taxpayers yet unborn will have to come up with something under US$1 trillion to repair the damage.

All through the last three decades, US banks pursued another strategy to escape the regulators. They shifted more and more of their activities beyond US shores, well out of reach of the treasury or the Federal Reserve. Here, too, regulators inadvertently spurred the process. As US corporations, armies, military installations and government aid programmes spread around the world in the 1950s, all spending billions in US currency in other countries, the glut of dollars in the hands of foreigners became a serious world problem. By this time, Germany, Japan, and the other industrial countries were recovering from the shocks of World War II and were producing a flood of goods. It was neither necessary nor advantageous to import so much from the US. Non-Americans had accumulated hundreds of billions of dollars more than they could possibly use to buy goods and services from the US. Except for the fact that the dollar was the world's reserve currency backed by gold, the overvalued offshore dollars were becoming risky holdings. If the holders of offshore dollars were to cash them in, the US would face financial catastrophe, because the treasury promised to redeem dollars with gold at US$35 an ounce. The obvious alternatives for the federal government were either to scale back expensive military commitments or to devalue the dollar. Both were inconsistent with America's self-image in the 1960s as the world's number one superpower.

For the first time, the nation experienced severe balance of payments problems. As foreigners piled up unwanted, overvalued dollars in banks in London, Paris, Geneva and Hong Kong, the doors of the gold depository at Fort Knox kept swinging open to accommodate the heavy traffic in gold bars bound for Europe. To stem the flow of gold, the Kennedy and Johnson administrations tried to limit the amount of dollars US banks could lend to foreigners and taxed foreign bonds issued in the United States. But these measures only succeeded in accelerating the outflow of dollars. US banks, led by Citibank, were now firmly established in Europe and Asia, and offshore lending exploded in reaction to the US government's efforts to keep Wall Street banks from lending to foreigners.

By the 1970s, for every dollar US banks were lending to non-Americans from their domestic bank offices, they were lending six or seven more from vast offshore facilities that collectively came to be called the Euromarket. This pooling of funds, mostly in dollars, started in Europe to accommodate the financial needs of communist China, but it soon became a global money pool that could be used by borrowers anywhere. The distinguishing feature of the Euromarket is that the money is denominated in a currency different from the official currency where the deposits are located. All such money is largely beyond the reach of national regulators in the countries of origin. When US companies in need of capital abroad resorted to the Euromarket, they were complying with the US policy to restrict capital outflow from the United States. But the buildup of this huge pool of offshore dollars created a formidable alternative to the US capital market. IBM was the pioneer among US-based companies to make creative use of the Euromarket, but soon many US companies operating outside the United

States were financing their overseas operations without resorting to banks in their home country. The Euromarket expanded into bond issues and then began offering a menu of increasingly arcane money products. Soon it was serving as a 'connecting rod' for financial markets around the world that once were entirely separate.

EMERGENCE OF CASINO ECONOMICS

Money itself was becoming a truly global product. In 1973, the gross sum in Eurocurrency accounts all over the world was US$315 billion; by 1987, the total was nearly US$4 trillion. This fantastic expansion was hastened by the series of deregulations of international money transactions that began when the Nixon administration forced the end of fixed exchange rates in August 1971, and governments everywhere lost much of their power over money. The value of money was now set in increasingly integrated global marketplaces, as foreign exchange traders all around the world haggled over how many lire or drachmas an ever fluctuating dollar could buy at any instant in time. In the 1970s, the eminent economist Milton Friedman convinced the Chicago Mercantile Exchange, which had established a lively futures market in hog bellies and other agricultural products in order to protect farmers and food companies from the volatility of farm prices, that a futures market for money products would be a smart idea. The more exchange rates fluctuated, the more interested investors would become in hedging their bets with contracts to buy or sell at a set price on a set date. The betting possibilities were limitless. By 1989, 350 varieties of futures contracts, most of which were financial, were traded in Chicago and in the 70-plus new exchanges that had sprouted up across the world.

US officials played the key role in the transformation of world financial markets, most notably on two occasions. The first was in 1971, when Nixon closed the 'gold window'. No longer was it possible to redeem dollars for gold. This meant that non-Americans had to keep their dollars on deposit somewhere in the world or convert them into some other currency. The second event came eight years later when Paul Volcker, then chair of the Federal Reserve Board, tried to fight inflation in the US by cutting the money supply. He used the standard tool – charging substantially higher interest rates to commercial banks to obtain dollars from the Federal Reserve. Since the dollar was the reserve currency for the world, however, the 'Fed' had unwittingly raised interest rates everywhere, and both interest rates and exchange rates began fluctuating wildly. As Michael Lewis puts it in his book *Liar's Poker* (1989), 'Overnight the bond market was transformed from a backwater into a casino. The buying, selling and lending of monetary products worldwide became businesses in themselves. Most of it had little or nothing to do with investment in either production or commerce. (However, as exchange rates became more volatile, hedging became almost a necessity for some transnational businesses.) Foreign direct investment in the developing world fell as the leading commercial banks of the world saw that they could reap quicker profits in commissions, fees and interest by 'recycling' tens of billions of 'petrodollars' from the coffers of Kuwait and Saudi Arabia to the governments and their business associates in poor countries.

As Richard O'Brien, chief economist of American Express Bank, notes (1992), 'Deregulation and liberalization clearly encourage globalization and integration. Liberal markets and systems tend to be open, providing greater ease of access, greater transparency of pricing and information.' The flow of accessible information offers a global environment that is hospitable to homeless money, promoting what O'Brien calls 'the end of geography' in the finance and investment business.

The rise of global financial markets makes it increasingly difficult for national governments to formulate economic policy, much less to enforce it. In the increasingly anarchic world of high-speed money, the dilemma facing national political leaders is clear: impose regulations, then sit back and watch how quickly financial institutions slip away by changing their looks, disappearing into other corporations, or otherwise rearranging their affairs to make life difficult for the regulators. At the same time, bankers argue that to the extent the regulations are observed, they pose a handicap in international competition. Yet, the history of deregulation is littered with scandals and financial foolishness for which a handful of bankers, but mostly millions of taxpayers and depositors, have paid a heavy price.

GLOBAL RACE TO DEREGULATE

On 27 October 1986, the 'Big Bang', as the chair of the London Stock Exchange first called it, went off in the city of London, ending 200 years of comfortable, stately, and expensive trading practices on the London Stock Exchange. Overnight, the market was deregulated and opened to foreign banks and securities firms of all sorts. An electronic marketing system modelled on the new US computer-age stock exchange, NASDAQ, was installed to take the place of old-fashioned floor trading. Traders could now bypass London and deal directly with markets in New York and Tokyo at much less cost. Deregulation was a strategy for trying to get lost business back. As the New York Stock Exchange had done more than ten years earlier, the London Stock Exchange abolished fixed commissions for traders, and it now permitted firms to act as both wholesale dealers and brokers. Suddenly, US commercial banks that were barred from the securities business at home could plunge into this market in London, neatly jumping over the wall of separation between investment and commercial banking provided under the Glass-Steagall Act of 1933, the cornerstone of modern US banking regulation. (With the Great Crash and its consequences still fresh in mind, the act was intended to forbid banks to act as underwriters for corporate securities.)

The global expansion through large corporate mergers and acquisitions gathered steam in the 1970s, and this global restructuring of industry required the amassing of huge amounts of capital. At first, large banks dominated this market because they were the ones with the financial power and connections to syndicate large loans through networks of foreign banks. But in the 1980s, as capital needs mushroomed, corporations in search of funds found that it was much cheaper to raise the capital by issuing bonds and other sorts of commercial paper. Financial institutions of all sorts packaged a bunch of small loans and sold them as securities on world markets.

Borrowers all over the world, including the largest corporations, could now shop around the world for money, and they could borrow it in many different forms on a wide variety of terms. Investors could hedge against risks in one national economy or in one industry by buying foreign stocks. Global markets in securities offered opportunities for diversification. Laws and regulations that had previously put international investments out of bounds came tumbling down. Markets in securities were losing what few geographical ties were left. It was now possible to invest in the New York market by buying New York Stock Exchange index shares on the Chicago Board Options Exchange.

The Big Bang triggered an explosion of deregulation in other financial centres all over the world. Screen-based markets offering instantaneous flows of global information took over an ever larger share of business from traditional floor trading. In addition to the speed and convenience, there were fees and taxes to be saved. Stocks in foreign companies became internationally traded products. London, Amsterdam, Paris, Frankfurt and Zurich competed in offering the most cosmopolitan menu of stocks, options, swaps, and futures in companies around the world. By 1990, the buying and selling of foreign equities on the London Exchange exceeded that of British equities.

THE FINAL BARRIER

With the juggernaut of deregulation having just about completed its sweep across the developed world, there remained one final barrier to ultimate freedom of movement for money and for the ability of the great financial conglomerates to control world markets. That barrier was among the poor countries of the developing world, who still stubbornly refused to open their commercial banking sector to outside domination. The Uruguay Round of the GATT took care of that.

In most of the world's poorest countries, foreign banks were traditionally welcomed for the services they performed, but only up to a certain point. The foreign banks were appreciated as sellers of retail credit and providers of capital under controlled, specific conditions. But foreign banks, with few exceptions, had been prohibited from buying into ownership positions in commercial banking. Developing world governments argued that since finance is central to development, the financial services industry should remain firmly in domestic hands, serve domestic interests, and keep money within the economy.

The US led the challenge against the developing world's control of its own financial markets during the Uruguay Round of GATT negotiations. The US and other Western nations argued that 'efficiency' and 'fairness' required that all foreign banks be accorded national treatment in every country. *National treatment* essentially means that foreign banks must be treated just as if they were local banks, so, for example, US banks must be permitted entry into developing world financial markets even if they gain full control of the local institutions. Local governments would have to give up all attempts to sustain control over local financing activity.

This was one of several important points that kept GATT negotiations stalled for seven years; but eventually the US and the other Western powers forced the poor nations to cave in and, under the WTO, a financial invasion is now underway.

While those negotiations proceeded, the US pushed hard for deregulation of financial services with Mexico and secured an agreement that the US negotiator said would give US banks 'dramatic new opportunities', a situation later solidified by NAFTA. As a result, one treasury official bragged at an off-record briefing, 'They [Mexico] gave us their financial system.' Indeed they had, and in January 1995 the world was given a taste of the consequences. The Mexican economy will not recover for a long while. Ordinary Mexican citizens will ultimately pay the bills for the bailout by the US of hundreds of its own speculators, notably Chase Manhattan and Goldman Sachs.

Clearly, Mexico in 1995 and much of the rest of the world in 1997–1998 were just the first of many such debacles to come. In a globalized economy, wired together by technologies capable of moving unimaginable funds instantaneously around the globe at the behest of speculators and immune to any ability to regulate or control this movement, we are in for more frequent catastrophes. Yet, this is a condition the world will not be able to tolerate for long. It makes banking services even more difficult and distant for local communities, small businesses and ordinary people. Worst of all, it puts the entire international economic apparatus into a most precarious situation. Global finance could tumble down quickly, like the house of cards it has become.

Ultimately, change must come in the form of a financial system not based on speculation, but a system that uses funds with geographic roots and some connection to goods and services that cater, as they once did, to the interests of local and regional economies. The examples of the Grameen Bank in Bangladesh and the South Shore Bank in Chicago, running directly counter to the trend, are informative, optimistic models. Only by such a change in direction can the financial community be remotely in service to ecological and social sustainability.

Chapter 5

Mechanisms of Corporate Rule

Tony Clarke

In this comprehensive overview, Canadian scholar and activist Tony Clarke surveys the growing power of the transnational corporations. No longer ordinary players on the international scene, corporations have achieved effective global governance by virtue of their control of economic processes, of financial markets, of the new global trade bureaucracy, of the media, and, increasingly, of education.

Tony Clarke brings to bear on this issue more than two decades of experience in social activism and leadership. After receiving his PhD degree in social ethics and professional ministry from the University of Chicago in 1974 he became director of the Social Affairs Department of the Canadian Conference of Catholic Bishops and later chair of the Justice and Peace Commission of the Canadian Council of Churches. From 1987 to 1993, he led Action Canada Network, a coalition of labour and social groups that fought to prevent Canada's adherence to the Canada–US Free Trade Agreement and NAFTA. Clarke is also chair of the Corporations Committee of the International Forum on Globalization. His books include Behind the Mitre: The Moral Leadership Crisis in the Canadian Catholic Church *(1995) and* Witness to Justice *(1979, with Theresa Clarke).*

In their famous book *Global Reach* (1974), Richard Barnet and Ronald Mueller state this: 'The men who run global corporations are the first in history with the organization, technology, money, and ideology to make a credible try at managing the world as an integrated economic unit.'

In the 20-odd years since these words were penned, TNCs have consolidated their power and control over the world. Today, 47 of the top 100 economies in the world are actually transnational corporations; 70 per cent of global trade is controlled by just 500 corporations; and a mere 1 per cent of the TNCs on this planet own half the total stock of foreign direct investment.

And their location is concentrated around the industrialized world's power axis. Based on the 1998 rankings, 443 of the Global Fortune 500 corporations are still home based in either the US (185), Europe (158) or Japan (100). At the same time, the new free market and free trade regimes (such as GATT and NAFTA) have created global conditions in which TNCs and banks can move their capital, technology, goods and services freely throughout the world, unfettered by the regulations of nation states or democratically elected governments.

In effect, what has taken place is a massive shift in power out of the hands of nation states and democratic governments and into the hands of TNCs and banks. It is now the TNCs that effectively govern the lives of the vast majority of the people on Earth; yet these new world realities are seldom reflected in the strategies of citizen movements for democratic social change. All too often, strategies are aimed primarily at changing government policies, while the real power being exercised by TNCs behind the scenes is rarely challenged, let alone dismantled. When the operations of TNCs do become a prime target for citizen action campaigns, there is a tendency to employ a rather piecemeal approach to what is a deeply systemic problem.

As we approach the 21st century, it is imperative that social movements in both the North and the South develop new politics for challenging the dominant global rule of transnational enterprises.

The following overview examines some of the salient ingredients of the new powers that now give corporations effective control over the lives of peoples and nations in this age of globalization, and then offers some suggestions as to changing the situation.

· · ·

Over the past three decades, as David C Korten points out (in Chapter 2), the world's leading business and governmental elites have been gathering on a regular basis in elite forums, such as the Council on Foreign Relations and the Trilateral Commission, to develop a consensus on an agenda for globalization.

Behind closed doors, these leaders have been able to agree on certain common approaches, which include global economic integration; the 'harmonization' of various trade, tax and regulatory measures; and an economic philosophy that should guide all nations, combined with political strategies to achieve such changes. With passage of the new free trade agreements to augment the Bretton Woods agreement and to establish the WTO, this unelected and unaccountable global elite has effectively seized important instruments of governance in the three dominant regions of the world.

Regardless of their nominal home bases, Japanese, North American and European corporations have increasingly become stateless, juggling multiple national identities and loyalties to achieve their global competitive interests. No matter where they operate in the world, these transnational conglomerates can use their overseas subsidiaries, joint ventures, licensing agreements and strategic alliances to assume foreign identities whenever it suits their purposes. In so doing, they develop chameleon-like abilities to change their identities to resemble insiders wherever they are operating. As one CEO put it, 'When we go to Brussels, we're member states of the EEC and when we go to Washington we're an American company too.' Whenever they need to, they will wrap themselves up in the national flag of choice to get support for tax breaks, research subsidies or governmental representation in negotiations affecting their marketing plans. Through this process, stateless corporations are effectively transforming nation states to suit their interests.

THE CORPORATE–STATE ALLIANCE

In most of the industrialized countries, business councils composed of the CEOs of the largest corporations and banks have formed new corporate–state alliances. In the US, for example, the powerful US Business Round Table, which represents the 200 largest corporations, has direct influence at the highest levels of Washington decision-making on international trade, investment and finance. In Japan, direct links between the big Japanese corporations and the government are well institutionalized through the Keidanren, the Japan Federation of Economic Organizations. In Europe, the leading big business lobby machine is the European Round Table of Industrialists, which comprises the continent's 50 largest transnational corporations, while in Canada it's the Business Council on National Issues, which represents the country's major 150 corporations.

Once a policy consensus is reached among the principal TNCs, massive lobbying and advertising campaigns are mounted around key policy issues. Armed with a network of policy research institutes and public relations firms, such business coalitions mobilize facts, policy positions, expert analysis and opinion polls and organize citizen-front groups for their campaigns to change national governments and their policies. By campaigning for debt elimination, privatization and deregulation, business coalitions have effectively dismantled many of the powers and tools of national governments.

The fundamental purposes of the new free trade deals (such as GATT and NAFTA) are to enable TNCs and banks to act unhindered by national laws and constitutions. As Caria Hills, when former chief US negotiator for both NAFTA and GATT, put it, 'We want corporations to be able to make investments overseas without being required to take a local partner, to export a given percentage of their output, to use local parts or to meet a dozen other restrictions.' As a result, the 'national treatment' clauses in NAFTA and GATT guarantee that foreign investors have the same rights and freedoms as domestic firms. The investment codes in the new free trade regimes ensure that various regulations of nation states are removed, including foreign investment requirements, export quotas, local procurement, job content and technology specifications. Through this new kind of constitutional protection, the rights of TNCs take precedence over the rights of citizens in their respective nation states. In addition, the legislative authority of GATT and NAFTA supersedes the legislation of participating nation states when matters of conflict arise.

The creation of a globalized consumer culture is another key element of the new corporate tyranny. The transnationals want to be able to sell their products with the same basic advertising design in Bangkok and Santiago as in Paris, Tokyo, New York or London. The prime example is the way Coca-Cola has become a global symbol transcending all national and cultural boundaries. Through television images and satellite communications, a homogeneous set of perspectives, tastes and desires can be transmitted to all corners of the globe to create a worldwide culture of corporate-friendly consumers. It is now estimated that transnationals spend well over half as much money in advertising as the nations of the world combined spend on public education. In turn, all this corporate advertising tends to forge a connection in people's mind-sets between private interests (those of the TNCs) and the public interest. As a result, a global monoculture is emerging which not only disregards local tastes and cultural differences, but threatens to serve as a form of social control over the attitudes, expectations and behaviour of people all over the world.

. . .

Until the setting up of the WTO, the two main Bretton Woods institutions, the World Bank and the IMF, have been the principal tools by which the new global managers maintain corporate control over nations and peoples, especially in countries of the South. Both the bank and the fund are directly linked to the transnational financial sector vis-à-vis the borrowing and lending ends of their operations. Loan agreements are routinely negotiated in secret between banking and government officials who, for the most part, are not accountable to the people on whose behalf they are obligating the national treasury to foreign lenders. The bank and the fund must be regarded, as one observer puts it, 'as governance institutions, exercising power through [their] financial leverage to legislate entire legal regimens and even to alter the constitutional structure of borrowing nations'. The officials of these organizations often have the power to 'rewrite a country's trade policy, fiscal policies, civil service requirements, labour laws, health care arrangements, environmental regulations, energy policy, resettlement requirements, procurement rules and budgetary policy'.

In the 1980s, the World Bank and the IMF used debt renegotiations as a club to force the developing nations into implementing SAPs in their economies. Each SAP package called for sweeping economic and social changes designed to channel the country's resources and productivity into debt repayments and to enhance transnational competition. The SAP measures included large-scale deregulation, privatization, currency devaluation, social spending cuts, lower corporate taxes, expansion of the export of natural resources and agricultural products, and removal of foreign investment restrictions. In order to obtain the foreign exchange to service their massive debts, developing countries were compelled to become export-oriented economies, selling off their natural resources and agricultural commodities on global markets while rapidly increasing their dependency on the imports of goods and services. In effect, the SAPs have become instruments for the recolonization of many developing countries in the South in the interests of TNCs and banks. (See Chapters 1 and 10 by Edward Goldsmith and Walden Bello, respectively.)

The new WTO established by the Uruguay Round of GATT is designed, in effect, to serve as a global governing body for transnational corporate interests. The WTO will have both legislative and judicial powers and a mandate to eliminate all barriers to international investment and competition. Under the WTO, a group of unelected trade representatives will act as a global parliament with the power to override economic and social policy decisions of nation states and democratic legislatures around the world. At the same time, the world's major TNCs will have a powerful role to play in the new WTO through direct linkages with the trade representatives of participating countries. In the case of the US, for example, members of the Advisory Committee for Trade Policy and Negotiations include such corporate giants as IBM, AT&T, Bethlehem Steel, Time Warner, Corning, Bank of America, American Express, Scott Paper, Dow Chemical, Boeing, Eastman Kodak, Mobil Oil, Amoco, Pfizer, Hewlett-Packard, Weyerhauser, and General Motors – all of which are members of the Business Roundtable.

Systems of Corporate Rule

The sections that follow describe some of the ways that global systems have been effectively usurped by transnational corporations and banks.

Global finance

The globalization of finance markets has been nothing short of revolutionary. The days when national authorities could stabilize financial markets through banking regulations, reserve requirements, deposit insurance, limits on interest rates, and the separation of commercial and investment banking are all but gone. In country after country there has been a massive deregulation of finance and mergers between commercial and investment banking. In addition, TNCs are now bypassing banks altogether and issuing their own commercial paper. Information technology has transformed global banking to the point where US$1.5 trillion is transferred every day around the world. Electronic transfer systems make more than 150,000 international transactions in a single day. The speed and frequency of these transactions – from Malaysia to Toronto to New York to Miami to the Cayman Islands to the Bahamas to Switzerland – makes the money trail difficult to trace, let alone regulate. But this deregulated, global finance market has become fragile and unstable to the point where a financial shock in one country (such as Mexico) can dramatically upset financial markets in other countries before national authorities have a chance to intervene. Unless radically new regulatory measures are introduced, the fiscal policies of national governments will not only be dictated but also threatened by a volatile global finance system. (See Chapter 4.)

Global industrial production

As the auto, electronics, textile and clothing industries have outgrown their home countries and shifted their production and supplier operations off-shore to independent contractors, the 'global factory', coupled with a radically new international division of labour, has emerged. With the globalization of production networks, transnational manufacturing firms can quickly move their operations around the world, in search of cheap labour, more profitable investment opportunities and freedom from the demands of unionized workers. The new global factory has resulted in a dramatic loss of manufacturing jobs in the industrial North (the US, Japan and Europe) as manufacturing companies move their production to low-wage, tax-free countries in the South. Increasingly, workers around the world find themselves lumped together in the same global labour pool to the point where exploitation in Guatemala, Malaysia or China is felt as wage competition by workers in London, New York or Montreal. While the staggering wage gap between workers in the North and the South has begun to narrow, there is a very real danger that the forces of global competition will drag workers everywhere down to the lowest common wage standards.

Global product distribution

In *Global Dreams* (1994), Richard Barnet and John Cavanagh describe the global supermarket that is transforming agricultural production throughout the world while undercutting the capacity of nations to meet the basic food needs of their populations. Transnational food corporations are demanding an end to the system of agricultural subsidies, regulation and protection that has maintained a relatively cheap food policy in the industrial North. At the same time, poor countries in the South who were once self-sufficient in food, but are now desperate for foreign exchange to pay down their debts, are forced to turn over valuable agricultural lands to transnational agribusinesses and to convert to cash-crop production while importing food products to feed their own peoples. 'Export or die' is the message, but 'export and die' is the reality. The introduction of biotech production methods – laboratory-produced vanilla, bioengineered celery, freeze-resistant flowers and tomatoes and bovine growth hormone for cows, combined with long-distance food transportation – poses further threats not only to the livelihood of traditional farmers in poor countries but also to the quality and safety of food products in general. Meanwhile, the giant food corporations – General Foods, Kraft, Pillsbury, Philip Morris, Del Monte, President's Choice, Procter and Gamble, Pepsico, and others – have merged their operations and expanded their marketing strategies on a global basis. National authorities are also finding it increasingly difficult to maintain adequate food inspection at the border, especially for the massive imports of fruits and vegetables, thereby requiring expanded use of ozone-depleting chemical fumigants such as methyl bromide.

The corporate dream of turning the whole world into a global shopping paradise is also near at hand. Not only have Coca-Cola and Marlboro become universally recognized brand names through massive corporate advertising, but global retailers such as Procter and Gamble, Philip Morris, RJR Nabisco, Kellogg, General Motors, Scars, Unilever, Pepsico, Nestlé and McDonald's have been spending billions of advertising and promotion dollars each year to create a steadily expanding global market based on mass consumption. The strategy is to sell the same things in the same way everywhere, with little or no regard for local customs, tastes or cultural or religious differences.

Resource control

Transnational resource giants such as Exxon, Mitsubishi, Texas Gulf, Shell, Rio Tinto Zinc and Alcan and a host of energy, mining, forestry, and hydro corporations have expanded their operations to the four corners of the Earth, posing serious threats to the environment by causing massive oil spills, reversing river flows, flooding huge land tracts, depleting vast forest areas, eliminating fish stocks and destroying vegetation and wildlife. The only thing new about this is the new atmosphere of deregulation in areas such as environmental protection. The resource and energy codes built into NAFTA and GATT are designed to accelerate the rapid development and export of natural resources. Moreover, 'the export or die' demands of the IMF mean that poor countries with resource-based economies have no choice but to open their doors to transnational resource companies without regulation or environmental protection. Rapid exports not only accelerate the depletion of non-renewable resources but greatly intensify the global demand for supplies of freshwater that are now being targeted by TNCs. Add to this the persistent destruction of the last rainforests plus the continuous dumping of hazardous wastes into the ecosystem by companies such as Union Carbide, Dow Chemical and DuPont. It leaves little wonder why the world is on the verge of an ecological holocaust.

Banking, insurance, education

Transnational corporations are also rapidly taking control of basic services such as health care and education, which have been the public responsibility of governments in most countries. Through a series of vertical and horizontal mergers, a system of large-scale health care corporations is emerging. In the US, the major drug companies such as Eli Lily are merging with health insurance industries such as PCS for the take-over of hospitals, pharmacies, free-standing clinics, nursing homes and doctors' practices. The world's largest profit-oriented hospital companies, Columbia and Health Trust, have merged to form a giant health care corporation with sales exceeding that of Eastman Kodak or American Express. In a deregulated global economy, these new health care giants are poised to swallow up pieces of the public health care system in countries such as Canada, where there is enormous pressure to privatize. At the same time, TNCs are also invading the education system. In the US, organizations such as the Business Higher Education Forum and the New American Schools Development Corporation (which funnels corporate finances into profit-oriented elementary schools) are composed of TNCs such as AT&T, Ford, Eastman Kodak, Pfizer, General Electric, Heinz and many others. Companies that sport household brand names such as Coca-Cola, Pepsi, McDonald's, Burger King and Procter and Gamble are also directly involved in developing curricula for schools along with advertising promotions to help kids grow up corporate. (See Chapter 19.)

Patenting of life forms

While government regulations over TNCs are being dismantled in countries all over the world, the monopoly rights of the transnationals over information and technology are now internationally protected under the intellectual property rights components of GATT. Moreover, the international patent right protection has been extended to genetic materials, including seeds and natural medicines. The patenting of life forms allows TNCs to secure widespread control over genetically engineered organisms, from microorganisms to plants and animals. Worse still, transnationals are now able to obtain monopoly rights over generic research, plus any products derived from that research, concerning an entire species. The W R Grace Corporation, for example, through its subsidiary Agracetus Inc, has secured a US patent on all genetically engineered or 'transgenic' cotton varieties (1992) and a European patent on all transgenic soybeans (1994). In addition, it has applications pending in other countries including India, China and Brazil to take control of 60 per cent of the world's cotton crop. Under these conditions, farmers who traditionally save seed from one harvest to replant for the next crop find themselves in violation of international patent law. Unless they pay a royalty to the TNC that owns the patented seed, farmers around the world are now prohibited from growing their own seed stocks. Furthermore, there are moves to have these global monopoly rights and patent protection laws extended to include the cloning of human embryos.

Cultural cloning

Armed with satellite communications, global entertainment corporations are selling their pop music cultural products all over the world. The target audience of this global entertainment industry is the two-fifths of the world's population who are under the age of 20. The biggest technological leap in the global entertainment industry came with MTV in the 1980s. By 1993, MTV programmes were reaching 210 million households in 71 countries throughout the world. Bertelsmann's pop music empire presently dominates youth markets throughout Europe, North America and Latin America and is now moving into Asia. Sony, Philips and Matsushita have also been expanding into these markets.

Increasingly, the big six global entertainment corporations are focusing their energies on opening up markets in Latin America and Asia, where the greatest growth potential exists. But this expansion is also being challenged as a new form of cultural imperialism. For the poor countries of Asia, Africa and Latin America, the big six's penetration of transnational sound will choke off traditional music of the local culture and restrict employment opportunities for local artists. At the same time, the global entertainment industry will increasingly generate a homogenized culture that reflects Western corporate values and priorities. (See Chapter 4.)

NEW BASES FOR SOCIAL ACTION

The best hope for countering growing corporate domination lies in the building of social movements in which people reclaim their sovereign rights over TNCs and banks.

Most people now feel that they have lost control over their economic, social and ecological future. This is not only true among the poor majority in the South, following the damage done by massive SAPs, but increasingly among the majority of working, middle-class peoples in the North. For many, the dream of securing a full-time job, a relatively stable and crime-free community or a clean environment with a bright future for their children has been shattered. In this climate, the politics of fear and insecurity have become rampant in most of our countries, expressing themselves sometimes as ethnic violence or, more recently, as right-wing citizen militias.

Underlying the politics of fear and insecurity is the fundamental question of democracy itself. These conditions, in turn, could create new political opportunities for building social movements to re-establish democratic control.

Popular sovereignty

In the building of social movements today, emphasis must be placed on the notion of popular sovereignty as a common base for action. Throughout this century alone, peoples all over the world have fought for the recognition of fundamental democratic and human rights – the right to adequate food, clothing and shelter; the right to employment, education, and health care; the right to a clean environment, social equality, and public services – and the right to self-determination and participation in the decisions that affect these rights. Together, these basic communal rights, which constitute the core of popular sovereignty, have been codified and enshrined in the Universal Declaration of Human Rights, the International Covenant on Economic, Social and Cultural Rights, and the International Covenant on Civil and Political Rights.

The emergence of the corporate state, however, in which the reins of democratic governance have been taken over by corporations and banks, has completely disfigured and distorted the responsibilities of the national governments. The moral and political obligations of nation states to intervene in the market economy have been eliminated in order to ensure that the entire national system – economic, fiscal, social, cultural, environmental, political – functions for the purpose of providing a profitable climate for transnational investment and competition in the new global economy. As the politics of insecurity unfold, however, a brand of right-wing nationalism is likely to arise with new forms of protectionism against immigration and cheap imports for the major TNCs – in other words, protectionism for the powerful. In this climate, social movements must focus their energies on resisting the corporate state and the rise of the new right-wing nationalism. People's energies need to be mobilized around a new social vision of the nation state in an age of global interdependence, where governments reclaim the power and tools necessary to exercise democratic control over TNCs and banks. In effect, the nation state must be retooled to serve the people's rights to determine their economic, social and ecological future. But this new nationalism must be simultaneously carried out in concert with social movements in other countries that are engaged in similar struggles.

Citizens' manifesto

In order to build social movements in both North and South that are committed to re-establishing democratic control, a common platform and agenda need to be developed. This could take the form of a common manifesto for citizens of the world, which would include:

1   a declaration of the fundamental rights of people to determine their own economic, social and ecological future;
2   the sovereign rights of peoples over TNCs and banks;
3   the demand that TNCs meet certain basic economic, social, and environmental conditions;
4   the insistence that governments develop and enact new regulatory measures for exercising democratic control over TNCs; and
5   the responsibility of social movements to take whatever forms of action are needed to ensure that people's basic rights are upheld and that democratic control over TNCs is maintained.

The core of this citizens' manifesto would be the spirit and practice of popular sovereignty. Its primary purpose would be to provide social movements in both the North and the South with a common platform for action in dismantling the corporate state and challenging the operations of TNCs at local, regional, national and international levels.

Chapter 6

The Rules of Corporate Behaviour

Jerry Mander

The main factors that determine corporate behaviour have far less to do with the people who work inside the corporate structure than they do with the corporate structure itself. The people inside corporations are simply following the legal and 'ethical' standards of corporate form. Profit comes first; growth is a close second; amorality – not morality – comes third: and there are quite a few more. To ask corporations to behave better by making growth and profit a lower priority or to act foremost in the interests of local communities, the environment, or the workers is like asking armies to give up guns. Managers who might personally like to develop more pro-social or pro-environment policies are constrained: they cannot give such factors higher priority than the bottom line, or they may find themselves out of work. This chapter describes some of the inherent rules that govern corporate behaviour.

For biographical details on Jerry Mander see Chapter 3, Technologies of Globalization.

In the previous chapter, Tony Clarke described in exquisite detail the global role corporations now play. Myriad other chapters in this book describe specific negative behaviours by corporations: factory closings and export of jobs; toxic dumpings; genetic piracy; terrible environmental destruction; and the abandonment of communities for 'free trade zones', where environmental and social laws are lax. But one important issue remains: Why do they behave this way?

Most people tend to see corporate behaviour as merely reflecting *human greed*, and the problems with corporations as stemming strictly from the makeup of the people within the corporate structure – people who are inevitably irresponsible, dishonest, overly ambitious or otherwise so self-interested as to eschew moral, ethical, social and environmental values.

To see corporate behaviour as rooted in the people who work within them is far too narrow a view and, in the end, excuses corporations from their ultimate responsibilities, for it puts the blame on individuals. In fact, the basic problems with corporations are structural and inherent in the forms and rules by which they are compelled to operate. The corporation is not as subject to human control as most people believe it is; rather, it is a largely autonomous technical structure that behaves by a system of logic uniquely well suited to its primary functions: to make profit, to give birth and impetus to new products and technologies, to expand its reach and powers, and to spread the consumer lifestyle around the globe. If all the problems of corporations could be traced to the personnel involved, they could be solved by changing the personnel. Unfortunately, all employees are obligated to behave in accordance with corporate form and corporate law. If someone attempted to revolt against them, the corporation would simply throw the person out and replace her or him with someone who would play by the rules. Form determines content. Corporations are machines.

CORPORATE CONSCIOUSNESS

The failure to grasp the nature and inevitabilities of corporate structure has left our society far too unconscious of, and passive towards, corporate desires and has helped corporations increase their global influence, power and freedom from accountability. More than any other institution (including government), corporations dominate our conceptions of how life should be lived. Corporate ideology, corporate priorities, corporate styles of behaviour, corporate value systems and corporate modes of organization have become synonymous with 'our way of life'. Corporate culture has become the virtual definition of American life, to be defended at all costs, even militarily. Now that global trade agreements have removed most obstacles to corporate invasion of all the countries of the world, and with the power of US media globally dominant, US corporate culture will soon be ubiquitous.

If you switch on your radio, flip on the television or open your newspaper, corporations speak to you. They do it through public relations and through advertising. US corporations spend more than US$150 billion yearly on advertising, which is far more than is spent on all secondary education in this country. In some ways, corporate advertising is the dominant educational institution in the US, surely in the realm of lifestyle.

According to *Advertising Age*, about 75 per cent of commercial network television time is paid for by the hundred largest corporations in the US. Many people do not react to this statistic as being important. But consider that there are presently 450,000 corporations in the US and some 250 million people with extremely diverse viewpoints about lifestyle, politics and personal and national priorities. Yet, only 100 corporations get to decide what will appear on television and what will not. These corporations do not overtly announce their refusal to finance programmes that contain views disconsonant with their own; their control is far more subtle. When television producers think about which programmes to produce, they have to subordinate other considerations to the need to sell the programmes to corporate backers. An effective censorship results.

While 100 corporations pay for 75 per cent of commercial broadcast time and thereby dominate the commercial channels, they now also pay for more than 50 per cent of public television. During the Reagan years, federal support for non-commercial television was virtually eliminated. leaving a void that public television filled by appealing to corporations. In 1995, the Gingrich-led Congress threatened to remove the remainder of public support, leaving the field entirely to corporations. As corporate influence grows in 'public' television, so do the visibility and length of the corporate commercial tags before and after the shows they sponsor. Whereas public television once featured such modest messages as, 'This programme has been brought to you through a grant by Exxon', now we see the Exxon logo, followed by an added advertising phrase or two and an audio slogan. Recently, several so-called 'non-commercial' TV stations, such as PBS affiliate KQED-TV in San Francisco, have announced that they will accept commercials. This, of course, was the original intention of defunding them, from Reagan to Gingrich.

The average US viewer already watches 22,000 commercials every year. Twenty-two thousand times, corporations place images in our brains to suggest that there is something great about buying commodities. Some commercials advertise cars; others advertise drugs – but all commercials agree that you should buy *something* and that human life is most satisfying when inundated with commodities. Between commercials there are programmes, also created by corporations, that espouse values consistent with the ads.

Corporations are also the major providers of educational materials for US schools and in other countries, too. Some of the largest corporations are now providing books, tapes, films and computer programs free of charge to public and private schools, as a 'public service' in these budget-conscious times. They get a lot of praise for these contributions. Oil and chemical companies have been particularly generous in providing materials to help explain nature to young people. The materials portray nature as a valuable resource for human use and celebrate concepts such as 'managing nature' through chemicals, pesticides, and large-scale agribusiness. Thus, a generation of American youngsters is trained to regard nature in a way that coincides with corporate objectives.

This same ideological training via television is inevitably becoming the norm all over the world. It is a further expression of the way corporations create the ideal conditions for their own expansion.

CORPORATE SHAME

I keep awaiting the day when the president of a Fortune 500 company expresses shame for a corporate transgression against the public or the environment. The statement would go something like this:

> *'On behalf of my company, its management, and its shareholders, I wish to express our grief concerning injuries suffered by people living downstream from our factory, along the Green River. We are ashamed to admit that over the years, our poisonous wastes have found their way into the river, putting the community in peril. We will do anything to relieve the suffering we have caused. We are also concerned that safe storage for such potent chemicals now seems impossible, and so henceforth we will use our facilities only for safer forms of manufacturing. Under no circumstances will we give thought to abandoning this community or its workers.'*

No such statements are made for several reasons. No manager of a publicly held company could *ever* place community welfare above corporate interest. An individual executive might personally wish to do so, but such a gesture could subject the company to seriously damaging lawsuits by victims. It could also open management to lawsuits from its shareholders. Corporate law holds that management of publicly held companies must act primarily in the economic interests of shareholders. So managers are actually legally *obligated* to *ignore* community welfare issues (such as worker health and satisfaction and environmental concerns) if those needs interfere with profitability. And corporate managers must deny that corporate acts have any negative impact if that impact might translate into costly damage suits that reduce profits.

As a result, we have witnessed countless cases in which companies deny any responsibility for corporate acts that caused death, injury or illness. We have heard cigarette company executives lie, with great transparency, about the products' harmful effects. We have heard the same from manufacturers of pesticides, chemicals, asbestos materials and birth-control technologies.

In instances such as these, withholding information means that people – perhaps tens of thousands of people – become sick. Some people die. In other contexts, murder charges would be in order.

CORPORATE SCHIZOPHRENIA

That murder charges are not levied against corporations, and that corporations do not express shame at their own actions, is a direct result of the peculiar nature of corporate form – its split personality. Though human beings work inside corporations, a corporation itself is not a person (except in the legal sense) and does not have feelings. A corporation is not even a thing. It may have offices and/or a factory where it may manufacture products, but a corporation does not have any physical existence or form – no *corporality*. So when conditions in a community or country become unfavourable – safety standards become too rigid or workers are not submissive – a corporation can dematerialize and rematerialize in another town or country. This tendency is dramatically accelerated under the new free trade regimes.

If a corporation is not a person or thing, what is it? It is basically a *concept* that is given a name, and a legal existence, on paper. Though there is no such actual creature, our laws recognize the corporation as an entity. So does the population. We think of corporations as having concrete form, but their true existence is only on paper and in our minds.

Even more curious than a corporation's ephemeral quality is the way our laws give this non-existent entity a great many rights similar to those given to human beings. The law in the US calls corporations *fictitious persons*, with the right to buy and sell property or to sue in court for injuries, slander, and libel. And *corporate speech* – advertising, public relations – is protected under the First Amendment to the US Constitution governing freedom of speech. This latter right has been extended to corporations despite the fact that when the US Bill of Rights was written in 1792, corporations as we now know them did not exist. (The First Amendment was originally intended to protect *personal* speech in a century when the media consisted only of single news sheets, handbills and books. The net result of expanding First Amendment protection to corporate speech is that US$150 billion worth of advertising from a relative handful of sources gets to dominate public perception, free from nearly all government attempts at regulation.)

Though corporations enjoy many 'human' rights, they have not been required to abide by human responsibilities. Even in cases of negligence causing death or injury, the state cannot jail or execute the corporation. In rare instances, individuals within a corporation can be prosecuted if they perpetrate acts that they know cause injury. And a corporation may be fined or ordered to alter practices, but its structure is never altered – its 'life' is never threatened. Unlike human beings, corporations do not die a natural death. A corporation usually outlives the human beings who have been a part of it, even those who own it. A corporation actually has the possibility of immortality.

Lacking the sort of physical, organic reality that characterizes human existence, this entity, this concept, this collection of paperwork called a *corporation* is not capable of feelings such as shame or remorse. Instead, corporations behave according to their own unique system of standards, rules, forms, and objectives, enshrined in state charters and confirmed through our legal structures.

THE INHERENT RULES OF CORPORATE BEHAVIOUR

The most basic rule of corporate operation is that it must show a profit over time. Among publicly held companies there is a second basic rule: it must expand and grow, since growth is the standard by which the stock market judges a company. All other values are secondary: the welfare of the community, the happiness of workers, the health of the planet and even the general prosperity.

So human beings within the corporate structure, whatever their personal morals and feelings, are prevented from operating on their own standards. Like the assembly-line workers who must operate at the speed of the machine, corporate employees are strapped onto the apparatus of the corporation and forced to operate by its rules.

In this sense, a corporation is essentially a machine, a technological structure, an organization that follows its own principles and its own morality. In such a structure, human morality is anomalous. Because of this double standard – one for real human beings and another for fictitious persons such as corporations – we sometimes see bizarre behaviour from executives who, though presumably knowing what is right and moral, behave in a contrary fashion.

For example, in 1986, Union Carbide's chemical plant in Bhopal, India, accidentally released methyl isocyanate into the air, injuring some 200,000 people and killing more than 6000. Soon after the accident, the chair of the board of Union Carbide, Warren M Anderson, was so upset at what happened he informed the media that he would spend the rest of his life attempting to correct the problems his company had caused and to make amends. Only one year later, however, Mr Anderson was quoted in *Business Week* as saying that he had 'overreacted', and was now prepared to lead the company in its legal fight *against* paying damages and reparations. What happened? Very simply, Mr Anderson at first reacted as a human being. Later he realized (and perhaps was pressed to realize) that this reaction was inappropriate for a chair of the board of a company whose obligations are not to the poor victims of Bhopal but to shareholders – that is, to its profit picture. If Mr Anderson had persisted in expressing his personal feelings or acknowledging the company's culpability, he certainly would have been fired.

Clearly, human beings within corporations are seriously constrained in their ability to act out of their personal sense of right and wrong. And yet, I have mentioned only two of the rules that serve to constrain this influence: the profit imperative and the need for growth. The following list is an attempt to articulate some of the obligatory rules by which corporations operate. Taken together, they help reveal why corporations behave as they do today and how they have come to dominate their environment and the human beings within it.

SEVEN RULES OF CORPORATE BEHAVIOUR

1 The Profit Imperative

This is the ultimate measure of corporate decisions. It takes precedence over community well-being, worker health, public health, peace, environmental preservation or national security. US corporations will even find ways of trading with national 'enemies' – Libya, Iran, Cuba – though public policy may abhor it. The profit imperative and the growth imperative are the most fundamental corporate drives; together they represent the corporation's instinct to live.

2 The Growth Imperative

Corporations live or die by whether they can sustain growth. Growth determines relationships to investors, to the stock market, to banks and to public perception. The growth imperative also fuels the corporate desire to find and develop scarce resources in obscure parts of the world.

This effect is now clearly visible, as the world's few remaining pristine places are sacrificed to corporate production. The peoples who inhabit these resource-rich regions are similarly pressured to give up their traditional ways and climb onto the production–consumption wheel. Corporate planners consciously attempt to bring 'less-developed societies into the modern world' in order to create both infrastructures for development and a cadre of new workers and consumers. Corporations claim they do this for altruistic reasons – to raise the living standard – but corporations have no altruism.

Theoretically, *privately held corporations* – those owned by individuals or families – do not have any intrinsic imperative to expand. In practice, however, the behaviour is usually the same. There are economies of scale and usually increased profits from growth. Privately held giants such as Bechtel Corporation have shown no propensity for moderate growth; their behaviour, in fact, shows quite the opposite. And even among smaller privately held companies – 'green' companies with 'enlightened' management – resistance to growth is difficult. Banks will resist funding companies that limit their growth. And even internally, middle managers and staff tend to see their opportunities for the future diminished. Corporate 'culture' abhors limiting goals and profits.

3 Amorality

Not being human, not having feelings, corporations do not have morals or altruistic goals. So decisions that may be antithetical to community goals or environmental health are made without misgivings. In fact, corporate executives tend to praise non-emotionality as a basis for 'objective' decisions.

Corporations, however, seek to hide their amorality and attempt to act as if they were altruistic. Lately, US industry has made a concerted effort to seem concerned with contemporary social issues such as environmental cleanups, community arts or drug rehabilitation programmes. Corporations' efforts to exhibit social responsibility occur precisely because they are innately *not* responsible to the public. They have little interest in community goals except the ones that serve their purposes.

For example, corporations have taken to advertising about how they work to clean the environment. A company that installs offshore oil rigs will run ads that show fish thriving under the rigs. Logging companies known for their clear-cutting practices will run millions of dollars' worth of ads about their tree farms, as if they were interested in renewable resources when they are not.

In fact, it is a fair rule of thumb that corporations will tend to advertise the very qualities they do not have in order to allay a negative public perception. When corporations say 'we care', it is almost always in response to the widespread perception that they do not care. And they don't. How could they? Corporations do not have feelings or morals. All their acts are in service to profit.

4 Quantification, Linearity and Segmentation

Corporations require that subjective information be translated into objective form, that is, into numbers. This excludes from the decision-making process all values that cannot be quantified in such a way. The subjective or spiritual aspects of forests, for example, cannot be quantified and so do not enter corporate equations. Forests are evaluated as 'board feet'. Production elements that pose a danger to public health or welfare – pollution, toxic waste, carcinogens – are translated to value-free objective concepts such as 'cost-benefit ratio' or 'trade-off'. Auto manufacturers evaluating the safety level of certain production standards calculate the number of probable accidents and deaths at each level of the standard. This number is then compared with the cost of insurance payments and lawsuits from dead drivers' families. A number is also assigned to the public relations problem, and a balance is sought.

The drive toward objectification enters every aspect of corporate activity. For example, on the production end, great effort is made, through time-and-motion studies, to measure each fragment of every process performed by a worker. The goal is to segment tasks sufficiently for them to be eventually automated and workers eliminated altogether. Where the task is not automated, it is reduced to its simplest repetitive form. As a result, workers become subject to intense comparisons with other workers. If they survive on the job, the repetitive task leaves them horribly bored and without a sense of participating in corporate goals. They feel like mere cogs in the machine, and they are.

5 Ephemerality and Mobility

Corporations exist beyond time and space. As we have seen, they are legal creations that exist only on paper. They do not die a natural death; they outlive their own creators. And, especially under the new rules of global trade, they have no commitment to locality, employees or neighbours. This makes the modern global corporation entirely different from the bakers or grocers of previous years who survived by cultivating relationships with their neighbours, their customers. Having no morality, no commitment to place and no physical nature (a factory someplace, while being a physical entity, is not the corporation), a corporation can relocate all of its operations to another place at the first sign of inconvenience: demanding employees, too high taxes, restrictive environmental laws. The traditional ideal of community engagement is antithetical to corporate behaviour.

6 Opposition to Nature

Though some individuals who work for corporations may personally love nature, corporations themselves and corporate societies are intrinsically committed to intervening in, altering and transforming the natural world. For corporations engaged in commodity manufacturing, profit comes from transmogrifying raw materials into saleable forms. Metals from the ground are converted into cars. Trees are converted into boards and then into houses, furniture and paper products. Oil is converted into energy. In all such activity, a piece of nature is taken from where it belongs and processed into a new form. In rare instances, elements of nature can be renewed or trees can be replanted, but even in such cases they do not return to their original forms. So all manufacturing activity depends upon intervention in, and reorganization of, nature. After natural resources are used up in one part of the globe, the corporation moves on to another part.

This transformation of nature occurs in all societies where manufacturing takes place. But in capitalist corporate societies, and especially in a global economy, the process is accelerated because capitalist societies and corporations must grow. Extracting resources from nature everywhere on Earth and reprocessing them at an ever quickening pace is intrinsic to corporate existence. Meanwhile, the consumption end of the cycle is also accelerated – corporations have an intrinsic interest in convincing people that commodities bring satisfaction. Modes of fulfilment that are based on self-sufficiency – inner satisfaction, contentment in nature or in relationships, satisfaction with one's material possessions – are subversive to corporate goals. The net effect is the corporate ravaging of nature.

7 Homogenization

US rhetoric claims that commodity society delivers greater choice and diversity than other societies. *Choice* in this context means product choice, choice in the marketplace: many brands to choose from and diverse features on otherwise identical products (such as flashing lights on toasters). Actually, corporations have a stake in all of us living our lives in a similar manner, achieving our pleasures from the things that we buy. While it is true that different corporations seek different segments of the market – elderly people, let's say, or organic food buyers – all corporations share an identical economic, cultural and social vision and seek to accelerate the social and individual acceptance of that vision.

Lifestyles and economic systems that emphasize sharing commodities and labour, that do not encourage commodity accumulation or that celebrate non-material values are not good for business. People living collectively, for example, sharing expensive hard goods such as washing machines, cars and appliances – or worse, getting along without them – are outrageous to corporate commodity society. The nuclear family is a far better idea for maintaining corporate commodity society: each family lives alone in a single-family home and has all the same machines as every other family on the block. Recently, the singles phenomenon has proved even more productive than the nuclear family, since each person duplicates the consumption of every other person.

As for native societies, which celebrate an utterly non-material relationship to life, the planet and the spirit, and whose lifestyles are completely antithetical to corporate ideology, they are regarded as inferior and unenlightened. Backward. We are told they envy the choices we have. To the degree native societies continue to exist, they represent a threat to the homogenization of worldwide markets and culture. Corporate society works hard to retrain such people in attitudes and values appropriate to corporate goals. But in the non-industrial parts of the world, where corporations are just arriving, the ideological retraining process is just getting underway. Satellite communications technology, which brings Western television and advertising, is combined with a technical infrastructure to speed up the pace of development. Most of this activity is funded by the World Bank and the IMF along with agencies such as USAID, the Inter-American Bank and the Asian-American Bank, all of which serve multinational corporate enterprise.

As for the ultimate goal? In the book *Trilateralism* (1980), editor Holly Sklar quotes the president of Nabisco Corporation: 'One world of homogeneous consumption. . . [I am] looking forward to the day when Arabs and Americans, Latins and Scandinavians will be munching Ritz crackers as enthusiastically as they already drink Coke or brush their teeth with Colgate.'

FORM IS CONTENT

The most important aspect of these rules is the degree to which they are inherent in corporate structure. Corporations are inherently bold, aggressive and competitive. Though they exist in a society that claims to operate by moral principles, they are structurally amoral. It is inevitable that they will dehumanize the larger society as well. They are disloyal to workers, including their own managers. If community goals conflict with corporate goals, then corporations are similarly disloyal to the communities they may have been a part of for many years. It is inherent in corporate activity that they seek to drive all consciousness into one-dimensional channels. They must attempt to dominate alternative cultures and effectively clone the world population into a form more to their liking. Corporations do not care about nations; they live beyond national boundaries. They are intrinsically committed to destroying nature. And they have an inexorable, unabatable, voracious need to grow and expand. In dominating other cultures, in digging up the Earth, corporations blindly follow the codes that have been built into them. It is as if such codes were part of their genetic programming.

Articulating these principles of corporate form gives us a picture we should have had a long time ago. Now that we see the inherent direction of corporate activity, we must abandon the assumption that the form of the corporate structure is neutral. Given the rules of corporate operation, to ask corporate executives to behave in a morally defensible manner is absurd. Corporations and the people within them are not subject to appeals toward moral behaviour. They are following a system of logic and rules that leads them inexorably toward dominant behaviour. Form is content.

Chapter 7

Monsanto: A Profile of Corporate Arrogance

Brian Tokar

The name Monsanto has become synonymous with corporate arrogance. Its story is one of a company that has consistently ignored and disguised the health and environmental impacts of its activities in the pursuit of ever-greater profits. After having foisted toxic PCBs, Agent Orange and dioxin-contaminated herbicides on the world, Monsanto aimed to do the same with genetically-engineered food. Despite highly inadequate testing and unanswered questions about the risks to human health and biodiversity, it saturated the media with adverts, influenced officials at the heart of governments, and intimidated critics in a bid to force the worldwide acceptance of its new products. But its arrogance back-fired: the public turned against it with dramatic results.

Brian Tokar is the author of Earth for Sale *(South End Press, 1997),* The Green Alternative *(New Society Publishers, 1992) and editor of a forthcoming collection on the politics of biotechnology (Zed Books, 2000). He teaches at the Institute for Social Ecology and Goddard College, both in Plainfield, Vermont. Tokar received a 1999 Project Censored Award for his investigative history of Monsanto, which originally appeared in* The Ecologist, *vol 28, no 5, Sept/Oct 1998.*

In the 1990s, the Monsanto corporation was feared and reviled as one of the world's largest chemical companies, and by far the most aggressive promoter of genetic engineering in agriculture. The company spent millions of pounds trying to convince people that the fate of the world's starving masses depended on the acceptance of its new, genetically engineered crop varieties. Monsanto tried to paint itself as a visionary, world-historical force, working to bring state-of-the-art science and a professed environmental responsibility to solving humanity's most intractable problems.

To activists concerned about the environmental and human health consequences of genetic engineering, Monsanto was evil incarnate. Campaigners in the UK caricatured the company as 'Nonsanto' and 'Monsatan'. The British ad campaign proclaiming Monsanto's mission to feed the world became such an object of derision that it had to be withdrawn.

Today, Monsanto is the agricultural subsidiary of Pharmacia, a transnational pharmaceutical company with dual origins in the US and Switzerland. Monsanto's 'visionary' CEO, Robert Shapiro, has been cast out on the short road toward early retirement, having gone from prophet to pariah in biotech corporate circles in less than three years. The story of Monsanto is an apt metaphor for the recent history of the chemical and biotechnology industries in the US and worldwide. To better understand its recent shifts in fortune, and its still-central role in the consolidation of global agribusiness and the promotion of genetically manipulated agriculture, it is necessary to first examine the historical record.

Headquartered just outside St Louis, Missouri, the Monsanto Chemical Company was founded in 1901 by John Francis Queeny. Queeny, a self-educated chemist, brought technology to manufacture saccharin, the first artificial sweetener, from Germany to the US. In the 1920s, Monsanto became a leading manufacturer of sulphuric acid and other basic industrial chemicals, and is one of only four companies to be listed among the top ten US chemical companies in every decade since the 1940s (*Chemical and Engineering News*, 1998, p193).

By the 1940s, plastics and synthetic fabrics had become a centrepiece of Monsanto's business. In 1947, a French freighter carrying ammonium nitrate fertilizer blew up at a dock 82 metres from Monsanto's plastics plant outside Galveston, Texas. More than 500 people died in what came to be seen as one of the chemical industry's first major disasters (Reisch, 1998, p90). The plant was manufacturing styrene and polystyrene plastics, which are still important constituents of food packaging and various consumer products. In the 1980s the US Environmental Protection Agency (EPA) listed polystyrene as fifth in its ranking of the chemicals whose production generates the most total hazardous waste (Peck, 1989).

In 1929, the Swann Chemical Company, soon to be purchased by Monsanto, developed polychlorinated biphenyls (PCBs), which were widely praised for their non-flammability and extreme chemical stability. The most widespread uses were in the electrical equipment industry, which adopted PCBs as a non-flammable coolant for a new generation of transformers. By the 1960s, Monsanto's growing family of PCBs were also widely used as lubricants, hydraulic fluids, cutting oils, waterproof coatings and liquid sealants. Evidence of the toxic effects of PCBs appeared as early as the 1930s, and Swedish scientists studying the biological effects of DDT began finding significant concentrations of PCBs in the blood, hair and fatty tissue of wildlife in the 1960s (Colborn et al, 1996, p90).

Research in the 1960s and 1970s revealed PCBs and other aromatic organochlorines to be potent carcinogens, and also traced them to a wide array of reproductive, developmental and immune system disorders (Allsopp et al, 1995; see also Cummins, 1998, pp 262–263). Their high chemical affinity for organic matter, particularly fat tissue, is responsible for their dramatic rates of bioaccumulation and their wide dispersal throughout the North's aquatic food web. Arctic cod, for example, carry PCB concentrations 48 million times that of their surrounding waters, and predatory mammals such as polar bears can harbour tissue concentrations of PCBs more than 50 times greater than that. Though the manufacture of PCBs was banned in the US in 1976, its toxic and endocrine disruptive effects persist worldwide (Colborn et al, 1996, pp 101–104).

The world's centre of PCB manufacturing was Monsanto's plant on the outskirts of East St Louis, Illinois. East St Louis is a chronically economically depressed suburb, across the Mississippi River from St Louis, bordered by two large metal processing plants in addition to the Monsanto facility. 'East St Louis,' reports education writer Jonathan Kozol, 'has some of the sickest children in America.' Kozol reports that the city has the highest rate of foetal death and immature births in the state, the third highest rate of infant death and one of the highest childhood asthma rates in the United States (Kozol, 1991, pp 7, 20).

DIOXIN: A LEGACY OF CONTAMINATION

The people of East St Louis continue to face the horrors of high-level chemical exposure, poverty, a deteriorating urban infrastructure and the collapse of even the most basic city services, but the nearby town of Times Beach, Missouri, was found to be so thoroughly contaminated with dioxin that the US government ordered it evacuated in 1982. Apparently, the town, as well as several private landowners, hired a contractor to spray its dirt roads with waste oil to keep dust down. The same contractor had been hired by local chemical companies to pump out their dioxin-contaminated sludge tanks. When 50 horses, other domestic animals and hundreds of wild birds died in an indoor arena that had been sprayed with the oil, an investigation ensued that eventually traced the deaths to dioxin from the chemical sludge tanks (*New York Times*, p36). Two young girls who played in the arena became ill, one of whom was hospitalized for four weeks with severe kidney damage, and many more children born to mothers exposed to the dioxin-contaminated oil demonstrated evidence of immune system abnormalities and significant brain dysfunction (Colborn et al, 1996, p116).

While Monsanto has consistently denied any connection to the Times Beach incident, the St. Louis-based Times Beach Action Group (TBAG) uncovered laboratory reports documenting the presence of large concentrations of PCBs manufactured by Monsanto in contaminated soil samples from the town (Times Beach Action Group, 1995). 'From our point of view, Monsanto is at the heart of the problem here in Missouri,' explains TBAG's Steve Taylor. Taylor acknowledges that many questions about Times Beach and other contaminated sites in the region remain unanswered, but cites evidence that close investigations of the sludge sprayed in Times Beach were limited to those sources traceable to companies other than Monsanto.

The coverup at Times Beach reached the highest levels of the Reagan administration in Washington. The nation's environmental agencies during the Reagan years became notorious for officials' repeated backroom deals with industry officials, in which favoured companies were promised lax enforcement and greatly reduced fines. Reagan's appointed administrator of the EPA, Anne Gorsuch Burford, was forced to resign after two years in office and her special assistant, Rita Lavelle, was jailed for six months for perjury and obstruction of justice. In one famous incident, the Reagan White House ordered Burford to withhold documents on Times Beach and other contaminated sites in the states of Missouri and Arkansas, citing 'executive privilege', and Lavelle was subsequently cited for shredding important documents (Shabecoff, 1993, pp 210–212; Tokar, 1997, pp 59–60; Times Beach Action Group, 1995). An investigative reporter for the *Philadelphia Inquirer* newspaper identified Monsanto as one of the chemical companies whose executives frequently hosted luncheon and dinner meetings with Lavelle (Martino-Taylor, 1997, p27). The evacuation sought by residents of Times Beach was delayed until 1982, 11 years after the contamination was first discovered, and 8 years after the cause was identified as dioxin.

Monsanto's association with dioxin can be traced back to its manufacture of the herbicide 2,4,5-T, beginning in the late 1940s. 'Almost immediately, its workers started getting sick with skin rashes, inexplicable pains in the limbs, joints and other parts of the body, weakness, irritability, nervousness and loss of libido,' explains Peter Sills, author of a forthcoming book on dioxin. 'Internal memos show that the company knew these men were actually as sick as they claimed, but it kept all that evidence hidden' (pers comm, 5 August 1998). An explosion at Monsanto's Nitro, West Virginia, herbicide plant in 1949 drew further attention to these complaints. The contaminant responsible for these conditions was not identified as dioxin until 1957, but the US Army Chemical Corps apparently became interested in this substance as a possible chemical warfare agent. A request filed by the *St. Louis Journalism Review* under the US Freedom of Information Act revealed nearly 600 pages of reports and correspondence between Monsanto and the Army Chemical Corps on the subject of this herbicide byproduct, going as far back as 1952 (Downs, 1998).

The herbicide Agent Orange, which was used by US military forces to defoliate the rainforest ecosystems of Vietnam during the 1960s, was a mixture of 2,4,5-T and 2,4-D that was available from several sources, but Monsanto's Agent Orange had concentrations of dioxin many times higher than that produced by Dow Chemical, the defoliant's other leading manufacturer (Warwick, 1998, pp 264–265). This made Monsanto the key defendant in the lawsuit brought by Vietnam War veterans in the US, who faced an array of debilitating symptoms attributable to Agent Orange exposure. When a US$180 million settlement was reached in 1984 between seven chemical companies and the lawyers for the veterans, the judge ordered Monsanto to pay 45.5 per cent of the total (Schuck, 1987, pp 86–87, 155–164).*

In the 1980s, Monsanto undertook a series of studies designed to minimize its liability, not only in the Agent Orange suit, but in continuing instances of employee contamination at its West Virginia manufacturing plant. A three-and-a-half-year court case brought by railroad workers exposed to dioxin following a train derailment revealed a pattern of manipulated data and misleading experimental design in these studies. An official of the US EPA concluded that the studies were manipulated to support Monsanto's claim that dioxin's effects were limited to the skin disease chloracne (Jenkins, 1990). Greenpeace researchers Jed Greer and Kenny Bruno describe the outcome (1996, p141):

> 'According to testimony from the trial, Monsanto misclassified exposed and non-exposed workers, arbitrarily deleted several key cancer cases, failed to verify classification of chloracne subjects by common industrial dermatitis criteria, did not provide assurance of untampered records delivered and used by consultants, and made false statements about dioxin contamination in Monsanto products.'

The court case, in which the jury granted a US$16 million punitive damage award against Monsanto, revealed that many of Monsanto's products, from household herbicides to the Santophen germicide once used in Lysol brand disinfectant, were knowingly contaminated with dioxin. 'The evidence of Monsanto executives at the trial portrayed a corporate culture where sales and profits were given a higher priority than the safety of products and its workers,' reported the Toronto *Globe and Mail* after the close of the trial (Ferguson, 1990, p49). The punitive damages in Kemner vs Monsanto were overturned on appeal two years later. 'They just didn't care about the health and safety of their workers,' explains author Peter Sills. 'Instead of trying to make things safer, they relied on intimidation and threatened layoffs to keep their employees working.'

A subsequent review by Dr Cate Jenkins of the EPA's Regulatory Development Branch documented an even more systematic record of fraudulent science. 'Monsanto has in fact submitted false information to EPA which directly resulted in weakened regulations under RCRA [Resources Conservation and Recovery Act] and FIFRA [Federal Insecticide, Fungicide and Rodenticide Act]' reported Dr Jenkins in a 1990 memorandum urging the agency to undertake a criminal investigation of the company. Jenkins cited internal Monsanto documents revealing that the company 'doctored' samples of herbicides that were submitted

---

* Monsanto's share of Agent Orange production was 29.5 per cent, compared to Dow's market share of 28.6 per cent; however, some batches of Agent Orange contained more than 47 times more dioxin than Dow's. The other defendants in the case were Hercules Chemical, Diamond Shamrock, T H Agriculture and Nutrition, Thompson Chemicals and Uniroyal.

to the US Department of Agriculture, hid behind 'process chemistry' arguments to deflect attempts to regulate 2,4-D and various chlorophenols, hid evidence regarding the contamination of Lysol, and excluded several hundred of its sickest former employees from its comparative health studies:

> *'Monsanto covered up the dioxin contamination of a wide range of its products. Monsanto either failed to report contamination, substituted false information purporting to show no contamination or submitted samples to the government for analysis which had been specially prepared so that dioxin contamination did not exist.'* (Jenkins, 1990)

New Generation Herbicides

In the late 1990s, glyphosate herbicides such as Roundup accounted for at least one-sixth of Monsanto's total annual sales and half of the company's operating income (stock analyst Dain Bosworth, quoted in Bruno, 1997; Arax and Brokaw, 1997). The importance of herbicide sales increased further after the company spun off its industrial chemicals and synthetic fabrics divisions as a separate company, called Solutia, in September 1997. Monsanto aggressively promotes Roundup as a safe, general purpose herbicide for use on everything from lawns and orchards, to large coniferous forest holdings, where aerial spraying of the herbicide is used to suppress the growth of deciduous seedlings and shrubs and encourage the growth of profitable fir and spruce trees (testimony of Champion Paper Company, 1996). The Oregon-based Northwest Coalition for Alternatives to Pesticides (NCAP) reviewed over 40 scientific studies on the effects of glyphosate, and of the polyoxyethylene amines used as a surfactant in Roundup, and concluded that the herbicide is far less benign than Monsanto's advertising suggests:

> *'Symptoms of acute poisoning in humans following ingestion of Roundup include gastrointestinal pain, vomiting, swelling of the lungs, pneumonia, clouding of consciousness and destruction of red blood cells. Eye and skin irritation has been reported by workers mixing, loading and applying glyphosate. EPA's Pesticide Incident Monitoring System had 109 reports of health effects associated with exposure to glyphosate between 1966 and October 1980. These included eye or skin irritation, nausea, dizziness, headaches, diarrhoea, blurred vision, fever and weakness.'* (Cox, 1991)

It is important to note that the 1966–1980 dates represent a time period well before Roundup came to be widely used.

A series of suicides and attempted suicides in Japan during the 1980s using Roundup herbicide allowed scientists to calculate a lethal dose of six ounces.

The herbicide is 100 times more toxic to fish than to people, toxic to earthworms, soil bacteria and beneficial fungi, and scientists have measured a number of direct physiological effects of Roundup in fish and other wildlife, in addition to secondary effects attributable to defoliation of forests. Breakdown of glyphosate into N-nitrosoglyphosate and other related compounds has heightened concerns about the possible carcinogenicity of Roundup products (Cox, 1991; see also Mendelson, 1998, pp 270–275).

A 1993 study at the University of California at Berkeley's School of Public Health found that glyphosate was the most common cause of pesticide-related illness among landscape maintenance workers in California, and the number three cause among agricultural workers (Cox, 1995). A 1996 review of the scientific literature by members of the Vermont Citizens' Forest Roundtable – a group which successfully lobbied the Vermont Legislature for a statewide ban on the use of herbicides in forestry – revealed updated evidence of lung damage, heart palpitations, nausea, reproductive problems, chromosome aberrations and numerous other effects of exposure to Roundup herbicide (Knight, 1996). In 1997, Monsanto responded to five years of complaints by the New York State attorney general that its advertisements for Roundup were misleading; the company altered its ads to delete claims that the herbicide is 'biodegradable' and 'environmentally friendly', and paid US$50,000 toward the state's legal expenses in the case (Pesticide Action Network North America, 1997).

In March 1998, Monsanto agreed to pay a fine of US$225,000 for mislabelling containers of Roundup on 75 separate occasions. The penalty was the largest settlement ever paid for violation of the Worker Protection Standards of the Federal Insecticide, Fungicide and Rodenticide Act (FIFRA). According to the *Wall Street Journal*, Monsanto distributed containers of the herbicide with labels restricting entry into treated areas for only four hours instead of the required 12 hours (*Wall Street Journal*, 1998, p39). This is only the latest in a series of major fines and rulings against Monsanto in the US, including a US$108 million liability finding in the case of the leukaemia death of a Texas employee in 1986, a US$648,000 settlement for allegedly failing to report required health data to the EPA in 1990, a US$1 million fine by the state attorney general of Massachusetts in 1991 in the case of a 200,000 gallon acid wastewater spill, a US$39 million settlement in Houston, Texas, in 1992 involving the deposition of hazardous chemicals into unlined pits, and numerous others (Greer and Bruno, 1996, pp 145–146). In 1995, Monsanto ranked fifth among US corporations in EPA's Toxic Release Inventory, having discharged 37 million pounds of toxic chemicals into the air, land, water and underground (cited in Anderson and Cavanagh, 1997, p8).

BIOTECHNOLOGY'S BRAVE NEW WORLD

Monsanto's aggressive promotion of its biotechnology products, from recombinant bovine growth hormone (rBGH), to Roundup Ready soybeans and other crops, to its insect-resistant varieties of cotton, has been described by many observers as a continuation of its many decades of ethically questionable practices. 'Corporations have personalities, and Monsanto is one of the most malicious,' explains author Peter Sills. 'From Monsanto's herbicides to Santophen disinfectant to BGH, they seem to go out of their way to hurt their workers and hurt kids.'

Originally, Monsanto was one of four chemical companies seeking to bring a synthetic bovine growth hormone, produced in *E. coli* bacteria genetically engineered to manufacture the bovine protein, to market. As Jennifer Ferrara described in the internationally acclaimed 'Monsanto Files' issue of *The Ecologist*, Monsanto's 14-year effort to gain approval from the US Food and Drug Administration (FDA) to bring recombinant BGH to market was fraught with controversy, including allegations of a concerted effort to suppress information about the hormone's ill effects (Ferrara, 1998, pp 280–286). One FDA veterinarian, Richard Burroughs, was fired after he accused both the company and the agency of suppressing and manipulating data to hide the effects of rBGH injections on the health of dairy cows (Canine, 1991, pp 41–47; Tokar, 1992, pp 27–32; Brighton, 1990, p21).

In 1990, when FDA approval of rBGH appeared imminent, a veterinary pathologist at the University of Vermont's agricultural research facility released previously suppressed data to two state legislators documenting significantly increased rates of udder infection in cows that had been injected with the then-experimental Monsanto hormone, as well as an unusual incidence of severely deforming birth defects in offspring of rBGH-treated cows (Christiansen, 1995; see also Tokar, 1992, pp 28–29). An independent review of the university data by a regional farm advocacy group documented additional cow health problems associated with rBGH, including high incidences of foot and leg injuries, metabolic and reproductive difficulties and uterine infections. The US Congress General Accounting Office (GAO) attempted an inquiry into the case, but was unable to obtain the necessary records from Monsanto and the university to carry out its investigation, particularly with respect to suspected teratogenic and embryotoxic effects. The GAO auditors concluded that cows injected with rBGH had mastitis (udder infection) rates one third higher than untreated cows, and recommended further research on the risk of elevated antibiotic levels in milk produced using rBGH (Christiansen, 1995, pp 10, 17; US General Accounting Office, 1992).

Monsanto's rBGH was approved by the FDA for commercial sale beginning in 1994. The following year, Mark Kastel of the Wisconsin Farmers Union released a study of Wisconsin farmers' experiences with the drug. His findings exceeded the 21 potential health problems that Monsanto was required to list on the warning label for its Posilac brand of rBGH. Kastel found widespread reports of spontaneous deaths among rBGH-treated cows, high incidences of udder infections, severe metabolic difficulties and calving problems, and in some cases an inability to successfully wean treated cows off the drug. Many experienced dairy farmers who experimented with rBGH suddenly needed to replace large portions of their herd (Kastel, 1995). Instead of addressing the causes of farmers' complaints about rBGH, Monsanto went on the offensive, threatening to sue small dairy companies that advertised their products as free of the artificial hormone, and participating in a lawsuit by several dairy industry trade associations against the first and only mandatory labelling law for rBGH in the US (Tokar, 1995, pp 49–55; Gershon, 1994, p384).* Still, evidence for the damaging effects of rBGH on the health of both cows and people continued to mount (Kronfeld, 1994, pp 116–130; Epstein, 1996, pp 173–185).

Monsanto's efforts to prevent labelling of genetically engineered soybean and maize exports from the US continued the same strategy that sought to squelch complaints against Monsanto's dairy hormone. While Monsanto argues that its 'Roundup Ready' soybeans will ultimately reduce herbicide use, herbicide-tolerant crop varieties are far more likely to increase farmers' dependence on herbicides. Weeds that emerge after the original herbicide has dispersed or broken down are often treated with further applications of herbicides (Schmitz, 1998). 'It will promote the overuse of the herbicide,' Missouri soybean farmer Bill Christison told Kenny Bruno of Greenpeace International. 'If there is a selling point for RRS, it's the fact that you can till an area with a lot of weeds and use surplus chemicals to combat your problem, which is not what anyone should be doing' (Bruno, 1997). Christison refutes Monsanto's claim that herbicide-resistant seeds are necessary to reduce soil erosion from excess tillage, and reports that Mid-Western farmers have developed numerous methods of their own for reducing overall use of herbicides. The pitfalls of these crops for farmers were further highlighted by a 1999 study at the University of Georgia, showing that the stems of 'Roundup Ready' soybean plants became unusually brittle at soil temperatures above 40 degrees Celsius, leading to cracked stems and sometimes drastic crop losses (*New Scientist*, 1999).

Monsanto, on the other hand, has stepped up its production of Roundup in recent years. With Monsanto's US patent for Roundup expiring in 2000, and competition from generic glyphosate products emerging worldwide, the packaging of Roundup herbicide with 'Roundup Ready' seeds became the centrepiece of Monsanto's strategy for continued growth in herbicide sales (Monsanto Annual Report, 1997, pp 16, 37). The possible health and environmental consequences of Roundup-tolerant crops have not been fully investigated, including allergenic effects, potential invasiveness or weediness and the possibility of herbicide

---

* The Vermont state labelling law was defended by the state on the grounds of consumer preference, rather than public health, and was ultimately struck down by a federal judge, who ruled that mandatory rBGH labelling was a violation of the companies' constitutional right to refuse to speak.

resistance being transferred via pollen to other soybeans or related plants (Greenpeace, 1997).

The experience of US cotton growers with Monsanto's genetically engineered seeds is even more striking. Monsanto released two varieties of genetically engineered cotton, beginning in 1996. One is a Roundup-resistant variety and the other, named 'Bollgard', secretes a bacterial toxin intended to control damage from three leading cotton pests. The toxin, derived from *Bacillus thuringiensis*, has been used by organic growers in the form of a natural bacterial spray since the early 1970s. But while *Bt* bacteria are relatively short lived, and secrete their toxin in a form that only becomes activated in the alkaline digestive systems of particular worms and caterpillars, genetically engineered *Bt* crops secrete an active form of the toxin throughout the plant's life cycle (Shand, 1989, pp 18–21; Steinbrecher, 1996, pp 273–281; Tokar, 1996, pp 50–55). Much of the genetically engineered maize currently on the market, for example, is a *Bt* secreting variety, designed to repel the corn rootworm and other common pests.

The first widely anticipated problem with these pesticide-secreting crops is that the presence of the toxin throughout the plant's life cycle is likely to encourage the development of resistant strains of common crop pests. The US EPA has determined that widespread resistance to *Bt* may render natural applications of *Bt* bacteria ineffective in just three to five years and requires growers to plant refuges of up to 40 per cent non-*Bt* cotton in an attempt to forestall this effect. Secondly, the active toxin secreted by these plants may harm beneficial insects, moths and butterflies, in addition to those species that growers wish to eliminate (Union of Concerned Scientists, 1998, p1, 4; 1995, pp 4–7).

But the damaging effects of *Bt*-secreting 'Bollgard' cotton have proved to be much more immediate, enough so that Monsanto and its partners pulled 2.3 million kilogrammes of genetically engineered cotton seed off the market in 1997 and 1998 and agreed to a multimillion dollar settlement with farmers in the southern US. Three farmers who refused to settle with Monsanto were awarded nearly US$2 million by the Mississippi Seed Arbitration Council (Myerson, 1998, p29; *Financial Times*, 1998; Union of Concerned Scientists, 1998, p1). Not only were plants attacked by the cotton bollworm, which Monsanto claimed they would be resistant to, but germination was spotty, yields were low, and plants were misshapen, according to several published accounts (Union of Concerned Scientists, 1996, p1; Benson et al, 1997; Reifenberg and Rundle, 1996). Some farmers reported crop losses of up to 50 per cent. Farmers who planted Monsanto's Roundup-resistant cotton also reported severe crop failures, including deformed and misshapen bolls that suddenly fell off the plant three-quarters of the way through the growing season (Union of Concerned Scientists, 1997, p1; Pesticide Action Network North America, 1997).

Despite these problems, Monsanto has advanced the use of genetic engineering in agriculture by taking control of many of the largest, most established seed companies in the US. In the late 1990s, Monsanto bought Holdens Foundation Seeds, supplier of germplasm used on 25–35 per cent of US maize acreage, and

Asgrow Agronomics, which Monsanto described as 'the leading soybean breeder, developer and distributor in the United States' (RAFI Communiqué, 1997; the comment about Asgrow was quoted by Brewster Keen, 1998, p2). In 1998, Monsanto completed its acquisition of De Kalb Genetics, the second largest seed company in the US and the ninth largest in the world, and spent more than two years trying to acquire Delta and Pine Land, the largest US cotton seed company (Monsanto Annual Report, 1997, p17; RAFI Communiqué, 1997; Union of Concerned Scientists, 1996, p11). By acquiring this company, Monsanto sought control over 85 per cent of the US cotton seed market, and also would have gained the rights to the notorious 'Terminator' sterile seed technology, jointly developed by Delta Pine and the USDA (Hammond et al, 1998; for an update, see RAFI Communiqué, 2000).

Monsanto aggressively pursued corporate acquisitions and product sales in other countries as well. In 1997, Monsanto bought Sementes Agroceres S A, described as 'the leading seed corn company in Brazil', with a 30 per cent market share (RAFI Communiqué, 1997). The following year, the Brazilian Federal Police investigated an alleged illegal importation of at least 200 bags of transgenic soybeans, some of which were traced to an Argentine subsidiary of Monsanto (*Correio Braziliense*, 1998). According to Brazilian law, foreign transgenic products can only be introduced after a period of quarantine and testing to prevent possible damage to native flora. In Canada, Monsanto had to recall 60,000 bags of genetically engineered rape ('canola') seed in 1997, because the shipment of Roundup-resistant seed contained an inserted gene different from the one that had been approved for consumption by people and livestock (Montague, 1997).

While Monsanto's herbicides and genetically engineered products have been the focus of public controversy for many years, its pharmaceutical products also have a troubling track record. For many years, the flagship product of Monsanto's G D Searle pharmaceuticals subsidiary (now a separate division of Pharmacia) was the artificial sweetener aspartame, sold under the brand names Nutrasweet and Equal. In 1981, four years before Monsanto purchased Searle, a Food and Drug Administration Board of Inquiry consisting of three independent scientists confirmed reports that had been circulating for eight years that 'aspartame might induce brain tumors' (quoted in Montague, 1996). The FDA revoked Searle's licence to sell aspartame, only to have its decision reversed under a new commissioner appointed by President Ronald Reagan.

A 1996 study in the *Journal of Neuropathology and Experimental Neurology* has renewed this concern, linking aspartame to a sharp increase in brain cancers shortly after the substance was introduced. Dr Erik Millstone of the University of Sussex Science Policy Research Unit cites a series of reports from the 1980s linking aspartame to a wide array of adverse reactions in sensitive consumers, including headaches, blurred vision, numbness, hearing loss, muscle spasms and induced epileptic-type seizures, among numerous others (Millstone, 1996). In 1989, Searle again ran afoul of the FDA, which accused the company of misleading advertising in the case of its anti-ulcer drug, Cytotec. The FDA said that the ads were designed to market the drug to a much broader and younger population than the agency had advised. Searle/Monsanto was required to place an ad in a number of medical journals, which was headed 'Published to Correct a Previous Advertisement which the Food and Drug Administration Considered Misleading' (Koenig, 1990).

MONSANTO'S GREENWASH

Given this long and troubling history, it is easy to understand why informed citizens throughout Europe and the US refused to trust Monsanto with the future of our food and our health. But Monsanto has gone to great lengths to appear unperturbed by this opposition. Through efforts such as their UK£1 million advertising campaign in Britain, their involvement with the prestigious Missouri Botanic Garden, and their sponsorship of a state-of-the-art biodiversity exhibit at the American Museum of Natural History in New York, they sought to appear greener, more righteous and more forward looking than even their opponents.

In the US they gained the support of people at the highest levels of the Clinton administration. In May 1997, Mickey Kantor, an architect of Bill Clinton's 1992 election campaign and US trade representative during Clinton's first term, was elected to a seat on Monsanto's board of directors. Marcia Hale, formerly a personal assistant to Clinton, has served as Monsanto's public affairs officer in Britain (Burrows, 1997). Al Gore, who is well known in the US for his writings and speeches on the environment, has been a vocal supporter of biotechnology at least since his days in the US Senate (see, for example, Gore, 1991, pp 19–30). Gore's chief domestic policy advisor in the late 1990s, David W Beier, was formerly the senior director of government affairs at Genentech, Inc (Genentech press release, 1998).

Under CEO Robert Shapiro, Monsanto pulled out all the stops to transform its image from a purveyor of dangerous chemicals to an enlightened, forward-looking institution crusading to feed the world. Shapiro, who went to work for G D Searle in 1979 and became the president of its Nutrasweet Group in 1982, sat on the President's Advisory Committee for Trade Policy and Negotiations and served a term as a member of the White House Domestic Policy Review (Monsanto worldwide web page). He would describe himself as a visionary and a Renaissance man, with a mission to use the company's resources to change the world: 'The only reason for working at a large company is that you have the capability of doing things on a large scale that really are important,' he told an interviewer for *Business Ethics*, a flagship journal for the 'socially responsible business' movement in the US (Scott, 1996, p49).

Monsanto's 1997 annual report was a veritable case study in corporate greenwash. Roundup is not a herbicide, it is a tool to minimize tillage and decrease soil erosion. Genetically engineered crops are not just about profits for Monsanto, they're about solving the inexorable problem of population growth. Biotechnology is not reducing everything alive to the realm of commodities – items to be bought and sold, marketed and patented – but is, in fact, a harbinger of 'decommoditization': the replacement of single mass-produced products with a vast array of specialized, made-to-order products (Monsanto Annual Report, 1997, p10). This is newspeak of the highest order, and an odd achievement for a company that is best known for its aggressive promotion of genetically engineered food, whose most profitable product is a herbicide, and that is world famous for its attempts to intimidate critics and suppress criticism in the media (see articles by Montague, Gorelick and Rowell, 1998, pp 299–303).

Finally, Monsanto's aggressive promotion of biotechnology is not a matter of mere corporate arrogance, but rather the realization of a simple fact of nature. Readers of the 1997 annual report were presented with an analogy between today's rapid growth in the number of identified DNA base pairs and the exponential trend of miniaturization in the electronics industry, a trend first identified in the 1960s. Monsanto dubbed the apparent exponential growth of what it terms 'biological knowledge' to be nothing less than 'Monsanto's Law'. Like any other putative law of nature, one has little choice but to see its predictions realized and, here, the prediction is nothing less than the continued exponential growth of Monsanto's global reach.

By 1999, however, Shapiro and his colleagues were increasingly on the defensive. Several attempts to merge with larger companies – ostensibly to help pay for more than US$8 billion in recent seed company acquisitions – had fallen through.* The company's aggressive, and often rather secretive, promotion of genetically engineered corn and soybeans had made the name Monsanto synonymous throughout Europe with everything that is threatening and out of control about genetic engineering. The 'Terminator' seed technology that Monsanto was attempting to acquire from Delta and Pine Land (while also developing similar technologies of its own) had become the focus of a growing worldwide resistance to genetically engineered crops. Germany's Deutsche Bank declared genetically modified crops an economic 'liability to farmers', advising its investors to stop buying agricultural biotech stocks, and the *Wall Street Journal* announced that Monsanto, once the seemingly invincible world leader in biotechnology, would be worth significantly more to investors if it were to simply be broken up (Deutsche Bank Alex Brown's investor report on DuPont Chemical, 1999, p18 – this appendix was apparently released by Deutsche Bank as an independent report to investors on 21 May 1999; Kilman and Burton, 1999).

In October 1999, the company made world headlines with the announcement that it would not seek to market 'Terminator' plants that would produce sterile

---

* After a failed attempt to merge with the pharmaceutical giant, American Home Products, Monsanto became involved in merger talks with DuPont, Novartis and several other companies. See, for example, Langreth and Deogun, 1999.

seeds, and Robert Shapiro appeared via interactive video at a Greenpeace Business Conference in London to seek 'dialogue' and a 'common ground' (Feder, 1999, p1; Vidal, 1999, p15; Greenpeace business conference transcript, 1999). Monsanto received considerable acclaim for bowing to its critics, most notably Rockefeller Foundation President (and former Sussex University vice-chancellor) Gordon Conway, who reportedly convinced Shapiro that 'Terminator' had to go. But Monsanto was already in serious trouble, and the apparent concession on 'Terminator' was a small price to pay in the hope of salvaging a future of genetically engineered crops. It was almost a textbook case of modern corporate public relations, in which companies are urged to admit mistakes and seek wider credibility by appearing to involve activist groups in corporate decision-making (Burton, 1999, pp 1–6).

By the end of the year, Monsanto's acquisition of Delta and Pine Land – the real patentholder on the 'Terminator' – had been abandoned, and Shapiro had to accept a non-executive chairmanship of Pharmacia, the company formed from the merger of Monsanto with Pharmacia and Upjohn. Pharmacia sought to cushion the blow to its own stock value by pledging to begin selling off up to 20 per cent of the merged company's agricultural division, which retained the name Monsanto. This predicament posed the real possibility that, in the search for new sources of capital, Monsanto might ultimately be forced to break up its notorious seed monopoly.

Whatever the outcome, these developments confirm that the development of biotechnology is nothing even remotely like a 'law of nature'. Technologies are not social, much less 'natural' forces unto themselves, nor are they merely neutral 'tools' that can be used to satisfy any social end we desire. Rather they are products of particular social institutions and economic interests. Once a particular course of technological development is set in motion, it can have much wider consequences than its creators could have predicted: the more powerful the technology, the more profound the consequences.

In rejecting Monsanto and its biotechnology, we are not necessarily rejecting technology *per se*, but seeking to replace a life-denying technology of manipulation, control and profit with a genuinely ecological technology that will respect the patterns of nature, improve personal and community health, sustain land-based communities and operate at a genuinely human scale. If we believe in democracy, it is imperative that we have the right to choose which technologies are best for our communities, rather than having unaccountable institutions such as Monsanto, DuPont, Novartis and other transnational biotech giants decide for us. Rather than technologies designed for the continued enrichment of a few, we can ground our technology in the hope of a greater harmony between our human communities and the natural world. Our health, our food and the future of life on Earth truly lie in the balance.

Chapter 8

The Wal-Martians Have Landed

Andrew Rowell

Faced with few, if any, remaining national barriers to trade or investment, corporations, such as the giant retailer Wal-Mart, have wasted no time in expanding their web of parasitic activities worldwide, with complete disregard for the social consequences. With its 'low cost at any price' culture, Wal-Mart has become infamous in the US for destroying small stores and the jobs they provide, ruining local communities, paying low wages and leaving a sprawling suburban wasteland in its wake. Exploiting the new opportunities provided by the global economy, Wal-Mart has exported this novel brand of strip-mining to the rest of the Americas and to parts of East Asia. The local economies and cultures of Britain look set to be its next victims.

Andrew Rowell is a freelance writer and author of Green Backlash: Global Subversion of the Environment Movement *(Routledge, 1996). He has written extensively on the environmental, social and health impacts of the car, oil, biotech, retail and tobacco industries.*

On 24 July 2000, the world's largest retailer, Wal-Mart, opened its first American-style supercentre in the UK, located on the outskirts of Bristol. As queues of cars choked the July sunshine, clamouring to squeeze into the 1000-space car park, both the local and national media, with a disturbing unanimity of message, warmly welcomed the behemoth's arrival. 'Store wars as US giant offers 60 per cent off', blazed the approving headline in the *Daily Mail*. 'Shoppers set for cut-price bonanza', yelled the *Bristol Evening News*. The pundits agreed with the journalists, who in turn agreed with the City analysts and senior members of Britain's government: Wal-Mart's arrival in Britain was a Good Thing. The 50,000 people who visited the Bristol store in its first two weeks apparently agreed.

This chorus of almost adulatory approval from all sides of British public life is not that hard to explain. After all, Wal-Mart, the vast megastore chain which, in its 40 years of existence, has risen to dominate and revolutionize American shopping, appeals to that most basic of consumer interests: the purse. Wal-Mart is cheap; very cheap. It lives and thrives by undercutting all and any competitors.

Ever since June 1999, when it was announced that Wal-Mart was taking over Britain's third-largest supermarket chain, Asda, in a deal worth UK£6.7 billion – a deal that doubled its overseas business overnight (Institute of Grocery Distribution, 2000, p78) – we have heard the same message from all sides: Wal-Mart is good for the consumer. The government thinks so – Wal-Mart's executives held a top-level personal meeting with Tony Blair before the Asda takeover, during which they were given the green light for expansion in the UK. The media thinks so too – national papers from the *Guardian* to the *Daily Telegraph* have praised the store.

We have heard less, though, about what Wal-Mart will be bad for. And when its record in the US and elsewhere is examined, we can begin to get a good idea. Wal-Mart will, in all likelihood, be bad for the British countryside and the wider environment; bad for workers, both in Britain and abroad; bad for jobs; bad for small communities and independent shops; bad for local economies; bad, even, for other supermarkets. Bad, in other words, for almost everyone but Wal-Mart.

Wal-Mart's takeover of Asda is more – much more – than one supermarket merging with, or even being swallowed by, another. It is the likely beginning of a retail revolution, which could change more than just shopping habits. Wal-Mart's aggressive 'low cost at any price' culture, according to serious retail analysts, looks set to force a series of mega-mergers that could within a decade or less leave only Wal-Mart and possibly one competitor standing. Britain could be on the verge of a vast upheaval that it is utterly unprepared for.

THE DRIVE TO DOMINATE

It is just under 40 years since Sam Walton, Wal-Mart's founder, opened his first store in Arkansas. Since then, the company has grown into the United States' largest private employer with over 920,000 staff. Every week some 93 million Americans shop at Wal-Mart and every three days another Wal-Mart opens (Norman, 1999). Just before he died in 1992, Walton, who had amassed the greatest personal fortune in American history, accepted one of the country's highest civilian honours, the Medal of Freedom, saying that:

> *'We're all working together; that's the secret. And we'll lower the cost of living for everyone, not just in America, but we'll give the world an opportunity to see what it's like to save and have a better lifestyle, a better life for all. We're proud of what we've accomplished; we've just begun.'**

---

* See www.walmartstores.com, The Wal-Mart Story.

This was prophetic. Having saturated its home market, in a country that has more shopping centres than high schools, Wal-Mart now set its sights overseas. Over the last decade it has acquired over 700 stores outside the US, expanding into Mexico in 1991, Puerto Rico in 1992, Canada in 1994, Argentina and Brazil in 1995, and China and Indonesia in 1996. In the following year it moved into Germany and now it is the turn of the UK. With over 3600 stores on four continents, in the next five to ten years Wal-Mart is set to become the world's largest corporation (Ortega, 1999).

But the company's phenomenal success comes at a huge ecological, cultural and social price. Its growing legion of critics has consistently pointed out that Wal-Mart, in its drive to dominate, has systematically destroyed downtown America. Furthermore, it is notorious for its low wages, and there is evidence that it imports its good from nations where the workers are either enslaved or paid a pittance. In its wake the company has destroyed thousands of competitors, crippled and depersonalized local communities and left a sprawling suburban wasteland. Wal-Mart, says ex-*Rolling Stone* editor James Howard Kunstler, is 'the exemplar of a form of corporate colonialism. . . going into distant places and strip-mining them culturally and economically' (Ortega, 1999).

RETAIL REVOLUTIONARIES

But this is not Sam Walton's worst legacy, says journalist Bob Ortega in his book *In Sam We Trust* (1999):

> '*Walton and Wal-Mart transformed retailing in the way Henry Ford revolutionised transportation. Wal-Mart's way of doing business is the new paradigm, and the company embodies both the shining success and the dark underbelly of modern American business.*'

This revolution is now set to sweep the UK. And in case there was any doubt about its significance, listen to the understated words of the Institute of Grocery Distribution (IGD), which analyses the sector. Wal-Mart's takeover, it says, 'is the most significant entry into the UK by a foreign retailer to date' (Institute of Grocery Distribution, 2000, p77). Translated, this means: big changes ahead. But what changes? Wal-Mart is playing its cards characteristically close to its chest, and its message is one of caution. Its communications strategy appears to be to reassure: it wants the British consumer to rest safe in the knowledge that it will not change too much, or too fast. It is unlikely, though, based on its record, that this is anything like the truth.

So, although the company maintains that it only plans to open ten stores in five years, the company's real aim, says the IGD, is 'very clear' – to become the 'leading retailer' in the UK (Institute of Grocery Distribution, 2000, p82). 'Keep in mind', writes Bob Ortega, 'that Wal-Mart started small in Canada and Mexico too, and that despite stumbling early on, in less than seven years it had become the largest retailer in both countries.'

In Germany the company moved from the 15th to the 4th largest retailer in just two years (Ortega, 1999).

In order to become number one, Wal-Mart will try its best to destroy the competition. But that's not all it will destroy. It also has its eyes on Britain's planning restrictions. Its success in the US had been based on the vast size of its stores, which can sell all and everything under one roof. In the UK, tight planning restrictions on out-of-town superstores seem to preclude such expansion – at present. However, the company is clear on this point: 'If you really want to make it more competitive, the thing to do is loosen planning,' says Alan Leighton, CEO of Wal-Mart Europe (Institute of Grocery Distribution, 2000, p85). If that happens, Wal-Mart will be given the green light to move in on Britain's small towns and cannibalize local businesses – with potentially devastating reults.

THE CONSUMER'S FRIEND?

Wal-Mart's claim to be the consumer's friend is the bedrock of its success. But how true is it? Tim Lang, Professor of Food Policy at Thames Valley University, has his doubts:

> '*It is dubious whether Wal-Mart's take-over of Asda will be of benefit to consumers. . . Consumers should ask themselves whether a six pence reduction in the price of baked beans is worth the environmental cost of having to buy a car and travel even further to get to the tin shed to buy the tin can on the edge of a motorway. Is it really worth it?*'
> (personal communication, 24 June 1999)

The message from the company's home country is the same. Al Norman, founder of the community group Sprawl-Busters, which has helped 88 communities in North America fight the company over the last eight years, argues:

> '*The idea that Wal-Mart will be an inducement to lower prices is ridiculous. . . Prices will only remain low while there is active competition. Wal-Mart is not the beginning of competition, it is the end of competition. Once it has driven out the competitors, it is free to do whatever it wants with its prices.*' (personal communication, 23 June 1999)

Only one other UK retailer is prepared to say anything at all about Wal-Mart's arrival in the UK. A spokesperson for Iceland says: 'From what we have seen in the States, we can see that Wal-Mart does affect the high street. They are going to be quite detrimental to consumer choice at the end of the day' (personal communication, August 1999).

Al Norman's evidence is based on his experience in the US where, using brutal economies of scale, Wal-Mart has flexed its economic muscle to squash competitors. The company has a history of undercutting the local competition until it goes bankrupt. An employee song goes: 'Stack it deep, sell it cheap, watch it fly and hear those downtown merchants cry.' Norman continues:

> *'For saving a few cents, we are supposed to sacrifice 20 to 30 acres of land, lose jobs in other stores, and support low wage labour… It is a quality of life issue. You're surrounded by gridlock, and the architectural graffiti of a windowless Wal-Mart store. People in America have lamented for years that Wal-Mart is scarring the face of home-town America and turning one community into a look-alike for every community.'* (personal communication, 23 June 1999)

Since 1962, writes Norman in his book *Slam-dunking Wal-Mart*, the corporation has 'cannibalized the retail food chain from the Mom and Pops on the bottom to the mid-level regional chains to the very top national chains' in every county in America (Norman, 1999). His message is clear: local communities pay a big price for low prices.

CRUSHING COMPETITION, CRUSHING JOBS

No company is immune. The Wal-Mart 'casualty department' is overflowing with those who could not compete. According to Iowa State University Professor Ken Stone, for example, in the 10 years after Wal-Mart moved into Iowa, the state lost over 555 grocery stores, 298 hardware stores, 293 building suppliers, 161 variety stores and 158 women's clothing stores, 153 shoe stores, 116 drug stores and 111 children's clothing stores. In total, some 7326 businesses went to the wall. There is no reason to believe that the company intends to spare Britain's beleaguered High Street the same fate.

Ironically, study after study has shown that the retail giant also destroys other jobs. Last year, in a study in Virginia, economist Tom Muller showed that while Wal-Mart's arrival would create 246 part-time jobs, 248 jobs in local businesses would be destroyed as a result. Another survey by Muller found that in nine counties examined, on average 84 per cent of Wal-Mart's sales came from existing businesses. In some areas it was as high as 100 per cent (Norman, 1999). In other words, in a saturated retail market, Wal-Mart's gains are another store's losses.

Another study by Muller and Beth Humstone, into a proposed Wal-Mart in Franklin County, Vermont, projected that:

> 'over time, the number of jobs in the county would decline by a net
> 200 jobs... This is due to the fact that the existing retail businesses
> are more labour intensive than Wal-Mart. For every US$10 million
> in sales in a typical Franklin County retail business, 106 people are
> employed. For every US$10 million sales at a Wal-Mart, 70 people
> are employed.'

In other words, for every job generated at Wal-Mart one and a half jobs are lost elsewhere (Muller and Humstone, 1993).

Even studies connected to Wal-Mart admit that job losses are a problem. In the town of Greenfield, near Boston, an economic survey underwritten by Wal-Mart in 1993 found that, despite creating a promised 293 new jobs, the net impact of the store would be just 27 jobs, because of jobs lost from other businesses. The study also concluded that 232,000 square feet of retail space would close because of Wal-Mart's store. Nearly half the sales for the new store would be poached from existing businesses (Norman, 1999). What's more, just as Wal-Mart can come in and close down the competition, it can also leave once all the competition has gone. There are over 4000 abandoned shopping malls in America, with 22 empty Wal-Mart stores in Alabama alone. 'They came in and ravaged all the small businesses,' says the president of the First National Bank in Nowata, Oklahoma. 'And when it came to the point when they were not satisfied, they left' (Norman, 1999).

Wal-Mart UK, though, denies that jobs are an issue. Nick Agarwal from Asda/Wal-Mart wants us to believe that Wal-Mart is good for surrounding businesses. 'The evidence is,' he says, without producing any evidence, 'that the [Bristol] store is attracting trade to the shopping centre in and around the area. That is part of its success' (personal communication, 9 August 2000).

But claiming that large, out-of-town superstores are good for local businesses flies in the face of the evidence. UK government research published in 1998 showed that edge-of-town and out-of-town supermarkets have a serious impact on between 13 and 50 per cent of the local market in market towns and centres (Hillier Parker, 1988). The industry's own figures, from the National Retail Planning Forum report, say that a superstore costs on average 276 local jobs (Porter and Raistrick, 1998).

The Sussex Rural Community Council has predicted that a new supermarket in its region would close all village shops within a 7-mile radius. The Cornwall Association of Village Shopkeepers found that 202 jobs out of 270 were at risk from a supermarket (Breed, 1998). One of Britain's leading think-tanks has calculated that a typical out-of-town supermarket has a subsidy of UK£25,000 per week over its town centre equivalent, because of pollution and congestion caused by the car culture that out-of-town stores rely on and encourage (Raven et al, 1995).

Wal-Mart's record, then, tells a clear story: the arrival of Wal-Mart in a community doesn't create new jobs, it just steals other people's. And its commitment to that community lasts only as long as its profits and its retail strategy allow it to. In Bristol, the company boasts of employing an extra 200 people at its new store. But how many of these will be at the expense of job losses in the surrounding area? And how long will they last? Only Wal-Mart knows – and it's not telling. Meanwhile, local businesses, led by the Bristol Chamber of Commerce, are already publicly expressing their worries.

Exploitation

Whilst it destroys jobs elsewhere, the jobs Wal-Mart does create are often low-wage and part-time. Jill Cashen from the United Food and Commercial Workers Union (UFCW) in the US explains:

> *'They are pushing down US labour standards. This is a company that pays low wages – on average two to three dollars an hour less than a union employer. . . Wal-Mart has gone to tremendous lengths to deny their own employees a union. Only 10 people out of 920,000 workers at Wal-Mart are members of a union in the US.'* (personal communication, 4 August 2000)

Other Wal-Mart business practices also leave much to be desired. In his Wal-Mart exposé, *Wall Street Journal* journalist Bob Ortega (1999) wrote:

> *'Wal-Mart's executives have demonstrated an often breathtaking contempt for laws and regulations. In the US, courts again and again have found the company to have lied, to have illegally falsified, destroyed or withheld documents, to have committed civil fraud, to have wilfully sold counterfeit goods, to have deliberately discriminated against disabled job applicants, to have illegally fired workers for interracial dating, to have discriminated against black and Mexican employees in other ways, to have allowed managers to sexually harass women workers – and to have fired women who had the temerity to complain.'*

Now Wal-Mart has brought its anti-union agenda to Europe. In July 2000, German Wal-Mart workers launched a two-day 'warning' strike against the company because it had refused to sign the German wage agreement and join the German employers' association. In a letter of support, the president of the UFCW, Doug Dority said:

'Your struggle demonstrates that Wal-Mart is committed to spreading its anti-union, anti-worker operation to any country it does business with, regardless of national labour laws or international labour standards protecting the rights of workers to organise.'*

Not content with bullying its domestic workers, Wal-Mart has also taken its attitude to workers' rights to less-developed countries, where factories producing clothes for Wal-Mart have consistently been found using forced or child labour. A 1992 American ABC investigation found garments sewn by 12 year olds in Bangladesh for Wal-Mart being proudly touted as 'Made in the USA'. The factory children were locked in at night until they had finished their production quotas. Only a year before Wal-Mart had shifted production to the notorious Saraka factory in the country, 25 child workers had died in a fire at the facility, unable to escape. The reaction of Wal-Mart's chief executive, David Glass, to this was as tactful as could be: 'There are tragic things that happen all over the world,' he spluttered. And anyway, 'You and I might define children differently' (Norman, 1999).

Subsequent investigations by the human rights group, the National Labour Committee (NLC) in the US looked at factory conditions in Honduras and Bangladesh where Wal-Mart clothing is sewn. In Honduras the NLC found that women as young as 14 were employed in up to 14-hour daily shifts, with occasional mandatory 24-hour shifts. They had to work seven days a week, and if they could not, they would be fired (Norman, 1999).

In response to these allegations Wal-Mart introduced a much-trumpeted Code of Conduct for its suppliers. But the evidence is that sweatshop labour continues to be used. In 1999 the NLC released reports on the continuing use of sweatshop labour for clothes made for Wal-Mart in Honduras, Mexico, El Salvador, Guatemala, China and Bangladesh. Wal-Mart continues to be 'one of the worst sweatshop abusers in the world, if not the worst', says a spokesperson for the NLC (personal communication, 8 August 2000). Meanwhile, in July 2000, the UFCW announced that Wal-Mart Canada had imported 60 tonnes of garments from Burma, a country reviled for its appalling human rights record and the use of forced labour.

In the UK the company has followed the same strategy. Asda recently announced a new Code of Practice on sourcing and labour, even though Wal-Mart's similar code in the US has been found to be effectively meaningless. All of this perhaps goes some way towards explaining how Wal-Mart keeps its prices so low.

---

* For more details see www.walmartwatch.com, maintained by the UFCW.

WATCH OUT, BRITAIN

So what is in store for Britain as the Wal-Mart noose begins to tighten around its local communities? Despite all the positive rhetoric by Asda/Wal-Mart, Al Norman from Sprawl-Busters believes that the company will behave no differently from its operations in the US. In an interview with the author (6 August 2000) he concluded:

> '*I don't see why the experience in the UK will be any different from the States, unless consumers in the UK reject the American company and its philosophy. . . This is not really a debate about stores at all, it is a debate about what communities in the UK are going to look like ten years from now. We are talking about community control, quality of life and a unique sense of place. It all adds up to what scale of commercial activity we want in our lives, forcing conspicuous over-consumption. I would hate to see that become the dominant mentality in England. There is a lot at risk here that goes beyond cheap underwear.*'

Chapter 9

Free Trade: The Great Destroyer

David Morris

One of the greatest unquestioned assumptions of modern policy-making is the necessity of global free trade. To doubt it is to commit an act of heresy. Yet for all its supposed and often vaunted 'superior efficiency' over other systems of economic organization, free trade, especially when practised globally, is grossly inefficient *in real terms. By prioritizing large-scale production for export over small-scale production for the fulfilment of local needs, and by engendering global competitive pressures that pit communities against communities worldwide, the* price of consumer products to individuals may fall, but the costs *to society and the natural environment rise enormously.*

David Morris has been one of the most widely quoted critics of the new free trade agreements, arguing his case on the grounds of environmental harm and the devastating effects upon local communities. Morris is director and vice president of the Institute for Local Self-Reliance (ISLR) in Minneapolis, a research and educational organization that provides technical assistance and information on environmentally sustainable economic practices. ISLR works with citizen groups, governments and businesses to develop policies that extract maximum economic value from resources drawn and used locally.

Free trade is the religion of our age. With its heaven as the global economy, free trade comes complete with comprehensive analytical and philosophical under-pinnings. Higher mathematics are used in stating its theorems. But in the final analysis, free trade is less an economic strategy than a moral doctrine. Although it pretends to be value free, it is fundamentally value driven. It assumes that the highest good is to shop. It assumes that mobility and change are synonymous with progress. The transport of capital, materials, goods and people takes precedence over the autonomy, the sovereignty and, indeed, the culture of local communities. Rather than promoting and sustaining the social relationships that create a vibrant community, the free trade theology relies on a narrow definition of efficiency to guide our conduct.

The Postulates of Free Trade

For most of us, after a generation of brainwashing about its supposed benefits, the tenets of free trade appear almost self-evident:

- Competition spurs innovation, raises productivity, and lowers prices.
- The division of labour allows specialization, which raises productivity and lowers prices.
- The larger the production unit, the greater the division of labour and specialization, and thus the greater the benefits.

The adoration of bigness permeates all political persuasions. The US Treasury Department proposes creating five to ten giant US banks. 'If we are going to be competitive in a globalized financial services world, we are going to have to change our views on the size of American institutions,' it declares (Nash, 1987). The vice chair of Citicorp warns us against 'preserving the heartwarming idea that 14,000 banks are wonderful for our country' (Nash, 1987). The liberal *Harper's* magazine agrees: 'True, farms have gotten bigger, as has nearly every other type of economic enterprise. They have done so in order to take advantage of the economies of scale offered by modern production techniques.' Democratic presidential advisor Lester Thurow criticizes antitrust laws as an 'old Democratic conception [that] is simply out of date'. He argues that even IBM, with US$50 billion in sales, is not big enough for the global marketplace. 'Big companies do sometimes crush small companies,' Thurow concedes, 'but far better that small American companies be crushed by big American companies than that they be crushed by foreign companies' (Thurow, 1980). The magazine *In These Times*, which once called itself an independent socialist weekly, concluded, 'Japanese steel companies have been able to outcompete American steel companies partly by building larger plants.'

The infatuation with large-scale systems leads logically to the next postulate of free trade: the need for global markets. Anything that sets up barriers to ever wider markets reduces the possibility of specialization and thus raises costs, making us less competitive.

The last pillar of free trade is the law of comparative advantage, which comes in two forms: absolute and relative. Absolute comparative advantage is easier to understand: differences in climate and natural resources suggest that Guatemala should raise bananas and Minnesota should raise walleyed pike. Thus, by specializing in what they grow best, each region enjoys comparative advantage in that particular crop. Relative comparative advantage is a less intuitive but ultimately more powerful concept. As the 19th-century British economist David Ricardo, the architect of free trade economics, explained:

'Two men can both make shoes and hats and one is superior to the other in both employments; but in making hats he can only exceed his competitor by one-fifth or 20 per cent, and in making shoes he can exceed him by one-third or 33 per cent. Will it not be for the interest of both that the superior man should employ himself exclusively in making shoes and the inferior man in making hats?' (Ricardo, 1996)

Thus, even if one community can make every product more efficiently than another, it should specialize only in those items it produces most efficiently, in relative terms, and trade for others. Each community, and ultimately each nation, should specialize in what it does best.

What are the implications of these tenets of free trade? That communities and nations abandon self-reliance and embrace dependence. That we abandon our capacity to produce many items and concentrate only on a few. That we import what we need and export what we produce.

Bigger is better. Competition is superior to cooperation. Material self-interest drives humanity. Dependence is better than independence. These are the pillars of free trade. In sum, we make a trade. We give up sovereignty over our affairs in return for a promise of more jobs, more goods, and a higher standard of living.

. . .

The economic arguments in favour of free trade are powerful. Yet for most of us it is not the soundness of its theory but the widely promoted idea that free trade is an inevitable development of our market system that makes us believers. We believe that economics, like natural organisms, evolve from the simple to the complex.

From the Dark Ages, to city states, to nation states, to the planetary economy and, soon, to space manufacturing, history has systematically unfolded. Free trade supporters believe that trying to hold back economic evolution is like trying to hold back natural evolution. The suggestion that we choose another developmental path is viewed, at best, as an attempt to reverse history and, at worst, as an unnatural and even sinful act.

This kind of historical determinism has corollaries. We not only move from simple to complex economics. We move from integrated economics to segregated ones, separating the producer from the consumer, the farmer from the kitchen, the power plant from the appliance, the dump site from the garbage can, the banker from die depositor, and, inevitably, the government from the citizenry. In the process of development we separate authority and responsibility – those who make the decisions are not those who are affected by the decisions.

Just as *Homo sapiens* is taken to be nature's highest achievement, so the multinational and supranational corporation becomes our most highly evolved economic animal. The planetary economy demands planetary institutions. The nation state itself begins to disappear, both as an object of our affection and identification and as a major actor in world affairs.

The planetary economy merges and submerges nations. Yoshitaka Sajima, vice president of Mitsui and Company US, asserts, 'The US and Japan are not just trading with each other anymore – they've become a part of each other' (Holstein, 1986a). Lamar Alexander, former Republican governor of Tennessee, agreed with Sajima's statement when he declared that the goal of his economic development strategy was 'to get the Tennessee economy integrated with the Japanese economy' (Holstein, 1986b).

In Europe, the common market has grown from 6 countries in the 1950s to 10 in the 1970s to 16 today, and barriers between these nations are rapidly being abolished. Increasingly, there are neither Italian nor French nor German companies, only European supracorporations. The US, Canadian and Mexican governments formed NAFTA to merge the countries of the North American continent economically.

Promotion of exports is now widely accepted as the foundation for a successful economic development programme. Whether for a tiny country such as Singapore or a huge country such as the US, exports are seen as essential to a nation's economic health.

Globalism commands our attention and our resources. Our principal task, we are told, is to nurture, extend and manage emerging global systems. Trade talks are on the top of everybody's agenda. Political leaders strive to devise stable systems for global financial markets and exchange rates. The best and the brightest of this generation use their ingenuity to establish the global financial and regulatory rules that will enable the greatest uninterrupted flow of resources among nations.

The emphasis on globalism rearranges our loyalties and loosens our neighbourly ties. 'The new order eschews loyalty to workers, products, corporate structure, businesses, factories, communities, even the nation,' the *New York Times* announces (Prokesch, 1987). Martin S Davis, chair of Gulf and Western, declares, 'All such allegiances are viewed as expendable under the new rules. You cannot be emotionally bound to any particular asset' (Waters, 1993).

We are now all assets.

Jettisoning loyalties isn't easy, but that is the price we believe we must pay to receive the benefits of the global village. Every community must achieve the lowest possible production cost, even when that means breaking whatever remains of its social contract and long-standing traditions.

The revised version of the American dream is articulated by Stanley J Mihelick, executive vice president for production at Goodyear: 'Until we get real wage levels down much closer to those of the Brazils and Koreas, we cannot pass along productivity gains to wages and still be competitive' (Mihelick, 1987).

Wage raises, environmental protection, national health insurance, and liability lawsuits – anything that raises the cost of production and makes a corporation less competitive – threaten our economy. We must abandon the good life to sustain the economy. We are in a global struggle for survival. We are hooked on free trade.

THE DOCTRINE FALTERS

At this very moment in history, when the doctrines of free trade and globalism are so dominant, the absurdities of globalism are becoming more evident. Consider the case of the toothpick and the chopstick.

A few years ago I was eating at a St Paul, Minnesota, restaurant. After lunch, I picked up a toothpick wrapped in plastic. On the plastic was printed the word *Japan*. Japan has little wood and no oil; nevertheless, it has become efficient enough in our global economy to bring little pieces of wood and barrels of oil to Japan, wrap the one in the other, and send the manufactured product to Minnesota. This toothpick may have travelled 80,000 kilometres. But never fear, we are now retaliating in kind. A Hibbing, Minnesota, factory now produces one billion disposable chopsticks a year for sale in Japan. In my mind's eye, I see two ships passing one another in the northern Pacific. One carries little pieces of Minnesota wood bound for Japan; the other carries little pieces of Japanese wood bound for Minnesota. Such is the logic of free trade.

Nowhere is the absurdity of free trade more evident than in the grim plight of the developing world. Developing nations were encouraged to borrow money to build an economic infrastructure in order to specialize in what they do best (comparative advantage, once again) and thereby expand their export capacity. To repay the debts, developing world countries must increase their exports.

One result of these arrangements has been a dramatic shift in food production from internal consumption to export. Take the case of Brazil. Brazilian per capita production of basic foodstuffs (rice, black beans, manioc and potatoes) fell 13 per cent from 1977 to 1984. Per capita output of exportable foodstuffs (soybeans, oranges, cotton, peanuts and tobacco) jumped 15 per cent. Today, although some 50 per cent of Brazil suffers malnutrition, one leading Brazilian agronomist still calls export promotion 'a matter of national survival'. In the global village, a nation survives by starving its people.

. . .

What about the purported benefits of free trade, such as higher standards of living?

It depends on whose standards of living are being considered. Inequality between and, in most cases, within countries has increased. Two centuries of trade has exacerbated disparities in world living standards. According to economist Paul Bairoch, per capita GNP in 1750 was approximately the same in the developed countries as in the developing ones. In 1930, the ratio was about 4 to 1 in favour of the developed nations. Today it is 8 to 1.

Inequality is both a cause and an effect of globalism. Inequality within one country exacerbates globalism because it reduces the number of people with sufficient purchasing power; consequently, a producer must sell to wealthy people in many countries to achieve the scale of production necessary to produce goods at a relatively low cost. Inequality is an effect of globalism because export industries employ few workers, who earn disproportionately higher wages than their compatriots, and because developed countries tend to take out more capital from developing world countries than they invest in them.

Free trade was supposed to improve our standard of living. Yet even in the US, the most developed of all nations, we find that living standards have been declining since 1980. More dramatically, according to several surveys, in 1988 US workers worked almost half a day longer for lower real wages than they did in 1970. We who work in the US have less leisure time in the 1990s than we had in the 1790s.

A New Way of Thinking

It is time to re-examine the validity of the doctrine of free trade and its creation, the planetary economy. To do so, we must begin by speaking of values. Human beings may be acquisitive and competitive, but we are also loving and cooperative. Several studies have found that the voluntary, unpaid economy may be as large and as productive as the paid economy.

There is no question that we have converted more and more human relationships into commercial transactions, but there is a great deal of uncertainty as to whether this was a necessary or beneficial development.

We should not confuse change with progress. Bertrand Russell once described change as inevitable and progress as problematic. Change is scientific. Progress is ethical. We must decide which values we hold most dear and then design an economic system that reinforces those values.

Reassessing Free Trade's Assumptions

If price is to guide our buying, selling and investing, then price should tell us something about efficiency. We might measure efficiency in terms of natural resources used in making products and the lack of waste produced in converting raw material into a consumer or industrial product. Traditionally, we have measured efficiency in human terms – that is, by measuring the amount of labour-hours spent in making a product.

But price is actually no measure of real efficiency. In fact, price is no reliable measure of anything. In the planetary economy, the prices of raw materials, labour, capital, transportation and waste disposal are all heavily subsidized. For example, wage-rate inequities among comparably skilled work forces can be as disparate as 30 to 1. This disparity overwhelms even the most productive worker. An American worker might produce twice as much per hour as a Mexican worker but is paid ten times as much.

In Taiwan, for example, strikes are strictly regulated. In South Korea, unions cannot be organized without government permission. Many developing nations have no minimum wage, maximum hours or environmental legislation. As economist Howard Wachtel notes, 'Differences in product cost that are due to totalitarian political institutions or restrictions on economic rights reflect no natural or entrepreneurial advantage. Free trade has nothing to do with incomparable political economic institutions that protect individual rights in one country and deny them in another.'

The price of goods in developed countries is also highly dependent on subsidies. For example, we in the US decided early on that government should build the transportation systems of the country. The public, directly or indirectly, built our railroads, canals, ports, highways and airports.

Heavy trucks do not pay taxes sufficient to cover the damage they do to roads. California farmers buy water at as little as 5 per cent of the going market rate; the other 95 per cent is funded by huge direct subsidies to corporate farmers. In the US, society as a whole picks up the costs of agricultural pollution. Having intervened in the production process in all these ways, we then discover it is cheaper to raise produce near the point of sale.

Prices don't provide accurate signals within nations; they are not the same as cost. Price is what an individual pays; *cost* is what the community as a whole pays. Most economic programmes in the industrial world result in an enormous disparity between the price of a product or service to an individual and the cost of that same product or service to the society as a whole.

It is often hard to quantify social costs, but this doesn't mean they are insignificant. Remember urban renewal? In the 1950s and 1960s inner-city neighbourhoods were levelled to assemble sufficient land area to rebuild our downtowns. Skyscrapers and shopping malls arose; the property tax base expanded; and we considered it a job well done. Later, sociologists, economists and planners discovered that the seedy areas we destroyed were not fragmented, violence-prone slums but more often cohesive ethnic communities where generations had grown up and worked and where children went to school and played. If we were to put a dollar figure on the destruction of homes, the pain of broken lives and the expense of relocation and recreation of community life, we might find that the city as a whole actually lost money in the urban renewal process. If we had used a full-cost accounting system, we might never have undertaken urban renewal.

Our refusal to understand and count the social costs of certain kinds of development has caused suffering in rural and urban areas alike. In 1944, Walter Goldschmidt, working under contract with the USDA, compared the economic and social characteristics of two rural California communities that were alike in all respects, except one. Dinuba was surrounded by family farms, Arvin by corporate farms. Goldschmidt found that Dinuba was more stable, had a higher standard of living, more small businesses, higher retail sales, better schools and other community facilities, and a higher degree of citizen participation in local affairs. The USDA invoked a clause in Goldschmidt's contract forbidding him to discuss his finding. The study was not made public for almost 30 years. Meanwhile, the USDA continued to promote research that rapidly transformed the Dinubas of our country into Arvins. The farm crisis we now suffer is a consequence of this process. Economists like to talk about externalities. The costs of job dislocation, rising family violence, community breakdown, environmental damage, and cultural collapse are all considered 'external'. External to what, one might ask?

The theory of comparative advantage itself is fast losing its credibility. Time was when technology spread slowly. Three hundred years ago in northern Italy, stealing or disclosing the secrets of silk-spinning machinery was a crime punishable by death. At the beginning of the Industrial Revolution, Britain protected its supremacy in textile manufacturing by banning both the export of machines and the emigration of men who knew how to build and run them. A young British apprentice, Samuel Slater, brought the Industrial Revolution to the US by memorizing the design of the spinning frame and migrating here in 1789.

Today, technology transfer is simple. According to Dataquest, a market research firm, it takes only three weeks after a new US-made product is introduced before it is copied, manufactured and shipped back to the US from Asia. So much for comparative advantage.

THE EFFICIENCIES OF SMALL SCALE

This brings us to the issue of scale. There is no question that when I move production out of my basement and into a factory, the cost per item produced declines dramatically. But when the factory increases its output a hundredfold, production costs no longer decline proportionately. The vast majority of the cost decreases are captured at fairly modest production levels.

In agriculture, for example, the USDA studied the efficiency of farms and concluded, 'Above about US$40–50,000 in gross sales – the size that is at the bottom of the end of medium-sized sales category – there are no greater efficiencies of scale' (Miller, 1979). Another USDA report agreed: 'Medium-sized family farms are as efficient as the large farms' (USDA, 1973).

Harvard Professor Joseph Bain's pioneering investigations in the 1950s found that plants far smaller than originally believed can be economically competitive. Furthermore, it was found that the factory could be significantly reduced in size without requiring major price increases for its products. In other words, we might be able to produce shoes for a region rather than for a nation at about the same price per shoe. If we withdrew government subsidies to the transportation system, then locally produced and marketed shoes might actually be less expensive than those brought in from abroad.

Modern technology makes smaller production plants possible. For instance, traditional float glass plants produce 550 to 600 tons of glass daily, at an annual cost of US$100 million. With only a US$40 to US$50 million investment, new miniplants can produce about 250 tons per day for a regional market at the same cost per ton as the large plants.

The advent of programmable machine tools may accelerate this tendency. In 1980, industrial engineers developed machine tools that could be programmed to reproduce a variety of shapes so that now a typical Japanese machine tool can make almost 100 different parts from an individual block of material. What does this mean? Erich Bloch, director of the National Science Foundation, believes manufacturing 'will be so flexible that it will be able to make the first copy of a product for little more than the cost of the thousandth' (Brandt, 1986). 'So the ideal location for the factory of the future,' says Patrick A Toole, vice president for manufacturing at IBM, 'is in the market where the products are consumed' (Brandt, 1986). Again, so much for 'comparative advantage'.

CONCLUSION

When we abandon our ability to produce for ourselves, when we separate authority from responsibility, when those affected by our decisions are not those who make the decisions, when the cost and the benefit of production or development processes are not part of the same equation, when price and cost are no longer in harmony, we jeopardize our security and our future.

You may argue that free trade is not the sole cause of all our ills. Agreed. But free trade as it is preached today nurtures and reinforces many of our worst problems. It is an ideological package that promotes ruinous policies. And, most tragically, as we move further down the road to giantism, globalism and dependence, we make it harder and harder to back up and take another path. If we lose our skills, our productive base, our culture, our traditions, our natural resources, if we erode the bonds of personal and familial responsibility, it becomes ever more difficult to recreate community. It is very, very hard to put Humpty Dumpty back together again.

Which means we must act now. The unimpeded mobility of capital, labour, goods and raw materials is not the highest social good. We need to challenge the postulates of free trade head on, to propose a different philosophy, to embrace a different strategy. There is another way. To make it the dominant way, we must change the rules; indeed, we must challenge our own behaviour. And to do that requires not only that we challenge the emptiness of free trade but that we promote a new idea: economics as if community matters.

Part 2

Impacts of Globalization

Chapter 10

Structural Adjustment Programmes

Walden Bello

Judged by their official goals of increasing economic growth and relieving debt in the less-developed world, the IMF and World Bank's structural adjustment programmes have failed utterly. In fact, the free market reforms they have prescribed in over 100 less-developed countries have destroyed domestic economies and increased debt, unemployment and poverty. But in their real objectives – of ensuring continued interest payments to Northern banks and, above all, the integration of less-developed countries into the global economy – they have been a resounding success. The staggering human costs involved are thus a chilling illustration of the true costs of economic globalization.

Walden Bello is a Philippine activist, scholar and writer. He obtained his PhD degree in sociology from Princeton University in 1975, and he has taught at the University of California at Berkeley and, presently, at the University of the Philippines. During the Marcos dictatorship, Bello worked in Washington, DC, as a lobbyist advocating democratic rights in the Philippines. Until recently, Bello was executive director of the San Francisco-based Institute for Food and Development Policy, also known as Food First. He is the author of A Siamese Tragedy: Development and Disintegration in Modern Thailand *(1998) and* Dragons in Distress *(1990, with Stephanie Rosenfeld), a book that documents the terrible social and ecological costs that the newly industrialized countries have incurred as byproducts of their much-publicized economic 'success', as well as* Development Debacle: The World Bank in the Philippines *(1982, with David Kinley and Elaine Elison). He also co-authored* Dark Victory: the US Structural Adjustment, and Global Poverty *(1994, with Shea Cunningham and Bill Rau), a critique of structural adjustment programmes.*

Structural adjustment loans (SALs) began to be provided to debtor countries in the early 1980s. The immediate objective was to rescue Northern banks that had become overextended in the developing world; the longer-term objective was to further integrate Southern countries into the North-dominated world economy. To accomplish these twin goals, the World Bank and the IMF became the linchpin of a strategy that involved providing compliant developing world debtors with billions of dollars in quick-disbursing SALs or 'standby loans' that would then be transferred as interest payments to the private banks. But to receive SALs, the Southern governments had to agree to undergo structural adjustment pro-grammes, which were ostensibly designed to make their economies more efficient and better capable of sustained growth.

The conditions usually attached to SALs included:

- Removing restrictions on foreign investments in local industry, banks, and other financial services. No longer could local industry or banks be favoured or protected against giant foreign intervention.
- Reorienting the economy toward exports in order to earn the foreign exchange required for servicing the debt and to become correspondingly more dependent on the global economy. The effect was to reduce self-sufficiency and diverse local production in favour of single-product manufacture or single-crop agriculture.
- Reducing wages or wage increases to make exports more 'competitive'. Radically reducing government spending, including spending on health, education and welfare, combined with wage reduction, would control inflation and ensure that all available money would be channelled into increasing production for export. But the few social services that remained were gutted.
- Cutting tariffs, quotas and other restrictions on imports to grease the way for global integration.
- Devaluing the local currency against hard currencies such as the US dollar in order to make exports still more competitive.
- Privatizing state enterprises, thereby providing further access for foreign capital.
- Undertaking a deregulation programme to free export-oriented corporations from government controls that protect labour, the environment, and natural resources, thereby cutting costs and further increasing export competitiveness. (This had the secondary effect of forcing down wages and standards in other countries – including industrialized countries – to maintain their competitiveness.)

Since structural adjustment programmes covered so many dimensions of economic policy, agreeing to an SAL virtually meant turning over a country's economic control to the World Bank and the IMF.

THE GLOBALIZATION OF 'ADJUSTMENT'

Initially, few governments felt eager to receive SALs. But the eruption of the debt crisis in the less-developed world mid-1982 provided a grand opportunity to further the Reaganite agenda of resubordinating the South via structural adjustment schemes. As more and more less-developed countries ran into ever greater difficulties in servicing the huge loans made to them by northern banks in the 1970s, the US government via the Bretton Woods institutions took advantage of 'this period of financial strain to insist that debtor countries remove the government from the economy as the price of getting credit' (Sheahan, 1992).

In accordance with guidelines set by the US Treasury Department, the US private banks invariably made (and continue to make) World Bank consent a prerequisite for debt rescheduling. Predictably, the World Bank's seal of approval and its cash, which debtor countries desperately needed to make interest payments to the private banks, came dearly. As one treasury official involved in the debt negotiations with Mexico put it, 'Only countries that commit to market-oriented economic reform will get the [World Bank's] help' (Miller 1991).

Debtor countries had no choice but to capitulate. By the beginning of 1986, 12 of the 15 countries designated by then Secretary of the Treasury James Baker as top-priority debtors – including Brazil, Mexico, Argentina, and the Philippines – had agreed to SAPs. From 3 per cent of total World Bank lending in 1981, structural adjustment credits rose to 25 per cent in 1986. By the end of 1992, about 267 SALs had been approved.

Thirteen years after the World Bank's first SAP was introduced, the bank declared structural adjustment a success. In its publication *Global Economic Prospects and the Developing Countries* (1993), the bank asserted that developing countries face brighter prospects that can be attributed mainly to the widespread economic reforms, notably privatization, greater openness to trade, reduction of fiscal deficits and commercial debt overhangs. This was, needless to say, a minority opinion.

A number of comprehensive studies, including one conducted by the IMF itself, admits that SALs did not achieve their overt goal of stimulating growth. Comparing countries who underwent stabilisation and adjustment programmes with those who did not over the period 1973 to 1988, IMF economist Mohsin Khan found that economic growth was higher in the latter than in the former.

Focusing on the African experience in the 1980s, UNICEF economist Eva Jespersen assessed a sample of 24 countries that were subjected to structural adjustment programmes, on three counts: the rate of capital accumulation, the share of manufacturing in GDP and the growth of exports (Cornia et al, 1992). The data showed that capital accumulation slowed in 20 countries; the share of manufacturing in GDP stagnated in 18 countries; exports fell in 13 countries; and the increases experienced in 11 countries did not compensate for the increase in imports.

EXPLAINING STAGNATION

Why such a dismal record? The problem, according to Massachusetts Institute of Technology economist Lance Taylor and his associates, is that the World Bank and the IMF misdiagnosed the problem. The main barrier to growth in the pre-SAL period was not that developing world economies had been insufficiently integrated into the global economy, as the IMF and the World Bank insisted, but above all that they had been subjected to two great shocks: the OPEC oil price rise in the 1970s and the debt crisis in the early 1980s (Fanelli, 1992). Using the bank's own data, Taylor and his associates found that the much-derided prior strategy called *import substitution* had been effective at fostering productivity. (Import substitution policies emphasized local production for local consumption and thereby promoted diverse production and national self-sufficiency, especially in the area of key goods and services. This was the common practice in Latin America from 1960 to 1973.) After the 1982 debt crisis, on the other hand, private investment fell dramatically in developing countries, while the money made available by multinational development banks was mainly designated to repay old debts. At the same time, there was a massive outflow of resources to the industrial countries that could otherwise have gone to domestic local investment.

Taylor and his associates, along with other academic critics of structural adjustment programmes, have also stressed the way SAPs trigger a range of adverse consequences that cannot be predicted on the basis of IMF and World Bank theories, but that must seem inevitable to anyone with a common-sense view of economics.

By reducing government spending, cutting wages and literally destroying the domestic economy in order to build up a new export-oriented economy, a structural adjustment programme must necessarily lead to an overall economic contraction and cause increased unemployment. Even in such conditions, the programmes prevent the state from stepping in to reverse the decline in private investment. The absence of intervention further accentuates all these trends and creates a vicious cycle of stagnation and decline rather than growth, rising employment and rising investment, as World Bank theory originally predicted.

To further promote exports, when devaluation and the lifting of price controls on imports are added to this policy of monetary and fiscal austerity, the economy has to contract still further. This must raise the local costs of both imported capital and the raw materials and components used in local assembly plants. For instance, letting the market determine fertilizer prices has led, in many countries, to reduced applications, lower yields and reduced investment in agriculture.

At the same time, rising exports of the small range of crops (such as sugar, palm oil and bananas) that the World Bank encourages developing countries to produce (regardless of a market need) have led to a continuous fall in prices and thus often to reduced foreign earnings. Much of the earnings are, in any case, used for servicing debt rather than for productive domestic investment.

CHILE: AN ECONOMIC LABORATORY

The sharp disparity between the expected and the actual results of a structural adjustment programme is illustrated by the case of Chile in the 1980s. Chile is probably the country with the longest-running structural adjustment programme in the world, one that began immediately after General Augusto Pinochet's 1973 bloody coup against the democratically elected government of President Salvador Allende. Adjustment took a particularly radical form in Chile, as Chilean economists trained at the University of Chicago sought to transform, vis-à-vis the new government's dictatorial powers, an economy dependent on heavy state intervention into a free market paradise. All the standard paraphernalia of structural adjustment programmes was called into play and applied with ideological fervour.

By the end of the 1980s, Chile's economy had indeed been transformed:

- Some 600 state enterprises had been sold off, with fewer than 50 remaining in state hands.
- Chile had gone from being one of the most protected to one of the least protected of Latin American economies, with all quantitative restrictions on trade abolished and tariffs set at a single flat rate of 10 per cent on all items.
- Foreign investors had achieved a strong presence in the economy as part owners of former state enterprises in strategic sectors such as steel, telecommunications and airlines.
- The radical deregulation of the domestic financial market had been accomplished.
- The economy had become substantially more integrated into the international economy, with total trade amounting to 57.4 per cent of GDP in 1990 compared to 35 per cent in 1970.

The World Bank and the IMF had been central to this transformation, and they were proud of the results of their policies. But were they really a success? It depends on the criterion one wishes to apply. If success is to be measured by the effects on Chile's external accounts, then structural adjustment has had dubious results. Chile's external debt rose to US$19 billion in 1991, which was 49 per cent of GNP, with close to 9 per cent of GDP flowing out of the country to service it. In reality, the situation was much worse, since a significant portion of the debt that is in fixed-interest bonds had been exchanged for ordinary shares (equity holdings) in strategic sectors of the Chilean economy via 'debt-equity swaps'.

If sustained growth is regarded as the key measure of success for structural adjustment, then Chile could hardly be considered successful. As Ricardo French-Davis and Oscar Munoz point out, the growth in GDP during the Pinochet years (1974 to 1989) averaged only 2.6 per cent per year as opposed to 4 per cent from 1950 to 1961 and 4.6 per cent from 1961 to 1971, the period before structural adjustment programmes had been applied. The result of the adjustment was even more dismal when viewed in terms of growth per capita GDP: this had averaged 1.1 per cent in the 1970s and only 0.9 per cent in the 1980s (Inter-American Development Bank, 1992).

These results are even more disappointing when one considers that in order to achieve them, free market policies plunged Chile into two major depressions in one decade: first in 1974–1975, when GDP fell by 12 per cent, then again in 1982–1983, when it dropped by 15 per cent. As Lance Taylor and his associates noted in their report for the UN Conference on Trade and Development, 'the [Chilean] economy reeled through a 12-year sequence of disastrous experiments amply supported by the [World] Bank and the [International Monetary] Fund' (Fanelli, 1992).

The reasons for the failure of the World Bank's and IMF's restructuring of the Chilean economy are clear. The combination of a lower rate of investment with draconian trade liberalization caused the manufacturing sector to lose ground, declining from an average of 26 per cent of GDP in the late 1960s to an average of 20 per cent in the late 1980s. Indeed, from 1979 to 1981, manufacturing shrank in absolute terms, and it was not until 1988 that gross profits in industry surpassed the level that had been attained in 1974. On the other hand, export-oriented enterprises involved in forestry, fishing, agriculture and mining greatly expanded. However, this led, among other things, to serious environmental problems. The logging of vast tracts of ancient *alerce* forests, the massive growth of agricultural monocropping and of large-scale intensive fish farming, the building of huge dams on wild rivers, and the replacement of natural forests with plantations of fast-growing exotics all drastically increased soil erosion, desertification and the pollution of rivers and estuaries while causing a massive reduction in biological diversity.

In addition, the transformed Chilean economy, with its extreme dependence on exports of primary and processed goods and its shrinking manufacturing base, was by the late 1980s far less stable than it had been before the Pinochet era.

However, the social impact of the radical free market policy may have been the least tolerable of all the consequences of structural adjustment. When the debt crisis broke out in 1983, the government (and hence the taxpayers) absorbed the massive debts (US$3.5 billion, or nearly 20 per cent of GDP) that had been incurred by private institutions whose owners and managers, rather than being penalized for their incompetence and irresponsibility, were allowed to carry on as before.

Also, in order to raise the money to pay for these losses, public spending was severely cut back, wages were frozen and the Chilean peso was drastically devalued, correspondingly reducing the standard of living of the poor. Indeed, the contraction of domestic expenditure that led to a 15 per cent drop in GDP put over 30 per cent of the work force out of work in a single year, with unemployment remaining at 25 per cent for three years. The 50 per cent devaluation of the peso in real terms caused the purchasing power of the work force to fall by nearly 20 per cent. At die same time, in contrast to the huge sums paid to subsidize the private institutions, benefits made available to the newly unemployed were minimal and were actually paid to less than half of those who should have received them.

Not surprisingly, between 1980 and 1990, the proportion of families below 'the line of destitution' had risen from 12 to 15 per cent and of those living below the poverty line (but above the line of destitution) from 24 to 26 per cent. This meant that at the end of the Pinochet era, some 40 per cent, or 5.2 million people out of 13 million, were now classified as poor in a country that had once boasted a large middle class. Increased poverty also meant increased hunger and malnutrition. Indeed, for 40 per cent of the population, the daily caloric intake dropped from 2019 in 1970 to 1751 in 1980 to 1629 in 1990 – well below international minimums for human nutrition.

Structural adjustment in Chile had a similar effect on income distribution. The share of the national income going to the poorest 50 per cent of the population declined from 20.4 per cent to 16.8 per cent, while the share going to the richest 10 per cent rose from 36.5 per cent to 46.8 per cent.

To all these costs must be added the replacement of a popular democratic government by a military dictatorship, which, as in the Philippines, was probably required in order to impose such a socially disruptive programme of economic transformation. Indeed, a study for the Organization for European Cooperation and Development (OECD), having asserted that the costs of the Chilean adjustment were 'among the largest in Latin America', actually asked whether 'this type of adjustment [could] have been feasible under a democratic regime' (Meller, 1992).

· · ·

The experience of Chile in the 1980s is by no means unique in this respect. During this period, except in East Asia and in some areas of South Asia, most countries in the South experienced stagnation or sharp reversals in growth, escalating poverty and increasing inequality both within and between countries.

With per capita income stagnant in the South and rising by 2.4 per cent per year in the North during 1980s, the gap between living standards in the North and the South widened, with the average income in the North reaching US$12,510, or 18 times the average in the South.

Especially ravaged during the decade were the regions that were most severely subjected to structural adjustment. In Latin America, the force of adjustment programmes struck with special fury, 'largely cancelling out the progress of the 1960s and 1970s' (Iglesias, 1992). The number of people living in poverty rose from 130 million in 1980 to 180 million at the beginning of the 1990s. In a decade of negative growth, income inequalities – already among the worst in the world – worsened. As Enrique Iglesias, president of the Inter-American Development Bank, reports, 'the bulk of the costs of adjustment fell disproportionately on the middle and low-income groups, while the top 5 per cent of the population retained or, in some cases, even increased its standard of living' (Iglesias, 1992).

With hunger and malnutrition on the rise, tuberculosis and cholera – diseases that were once thought to be banished by modern medicine – returned with a vengeance throughout the continent, with cholera claiming at least 1300 in Peru alone in 1991.

Sub-Saharan Africa has been even more devastated than Latin America, with total debt in 1994 amounting to 110 per cent of GNP, compared to 35 per cent for all developing countries. Cut off from significant capital flows except for aid, battered by plunging commodity prices, wracked by famine and civil war, and squeezed by structural adjustment programmes, Africa's per capita income declined by 2.2 per cent per annum in the 1980s. By the end of the decade it had plunged to the same level as at the time of independence in the early 1960s. Some 200 million of the region's 690 million people are now classified as poor, and even the least pessimistic World Bank projection sees the number of poor rising by 50 per cent to reach 300 million by the year 2000.

Adjustment: the Outcome

Judged by its ostensible objectives – resolving the debt problems of developing world economies and bringing about renewed and sustained growth while reducing poverty and unemployment – structural adjustment has been a resounding failure.

Judged by its concealed underlying strategic goals, however, it has been a resounding success. From Argentina to Ghana, state participation in the economy has been drastically curtailed; government enterprises are passing into private hands; protectionist barriers on Northern imports have been eliminated wholesale; restrictions on foreign investments have been lifted; and export-first policies have been implemented with quasi-religious zeal. As a result, debtor countries have, on the whole, been able to pay interest on the loans contracted to Northern banks, and, most important of all, they have become more tightly integrated within the capitalist world market and thereby made increasingly dependent for their sustenance on the Northern powers and the transnational corporations that effectively control them.

Chapter 11

Jurassic Fund

Walden Bello

The IMF now claims that it has changed; that poverty reduction, not structural adjustment, has become its overarching goal. In practice, however, the conversion has been largely cosmetic. The IMF's macroeconomic approach remains fundamentally unchanged; trade and investment liberalization, privatization and deregulation are still the order of the day. It is time for governments to decide once and for all: the IMF must either undergo radical reform or be decommissioned.

For biographical details on Walden Bello see Chapter 10, Structural Adjustment Programmes.

When the IMF, in a surprise announcement at the World Bank–IMF annual meeting at the end of September 1999, announced that henceforth it would put 'poverty reduction' at the centre of its approach toward developing countries, there was widespread speculation among Washington watchers that Michel Camdessus's days as managing director of the fund were numbered.

Indeed, Camdessus – whose 13-year reign was so closely identified with the paradigm of structural adjustment – resigned in mid November 1999, shortly after Larry Summers, the then new US secretary of the treasury and one of Camdessus's biggest backers, told the US Congress that the US would support a 'new framework for providing international assistance to [developing] countries – one that moves beyond a closed IMF-centred process that has too often focused on narrow macroeconomic objectives at the expense of broader human development' (*Washington Post*, 1999).

CRISIS OF LEGITIMACY

While self-doubt had already begun to engulf the World Bank under James Wolfensohn in the mid 1990s, the IMF, in contrast, ploughed confidently on, and the lack of evidence for the success of its structural adjustment programmes was interpreted to mean simply that a government lacked political will to push adjustment. Through the establishment of the extended structural adjustment facility (ESAF), the IMF actually sought to fund countries over a longer period in order to more fully institutionalize the desired free-market reforms and make them permanent.

It was the Asian financial crisis that finally forced the IMF to confront reality. In 1997–1998 the IMF moved with grand assurance into Thailand, Indonesia, and Korea, with its classic formula of short-term fiscal and monetary policy cum structural reform in the direction of liberalization, deregulation and privatization. This was the price exacted from their governments for IMF financial rescue packages that would allow them to repay the massive debt incurred by their private sectors. But the result was to turn a conjunctural crisis into a deep recession, as governments' capacity to counteract the drop in private-sector activity was destroyed by budgetary and monetary repression. If some recovery is now discernible in a few economies, this is widely recognized as coming in spite of, rather than because of, the IMF.

For a world that had long been resentful of the IMF's arrogance, this was the last straw. In 1998–1999, criticism of the IMF rose to a crescendo and went beyond its stubborn adherence to structural adjustment and its serving as a bailout mechanism for international finance capital to encompass accusations of its being non-transparent and non-accountable. Its vulnerable position was exposed during the recent debate in the US Congress over a G-7 initiative to provide debt relief to 40 poor countries. Legislators depicted the IMF as the agency that caused the debt crisis of the poor countries in the first place, and some called for its abolition within three years. Said Representative Maxine Walters: 'Do we have to have the IMF involved at all? Because, as we have painfully discovered, the way the IMF works causes children to starve' (*Business World*, 1999).

In the face of such criticism from legislators in the IMF's most powerful member, the then US Treasury Secretary Larry Summers claimed that the IMF-centred process would be replaced by 'a new, more open and inclusive process that would involve multiple international organizations and give national policymakers and civil society groups a more central role' (*Washington Post*, 1999).

BUT IS THIS FOR REAL?

So, structural adjustment is dead and the Bretton Woods institutions have seen the light. But wait, isn't there something too easy about all of this?

The fact is, in the case of the IMF, as well as that of the World Bank and the Asian Development Bank (ADB), jettisoning the paradigm of structural adjustment has left them adrift, in the view of many critics, with just the rhetoric and broad goals of reducing poverty, but without an innovative macroeconomic approach. Wolfensohn and his ex-chief economist Joseph Stiglitz talk about 'bringing together' the 'macroeconomic' and 'social' aspects of development, but World Bank officials cannot point to a larger strategy beyond increasing lending to health, population, nutrition, education and social protection to 25 per cent of the World Bank's total lending. The ADB is even more of a newcomer in the anti-poverty approach, and its strategy paper issued this year is long on laudable goals but, even ADB insiders agree, breaks no new ground in terms of macro-economic innovation. Most at sea are IMF economists, some of whom openly admitted to non-governmental organization (NGO) representatives at the September IMF–World Bank meeting that so far the new approach was limited to relabelling the extended structural adjustment fund (ESAF) the 'poverty reduction facility', and that they were looking to the World Bank to provide leadership.

It is not surprising that, in these circumstances, the old framework would reassert itself, with, for example, the IMF telling the Thai government, already its most obedient pupil, to cut its fiscal deficit despite a very fragile recovery; the IMF's pushing Indonesia to open its retail trade to foreign investors, despite the consequences in terms of higher unemployment; and technocrats of the ADB making energy loans and Miyazawa funding contingent upon the Philippine government's acceleration of the IMF-promoted privatization of the National Power Corporation, despite the fact that consumers are likely to end up paying more to the seven private monopolies that will succeed the state enterprise.

'It's the old approach of deregulation, privatization, and liberalization but with safety nets' is the not inappropriate description made by one Filipino labour leader much consulted by the multilateral institutions.

Then, there is the issue of accountability. One cannot just walk away from the scene of the crime without admitting wrongdoing. The World Bank and the IMF have been responsible for tremendous economic and social damage wrought on developing world economies for over two decades. Shouldn't they be held to account for that? Should not Camdessus and the whole top leadership of the IMF, including his deputy Stanley Fischer and Asia-Pacific division chief Hubert Neiss, who blindly embraced adjustment to the end, take responsibility for their massive blunders? Despite their announced resignations, both Camdessus and Neiss are unrepentant when it comes to their policies.

Many of the IMF's long-time critics have a darker view of things. To them, Camdessus served as a sacrificial lamb to blunt real efforts for reform at a time when the IMF 'desperately needs' credibility and legitimacy, as the *Financial Times* put it. This fear is well grounded, for in his most recent statements, Larry Summers, the pivotal figure when it comes to the future of the IMF, appears to have forgotten about the need for a paradigm shift. When speaking about the elements of a 'new' IMF strategy, Summers says that the 'approach looks to the IMF to continue to certify that a country's macroeconomic policies are satisfactory before debt is relieved and new concessional lending is advanced' (Summers, 1999a). Is this what is meant by 'moving away from an IMF-centred process that has too often focused on narrow macroeconomic objectives at the expense of broader human development'?

Bearing in mind that trade liberalization was one of the most controversial dimensions of the old structural adjustment approach, even more revealing is Summers's view that the new IMF must have as one of its priorities 'strong support for market opening and trade liberalization'. Trade liberalization, Summers continues,

> '. . . is often a key component of IMF arrangements. In the course of negotiations, the IMF has sought continued compliance with existing trade obligations and further commitments to market opening measures as part of a strategy for spurring growth. For example: As part of its IMF programme, Indonesia has abolished import monopolies for soybeans and wheat; agreed to phase out all non-tariff barriers affecting imports; dissolved all cartels for plywood, cement and paper; removed restrictions on foreign investment in the wholesale and resale trades; and allowed foreign banks to buy domestic ones. Zambia's 1999 programme with the IMF commits the government to reducing the weighted average tariff on foreign goods to 10 per cent, and to cutting the maximum tariff from 25 per cent to 20 per cent by 2001. In July, the import ban on wheat flour was eliminated.'* (Summers, 1996)

Calling this a 'new approach' is, let us face it, stretching the truth.

RADICAL REFORM OR DECOMMISSIONING?

Now, what would a real process of transformation look like? It would be something that would include more than the open selection process for the new managing director – one that would open the recruitment process to non-Europeans – endorsed by Jeffrey Sachs. For the problem lies in the very structure and culture of the institution: a lack of accountability except to the US Treasury Department; a belief in non-transparency as a condition for effectiveness; and a deeply ingrained elitism that renders the bureaucracy incapable of learning from outsiders.

If this is the heart of the matter, then surgery must be more radical. I would propose the following measures:

● Firstly, so embedded is the old adjustment framework in current programmes that a clean break with the past can only take place, not just with a renaming but with the immediate dismantling of all structural adjustment programmes in the developing world and the ex-socialist world, as well as the IMF adjustment programmes imposed on Indonesia, Thailand and Korea following the Asian financial crisis.

- Secondly, there should be an immediate reduction of the IMF professional staff from over 1000 to 200, and major cuts in both capital expenditures and operational expenses of the agency. Most of the IMF's economists are today employed in micromanaging adjustment programmes and would definitely cease to be necessary if, as the G-7 finance ministers and Central Bank governors suggest, developing countries be given more authority in formulating and implementing their poverty reduction programmes; and if, as Jeffrey Sachs advises, the IMF's main work is limited to monitoring world capital markets and the world's monetary system.

- Thirdly, and most importantly, there should be created a global commission on the future of the IMF to decide if it is to be reformed along the lines suggested by Sachs and others or, to borrow a phrase applied to ageing nuclear plants, it is to be decommissioned, which this author favours. Half of the members of such a body should come from civil society organizations since it is these groups that were instrumental in bringing to light the destructive impact of adjustment programmes and are now engaged in many of the most innovative experiments in grassroots social development. Energy from below and decentralized operations are the trademarks of so many successful organizations that the top-down centralized IMF looks positively Jurassic.

With its credibility and legitimacy in tatters, the IMF is in severe crisis. Unless international civil society intervenes, and intervenes forcefully now, the powers that be will wait for the storm to blow over while talking, as Larry Summers has done, about reform. Radical reform or decommissioning? That is the question of the hour around which we must frame our strategies for intervention.

Chapter 12

Seeds of Exploitation: Free Trade Zones in the Global Economy

Alexander Goldsmith

Free trade zones provide the starkest illustration of the social, ecological and human consequences of almost total deregulation, which governments worldwide now seek to achieve as a means of maximizing global trade. The most notorious free trade zones, the maquiladoras *of Mexico, populated mostly by US-owned factories, represent a terrible indictment of the modern global economy.*

Alexander Goldsmith studied anthropology at Jesus College, Cambridge. He went into journalism, specializing in environmental issues, founded the Environmental Digest *with Martin Wright, became the editor of the* Geographical Magazine, *which is produced in conjunction with the Royal Geographic Society, and was then the editor of* Green Futures, *the magazine of Forum for the Future.*

Free-trade zones (FTZs), also known as export-processing zones, were first created in the early 1970s, officially as a means of attracting foreign investment to 'undeveloped' regions. In the words of Sri Lanka's President Jayawardene, when he created the Katunayake FTZ in 1978, 'Foreign investment in our country will help us acquire higher technology, develop new export markets and generate employment.'

Free-trade zones are regions that have been fiscally or juridically redefined by their 'host country' to give them a comparative advantage over neighbouring regions and countries in luring transnational corporate activity. Most FTZs share the following characteristics: lax social, environmental and employment regulations; a ready source of cheap labour; and fiscal and financial incentives that can take a huge variety of forms, although they generally consist of the lifting of customs duties, the removal of foreign exchange controls, tax holidays and free land or reduced rents.

Today, there are some 800 FTZs worldwide, compared to 116 in 1986 in 40 different countries. Then, about 48 per cent of them were located in Latin America and the Caribbean, and 42 per cent were in Asia. At that time, the total direct employment in FTZs exceeded one million. Sizes of FTZs vary enormously. Some employ over 30,000 people, others as few as 100.

FTZs attract labour-intensive work, such as textile and clothing manufacture and the assembly of electronic goods. Nearly 50 per cent of the total labour force in the FTZs of Asia are engaged in the electronics industry. The work force is mostly composed of unmarried women between the ages of 17 and 23. In Mexican FTZs, these women account for about 50 per cent of the work force. They are the preferred workers, as their wages tend to be lower (often less than US$1 per day), and they are considered better suited to repetitive tasks that require nimble fingers.

Mexico's *maquiladoras* are some of the best-documented FTZs. They consist mainly of US-owned factories that import US materials for assembly and re-export. At the North American Free Trade Agreement's (NAFTA's) birth, the *maquiladoras* numbered more than 2100 and represented Mexico's second-largest source of foreign exchange after oil, earning the country US$3 billion in 1989. They quadrupled in number after 1982, employing a half-million Mexicans and accounting for 20 per cent of Mexico's manufacturing industry. Prior to NAFTA, no Mexican duties were charged on the imports, and US duties were levied only on the value added.

The *maquiladoras* are characterized by providing poor living and working conditions and strong restrictions on union activities. Health and safety regulations are routinely ignored. A 1993 random examination of 12 US-owned plants showed that not one was in compliance with Mexican environmental law. An Arizona-based environmental group, the Border Ecology Project, found that *maquiladoras* are unable to account for 95 per cent of the waste they generated between 1969 and 1989. The average productive work life of a worker is ten years. Employee turnover is nearly 180 per cent annually, in spite of the lack of alternative forms of employment.

Maquiladoras import most of their raw materials from the US and are supposed to return waste there for disposal, but, according to the US EPA, a tiny percentage is actually returned. The EPA's Mexican counterpart, Sedesol, estimated that while half of the 2100 plants generate hazardous waste, only 307 have obtained official licences.

In the mid 1990s, the US National Toxics Campaign detected high levels of pollutants outside the plants, including drainage water containing xylene, an industrial solvent, at concentrations 6000 times the US drinking water standard. Tests carried out by an EPA-certified laboratory revealed levels of xylene up to 50,000 times what is allowed in the US, and of methylene chloride up to 215,000 times the US standard.

Pollution-related health problems were the inevitable result. In Brownsville, Texas, between 1990 and 1992, 30 babies were born with anencephaly, a fatal birth condition in which the brain fails to develop and is filled with liquid. This is four times the US national average. During the same period in Matamoros, on the Mexican side of the border, 53 cases were recorded. In March 1993, 27 Brownsville families filed a lawsuit against 88 different *maquillas* in Matamoros. They claimed that an airborne cocktail of solvents, acids and heavy metals, blown over the Rio Grande by prevailing winds, was responsible for the high incidence of children with spina bifida and anencephaly. Among those accused were companies twinned with such international household names as General Motors, Union Carbide, Fisher Price and Zenith Electronics. All of them deny responsibility.

Also in Matamoros, social workers identified 110 children who shared certain deformity symptoms: mongoloid features and a range of physical and mental defects. The worst-affected boys have only one testicle and the girls have only partially developed vaginas. All 76 mothers had worked while pregnant at Mallory Capacitors, a *maquilla* that produces electronic components. Workers there, almost entirely young women, said they had handled highly toxic polychlorinated biphenyls without proper safety equipment or clothing.

Clearly, then, part of the 'incentive' package that a government offers to companies when it creates FTZs is the right to despoil the environment, the right to flout basic standards of social welfare and the right to poison workers. These, along with attractive financial and fiscal incentives, form an integral part of the 'subsidy' offered by a government to attract industry to its territory. As David Korten writes in his book *When Corporations Rule the World* (1995), 'Mexican workers, including children, have become world-class competitors by sacrificing their health, lives and futures to subsidize the profits of investors.'

So, five years on since NAFTA and the WTO, is there evidence of the oft-promised rising tide of prosperity and improving social and environmental conditions across the NAFTA area? Far from it. As Lori Wallach described in 1998, the US had lost 400,000 jobs through NAFTA, against a few thousand new jobs that could be satisfactorily attributed to the agreement. Equally, against all the official predictions, there was no improvement in the environmental running sore represented by the *maquiladora* region. Instead, increased volume in toxic waste production and disposal had resulted in diminished water quality and a greater incidence of environmentally related disease. Tuberculosis, for instance, soared on both sides of the border, while the number of babies born with deadly anencephaly continued to rise.

Meanwhile, the increased porosity of the US–Mexican border had resulted in a massive increase in the volume of tainted food and illegal drugs entering the US and in illegal handguns entering Mexico.

The arguments in favour of FTZs are based on a contradiction: that relaxing social and environmental obligations creates prosperity which leads (in the fullness of time, presumably) to those social and environmental conditions being reimposed. Isn't it rather the opposite? FTZs are social and environmental 'black holes' which suck in and subvert the higher standards of neighbouring regions.

When a government sets up an FTZ it renounces its sovereignty over the area involved. The role of FTZs in the global economy is similar to that of tax havens, which provide boltholes for capital that is beyond the purview of government. FTZs provide locales where such capital can be invested.

In *Global Dreams*, Richard Barnet and John Cavanagh note (1994):

> *'Leaders of nation states are losing much of the control over their own territory they once had. More and more, they must conform to the demands of the outside world because the outsiders are already inside the gates. Business enterprises that routinely operate across borders are linking far-flung pieces of territory into a new world economy that bypasses all sorts of established political arrangements and conventions. Tax laws intended for another age, traditional ways to control capital flows and interest rates, full employment policies, and old approaches to resource development and environmental protection are becoming obsolete, unenforceable or irrelevant.'*

The complex interplay between trade, territory and sovereignty can be well discerned in South-East Asia's growth triangles. These are quasi-FTZs whose operations bring together regions from different nation states. One of these is the Singapore–Batam–Johor growth triangle, which seeks to establish a synergistic relationship between three politically divided but geographically adjacent regions.

It was Singapore's deputy prime minister who first proposed a growth triangle in 1989. According to William Mellor, senior writer for *Asia, Inc* magazine, Singapore was running short on land and labour but possessed high-tech skills, financial muscle and excellent international transport links. Batam Island, only 20 kilometres from Singapore, had been given 'freeport' status by Indonesia in 1978 in its attempt to compete with Singapore. Batam could supply plenty of land, freshwater and a cheap labour force, courtesy of Indonesia's Transmigration Programme. On the mainland, connected to Singapore by road and rail, was Malaysia's Johor state, which equally had plentiful land and a large skilled and semi-skilled labour force.

The triangle was established in spite of considerable suspicion on the part of the nations involved. Malaysia was worried that Johor would grow closer to Singapore than to its federal government. Indonesia was concerned that it was being exploited by Singapore. But business pressures made it inevitable. Mellor quotes Noordin Sopiee from the Kuala Lumpur-based Institute of Strategic and International Studies: 'Nationalism and national governments will remain very important. But business is going to flow according to its own rules – like water.'

The Singapore–Batam–Johor growth triangle was only one of several developing in South-East Asia. Of course, many of these made good sense, insofar as they represent a renewal of links between regions whose historical trade and cultural relations were fractured by the colonial and postcolonial era. But at the same time, they represented new configurations of exploitation that were subject to few controls. And, needless to say, in regions that still possess relatively unexploited natural resources, the environment is as important a part of the equation as cheap labour, investment capital and tax breaks.

FTZs also affect the global economy through the straightforward mechanism of competition. By offering lower production costs through the elimination of basic standards, FTZs take work away from regions in which those standards are maintained. A 1980 World Bank report on Sri Lanka stated with diplomatic caution that 'some of the exports by foreign garment firms may have been at the expense of potential exports by Sri Lankan firms'.

The phenomenon of free-trade zones is no longer limited to 'developing' nations. In an effort to adapt to the competitive environment engendered by the creation of FTZs, the same variables are being manipulated in different places and on different scales in the industrialized countries. In the US, towns, counties and even states fall over themselves in an effort to attract corporations to their respective areas, regardless of the social and ecological costs. In *When Corporations Rule the World*, David Korten cites the case of Moore county in South Carolina (1995):

> *'It benefited handsomely when large manufacturers fled the unionized industrial regions of the north-eastern US in the 1960s and 1970s, lured south by promises of tax breaks, lax environmental regulations and compliant labour. Not only did Moore county offer attractive tax breaks to prospective investors, it worked with them to provide publicly financed facilities tailored to their individual needs. When Proctor Silex expanded its local plant, Moore county floated a US$5.5 million bond to finance the necessary sewer and water hookups – even though nearby residents were without tap water and other basic public services. Then in 1990, NACCO Industries, the parent company of Proctor Silex, decided to move its assembly lines to Mexico, eliminating the jobs of 800 workers and leaving behind drums of toxic waste and the public debts the county incurred on the company's behalf.'*

Equally, whole countries are no longer immune to using similar techniques, as demonstrated by the deregulatory frenzy initiated by President Reagan. The Quayle Council on Competitiveness was the direct successor of Reagan's Task Force on Regulatory Relief, which was chaired by then Vice-President George Bush. These measures, according to citizens' groups such as Public Citizens' Congress Watch in Washington, DC, succeeded in thwarting worker safety regulations, obstructing consumer product safety controls, rolling back highway safety initiatives and weakening environmental protection (Watzman and Triano, 1991).

So there can be little surprise that post-NAFTA, various North American social and environmental regulations have suffered sustained attacks. Witness the 1998 lawsuit brought against the Canadian government by the Ethyl corporation, which took offence against that government's ban of one of its fuel additives.

The UK has its own deregulatory programme. Initiated in 1993, the taskforce overseeing the process made 605 different recommendations. The majority of these affected the now Department of the Environment, Transport and the Regions (DETR). They included measures relaxing regulations in such fields as health and safety, biotechnology, advertising in sensitive areas, hedgerow preservation and energy efficiency in buildings.

A brochure produced in 1994 by the UK Department of Trade and Industry-funded Invest in Britain Bureau trumpeted Britain's numerous advantages for multinational companies looking for a home. It boasted of a 'pro-business environment' and highlighted 'liberal and undemanding labour regulations', 'labour costs significantly below other European countries, no exchange controls on repatriated profits', and a 'commitment to reduce the burdens on business'. To hammer home the point, the brochure went into detail: 'The UK has the least onerous labour regulations in Europe, with few restrictions on working hours, overtime and holidays. Many companies setting up in the UK have negotiated single union agreements. However, there is no legal requirement to recognize a trade union. Many industries operate shift work and 24 hour, seven-days-a-week production for both men and women.' Also, 'no new laws or regulations', it said, 'may be introduced without ascertaining and minimizing the costs to business'. The UK was thus already well on the way to becoming a national FTZ – with the usual consequences.

Free-trade zones have moved beyond specific locales and begun to encompass the entire globe. Under the rules by which countries (serving their corporations) can initiate challenges to other countries' trading practices or their environmental or consumer laws, an alarming process of mutual deregulation is underway. European corporate interests, among others, can now effectively deregulate US corporate interests via external challenges, while Americans can do likewise to Europeans and to others. By this friendly arrangement, corporations are effectively collaborating in transforming the entire world into a free-trade zone with all the opportunities to operate without controls that were formerly limited to Sri Lanka, small zones of Mexico and elsewhere. How far this global process will advance before a public reaction sets in remains to be seen.

Chapter 13

Global Economy and the Developing World

Martin Khor

Confronted with growing joblessness, Americans and Europeans often blame competition from low-wage developing world countries or the influx of immigrants from those countries. In fact, it is more directly the new round of economic colonialism that is the culprit, as it sets into motion changes that cause immigration and have dire effects on the poorest countries themselves – countries whose economies are controlled by foreign corporations and whose resources are raided and shipped north to the wealthy industrial nations. The new trade rules leave developing world countries unable to resist or protect themselves, or to seek alternative economic strategies. Martin Khor presents a summary review of the negative impacts on the environment and social structures.

Martin Khor is the director of Third World Network comprising NGOs in different parts of the developing world. An economist, trained at Cambridge University, who has lectured in economics at the Science University of Malaysia, he is the author of several books and articles on trade, development and the environment. He is honorary secretary of the Consumers' Association of Penang in Malaysia and a board member of the IFG. He was formerly vice-chairman of the UN Commission on Human Rights Expert Group on the Right to Development and a consultant to several research studies under the UN.

Before colonial rule and the infusion of Western systems, people in the developing world lived in relatively self-sufficient communities, planted rice and other staple crops, fished and hunted for other food, and satisfied housing, clothing and other needs through home production or small-scale industries that made use of local resources and indigenous skills. The modes of production and style of life were largely in harmony with the natural environment.

Colonial rule – accompanied by the imposition of new economic systems, new crops, the industrial exploitation of minerals and participation in the global market (with developing world resources being exported and Western industrial products imported) – changed the social and economic structures of developing societies. The new structures, consumption styles and technological systems became so ingrained in developing world economies that even after the attainment of political independence, the importation of Western values, products, technologies and capital continued and expanded. Developing world countries grew more and more dependent upon global trading and financial and investment systems, with transnational corporations setting up trading and production bases in the developing world and selling products there. With the aid of infrastructure programmes funded by industrial governments, multilateral institutions such as the World Bank and transnational banks, developing world governments were loaned billions of dollars to finance expensive infrastructure projects and to import highly capital-intensive technologies. They were also supported by foundations, research institutions and scientists in the industrialized countries who carried out research on new agricultural technologies that would 'modernize' the developing world – that is, that would create conditions whereby the developing world would become dependent on the transnational companies for technology and inputs.

To finance the import of modern technology and inputs, developing world countries were forced to export even more goods, mainly natural resources such as timber, oil and other minerals, and export crops that consumed a larger and larger portion of the total agricultural land area. Economically, financially and technologically, developing world countries were sucked deeper and deeper into the whirlpool of the world economic system and consequently lost or are losing their indigenous skills, their capacity for self-reliance, their confidence and, in many cases, the very resource base on which their survival depends. But the Western world's economic and technological systems are themselves facing a crisis. The developing world is now hitched onto these systems, over which they have very little control. The survival and viability of most developing world societies will thus be put to the test in the next few decades. Even now, there are numerous examples of how the Western system has caused the degradation of the environment and the deterioration of human health in the developing world.

IMPORT OF HAZARDOUS TECHNOLOGIES AND PRODUCTS

Many transnational companies have shifted their production operations to the developing world, where safety and environmental regulations are either very lax or non-existent. Some corporations are also concentrating their sales efforts on the markets of the developing world, where they can sell lower-quality products or products that are outright toxic and thus banned in the industrialized countries.

As a result, developing world people are now exposed to extremely toxic or dangerous technologies that could potentially cause great harm. The Bhopal gas tragedy, in which 6000 lives were lost and another 200,000 people suffered disabilities, is the most outstanding example to date of what can happen when a Western transnational company adopts industrial safety standards far below acceptable levels in its home country. There are hundreds of other substandard industrial plants sold to the developing world or relocated there by transnationals to escape health and pollution standards in their home countries. The Batoon nuclear plant in the Philippines is one such example.

Hazardous products are also being pushed on the developing world in increasing volume. There are many examples of these: pharmaceutical drugs, contraceptives and pesticides banned years ago in Europe, America or Japan but sold by companies of these same countries to the developing world; cigarettes with a far higher tar and nicotine content than in the rich countries; and, most recently, milk products contaminated with high radioactivity resulting from the Chernobyl nuclear disaster. The health effects on developing world peoples are horrendous. For example, it is estimated that 40,000 people in the developing world die from pesticide poisoning each year. Moreover, millions of babies have died of malnutrition or illness from diluted or contaminated baby formula pushed by transnational companies that persuaded mothers to give up breastfeeding on the argument that infant formula is a superior form of nourishment.

The hazardous technologies and products imported from the industrialized countries often displace indigenous technologies and products that may be more appropriate to meet the production and consumption needs of the developing world. Labour-intensive technologies that provide employment for the community and are in harmony with the environment (traditional fishing methods, for instance) are replaced with capital-intensive modern technologies that in many instances are ecologically destructive. Appropriate products or processes (such as breastfeeding) are replaced by modern products that are thrust upon the people through high-powered advertising, sales promotions and pricing policy. The developing world is thus losing many of its indigenous skills, technologies and products which are unable to survive the onslaught of the modern world.

THE GREEN REVOLUTION

The modern industrial system has changed the face of developing world agriculture. In many developing world societies, under the new plantation system, much of the lands formerly planted with traditional food crops have been converted into cash-crop production for export. If export prices are high, the incomes obtained could be higher for export-crop farmers; but when prices fall, as they have in recent years, the farmers are not able to buy enough food with their incomes, and also many agricultural workers lose their jobs.

The so-called Green Revolution is a package programme that makes it possible to grow more than one crop per year through the introduction of high-yielding seed varieties (especially of rice), high doses of chemical fertilizers and pesticides, agricultural machinery and irrigation. While its stated purpose was to increase food supply, the entire Green Revolution was little more than a market expansion programme of the US chemical industry, largely paid for by US aid programmes. In many areas where this 'revolution' was implemented there was an initial rise in production because more than a single crop could be produced in a year. But the corresponding rise in farmers' incomes was soon offset by the increasing costs of imported chemical inputs and machinery. High-input agriculture favoured richer farmers who could afford to pay for the chemicals and drove out poorer farmers who could not. The pesticides exacted a heavy toll in thousands of poisoning cases. In addition, the high-yielding crop varieties are very susceptible to pest attacks as insects become resistant to the pesticides. Yields in some areas have dropped. Meanwhile, thousands of indigenous rice varieties that had withstood generations of pest attacks have been abandoned and are now only preserved in research laboratories, most of which are controlled by international agencies and corporations in rich countries. Developing world farmers and governments will increasingly be at the mercy of the transnational food companies and research institutions that have collected and patented the seeds and germ plasm originating in the developing world itself (See Chapter 18).

BIOTECHNOLOGY: THE LATEST WEAPON

Although it is still relatively new, the application of biotechnology to agriculture has already had severely detrimental impacts on developing world economies. A few examples will illustrate this point.

Fructose produced by biotechnology has captured over 10 per cent of the world sugar market and caused sugar prices to fall, throwing tens of thousands of sugar workers in the developing world out of work. Over 70,000 farmers in Madagascar growing vanilla were ruined when a Texas firm produced vanilla in biotech labs. In 1986, the Sudan lost its export market for gum arabic when a New York company discovered a process for producing gum.

It is now estimated that biotechnology can find substitutes for US$14 billion worth of developing world commodities now exported to the rich countries. This will dramatically reduce the developing world's income.

MODERN FISHING DESTROYS FISHERY RESOURCES

In many developing world countries, fish is the main source of animal protein, and fishing was once a major economic activity. In traditional fishing, the nets and traps were simple and ecological principles were adhered to. The mesh size of the nets was large enough to avoid trapping small fish, the breeding grounds were not disturbed and fish stocks could multiply. Fishing required hard work and tremendous human skill, passed on through generations. Boats and nets were usually made from local materials, and the whole community was involved in fishing, fish preservation, mending nets, the making of boats and so on.

Then modern trawl fishing was introduced, in many cases funded by aid programmes. (In Malaysia, for instance, it was introduced through a German aid programme.) There was an explosive increase in the number of trawlers, usually owned by non-fishing businessmen and operated by wage-earning crews. This led to gross overfishing, and much of the fish caught by trawlers was not used for human consumption but sold to factories as feed-meal for animals. The criterion in trawl fishing was maximum catch for maximum immediate revenue. The mesh size is usually small so that even small fish could be netted and sold, and crews used destructive gear that scraped the bottom of the seabed and disturbed breeding grounds. As a result, there was a decrease in fish stocks in many parts of the developing world for both traditional and trawl fishermen.

Meanwhile, riverine fishery resources have also been destroyed by industrial toxic effluents, which kill off fish life and poison villagers' water supplies. In the rice ponds, where farmers used to catch freshwater fish to supplement their diet, the pesticides introduced by the Green Revolution have also killed off fish life. Thus, the livelihoods of millions of small-scale fishermen in the developing world have been threatened, while an important source of protein for the general population has been depleted. In Malaysia, where fish used to be abundant and considered a poor man's meat, the depletion of marine life has caused seafood to become one of the most expensive items on restaurant menus, seriously reducing poor people's access to fish protein.

LOGGING OF TROPICAL FORESTS

Another fast-disappearing developing world resource is the tropical forest. Traditionally, forests were inhabited by indigenous peoples practising *swidden agriculture,* which, contrary to modern propaganda, was an ecologically sound agricultural system that caused minimal soil erosion in the hilly tropical terrain and endured for millennia. Massive logging activities have threatened this system, as trees are chopped down by transnational corporations for log export to the industrialized countries or for conversion of primary forest to cattle-grazing land for the US hamburger industry. Between 1900 and 1965, half the forest area in developing countries was cleared, and since 1965 the destruction has further accelerated. Many millions of hectares are destroyed or seriously degraded each year, and by the end of this century little primary forest will be left.

The massive deforestation has myriad ecological and social consequences: the loss of land rights and way of life (or even life itself) for millions of tribal peoples throughout the developing world; massive soil erosion due to the removal of tree cover, thus causing the loss of invaluable topsoil; much-reduced intake of rainwater in catchment areas, as the loss of tree cover increases water runoff to rivers; extensive flooding in downstream rural and urban areas, caused by excessive silting of river systems; not to mention its contribution to climate change.

MODERN INDUSTRIAL PLANTS AND ENERGY MEGAPROJECTS

The introduction of Western consumer goods, industrial plants, and energy megaprojects has also greatly contributed to the loss of well-being in the developing world.

The indigenous, small-scale industries of the developing world produced simple goods that satisfied the basic needs of the majority of people. The technology employed to manufacture these goods was also simple and labour intensive. Many of these indigenous industries have been displaced by the entry of modern products that, when heavily promoted through advertising, became glamourized, rendering the local products low in status by comparison. With modern products capturing high market shares, modern capital-intensive industries (usually foreign owned) set up their bases in developing world countries and displace the traditional, locally owned industries.

But many developing world countries were not content simply with modern consumer-goods industries. They also copied the cities of the industrial nations and set up large infrastructure and industrial projects: steel mills, cement plants, vast highways, big bridges and super-tall buildings. The political leaders and elites of the developing world feel their countries need to have all this in order to appear 'developed', just like the industrial countries.

Huge amounts of energy are required by modern industrial plants and infrastructure, hence the need for the megaprojects in the energy sector – particularly large hydroelectric dams and nuclear power stations. Each project has its problems. The huge dams require the flooding of large tracts of forest and agricultural land, causing the displacement of many thousands of people living there. In any case, the dams do not last for long due to siltation, so they are usually not viable financially. Their costs far outweigh their benefits. There are also health effects, as ecological changes associated with dams and irrigation canals spread schistosomiasis (carried by snails), malaria and other waterborne diseases. Finally, there is the possibility of a major tragedy should the dam burst, as has occurred in India and elsewhere.

In the case of nuclear power plants, those sold to the developing world do not have the same quality and safety standards as those installed in industrialized countries, where there is stricter quality control and greater technical expertise. If a power plant installed in a developing world country is found unsafe, the government has a dilemma: stop its operation and incur a huge loss or continue using it but run the risk of a tragic accident. In the Philippines, Westinghouse Corporation built a nuclear power plant for US$2 billion, but there were so many doubts about its safety that the Aquino government decided to 'mothball' it. Even when a nuclear power plant is declared safe enough to start operating, there is no way of safely disposing of its radioactive wastes.

These huge industrial, infrastructural and energy projects often cost hundreds of millions or billions of US dollars. The projects are invariably marketed by transnational corporations that stand to gain huge sums in sales and profits per approved project. Financing is arranged by the World Bank, by transnational commercial banks or by developed world governments, usually under aid programmes. Such projects are rarely appropriate for genuine development, since they end up underutilized, grossly inefficient or too dangerous to use. Absorbing so much investment funding, they deprive communities of much-needed finance for genuine development projects while leading the borrowing developing world nations into the external debt trap. Finally, they cause widespread disruption and displacement of poor communities, especially indigenous peoples, who by the hundreds of thousands have to be 'resettled' as their forests and lands are flooded out by dams. Tens of millions have been displaced in this way in the last 50 years.

THE DRAIN OF RESOURCES FROM SOUTH TO NORTH

In this way, via their powerful technological capacity and their domination of the new global systems of trade and finance, the industrial countries have rapidly sucked out forest, mineral and metal resources from the developing world and used its land and labour resources to produce the raw materials that feed the machinery of industrialism. It is worth reminding readers that the industrial nations – approximately one-fifth of the world's population – use up four-fifths of the world's resources, mostly for making luxury products. The developing world, by contrast, with three-quarters of the world's population, uses only 20 per cent of the world's resources. Since incomes are also unequally distributed within developing world nations, a large part of these resources are used to make or import the same luxury products as are enjoyed in the industrial nations and to import capital-intensive technologies required to produce such elite consumer goods. Thus, only a small portion of the world's resources serves the basic needs of the poor majority in the developing world, who sink deeper into the trough of poverty and destitution. This is the ultimate environmental and social tragedy of our age.

Worse yet, the very processes of extracting developing world resources result in environmental disasters such as massive soil erosion and desertification, pollution of water supplies, and poisonings from toxic substances and industrial accidents. The resource base on which communities have traditionally relied for both production and home needs has been rapidly eroded. Soils required for food production become infertile; forests that are home to indigenous peoples are logged; water from the rivers and wells is clogged up with silt and toxic industrial effluents.

The transfer of resources from South to North takes place through many channels. Firstly, there is the transfer of physical resources. For example, only 20 per cent of the world's industrial wood comes from tropical forests, but more than half of that is exported to the richest nations. The developed countries produce and keep 80 per cent of the world's industrial wood but also import much of the rest of the world's timber harvest as well. Most of it is used for furniture, high-class joinery, housing, packing material, even matchsticks. Thus the wood that is exported to developed world countries mainly for luxury use is lost to developing world peoples, who now have difficulty getting wood for essential uses such as making houses, furniture and boats.

Secondly, there is a transfer of financial resources in that the prices of developing world commodities (often obtained at a terrible environmental cost) are low and declining even more. Between US$60 and US$100 billion per year were lost to developing world countries in 1985 and 1986 alone due to the fall in commodity prices. In human terms, this means drastic cuts in living standards, massive retrenchments of workers, and big reductions in government budgets in many developing world countries.

Thirdly, many of the 'development projects' that lead to the loss of resources are financed by foreign loans. It is rare for these projects to generate sufficient returns to enable repayment of debt, so debt repayments are ultimately met by the already impoverished developing world citizens.

THE NEW GATT

This deteriorating situation has been exacerbated by the passage of the Uruguay Round of GATT and the setting up of the WTO, which is in effect a world government controlled by the transnational corporations and has legislative, executive and judiciary powers that can overrule those of national governments in such major areas as banking, insurance, information and communications, the media, and professional services such as law, medicine, tourism, accounting, advertising and even health, education and environmental services (See Chapter 19).

It is now possible to predict that because of the new rules of the WTO, many of the service industries in the developing world will come under the direct control of the transnational service corporations within a few years. This means that the last sectors in the developing world that are still controlled by national corporations will be taken over by Northern transnationals. In terms of manufacturing and agriculture, many developing world countries are already controlled by Northern, many US, transnational corporations, either through investments or through dependence upon products from the global market. With the new world government in power, the problems faced by developing world countries since the beginning of the colonial era can only escalate (See Chapters 10, 11 and 18).

AN ALTERNATIVE VISION

The analyses just given clearly show that a radical reshaping of the international economic and financial order must occur so that economic power, wealth and income are more equitably distributed and so that the developed world will be forced to lower its irrationally high consumption levels. If this is done, the level of industrial technology will be scaled down, and there will be less need for the tremendous waste of energy, raw materials and resources that now go toward the production of superfluous goods simply to maintain 'effective demand' and to keep the monstrous economic machine going. If appropriate technology is appropriate for the developing world, it is even more essential as a substitute for the environmentally and socially obsolete high technology in the developed world.

But it is almost impossible to hope that the developed world will do this voluntarily. It will have to be forced to do so, either by a new unity of the developing world in the spirit of OPEC in the 1970s and early 1980s or by the economic or physical collapse of the world economic system.

In the developing world, there should also be a redistribution of wealth, resources and income, so that farmers have their own land to till and thus do not have to look for employment in timber camps or on transnational company estates. This will enable a redistribution of priorities away from luxury-oriented industries and projects and toward the production of basic goods and services. If the poor are allocated more resources, the demand for the production of such basic goods and services would increase. With people given the basic facilities to fend for themselves, at least in terms of food crop production, housing and health facilities, developing world governments can reduce their countries' dependence on the world market.

Thus, there could be a progressive reduction in the unecological exploitation of resources. With increasing self-reliance based on income redistribution and the resurgence of indigenous agriculture and industry, the developing world could also afford to be tough with transnationals; it would be able to insist that those invited adhere to other health and safety standards that now prevail in the industrial countries. It would be able to reject the kinds of products, technologies, industries and projects that are inappropriate for need-oriented, ecologically sustainable development.

In development planning, the principles of such ecologically sustainable development should be adopted: minimizing the use of non-renewable resources; developing alternative renewable resources; and creating technologies, practices and products that are durable and safe, and satisfy real needs.

In searching for the new environmental and social order we should realize that it is in the developing world that the new ecologically sound societies will be born. Within each developing world nation there are still large areas where communities earn their livelihoods in ways that are consistent with the preservation of their culture and of their natural environment. Such communities have nearly disappeared in the developed world. We need to recognize and rediscover the technological and cultural wisdom of our indigenous systems of agriculture, industry, shelter, water and sanitation, and medicine.

By this I do not mean here the unquestioning acceptance of everything traditional in a romantic belief in a past Golden Age. For instance, exploitative feudal or slave social systems also made life more difficult in the past. But many indigenous technologies, skills and processes are still part and parcel of developing world life and are appropriate for sustainable development and harmony with nature and the community. These indigenous scientific systems have to be accorded their proper recognition. They must be saved from being swallowed up by modernization.

Developing world governments and peoples in the developed world have first to reject their obsession with modern technologies, which absorb a bigger and bigger share of investment funds for projects such as giant hydrodams, nuclear plants and heavy industries that serve luxury needs.

We need to devise and fight for the adoption of appropriate, ecologically sound and socially equitable policies to satisfy our needs for such necessities as water, health, food, education and information. We need appropriate technologies and even more so the correct prioritizing of what types of consumer products to produce; we can't accept appropriate technology that produces inappropriate products. Products and technologies need to be safe to handle and use; they need to fulfill basic human needs and should not degrade or deplete the natural environment. Perhaps the most difficult aspect of this fight is the need to deprogramme developing world peoples away from the modern culture that has penetrated our societies, so that lifestyles, personal motivations and status structures can be delinked from the system of industrialism and its corresponding creation of culture.

. . .

The creation and establishment of a new economic and social order, based on environmentally sound principles, to fulfill human rights and human needs is not such an easy task, as we know too well. It may even be an impossible task, a challenge that cynics and even good-hearted folks in their quiet moments may feel will end in defeat. Nevertheless, it is the greatest challenge in the world today, for it is tackling the issue of the survival of the human species and of Earth itself. It is a challenge that we in the developing world readily accept. We hope that together with our friends in the developed countries we will grow in strength to pursue the many paths toward a just and sustainable social and ecological order.

Chapter 14

The Pressure to Modernize and Globalize

Helena Norberg-Hodge

Ladakh, known as 'Little Tibet', is politically part of Kashmir and hence of India. It is on the border with China, with which India has recently been at war, and hence is a particularly sensitive area. This explains why it was virtually closed off from the rest of the world until the early 1970s when Helena Norberg-Hodge first arrived there. Since then she has spent much of her time in the area and has been able to document how this fascinating Bhuddist society functioned prior to the advent of economic development and modernization. She has been able to document just as carefully the extent of the social, psychological and ecological degradation that has occurred as an inevitable consequence of that fatal process.

For 30 years, on three continents, Swedish philosopher, teacher and activist Helena Norberg-Hodge has been fighting the excesses of today's economic development models, particularly their effects on traditional societies and local culture. She was the first foreigner accepted to make her home in the Himalayan province of Ladakh (Kashmir). There, over three decades, she learned the native language and helped people study and resist the hidden perils and culturally destructive effects of modernization. Meanwhile, in Europe, she was a leading campaigner in the Norwegian vote opposing entry into the European Economic Community (EEC), and is now codirector of the International Forum on Globalization Europe. In the US, her organization the International Society for Ecology and Culture runs educational campaigns on globalization issues. She is the author of Ancient Futures: Learning from Ladakh *(1991), and coauthor of* From the Ground Up *(1993).*

Ladakh is a high-altitude desert on the Tibetan Plateau in northernmost India. To all outward appearances, it is a wild and inhospitable place. In summer the land is parched and dry; in winter it is frozen solid by a fierce, unrelenting cold. Harsh and barren, Ladakh's land forms have often been described as a 'moonscape'.

Almost nothing grows wild – not the smallest shrub, hardly a blade of grass. Even time seems to stand still, suspended on the thin air. Yet here, in one of the highest, driest and coldest inhabited places on Earth, the Ladakhis have for 1000 years not only survived but prospered. Out of barren desert they have carved verdant oases – terraced fields of barley, wheat, apples, apricots and vegetables, irrigated with glacial meltwater brought many kilometres through stone-lined channels. Using little more than Stone-Age technologies and the scant resources at hand, the Ladakhis established a remarkably rich culture, one that met not only their material wants but their psychological and spiritual needs as well.

Until 1962, Ladakh, or 'Little Tibet', remained almost totally isolated from the forces of modernization. In that year, however, in response to the conflict in Tibet, the Indian army built a road to link the region with the rest of the country. With the road came not only new consumer items and a government bureaucracy but, as I shall show, a first misleading impression of the world outside. Then, in 1975, the region was opened up to foreign tourists, and the process of 'development' began in earnest.

Based on my ability to speak the language fluently from my first year in Ladakh, and based on almost two decades of close contact with the Ladakhi people, I have been able to observe almost as an insider the effect of these changes on the Ladakhis' perception of themselves. Within the space of little more than a decade, feelings of pride gave way to what can best be described as a cultural inferiority complex. In the modern sector today, most young Ladakhis – the teenage boys, in particular – are ashamed of their cultural roots and desperate to appear modern.

TOURISM

When tourism first began in Ladakh, it was as though people from another planet suddenly descended on the region. Looking at the modern world from something of a Ladakhi perspective, I became aware of how much more successful our culture looks from the outside than we experience it on the inside.

Each day many tourists would spend as much as US$100 – an amount roughly equivalent to someone spending US$50,000 per day in America. In the traditional subsistence economy, money played a minor role and was used primarily for luxuries – jewellery, silver and gold. Basic needs – food, clothing and shelter – were provided for without money. The labour one needed was free of charge, part of an intricate web of human relationships.

Ladakhis did not realize that money meant something very different for the foreigners: that back home they needed it to survive; that food, clothing and shelter all cost money – a lot of money. Compared to these strangers, the Ladakhis suddenly felt poor.

This new attitude contrasted dramatically with the Ladakhis' earlier self-confidence. In 1975, I was shown around the remote village of Hemis Shukpachan by a young Ladakhi named Tsewang. It seemed to me that all the houses we saw were especially large and beautiful. I asked Tsewang to show me the houses where the poor people lived. Tsewang looked perplexed a moment, then responded, 'We don't have any poor people here.'

Eight years later I overheard Tsewang talking to some tourists. 'If you could only help us Ladakhis,' he was saying, 'we're so poor.'

Besides giving the illusion that all Westerners are multimillionaires, tourism and Western media images also help perpetuate another myth about modern life – that we never work. It looks as though our technologies do the work for us. In industrial society today, we actually spend more hours working than people in rural, agrarian economies; but that is not how it looks to the Ladakhis. For them, work is physical work: ploughing, walking carrying things. A person sitting behind the wheel of a car or pushing buttons on a typewriter doesn't appear to be working.

MEDIA IMAGES

Development has brought not only tourism but also Western and Indian films and, more recently, television. Together they provide overwhelming images of luxury and power. There are countless tools, magical gadgets, and machines – machines to take pictures, machines to tell the time, machines to make fire, to travel from one place to another, to talk with someone far away. Machines can do everything; it's no wonder the tourists look so clean and have such soft, white hands.

Media images focus on the rich, the beautiful and the mobile, whose lives are endless action and glamour. For young Ladakhis, the picture is irresistible. It is an overwhelmingly exciting version of an urban American dream, with an emphasis on speed, youthfulness, supercleanliness, beauty, fashion and competitiveness. 'Progress' is also stressed: humans dominate nature, while technological change is embraced at all costs.

In contrast to these Utopian images from another culture, village life seems primitive, silly and inefficient. The one-dimensional view of modern life becomes a slap in the face. Young Ladakhis – whose parents ask them to choose a way of life that involves working in the fields and getting their hands dirty for very little or no money – feel ashamed of their own culture. Traditional Ladakh seems absurd compared with the world of the tourists and film heroes.

This same pattern is being repeated in rural areas all over the South, where millions of young people believe contemporary Western culture to be far superior to their own. This is not surprising: looking as they do from the outside, all they can see is the material side of the modern world – the side in which Western culture excels. They cannot so readily see the social or psychological dimensions: the stress, the loneliness, the fear of growing old. Nor can they see environmental decay, inflation or unemployment. This leads young Ladakhis to develop feelings of inferiority, to reject their own culture wholesale, and at the same time to eagerly embrace the global monoculture. They rush after the sunglasses, walkmans and blue jeans – not because they find those jeans more attractive or comfortable but because they are symbols of modern life.

Modern symbols have also contributed to an increase in aggression in Ladakh. Young boys now see violence glamourized on the screen. From Western-style films, they can easily get the impression that if they want to be modern, they should smoke one cigarette after another, get a fast car, and race through the countryside shooting people left and right.

WESTERN-STYLE EDUCATION

No one can deny the value of real education – the widening and enrichment of knowledge. But today in the developing world, education has become something quite different. It isolates children from their culture and from nature, training them instead to become narrow specialists in a Westernized urban environment. This process has been particularly striking in Ladakh, where modern schooling acts almost as a blindfold, preventing children from seeing the very context in which they live. They leave school unable to use their own resources, unable to function in their own world.

With the exception of religious training in the monasteries, Ladakh's traditional culture had no separate process called education. Education was the product of a person's intimate relationship with the community and the ecosystem. Children learned from grandparents, family and friends and from the natural world.

Helping with the sowing, for instance, they would learn that on one side of the village it was a little warmer, on the other side a little colder. From their own experience children would come to distinguish different strains of barley and the specific growing conditions each strain preferred. They learned how to recognize and use even the tiniest wild plant, and how to pick out a particular animal on a faraway mountain slope. They learned about connection, process and change, about the intricate web of fluctuating relationships in the natural world around them.

For generation after generation, Ladakhis grew up learning how to provide themselves with clothing and shelter: how to make shoes out of yak skin and robes from the wool of sheep; how to build houses out of mud and stone. Education was location-specific and nurtured an intimate relationship with the living world. It gave children an intuitive awareness that allowed them, as they grew older, to use resources in an effective and sustainable way.

None of that knowledge is provided in the modern school. Children are trained to become specialists in a technological rather than an ecological society. School is a place to forget traditional skills and, worse, to look down on them.

Western education first came to Ladakhi villages in the 1970s. Today there are about 200 schools. The basic curriculum is a poor imitation of that taught in other parts of India, which itself is an imitation of British education. There is almost nothing Ladakhi about it.

Once, while visiting a classroom in Leh, the capital, I saw a drawing in a textbook of a child's bedroom that could have been in London or New York. It showed a pile of neatly folded handkerchiefs on a four-poster bed and gave instructions as to which drawer of the vanity unit to keep them in. Many other schoolbooks were equally absurd and inappropriate. For homework in one class, pupils were supposed to figure out the angle of incidence that the Leaning Tower of Pisa makes with the ground. Another time they were struggling with an English translation of *The Iliad*.

Most of the skills Ladakhi children learn in school will never be of real use to them. In essence, they receive an inferior version of an education appropriate for a New Yorker, a Parisian or a Berliner. They learn from books written by people who have never set foot in Ladakh, who know nothing about growing barley at 4000 metres or about making houses out of sun-dried bricks.

This situation is not unique to Ladakh. In every corner of the world today, the process called *education* is based on the same assumptions and the same Eurocentric model. The focus is on faraway facts and figures, on 'universal' knowledge. The books propagate information that is believed to be appropriate for the entire planet. But since the only knowledge that can be universally applicable is far removed from specific ecosystems and cultures, what children learn is essentially synthetic, divorced from its living context. If they go on to higher education, they may learn about building houses, but these 'houses' will be the universal boxes of concrete and steel. So too, if they study agriculture, they will learn about industrial farming: chemical fertilizers and pesticides; large machinery and hybrid seeds. The Western educational system is making us all poorer by teaching people around the world to use the same global resources, ignoring those that the environment naturally provides. In this way, Western-style education creates artificial scarcity and induces competition.

In Ladakh and elsewhere, modern education not only ignores local resources but, worse still, robs children of their self-esteem. Everything in school promotes the Western model and, as a direct consequence, makes children think of themselves and their traditions as inferior.

Western-style education pulls people away from agriculture and into the city, where they become dependent on the money economy. Traditionally, there was no such thing as unemployment. But in the modern sector there is now intense competition for a very limited number of paying jobs, principally in the government. As a result, unemployment is already a serious problem.

Modern education has brought some obvious benefits, such as improvement in the literacy rate. It has also enabled the Ladakhis to be more informed about the forces at play in the world outside. In so doing, however, it has divided Ladakhis from each other and the land and put them on the lowest rung of the global economic ladder.

LOCAL ECONOMY VERSUS GLOBAL ECONOMY

When I first came to Ladakh, the Western macroeconomy had not yet arrived, and the local economy was still rooted in its own soils. Producers and consumers were closely linked in a community-based economy. Two decades of development in Ladakh, however, have led to a number of fundamental changes, the most important of which is perhaps the new dependence on food and energy from thousands of kilometres away.

The path toward globalization depends upon continuous government investments. It requires the buildup of a large-scale industrial infrastructure that includes roads, mass communications facilities, energy installations and schools for specialized education. Among other things, this heavily subsidized infrastructure allows goods produced on a large scale and transported long distances to be sold at artificially low prices – in many cases at lower prices than goods produced locally. In Ladakh, the Indian government is not only paying for roads, schools and energy installations but is also bringing in subsidized food from India's bread basket, the Punjab. Ladakh's local economy – which has provided enough food for its people for 2000 years – is now being invaded by produce from industrial farms located on the other side of the Himalayas. The food arriving in lorries by the ton is cheaper in the local bazaar than food grown a five-minute walk away. For many Ladakhis, it is no longer worthwhile to continue farming.

In Ladakh this same process affects not just food but a whole range of goods, from clothes to household utensils to building materials. Imports from distant parts of India can often be produced and distributed at lower prices than goods produced locally – again, because of a heavily subsidized industrial infrastructure. The end result of the long-distance transport of subsidized goods is that Ladakh's local economy is being steadily dismantled, and with it goes the local community that was once tied together by bonds of interdependence.

Conventional economists, of course, would dismiss these negative impacts, which cannot be quantified as easily as the monetary transactions that are the goal of economic development. They would also say that regions such as the Punjab enjoy a 'comparative advantage' over Ladakh in food production, and it therefore makes economic sense for the Punjab to specialize in growing food, while Ladakh specializes in some other product, and that each trade with the other. But when distantly produced goods are heavily subsidized, often in hidden ways, one cannot really talk about comparative advantage or, for that matter, 'free markets', 'open competition in the setting of prices', or any of the other principles by which economists and planners rationalize the changes they advocate. In fact, one should instead talk about the unfair advantage that industrial producers enjoy, thanks to a heavily subsidized infrastructure geared toward large-scale, centralized production.

In the past, individual Ladakhis had real power, since political and economic units were small and each person was able to deal directly with the other members of the community. Today, 'development' is hooking people into ever-larger political and economic units. In political terms, each Ladakhi has become one of a national economy of 800 million, and, as part of the global economy, one of about six billion.

In the traditional economy, everyone knew they had to depend directly on family, friends and neighbours. But in the new economic system, political and economic interactions take a detour via an anonymous bureaucracy. The fabric of local interdependence is disintegrating as the distance between people increases. So, too, are traditional levels of tolerance and cooperation. This is particularly true in the villages near Leh, where disputes and acrimony within close-knit communities and even families have dramatically increased in the last few years. I have even seen heated arguments over the allocation of irrigation water, a procedure that had previously been managed smoothly within a cooperative framework.

As mutual aid is replaced by dependence on faraway forces, people begin to feel powerless to make decisions over their own lives. At all levels, passivity, even apathy, is setting in; people are abdicating personal responsibility. In the traditional village, for example, repairing irrigation canals was a task shared by the whole community. As soon as a channel developed a leak, groups of people would start shovelling away to patch it up. Now people see this work as the government's responsibility and will let a channel go on leaking until the job is done for them. The more the government does for the villagers, the less the villagers feel inclined to help themselves.

In the process, Ladakhis are starting to change their perception of the past. In my early days in Ladakh, people would tell me there had never been hunger. I kept hearing the expression *tungbos zabos*: 'enough to drink, enough to eat'. Now, particularly in the modern sector, people can be heard saying, 'Development is essential; in the past we couldn't manage, we didn't have enough.'

The cultural centralization that occurs through the media is also contributing both to this passivity and to a growing insecurity. Traditionally, village life included lots of dancing, singing and theatre. People of all ages joined in. In a group sitting around a fire, even toddlers would dance, with the help of older siblings or friends. Everyone knew how to sing, to act, to play music. Now that the radio has come to Ladakh, people do not need to sing their own songs or tell their own stories. Instead, they can sit and listen to the *best* singer, the *best* storyteller. As a result, people become inhibited and self-conscious. They are no longer comparing themselves to neighbours and friends, who are real people – some better at singing but perhaps not so good at dancing – and they never feel themselves to be as good as the stars on the radio. Community ties are also broken when people sit passively listening to the very best rather than making music or dancing together.

ARTIFICIAL NEEDS

Before the changes brought by tourism and modernization, the Ladakhis were self-sufficient, both psychologically and materially. There was no desire for the sort of development that later came to be seen as a 'need'. Time and again, when I asked people about the changes that were coming, they showed no great interest in being modernized; sometimes they were even suspicious. In remote areas, when a road was about to be built, people felt, at best, ambivalent about the prospect. The same was true of electricity. I remember distinctly how, in 1975, people in Stagmo village laughed about the fuss that was being made to bring electric lights to neighbouring villages. They thought it was a joke that so much effort and money was spent on what they took to be a ludicrous gain: 'Is it worth all that bother just to have that thing dangling from your ceiling?'

More recently, when I returned to the same village to meet the council, the first thing they said to me was, 'Why do you bother to come to our backward village where we live in the dark?' They said it jokingly, but it was obvious they were ashamed of the fact they did not have electricity.

Before people's sense of self-respect and self-worth had been shaken, they did not need electricity to prove they were civilized. But within a short period the forces of development so undermined people's self-esteem that not only electricity but Punjabi rice and plastic have become needs. I have seen people proudly wear wristwatches they cannot read and for which they have no use. And as the desire to appear modern grows, people are rejecting their own culture. Even the traditional foods are no longer a source of pride. Now when I'm a guest in a village, people apologize if they serve the traditional roasted barley, *ngamphe*, instead of instant noodles.

Surprisingly, perhaps, modernization in Ladakh is also leading to a loss of individuality. As people become self-conscious and insecure, they feel pressure to conform, to live up to the idealized images – to the American dream. By contrast, in the traditional village, where everyone wears the same clothes and looks the same to the casual observer, there seems to be more freedom to relax, and villagers can be who they really are. As part of a close-knit community, people feel secure enough to be themselves.

A PEOPLE DIVIDED

Perhaps the most tragic of all the changes I have observed in Ladakh is the vicious circle in which individual insecurity contributes to a weakening of family and community ties, which in turn further shakes individual self-esteem. Consumerism plays a central role in this whole process, since emotional insecurity generates hunger for material status symbols. The need for recognition and acceptance fuels the drive to acquire possessions that will presumably make you somebody. Ultimately, this is a far more important motivating force than a fascination for the things themselves.

It is heartbreaking to see people buying things to be admired, respected and, ultimately, loved, when in fact the effect is almost inevitably the opposite. The individual with the new shiny car is set apart, and this furthers the need to be accepted. A cycle is set in motion in which people become more and more divided from themselves and from one another.

I've seen people divided from one another in many ways. A gap is developing between young and old, male and female, rich and poor, Buddhist and Muslim. The newly created division between the modern, educated expert and the illiterate, 'backward' farmer is perhaps the biggest of all. Modernized inhabitants of Leh have more in common with someone from Delhi or Calcutta than they do with their own relatives who have remained on the land, and they tend to look down on anyone less modern. Some children living in the modern sector are now so distanced from their parents and grandparents that they don't even speak the same language. Educated in Urdu and English, they are losing mastery of their native tongue.

Around the world, another consequence of development is that the men leave their families in the rural sector to earn money in the modern economy. The men become part of the technologically based life outside the home and are seen as the only productive members of society. In Ladakh, the roles of male and female are becoming increasingly polarized as their work becomes more differentiated.

Women become invisible shadows. They do not earn money for their work, so they are no longer seen as 'productive'. Their work is not included as part of the gross national product. In government statistics, the 10 per cent or so of Ladakhis who work in the modern sector are listed according to their occupations; the other 90 per cent – housewives and traditional farmers – are lumped together as non-workers. Farmers and women are coming to be viewed as inferior, and they themselves are developing feelings of insecurity and inadequacy.

Over the years I have seen the strong, outgoing women of Ladakh being replaced by a new generation – women who are unsure of themselves and extremely concerned with their appearance. Traditionally, the way a woman looked was important, but her capabilities – including tolerance and social skills – were much more appreciated.

Despite their new dominant role, men also clearly suffer as a result of the breakdown of family and community ties. Among other things, they are deprived of contact with children. When men are young, the new macho image prevents them from showing any affection, while in later life as fathers, their work keeps them away from home.

BREAKING THE BONDS BETWEEN YOUNG AND OLD

In the traditional culture, children benefited not only from continuous contact with both mother and father but also from a way of life in which different age groups constantly interacted. It was quite natural for older children to feel a sense of responsibility for the younger ones. A younger child, in turn, looked up to the older ones with respect and admiration and sought to be like them. Growing up was a natural, non-competitive learning process.

Now children are split into different age groups at school. This sort of levelling has a very destructive effect. By artificially creating social units in which everyone is the same age, the ability of children to help and to learn from each other is greatly reduced. Instead, conditions for competition are automatically created, because each child is put under pressure to be just as good as the next one. In a group of ten children of quite different ages, there will naturally be much more cooperation than in a group of ten 12-year olds.

The division into different age groups is not limited to school. Now there is a tendency to spend time exclusively with one's peers. As a result, a mutual intolerance between young and old has emerged. Young children have less and less contact with their grandparents, who often remain behind in the village. Living with many traditional families over the years, I have witnessed the depth of the bond between children and their grandparents. It is clearly a natural relationship that has a very different dimension from that between parent and child. To sever this connection is a profound tragedy.

Similar pressures contribute to the breakdown of the traditional family. The Western model of the nuclear family is now seen as the norm, and Ladakhis are beginning to feel ashamed about their traditional practice of polyandry, one of the cultural controls on population growth. As young people reject the old family structure in favour of monogamy, the population is rising significantly. At the same time, monastic life is losing its status, and the number of celibate monks and nuns is decreasing. This too contributes to population increase.

VIOLENCE

Interestingly, a number of Ladakhis have linked the rise in birth rates to the advent of modern democracy. 'Power is a question of votes' is a current slogan, meaning that in the modern sector, the larger your group, the greater your access to power. Competition for jobs and political representation within the new centralized structures is increasingly dividing Ladakhis. Ethnic and religious differences have taken on a political dimension, causing bitterness and envy on a scale hitherto unknown.

This new rivalry is one of the most painful divisions that I have seen in Ladakh. Ironically, it has grown in proportion to the decline of traditional religious devotion. When I first arrived, I was struck by the mutual respect and cooperation between Buddhists and Muslims. But within the last few years, growing competition has actually culminated in violence. Earlier there had been individual cases of friction, but the first time I noticed any signs of group tension was in 1986, when I heard Ladakhi friends starting to define people according to whether they were Buddhist or Muslim. In the following years, there were signs here and there that all was not well, but no one was prepared for what happened in the summer of 1989, when fighting suddenly broke out between the two groups. There were major disturbances in Leh bazaar, four people were shot dead by police, and much of Ladakh was placed under curfew.

Since then, open confrontation has died down, but mistrust and prejudice on both sides continue to mar relations. For a people unaccustomed to violence and discord, this has been a traumatic experience. One Muslim woman could have been speaking for all Ladakhis when she tearfully told me, 'These events have torn my family apart. Some of them are Buddhists, some are Muslims, and now they are not even speaking to each other.'

The immediate cause of the disturbances was the growing perception among the Buddhists that the Muslim-dominated state government was discriminating against them in favour of the local Muslim population. The Muslims for their part were becoming anxious that as a minority group they had to defend their interests in the face of political assertiveness by the Buddhist majority.

However, the underlying reasons for the violence are much more far-reaching. What is happening in Ladakh is not an isolated phenomenon. The tensions between the Muslims of Kashmir and the Hindu-dominated central government in Delhi, between the Hindus and the Buddhist government in Bhutan, and between the Buddhists and the Hindu government in Nepal, along with countless similar disturbances around the world, are, I believe, all connected to the same underlying cause: the intensely centralizing force of the present global development model is pulling diverse peoples from rural areas into large urban centres and placing power and decision-making in the hands of a few. In these centres, job opportunities are scarce, community ties are broken and competition increases dramatically. In particular, young men who have been educated for jobs in the modern sector find themselves engaged in a competitive struggle for survival. In this situation, any religious or ethnic differences quite naturally become exaggerated and distorted. In addition, the group in power inevitably tends to favour its own kind, while the rest often suffer discrimination.

Most people believe that ethnic conflict is an inevitable consequence of differing cultural and religious traditions. In the South, there is an awareness that modernization is exacerbating tensions; but people generally conclude that this is a temporary phase on the road to 'progress', a phase that will only end once development has erased cultural differences and created a totally secular society. On the other hand. Westerners attribute overt religious and ethnic strife to the liberating influence of democracy. Conflict, they assume, always smouldered beneath the surface, and only government repression kept it from bursting into flames.

It is easy to understand why people lay the blame at the feet of tradition rather than modernity. Certainly, ethnic friction is a phenomenon that predates colonialism, modernization and globalization. But after nearly two decades of firsthand experience on the Indian subcontinent, I am convinced that 'development' not only exacerbates tensions but actually creates them. As I have pointed out, development causes artificial scarcity, which inevitably leads to greater competition. Just as importantly, it puts pressure on people to conform to a standard Western ideal – blond, blue-eyed, 'beautiful' and 'rich' – that is impossibly out of reach.

Striving for such an ideal means rejecting one's own culture and roots – in effect, denying one's own identity. The inevitable result is alienation, resentment and anger. I am convinced that much of the violence and fundamentalism in the world today is a product of this process. In the industrialized world we are becoming increasingly aware of the impact of glamorous media and advertising images on individual self-esteem: problems that range from eating disorders such as anorexia and bulimia to violence over high-priced and 'prestigious' sneakers and other articles of clothing. In the South, where the gulf between reality and the Western ideal is so much wider, the psychological impacts are that much more severe.

COMPARING THE OLD WITH THE NEW

There were many real problems in the traditional society, and development does bring some real improvements. However, when one examines the fundamentally important relationships – to the land, to other people, and to oneself – development takes on a different light. Viewed from this perspective, the differences between the old and the new become stark and disturbing. It becomes clear that the traditional nature-based society, with all its flaws and limitations, was more sustainable, both socially and environmentally. It was the result of a dialogue between human beings and their surroundings, a continuing coevolution that meant that, during 2000 years of trial and error, the culture kept changing. Ladakh's traditional Buddhist worldview emphasized change, but that change occurred within a framework of compassion and a profound understanding of the interconnectedness of all phenomena.

The old culture reflected fundamental human needs while respecting natural limits. And it worked. It worked for nature and it worked for people. The various connecting relationships in the traditional system were mutually reinforcing and encouraged harmony and stability. Most importantly, having seen my friends change so dramatically, I have no doubt that the bonds and responsibilities of the traditional society, far from being a burden, offered a profound sense of security, which seems to be a prerequisite for inner peace and contentment. I am convinced that people were significantly happier before development and globalism than they are today. The people were cared for, and the environment was well sustained – which criteria for judging a society could be more important?

By comparison, the new Ladakh scores very poorly when judged by these criteria. The modern culture is producing environmental problems that, if unchecked, will lead to irreversible decline; and it is producing social problems that will inevitably lead to the breakdown of community and the undermining of personal identity.

Chapter 15

Homogenization of Global Culture

Richard Barnet and John Cavanagh

An intrinsic part of the process of economic globalization is the rapid homogenization of global culture. In this chapter, Richard Barnet and John Cavanagh look particularly at the role the entertainment industry plays in that process. As Western transnational corporations are given full access to all other countries of the world, the cultural transmissions conveyed in Western television, film, fashion and music ride right in with them, overpowering local media. The effect is to diminish the viability of traditional local cultures and tastes and to accelerate the standardization of markets within the Western conceptual framework.

For biographical details on Richard Barnet and John Cavanagh see Chapter 4, Electronic Money and the Casino Economy.

Satellites, cables, walkmans, videocassette recorders, CDs and other marvels of entertainment technology have created the arteries through which modern entertainment conglomerates are homogenizing global culture. With the toppling of the Berlin Wall and the embrace of free market ideologies in former and current communist countries, literally the entire planet is being wired into music, movies, news, television programmes and other cultural products that originate primarily in the film and recording studios of the US. The impact of this homogenization on the rich cultural diversity of communities all around the world is immense, and its contours are beginning to emerge.

Unlike American automobiles, television sets and machine tools, American cultural products are sweeping the globe. Reruns of *Dallas* and the *Bill Cosby Show* fill the television screens on every continent. The 1990 fairy-tale hit *Pretty Woman* became the all-time best-selling film in Sweden and Israel within weeks of its release. Disneyland is now a global empire; its Japanese incarnation outside Tokyo draws 300,000 visitors a week, and Euro Disneyland, a theme park on the outskirts of Paris occupying a space one-fifth the size of the city itself, hoped to draw more tourists than the Eiffel Tower, Sistine Chapel, British Museum and the Swiss Alps combined.

When the Berlin Wall came down in late 1989, East German families flocked to West Berlin to taste the fruits of capitalism; what they wanted most were oranges and pop-music records. In Rio, school kids adorn their workbooks with pictures of Michael Jackson. In Kashmir, teenagers hum Beatles songs. All over the world, people are listening to pop music and watching videos that offer excitement and a feeling of connectedness to a larger world. Most of the consumers of these global cultural products are young.

As governments, families and tribal structures are thrown into crisis by the sweeping changes of late 20th-century society, pop artists have emerged as global authority figures. Thanks to the microphone and the camera, a few megastars can communicate the appearance of power and strong commitment at great distance. Unlike parents, mullahs, chiefs, bureaucrats and politicians, they ask little of their fans except that they enjoy themselves and keep buying. On the few occasions when rock stars call upon their worldwide audiences for personal contributions – for rainforests, famine relief, AIDS or political prisoners – the global outpouring is astounding.

Global entertainment companies are pinning their hopes on the two-fifths of the world's population who are under the age of 20. The competition to hook millions of new fans at increasingly early ages is intense. Sony has expanded into the children's market with its 'My First Sony' line of toy-like radios, its new Sony Kids' Music label and an expanding children's library of videos.

The most spectacular technological development of the 1980s for expanding the reach of global entertainment was MTV. By the beginning of 1993, MTV programming was beamed daily to 210 million households in 71 countries. The cable network, which began in August 1981, claims to have 39 million viewers in Europe and well over 50 million in the US. It has already spun off a second network called VH-1. Viacom, the parent company, also has a channel aimed at children called Nickleodeon. (In the early 1990s, Nickleodeon's hit attraction was the *Ren & Stimpy Show*, a cartoon saga of a hyperactive chihuahua and a cat that spits up hair balls.)

The owner of this global network of networks is Sumner Redstone, a Boston multibillionaire who made a fortune in movie theatres. Although his name is unknown to the general public, he has become one of the most influential educators of young people in the world. As MTV was announcing plans to extend its worldwide home entertainment networks to China, Korea and Taiwan and to launch *Ren & Stimpy* in Europe, Redstone was celebrating the arrival of the global child. 'Just as teenagers are the same all over the world, children are the same all over the world', he declared.

Although hundreds of millions of children and teenagers around the world are listening to the same music and watching the same films and videos, globally distributed entertainment products are not creating a positive new global consciousness – other than a widely shared passion for more global goods and vicarious experience. The exotic imagery of music videos offers their consumers the illusion of being connected to cultural currents sweeping across the world, but this has little to do with the creation of a new global identification with the welfare of the whole human species and with the planet itself, as consciousness philosophers, from Kant to McLuhan, had hoped for and predicted. So far, *commodity consciousness* is the only awareness that has been stimulated.

The spread of commercially produced popular music, most of it conceived in the US, is speeding up as once-formidable ideological barriers come down. The collapse of communism makes it easier to export music, film and video to Eastern Europe, the former Soviet Union and China. But integrating vast reaches of the world into a global story-and-song market is not a simple task. In 1990, Rudi Gassner was president of BMG International and in direct charge of Bertelsmann's music business. 'Our priority,' he stated, is 'signing acts on a worldwide basis exclusive to BMG for worldwide exploitation.' Months before the reunification of Germany was completed, Bertelsmann had hired someone to head its sales force for what had been the German Democratic Republic, where, Gassner says, he is counting on picking up an additional 15 million customers. 'Our next target group,' he wrote in an internal newsletter for BMG management in 1990, 'includes Hungary, Czechoslovakia and, to a certain extent, Poland.' But he anticipated 'enormous problems for us because of the currency constraints. . . We will not make money immediately; we will not be able to take money out. But I feel that long term we should be there and be one of the first, if not the first . . . for political and strategic reasons.'

The strongest remaining ideological barrier to American music, television and film is Islamic fundamentalism. In the Khomeini era in Iran, US cultural products were the supreme symbols of satanic decadence. The more fanatical Iranian and Saudi authorities became in their attempts to purify their traditional cultures, the more people were drawn to forbidden music and films. Underground video clubs sprang up all over Iran, and crowds came to watch tapes of the latest US network programmes and, of course, X-rated films. Pirated Michael Jackson videotapes were available for US$50, and underground discos flourished. The Islamic guards regularly raided all these activities, but in recent years there have been a few signs of liberalization. The technologies of penetration are so powerful that the industry is planning for the day when Iran will rejoin the global market in music and film.

The biggest growth potential for pop music is in Latin America and Asia. (Africa is almost never mentioned.) BMG Ariola Discos operates in Brazil and has 55 per cent of the market. About 80 per cent of the records sold are by local artists. A country with a yearly inflation rate of 1800 per cent is not an easy place in which to to do business, and when the rate suddenly drops to zero it is no easier. One has to assume that next year it will again be closer to 1800 per cent. But despite Brazil's political and economic difficulties, BMG remains bullish.

Today only 50 million of Brazil's 150 million people buy records. Nevertheless, in a few years, Gassner predicts, 'another half will be active economically, doubling our market potential.'

Musicians, social critics and politicians in poor countries of Asia, Africa and Latin America worry that the massive penetration of transnational sound will not only foreclose employment opportunities for local artists but will doom the traditional music of their local culture. 'My fear is that in another 10 or 15 years' time, what with all the cassettes that find their way into the remotest village, and with none of their own music available, people will get conditioned to this cheap kind of music.' This remark by a Sri Lankan musician typifies the anxiety felt throughout the non-industrialized world – that industrial musical products will sweep away hundreds, perhaps thousands, of years of traditional music. 'However small a nation we are, we still have our own way of singing, accompanying, intonating, making movements, and so on. We can make a small but distinctive contribution to world culture. But we could lose it.'

In the 1980s, the environmental movement began to popularize the important idea that biological diversity is a precious global resource, that the disappearance of snail darters, gorgeous tropical birds and African beetles impoverishes the Earth and possibly threatens the survival of the human species. The cultural–environmental movement has no powerful organizations promoting its message, but it has a large, unorganized global constituency. The feeling that world culture will be degraded if diversity is lost is widely shared among artists, cultural conservatives and nationalists. Yet these concerns are overwhelmed by the sheer power of global popular culture, which threatens local cultural traditions and the traditional communities from which they spring.

The impact of the global music industry on the character of local music has been significant. The Indian pop star Babydoll Alisha sings Madonna songs in a Hindi rendering. Tunisian artists now routinely use synthesizers to accompany the traditional bagpipes at live concerts. The need for financing for expensive electronic instruments and the dependence on access to electricity is changing local music cultures. In Trinidad, the introduction of multichannel recording has transformed the employment prospects of the famous steel bands. It used to be that a hundred musicians would crowd into someone's backyard, all with tuned oil drums, and two microphones would pick it all up to make local tapes. Now, as Roger Wallis of the Swedish Broadcasting Corporation, and Krister Malm, director of the Music Museum in Stockholm, report, a few of the best musicians are brought into a studio, and they 'record all the various parts on different channels on the tape recorder at different times. The final mix . . . might be technically perfect, but it no longer represents the collective communication of 100 musicians and their audiences.'

The globalization of the music market and the technology of multiple-channel recording have made it possible to create fresh sounds from all over the world. Everything from *zouk*, *rhi* and *jit* from Africa to *salsa* from the Caribbean islands to the chants of India known as *bhangra* are mixed with a variety of American pop genres to produce a blend that is promoted around the world as 'world beat'. *Lambada*, promoted by French entrepreneurs as the dance craze of Brazil, is Bolivian in origin. A recorded version of this music performed by mostly Senegalese musicians became a global hit. Paul Simon used South African singers and songs for his hit album *Graceland*, but he wrote his own words and the political message was diluted.

Local musicians are, of course, excited by the audiences, fame and money that the international record companies can provide, but some are concerned that their rich cultural traditions are being mined and skimmed to make an international product. The companies, though much agitated about protecting their own intellectual property from pirates, feel no compunction about uprooting the music of indigenous peoples from its native soil and treating it as a free commodity.

To be sure, painters and composers have often borrowed many different artistic traditions. Picasso's use of African images and Dvorak's renderings of folk dances in sophisticated works of chamber music are examples. But there is a line between tapping into an exotic musical tradition and stealing uncopyrighted songs, and sometimes the line is crossed.

The spectacular growth of global commercial entertainment has inspired myriad explanations. The role of technology clearly has been important. The wiring of the world through global transmission of pictures, talk and music by satellite greatly accelerated the spread of a global market for movies, videos and television programmes. The VCR turned homes, bars, daycare centres, buses, waiting rooms and nursing homes into a global chain of movie theatres. On the remote island of Siquijor in the Philippines, the inhabitants still gather at 'The Hangout' to eat *halo-halo* (chopped ice, corn flakes, fruit, and beans) and watch *Rambo* on videotape. In Colombia, long-distance buses keep their all-night movie fans on the edge of their seats (and the others grumpily awake) with *Robocop*. Hours once written off as commercially irrelevant were suddenly transformed into marketable time; insomniacs, housebound invalids, children with enough disposable income to rent a film, and couch potatoes of every variety could thrust a videocassette into their VCR at any time of the day or night. Old television programmes and movies bounce off satellites or travel by cable into homes, schools and prisons around the world, achieving a certain immortality previously denied to most cultural products. Not many dead poets, pundits or even departed best-selling novelists last long on the shelf, but, thanks to videotape and the near-universal hunger for American movies, music and television programmes, dead rock stars and movie actors go on forever.

One persuasive explanation is that it fills the vacuum left by the pervasive collapse of traditional family life, the atrophying of civic life and the loss of faith in politics that appears to be a worldwide trend. Others, such as Helena Norberg-Hodge, argue that the entertainment industry also causes the collapse of these traditions (see Chapter 14). Popular culture acts as a sponge to soak up spare time and energy that in earlier times might well have been devoted to nurturing and instructing children or to participating in political, religious, civic or community activities, or to crafts, reading and continuing self-education. Such pursuits may sound a bit old-fashioned today, although political theory still rests on the assumption that these activities are central to the functioning of a democratic society. Yet increasingly, vicarious experience via film, video and music is a substitute for civic life and community. As it becomes harder for young people in many parts of the world to carve out satisfying roles, the rush of commercial sounds and images offers escape.

In the US, global cultural products may outrage local sensibilities, but at least they are mostly made in the US. In Latin America and parts of Asia, American films and television programmes dominate the airways. It costs next to nothing to air an old Hollywood B film or a rerun of *I Love Lucy* or *Mr Ed*. Even less antique programmes such as *Dallas* or *LA Law* are much less expensive to run than local programmes with local talent, and the American product is likely to draw a bigger audience. Of the 4000 films shown on Brazilian television, according to the Brazilian film producer Luis Carlos Barreto, 99 per cent are from rich countries, mostly from Hollywood. Television is the most powerful force for mass education in most poor countries. Cultural nationalists in Latin America and in pockets of Asia are enraged that the most influential teachers of the next generation are Hollywood film studios and global advertising agencies. But recent trends all over the world – advances in intrusive technologies, privatization, deregulation and commercialization of electronic media – are making it increasingly difficult for families and teachers to compete with the global media for the attention of the next generation.

Chapter 16

The World Trade Organization's Five-Year Record: Seattle in Context

Lori Wallach

The World Trade Organization was founded in 1995 after the ratification of the GATT Uruguay round. Originally, 125 countries agreed to give it powers that are incomparably greater than have ever been granted to any international body. It has legislative powers, in that it can pass its own laws, executive powers, in that it can implement them, and judicial powers, in that it can penalize those countries who violate them. In addition, it is not only concerned with trade issues; its powers extend over investment policy, patent law and, by virtue of the General Agreement on Trade in Services (GATS), education, health services, environmental services and other critical services that have hitherto been provided for by national governments.

The WTO differs from other governments in that it is global, non-elected, totally controlled by transnational corporations, and in that its role is almost exclusively to create those conditions worldwide that best serve the latter's immediate interests. The author makes this quite clear by exposing the WTO's five-year record which has seen it undermine 'public policy worldwide'. She also describes how public opposition to this institution and to the global economy is building rapidly.

Lori Wallach is the director of Public Citizen's Global Trade Watch and is a leading US analyst and activist on trade and economic globalization issues. She played a leading role in the national citizens' campaigns in the US in opposition to NAFTA and the GATT–WTO, created the Public Citizens' Trade Programme in 1991 and became the first director of the new division of Public Citizen devoted to globalization issues. Wallach has recently published a book analysing in detail the WTO's five-year record: Whose Trade Organization: Globalization and the Erosion of Democracy *(Wallach et al, 1999).*

In 1997, after nearly a decade of public education and grassroots organizing, the US Congress rejected a request by President Clinton for a 'fast track' trade authority. It was the first time the elite consensus in favour of 'free trade' had been defeated in the Congress in decades. The uniquely undemocratic fast track process was essential in securing congressional approval of the Uruguay Round of GATT and the establishment of the WTO in 1994 and the NAFTA in 1993. Clinton particularly needs a 'fast track' to facilitate the further expansion of both NAFTA and GATT.

Eight months later, the US movement that defeated Fast Track, united with similar progressive environmental–consumer–labour–human rights and small farmer coalitions in numerous other countries, quashed a planned multilateral agreement on investment (MAI). The extreme globalization proposal, dubbed 'NAFTA on steroids', was nearly completed after four years of secluded talks at the OECD. The MAI withered when the citizens groups applied the 'dracula test' by exposing the previously secret, outrageous proposal to the sunshine of public scrutiny.

However, it was at Seattle in November 1999 that the promoters of globalization and corporate control suffered their worst humiliation to date. The WTO ministerial meeting at which all sorts of socially and environmentally destructive new regulations were to be enacted, and at which an agreement was sought for a new millennium round of trade negotiations, never got off the ground. This was largely as a result of huge demonstrations by groups representing many different sectors of civil society and of the refusal by the developing world leaders to sign the conference's final declaration.

Back in 1994, the Clinton administration had painted a very positive picture of how the Uruguay Round and the WTO would affect the US – and the rest of the world – on virtually all fronts. It would not erode sovereignty, undermine environmental health or food safety policy; it would lead to increased family income, unprecedented economic growth and the creation of thriving consumer societies that would purchase US goods.

FIVE YEARS OF THE WTO

The most powerful tool for organizing citizen opposition to WTO expansion has been the WTO's own five-year record. In virtually every key area where the US and other governments promised WTO benefits, the WTO instead undermined the status quo ante. The economic record is fairly well known: the world has been buffeted by unprecedented global financial instability, in part thanks to the investment and financial services deregulation that the Uruguay Round was designed to intensify. Income inequality is increasing rapidly between countries and within countries. Five years of WTO have seen the least developed countries' share of world trade diminished. Despite efficiency gains, wages in numerous countries have failed to rise and commodity prices are at an all time low, causing a decrease in the standards of living in real terms for a majority of people in the world. Per-capita income in Africa has declined and in Latin America is stagnant.

Indeed, recent data touted by defenders of the status quo on poverty are revealing. While emphasizing that the number of people living on less than US$1 per day has declined, these WTO boosters fail to reveal that the improvements are in China, a country that has rejected the neo-liberal model to date. Removing China, with its non-convertible currency, trade protections and industrial policy, from the calculations reveals that the numbers of those living on *de minimis* income in other countries has actually increased.

What is even less well known and very dramatic is the WTO's role as a cancer on democratic, accountable governance in all of its member nations, undermining a growing list of national, state and local policies regarding food safety, the environment, human rights, public health and more.

With only one interesting exception, the WTO has struck down as an illegal trade barrier every single domestic environmental, health or safety law that it has reviewed, including a European ban on artificial beef hormones, petrol cleanliness standards under the US Clean Air Act, and the US implementation of a global endangered species treaty concerning sea turtles. The mere threat of a WTO challenge has resulted in the weakening of numerous other policies, from Guatemala's implementation of the UNICEF–World Health Organization's (WHO's) baby formula marketing code, to EU humane trapping laws, to Thai consumer-medicines access policy, to Korean food safety rules. As the WTO approaches its fifth anniversary, the number of WTO threats and challenges is ballooning, including Canada's attack on France's asbestos ban, a US–EU attack on Japanese implementation of its Kyoto Treaty obligations and more.

Yet, despite this unacceptable record, few people living within the boundaries of the WTO member countries are aware that they are witness to a broad, slow-motion *coup d'etat* against democratic governance.

In part, this lack of awareness is caused by the lack of public understanding of the WTO. The 1995 formation of the WTO transformed the GATT – which was effectively a trade contract between nations – into a powerful new global commerce agency. The GATT, initiated in 1947 and expanded in scope and signatories through eight 'rounds' of negotiations, covered traditional trade matters: it lowered quotas and tariffs to facilitate trade in goods. The GATT also contained several simple principles, such as 'national treatment', which means not discriminating against foreign-made goods, but rather providing equal treatment to domestic and imported goods.

THE TRANSFORMATION OF THE GATT INTO THE WTO

The establishment of the WTO buried these basic trade rules, with over 800 pages of explicit new rules proscribing which goals countries could make policy and the means countries could use to further even WTO-allowed goals.

The transformation from GATT to WTO included a shift from the GATT's broad trade principles to the WTO's imposition of 'one size fits all' values and subjective policy decisions on countries.

Though different rules apply to different issue areas, the overall theme is trade *über alles*. Namely, instead of simply treating foreign and domestic goods the same, countries are required to put maximizing international commercial flows ahead of nearly all other policy goals. Indeed, many of the WTO provisions that constrain government action regarding health and environmental policy specifically require that such policies be the 'least trade-restrictive' alternative, meaning that policy-makers first must consider the trade impacts of a health law, not its effectiveness in protecting public health.

The WTO included numerous new agreements which set these new limits on government action in policy areas previously untouched by global international commercial rules. In some instances, by simply adding the prefix 'trade related', the WTO agreements dragged issues unrelated to trade under WTO jurisdiction. For instance, in direct contradiction to the notion of 'free' trade, the WTO established a new worldwide standard of a 20-year monopoly protection for patents and permitted almost anything to be submitted to patenting, including seeds and essential medicines in a 'trade-related intellectual property agreement'. The trade-related investment measures agreement forbids governments from setting even non-discriminatory conditions on investment, such as development policies previously used by the now-rich countries, and from regaining certain domestic content in products being manufactured, a rule that would apply equally to domestic and foreign producers.

As well, the new WTO rules moved beyond simply requiring equal treatment for foreign and domestic goods. Instead, in extensive new rules limiting food, worker health, product safety and environmental standards, the WTO legislated on the *level* of public health or environmental protection a country could choose. The WTO agreements also newly brought all service sectors – banking, transport, telecommunications and more – and government procurement under WTO disciplines.

WTO's Powerful, Secretive New Enforcement Bodies

This lengthy set of new constraints on government action is powerfully enforced through the threat of trade sanctions under the WTO's built-in dispute-resolution system. Unlike international environmental treaties, in which signatories take on commitments and then enforce them themselves at this national border, the WTO is 'self-executing'. This means that the WTO has its own built-in enforcement capacity. Under WTO rules, one member government can challenge the laws of another WTO member at a closed WTO dispute-resolution tribunal.

Cases are decided by panels of three trade bureaucrats meeting in secrecy who determine if a country's laws reach beyond the WTO's allowable parameters. There are no outside appeals, but rather a standing WTO appellate body which also operates in strict secrecy, with documents and hearings closed to the public and the press. The qualifications to become a WTO panellist – such as past employment at the GATT – ensure that panellists will have an interest in, and bias for, the primacy of trade rules over national policies. Indeed, the WTO's appellate body consists of panellists literally on the WTO payroll. There are no basic due-process guarantees – for instance, meaningful conflict of interest rules for panellists or guarantees of panellists' qualifications to determine the vast array of policy areas touched by WTO rules. Indeed, recent international law review articles have faulted the basic international law interpretations of WTO panellists as being ill-informed. Yet, despite these enormous structural faults, the WTO tribunal rulings are uniquely powerful – unlike other international agreements, WTO rules are enforceable with threat of trade sanction.

Once a law has been successfully challenged at the WTO, countries have three and only three options: eliminate or change the law, arrange to pay cash compensation to the winning country or face trade sanctions.

As critics feared, the WTO's built-in bias against public participation and the WTO's backwards rules have made the institution a perfect venue for industry and governments to pursue agendas that would fail in any open, democratic forum. According to a WTO official quoted in a recent *Financial Times* article (1998), the WTO 'is the place where governments collude in private against their domestic pressure groups'. The revelation of this mind-set, though entirely unacceptable, is refreshingly honest with regard to WTO's view of itself and the view of industry and WTO member governments of the WTO.

THE WTO'S RECORD OF UNDERMINING PUBLIC-INTEREST POLICY WORLDWIDE

In five years, a string of WTO challenges has resulted in a growing list of domestic environmental, health and development policies being weakened. Because the breadth of the existing and potential damage is hard to fathom, several of the cases are presented in some detail.

Artificial hormone-tainted beef

In 1997, the WTO ruled against the EU ban on beef containing artificial hormone residues. The existence of the case, brought to the WTO by the US at the behest of its agribusiness and pharmaceutical interests and against the strong opposition of US consumer and family farm groups, is fairly well known. However, its implications remain a mystery to many who will be directly affected by it.

Europe's ban on sale of beef from cattle treated with artificial growth hormones was declared WTO-illegal, even though the European ban treated domestic and foreign products alike. The artificial hormones, which are administered through tags clipped to cows' ears, were banned after incidents in Europe where consumption of high concentrations of the substances caused male toddlers to grow enlarged breasts and very young girls to begin menstruating. The artificial hormones have also been linked to cancer threats in both US and EU studies. The actual hormones used are known to cause cancer, although the human health effect of ingesting meat containing such hormone residues is unknown.

Under the WTO's decision, the EU was forced to decide on either eliminating its consumer-demanded ban on the artificial hormone-tainted beef or facing trade sanctions from the US. As of August 2000, the EU stands firm and US consumers and EU producers are suffering from a broad set of high retaliatory tariffs totalling US$180 million. Indeed, the US rejected a European offer to pay cash compensation to the US while the EU undertook risk-assessment studies that the WTO panel had suggested. The US argues that under WTO, a country must eliminate laws against which the WTO rules.

The beef hormone WTO ruling exposed the WTO's invasion into non-trade value judgements, such as the level of health protection the EU chose for its consumers. The ruling also put a stake through the heart of the precautionary principle, on which the EU's zero-risk standard was premised.

Precautionary principle

The precautionary principle, widely recognized in international environmental law and in US, EU and many other countries' domestic regulatory policies, is based on the premise that science does not always provide the complete information or insight necessary to take protective action effectively or in a timely manner. Under the precautionary principle, countries take action to *avoid* exposing people to unnecessary and potentially irreversible harm instead of waiting for science to provide more precise information about risk. Thus, under the precautionary approach, producers bear a burden of proving a product's long-term safety as a condition of getting it on the market, rather than the government having to prove it is dangerous in order to keep it off the market. By taking precautionary steps with respect to the use of the anti-nausea drug thalidomide, the US avoided a potentially disastrous epidemic of birth defects. Thalidomide is estimated to have been responsible for deformities in more than 10,000 babies in the countries in which it was approved. At the time of its approval in Europe and Canada, tests in laboratory animals showed no negative effects, but the long term dangers – not to pregnant women, but their children – were tragically discovered later.

Genetically Modified Organisms (GMOs)

The WTO's beef-hormone ruling declared that health regulations taken in advance of scientific certainty are not allowed under WTO rules. The potential boomerang effect of this WTO determination on a range of laws worldwide is immense – with the issue of the regulation and labelling of genetically modified organisms (GMOs) the likely next target. Around the world – in the EU, Japan, Australia and other countries – governments are beginning to regulate GMO foods and seeds. As evidence begins to accumulate – for instance, a recent study replicating an earlier study that demonstrated an increased fatality rate for monarch butterfly caterpillars which consumed GMO-tainted pollen – governments are acting to avoid potentially irreversible environmental or health threats.

Yet, the US has threatened the EU regulations on GMOs with a WTO challenge. The US position is that until specific human health or environmental risks are scientifically proven, governments' regulations – even the requirement to label food containing GMOs – violate WTO rules.

The WTO beef-hormone case also demonstrated that the WTO exalts the role of science far beyond the point that is appropriate, attempting to eliminate all 'non-science' factors from policy-setting. Despite the undisputed value of science in policy-making, scientific uncertainties – for instance, concerning the health threats posed by exposure to an array of chemicals – remain. Moreover, political judgements always play a central role in policy-making. While science plays a valuable role in informing such policy decisions, it is ultimately parliament or a local legislature that must make the political decision about how much risk society will face under a food safety or other law. Thus, the US Congress may make the political decision to allow zero risk from a particular hazard, rather than establishing an allowable level of risk. For example, the US has a zero tolerance level for listeria in cold smoked fish, canned lobster and ready-to-eat seafood combined with a more rigorous sampling regime than that currently practised in Canada. Canada considers the US policy to be unnecessarily severe and thus listed the US listeria policy in its 'Register of United States Barriers to Trade'.

Ecolabelling

Even as a US safeguard was being threatened by the inappropriate elevation of science in WTO rules, the US was presenting the same industry position before one of the WTO's numerous ongoing policy-making committees. The US wanted to add new WTO rules that would restrain food and product ecolabelling that is not premised on scientific evidence of a human health risk. Under the US proposal, merely providing consumers with information about the environmental impacts or production methods of a product in order to facilitate their choice would not be permitted. Happily, opposition to this proposal by other WTO member countries resulted in its rejection as WTO policy to date, and under consumer and environmental group pressure the US has stopped threatening a WTO challenge of Europe's ecolabelling regime.

Finally, by requiring food safety standards to be based on a risk assessment, the WTO ruling in the beef hormone case eliminates the possibility that a society's values – for example, prevention of exposure to low doses of a highly toxic substance in the presence of uncertain knowledge of the chemical's effects on humans – should outweigh the uncertain outcome of a risk assessment.

Invasive species

Already there have been two WTO rulings requiring certain WTO-specified risk assessments that a country must do *before* it can put in place regulations to halt invasive species attacks on biodiversity or to contain plant or animal disease. For instance, the WTO ruled against an Australian law forbidding the import of raw salmon; this was intended to keep known foreign bacteria which infected other regions' salmon from attacking Australian salmon stocks. The WTO declared that while Australia had performed a risk assessment and had proved scientifically that there was a risk to its salmon, it had not proved the probability of the actual damage occurring. Thus, the Australian law was declared a WTO-illegal trade barrier.

A similarly reasoned WTO ruling also labelled a Japanese law protecting against invasion by the devastating coddling moth an illegal trade barrier. The outcome in these cases has undoubtedly been considered by Hong Kong, who filed preliminary complaints against a new US policy aimed at halting the invasion of the voracious tree-eating Asian long-horned beetle. These beetles have entered the US in raw wood-packing materials from China, including some shipped through Hong Kong. The US has had to torch groves of trees near ports and airports in Illinois and New York because of infestations, which can only be halted by cutting and incinerating infested and surrounding trees. The US policy requires that wooden packing materials, such as shipping pallets, be treated before entry into the US. Hong Kong suggests that this US action, taken before the completion of all WTO-required risk assessments, violates its WTO rights.

France's asbestos ban

The one instance in which the WTO has not ruled against a country's challenging environmental or health rule is in the highly politicized Canadian challenge of France's ban on asbestos. Asbestos is a proven carcinogen for humans. Canada produces 95 per cent of asbestos exported worldwide. In 1996, France joined Germany, Austria, Denmark, the Netherlands, Finland, Italy, Sweden and Belgium to become the ninth EU member to ban all forms of asbestos. Canada claimed that under WTO rules, countries can regulate but not ban asbestos. The ruling in this case was expected before the late 1999 Seattle WTO ministerial meeting. Given the damage to the WTO that a ruling against the asbestos ban would cause, it was delayed. WTO defenders lobbied the WTO tribunal in the case to save the WTO by ruling in favour of the asbestos ban, even though WTO technical barrier to trade rules are so backwards that they require the opposite outcome. In mid 2000, the WTO ruling finally was announced, with the French asbestos ban permitted under extremely narrow grounds. While the result in the case is good, the jurisprudence it establishes sets an impossible standard before the WTO's already severely limited exceptions can be applied in defence of a health law. In addition to seeking prohibitive definitions of what comprises a human health risk, the ruling required legal contortions to avoid the WTO's requirements.

Threats of WTO action chill policy-making

In addition to outright challenges to countries' food or worker safety laws, the WTO's anti-public interest bias has chillingly emerged with regard to food and other health and safety standards. For instance, after US threats of WTO action, Korea changed its 30-day meat shelf-life rule to permit meat to remain in stock for 90 days. Korea also shortened its guaranteed produce-inspection turnaround time after a US WTO threat, so that now food is distributed to consumers before the results of microbial tests have arrived.

As the WTO continues to build on its history of ruling against public health and safety, a new trend is emerging where companies, as well as nations, use threats of WTO trade sanctions to force countries to drop or weaken health and safety laws without a formal challenge. This tactic has been used, for instance, to get Thailand to eliminate its consumer pricing board for medicines – and will most likely continue to be used against developing countries who often lack the resources and technical capacity to defend themselves against potentially costly formal WTO challenges.

In addition, a disturbing trend is emerging in which WTO intellectual property rules are being used to discourage the adoption of public health initiatives, including those advanced by world health bodies such as the WHO or those accepted as common practice elsewhere in the world. International law is being skewed in favour of the property rights of corporations vis-à-vis the rights of people to survive and the fiduciary responsibility of elected governments to provide for public health and welfare. Indeed, the prospect of the expense of defending policies before trade tribunals in Geneva, and the looming threat of sanctions, claimed one important public health measure even before the WTO was formally initiated.

The UNICEF–WHO Baby Formula Code

US-based Gerber Products Company sought to avoid compliance with a Guatemalan infant health law that banned the use of baby pictures on labels for baby food for children under two years' old. The Guatemalan law implemented the UNICEF–WHO Infant Formula Marketing Code, which was developed to help protect the lives of infants by promoting breastfeeding over artificial breast milk substitutes by, among other things, eliminating the packaging that could induce illiterate parents to associate formula with healthy, fat babies.

All of Guatemala's domestic and foreign suppliers of infant formula and other breast milk substitutes made the necessary changes to their packaging to comply with the Guatemalan law except Gerber. Guatemalan infant mortality rates dropped significantly after the law passed, with UNICEF holding up Guatemala as a model of the code's success in its literature.

After passing the law, the Guatemala Ministry of Health negotiated with Gerber to seek compliance. Gerber's trademark included the fat 'Gerber baby' face. After several years of watching Gerber refuse to abide by its regulations and remove the baby face from its labels, the government of Guatemala considered a total ban on the company's products. It was at this point that Gerber threatened the Guatemalan government with a challenge under the GATT (Kelly, 1994). Indeed, the nearly completed new WTO intellectual property rules required countries to provide protection for companies' trademarks, such as Gerber's familiar fat baby face. According to Gerber's letter to the president of Guatemala, failure to respect these rights would result in action at the GATT (Kelly, 1994).

By 1995, with the WTO coming into effect, Gerber's threats succeeded. To avoid the potential costs of defence or trade sanctions, the Guatamalan law was changed to exempt imported baby food products from Guatemala's otherwise stringent infant health laws.

WTO ATTACKS ON THE ENVIRONMENT

The WTO has ruled against every environmental law that it has reviewed. Trade rulings against dolphin and sea turtle conservation and against petrol cleanliness rules under the US Clean Air Act reveal a systemic bias – evidenced in the WTO rules and the WTO dispute-resolution process – against the rights of sovereign states to enact and effectively enforce environmental laws. All three rulings have led (or will lead, if implemented) to the weakening of the US laws in question. Four years after a 1992 GATT panel ruled against the US Marine Mammal Protection Act (MMPA) forbidding the sale in the US of tuna caught by domestic or foreign fishers using techniques that kill hundreds of thousands of dolphins, the Clinton administration lobbied Congress intensively to amend the MMPA to implement the GATT ruling after Mexican threats of a WTO enforcement case. In early 2000, the US again started allowing the sale of tuna caught using kilometre-long nets set around schools of dolphins. In fact, under the Clinton administration-pushed MMPA amendments, this tuna was supposed to be labelled as 'dolphin safe'. However, a lawsuit by environmentalists has halted the label change even through the dolphin-deadly tuna is once again permitted.

Endangered sea turtle protection

In the 'shrimp–turtle' case, a WTO panel ruled against the US Endangered Species Act provisions implementing US obligations under the multilateral environmental treaty CITES (Convention on International Trade in Endangered Species of Wild Fauna and Flora). The US law requires all foreign- and domestic-caught shrimp sold in the US to be harvested using techniques that safeguard endangered sea turtles. The Clinton administration tried to implement this WTO ruling by changing a domestic rule so that only individual shrimp boats must be certified, not countries, thus encouraging the practice of 'shrimp-laundering' where shrimp that are harvested using turtle-deadly techniques are imported on boats certified as 'turtle friendly'. However, environmentalists have also challenged this move in US courts and the administration has decided to wait until after the recent US Gore versus Bush presidential elections before trying to weaken the underlying law.

While the WTO secretary general publicly states its support for the principles of sustainable development ('the [environment] has been given and will continue to be given a high profile on the WTO agenda'), in a subsequent attack of candour, WTO Secretary General Renato Ruggiero professed that environmental standards in the WTO are 'doomed to fail and could only damage the global trading system'.

Multilateral environmental agreements and the WTO

Both the tuna–dolphin and the shrimp–turtle cases reveal a disturbing tendency within GATT/WTO dispute panels to ignore existing multilateral environmental agreements (MEAs). The tuna–dolphin panels refused to consider the US tuna embargo within the framework of multilateral agreements on dolphin protection. Instead, the panels ignored the international precedent in favour of species protection and found that US law violated GATT through the extraterritorial application of domestic law. It also ignored the US effort to multilateralize the tuna-fishing process and production methods (PPMs) within the Inter-American Tropical Tuna Commission.

In the shrimp–turtle case, the fact that the US has signed agreements mandating the use of turtle exclusion devices (TEDs) with 17 nations did not prevent the WTO from ruling that the US was still implementing the shrimp import ban in a unilateral, extraterritorial and, under WTO definitions, discriminatory manner, even though the law applied to both domestic and foreign shrimping vessels. In addition, the panel rejected the application of the narrow GATT Article XX exception that theoretically could safeguard some environmental laws from WTO attack, even though the shrimp embargo conforms with multilateral environmental agreements such as the CITES. The CITES allows the imposition of trade sanctions on nations who endanger species threatened with extinction.

Countries may not regulate on how a product is made

A key factor in the tuna–dolphin case is a WTO principle which prohibits a country from differentiating between physically similar products based on the way they are produced (this is called process and production methods or PPMs). Yet, the ability to distinguish between production methods is essential to environmental protection and sustainable development policies. One of the key components in setting the world on a sustainable and equitable development path involves changing the conditions and processes under which goods are produced and commodities are grown, harvested and extracted. Trade rules that forbid the differentiation between production methods make it impossible for governments to adopt an aggressive approach towards environmental protection or an enlightened and effective response to oppressive social practices such as child labour.

WTO undermining of national priorities

In January 1996, the very first WTO panel ruled against US clean air regulations governing petrol cleanliness. The US policy required the cleanliness of petrol sold in the most polluted cities in the US to improve by 15 per cent over 1990 levels, and all petrol sold elsewhere in the US to maintain levels of cleanliness at least equal to 1990 levels.

The US EPA's initial difficulty in designing the regulation was finding an enforceable, trustworthy and economically feasible way to ensure that all petrol sold in the US met the standards. In an attempt to minimize market disruptions and maximize health protection, the EPA settled on an interim solution: a preset standard for petrol from foreign and domestic refiners that lacked the necessary documentation. Petrol from those refiners had to match the average actual 1990 contaminant level of all petrol refiners able to provide full documentation. This rule was set to expire in 1998, giving refiners five years to meet a single cleanliness target.

However, Venezuela and Brazil, claiming that the EPA rule unfairly disadvantaged their petrol by possibly holding it to higher standards than some categories of US-refined petrol, challenged it in the WTO. The WTO panel sided with Venezuela and Brazil, holding that the EPA's mechanism to enforce the congressionally mandated air standards could inadvertently result in discriminatory *effects* favouring US refiners over foreign refiners. The US appealed, arguing that the policy was not discriminatory, placing US refineries without proper documentation in the same category as similar foreign refineries. However, the WTO substituted its judgement for that of the US environmental regulators, arguing that while air was a natural resource that could be protected, the means that the US designed were not WTO-permissible.

These rulings forced the US to choose between repealing the EPA regulation and permitting imports of dirtier Venezuelan petrol (and possibly placing US refiners at a competitive disadvantage for having implemented the EPA regulations), or keeping the EPA regulation and facing US$150 million in trade sanctions each year in the form of higher Venezuelan tariffs on US products. In August 1997, the US weakened the standard. The US adopted a policy towards limiting contaminants in foreign petrol that the EPA had earlier rejected as effectively unenforceable.

This case demonstrates the WTO's threat to national sovereignty in that the EPA regulation had withstood all the challenges available through the US democratic process. Firstly, opponents of the rule – including the Venezuelan government represented by the powerful US lobbying firm Arnold & Porter – lobbied the US Congress. Failing there, they participated in the rule-making process. When the government approved the regulation despite their efforts, opponents threatened a lawsuit. The opponents and their lobbyists went back to Congress to try to get the rule changed. At this point, domestic oil refiners concluded that they had just better implement the law and in doing so invested US$37 billion. In contrast, industry interests in Venezuela and Brazil renewed their attack at the WTO's secret tribunals before unaccountable, unelected trade bureaucrats. Only there, out of the public eye, could they find success in weakening the policy.

CONCLUSION

This chapter provides a small slice of the WTO's five-year record. Even this partial review provides a compelling case that the WTO's outcomes are unacceptable.

Recently, in countries around the globe, citizens' movements working with the extensive grassroots network and coordinating internationally have been able to make significant progress in educating their publics, the press and policy-makers about the implications of globalization and current international trade agreements. The year of public-interest campaigning and lobbying leading up to the Seattle WTO ministerial (called the 'WTO: No New Round, Turnaround' campaign) and its contribution to holding governments publicly accountable significantly contributed to the failure of the planned WTO millennium round expansion. Throughout, these many internationally united national campaigns shared a conviction: if the public were to understand the true nature and implication that the globalization project has on their lives, the project's political viability and its legitimacy would be severely undercut.

Indeed, growing public understanding has significantly undermined the version of globalization that was engineered through its proponents' PR campaigns: few believe that the corporate agenda of globalization is a positive force. More and more also realize that it is not inevitable, but rather that the globalization driven by the WTO is merely one version of how economies, legal systems and policies can be designed. If the outcomes are unacceptable, as are those of the WTO, then the design must be replaced.

As a result, the citizens' coalitions and many individual NGOs from 72 countries have launched an offensive called the 'WTO: Shrink or Sink' campaign which seeks 11 transformational changes to the WTO rules to limit the WTO's undermining of public interest.

Through numerous means, the struggle to reveal this version of corporate economic globalization as a carefully designed project with devastating consequences for democratically accountable governance, and the resulting environmental, health and other public interest accomplishments, hard won over the past decades, will go forward. Once public pressure has been mobilized, this insanity will be brought to an end.

Chapter 17

The Environmental Cost of Economic Globalization

Simon Retallack

Advocates of economic globalization claim that it is instrumental to ecological sustainability on the grounds that it makes environmental protection more affordable and desirable. In reality, however, the natural environment is one of the greatest casualties of economic globalization, which is accelerating the depletion of the planet's natural resource base and the exhaustion of its carrying capacity for wastes at the same time as preventing adequate mitigating action from being taken.

Simon Retallack is managing editor of The Ecologist's *special issues and is co-director of the Climate Initiatives Fund – a grant-making foundation dedicated to accelerating efforts to mitigate climate change. He graduated in government from the London School of Economics and was a researcher at the London-based think-tank Demos. He was also a visiting fellow at the International Forum on Globalisation in San Francisco, for which he has recently edited and cowritten a report on the environmental impact of economic globalization. He writes and speaks regularly on climate and trade related issues.*

The importance of the natural world, in intrinsic terms and for human life, is fundamental. Without it, we cannot survive. Yet we have sufficiently divorced ourselves from it to become capable of devising an economic system that is destroying it.

The revolutionary set of policies that has been implemented to create the global economy has brought into play new rules and dynamics that are incompatible with environmental protection. In particular, creating increasingly global and unfettered markets for trade and investment has significantly increased the destructive impact of economic activity upon the Earth, exhausting the world's natural resource endowment and ecological carrying capacity at such a voracious rate as to jeopardize the planet's ability to support generations to come.

To make matters worse, the new rules and dynamics of economic globalization have simultaneously led to the holding back or removal of regulations and taxes designed to protect the natural environment, just when they are most needed. The principal economic actors of today, corporations, are thus increasingly able to operate free of constraints. In the process, economic accountability, democracy and the possibility of democratically achieved environmental protection are being seriously eroded.

As a result, we now face chronic, uncontrolled global crises in deforestation, biodiversity loss, climate change, fisheries depletion, soil loss, land degradation and freshwater depletion. Perilously, economic globalization is pushing the Earth beyond its limits.

THE IMPACT OF LIBERALIZING TRADE AND INVESTMENT

National barriers to trade and investment have been dramatically reduced around the world in the past 20 years, following the adoption of IMF and World Bank SAPs across the developing world, the sweeping to power of neo-liberal governments in the North, the creation of free trade areas in Europe and North America, and the implementation of successive rounds of GATT (see Chapter 10).

As a result, FDI by transnational corporations in developing countries grew twelvefold between 1970 and 1992 (*World Investment Report 1996*, 1996). It then almost trebled between 1992 and 1997, rising to US$149 billion out of a worldwide FDI total of US$400 billion – itself nearly double the total for 1994 (*World Investment Report 1996* and *1998*, 1996; 1998). The opening of markets worldwide to foreign imports and the promotion of exports has caused a similar explosion in the volume of world trade, whose value has grown from US$380 billion in 1950 to US$5.86 trillion in 1997: a fifteenfold increase (*World Economic Outlook October 1997*, 1997; see also *Financial Statistics Yearbook*, 1997; *International Financial Statistics*, 1998).

The boom in world trade and investment that has resulted from economic globalization has contributed to a number of very specific ecological problems.

For trade to take place, it requires transportation. Given that current means of transportation are driven by fossil fuels – that when combusted release various harmful gases into the air including greenhouse gases – the increase in transport that has necessarily accompanied the increase in world trade has led directly to increased air pollution and global climate change (see Chapter 20). The same process has also led to increased bioinvasion – a primary cause of species extinction by which species from distant ecosystems are transported in the cargoes or ballasts of ships, planes and trucks to new places with often catastrophic results for local biodiversity.

Many endangered species are further threatened by another consequence of trade liberalization. The removal of border controls on trade – as, for example, within the European single market – and increased trade-related transport across North American and other international borders have seriously hindered the task of preventing illegal traffic in endangered species. The same processes have made it much harder to prevent illegal trade in hazardous wastes and in banned chlorofluorocarbons (CFCs) that play a leading role in destroying the ozone layer.

But trade liberalization is perhaps most serious because of its overall ecological impact. Because of the tearing down of barriers to trade, corporations – whose primary goal is to expand in order to increase their stock market value and profits for shareholders – are able to access two important new markets. The first is a vast new market of consumers, to whom they can sell a corresponding increase of manufactured products by persuading them, through advertisements, that commodity consumption brings satisfaction. And the second is a vast new market for natural resources to meet production for these new consumer markets and to continue to satisfy the high consumption levels of industrialized countries.

Consequently, products, technologies and lifestyles that were previously confined to industrialized countries, and that when used or followed are often highly polluting, are now exported and sold worldwide. That is the case, for example, of the motor car, whose numbers have increased from a few thousand worldwide in 1900 to 501 million today (cited by Brown and Flavin in *State of the World 1999*, 1999, p6). Since the opening of markets to foreign imports, car ownership has been booming in most industrializing countries. South Korea and Thailand, for instance, witnessed annual car growth rates of 25 and 40 per cent respectively in the early 1990s (Matthews and Rowell, 1992, p6). The result is crippling air pollution in urban centres and more greenhouse gas emissions, seriously exacerbating climate change.

Meanwhile, the unceasing flow of products that corporations sell to their traditional home markets, and the increasing flow to the new consumer markets that are opened to them by trade liberalization, require that a correspondingly unceasing and increasing flow of raw materials is produced. Metals must be mined from the ground to be converted into cars; trees must be felled to be converted into paper, packaging and furniture; oil and coal must be mined to be converted into electricity; fisheries are exploited for fish products; and soils are mined for cash crops. With the removal of barriers to exports and imports, those natural resources, many of which are non-renewable, are now accessible on a scale that they never were before. They are available to be purchased to meet corporate production needs, explaining in part, at least, why there has been an eighteenfold increase in the global consumption of materials (including minerals, metals, wood products and fossil-fuel-based materials) since 1900 (cited by Gardner and Sampat in *State of the World 1999*, 1999, pp43–49).

The consequence is much more rapid resource exploitation. Mineral and metal extraction is leaving an ever larger and more damaging environmental footprint, from the generation of vast quantities of pollution and waste to the destruction of huge tracts of land. Mining now strips more of the Earth's surface each year than natural erosion by rivers (cited by Gardner and Sampat in *State of the World 1999*, 1999, pp43–49). Global fish-stock depletion and deforestation have reached devastating levels, with overfishing now threatening most major commercial fishing grounds, and logging for wood products threatening more than 70 per cent of the world's large intact virgin forests (Bryant et al, 1997). The production of cash crops for export is also causing severe and unsustainable ecological damage, including soil erosion, land degradation from overgrazing, desertification, water depletion, chemical contamination, biodiversity loss and deforestation.

Yet, economic globalization ensures that this damage takes place. The imperative to export is the necessary outcome of the dismantling of export and import barriers; the logic of free trade is based on specialization according to comparative advantage; and the quest to earn foreign exchange is to pay off debts to Northern banks. Were it not for the resulting drive to export, we can be sure that most of the natural resources from which primary products are derived would not be exploited to the extent that they are. In 1990, all of the diamonds produced in Botswana, for example, were for export; 99 per cent of the coffee produced in Burundi; 93 per cent of the bananas grown in Costa Rica; 83 per cent of the cotton cultivated in Burkina Faso; 71 per cent of the tobacco produced in Malawi; half of the tress felled for timber in Malaysia; and half of Iceland's fish catch – all for export (cited by French in *Costly Tradeoffs, Reconciling Trade and the Environment*, 1993, p12).

Economic globalization further ensures increased natural resource depletion by dismantling barriers to foreign investment, enabling corporations engaged in resource extraction – either as primary commodity exporters or to meet their own manufacturing needs – to expand their operations around the world. Thus, transnational corporations such as Exxon–Mobil and Shell of the oil industry; Rio Tinto Zinc and BHP of the mining industry; Mitsubishi and Boise Cascade of the logging industry; Pescanova and Arctic-Tyson Foods of the fishing industry; Vivendi SA and Suez Lyonnaise des Eaux of the water industry; and Cargill and Monsanto of the food industry have expanded their operations to the four corners of the Earth. In a world with fewer barriers to investment, any business with sufficient capital, technology and expertise can haul away as much oil, gas, minerals, timber, fish, water and food, among other natural resources, as it wants. When the resources of one area have been thoroughly depleted, businesses simply move on to another. The consequence is massive and often permanent ecological damage.

That damage does not end with the extraction of primary commodities: processing them into more and more manufactured goods is also often highly polluting. It requires large quantities of energy, mostly in the form of fossil fuels, contributing to air pollution and climate change. In the US, for example, material processing and manufacturing alone claimed 14 per cent of the country's energy use in 1994 (cited by Gardner and Sampat in *State of the World 1999*, 1999, p48). Manufacturing also involves the use of large quantities of chemicals. As an exponentially rising number of manufactured products are made and exported worldwide, the annual world production of synthetic organic chemicals has increased enormously. From 7 million tons in 1950, chemical production has grown to nearly a billion tons today and is generating huge amounts of hazardous waste in the process (cited by Karliner in *The Corporate Planet*, 1997, p16). The consequences are a significant decrease in biodiversity and a horrifying growth in cancer rates. A white male in the US today, for example, is twice as likely to get cancer as his grandfather (Davis et al, 1994; cited in *Rachel's Hazardous Waste News*, 14 April 1994).

Economic globalization not only promotes these trends by stimulating increased commodity production for export. By liberalizing investment, it permits corporations to expand industrial production around the world, increasing the scale of ecological problems such activities cause. Thus, we have witnessed the global expansion of the computer, car, steel, paper, plastic, chemical and oil refining industries – all of which generate significant quantities of hazardous waste, with serious implications for public health and biodiversity.

Investment liberalization also permits Northern-based corporations which are engaged in activities that are so ecologically harmful that they incur heavy financial cleanup penalties, or are illegal in most industrialized countries, to continue to engage in them wherever in the world environmental laws or their enforcement are lax (see Chapter 12). Many cases have been documented in which particularly hazardous operations have relocated from the North to escape strict and costly environmental standards. They include producers of asbestos, benzidine dyes, ozone-destroying CFCs, certain pesticides such as DDT, as well as lead and copper smelters, and some mineral processors (Leonard, 1988). A number of serious environmental problems are thus perpetuated with devastating implications for public health and biodiversity.

Similarly appalling problems are caused by the disposal of increased municipal waste arising from the increased volume of consumer products and packaging entering markets worldwide, and the expansion of the industrial way of life that is taking place with the opening of markets to trade. The increased use of waste disposal methods such as incineration and landfill, pollutes more water supplies, leaches more mercury, generates more methane (a powerful greenhouse gas), and fills the air we breathe with more cancer-causing dioxins.

The tearing down of barriers to trade and investment around the world clearly contributes to all of these problems by providing growth-oriented corporations with unprecedented access to consumers and raw materials, and by maintaining the unsustainable industrialized way of life beyond its natural limits while extending it to the rest of the world.

If the consequent rising tide of ecological destruction is to be halted, the task of strengthening environmental regulations is more urgently needed than ever. Yet another key feature of economic globalisation is *de*regulation. The competitive dynamic that economic globalization creates, and the new trade rules of the global economy principally administered by the WTO, are causing governments around the world to roll back and hold back legislative and fiscal measures designed to protect the natural environment. Constraints on ecologically destructive corporate activity are thus being removed, just when they are needed most.

THE IMPACT OF GLOBAL COMPETITION

As the economy and corporate activity have become global, democratic government has remained nationally based, enabling corporations to function increasingly beyond the reach of public accountability and control, with very serious implications for the possibility of achieving the level of environmental protection that is so desperately needed.

In their battles to thwart environmental regulations or taxes, corporate executives tell regulators that if environmental costs, whether real or perceived, are imposed on them, they will be forced to reflect them in the price of their goods. Because their goods must compete in a global market with goods that do not carry such environmental costs, their company, they claim, will be at a systematic competitive disadvantage and, over time, will go out of business, shedding precious jobs. If that strategy fails, corporations can use the ultimate threat: to use their new freedom – created by the dismantling of barriers to trade and investment – to relocate to another country with less onerous environmental regulations or enforcement (see Chapter 12).

Governments in both the industrialized and the industrializing world have proven utterly susceptible to such arguments and threats. Once their countries are part of the global economy, they are invariably desperate to attract inward investment to generate jobs, facilitate the transfer of new technologies that improve productivity and increase economic growth and hence GDP. They are also invariably intimidated or bought off by the enormously increased wealth and economic power of transnational corporations that has resulted from economic globalization. The assets and sales of the largest transnational corporations are now far in excess of the GNP of most countries in the world. Indeed, 51 of the largest 100 economies in the world (excluding banking and financial institutions) are now corporations (cited by Karliner in *The Corporate Planet*, 1997, p5).

As corporations use their new strength and mobility in the global economy to exert political influence, notably by playing off states and communities against one another to leverage optimum investment conditions, a global 'race to the bottom' has been initiated, in which standards fall towards the level of the most desperate. Many environmental protections have been overturned or left unenforced and countless others prevented from seeing the light of day – all so that national companies remain or feel they remain competitive in the global economy, and foreign corporations are induced to invest.

Leading the drive to deregulate are developing countries. Whether prompted by IMF–World Bank structural adjustment programmes or unilateral governmental initiatives, the aim is the same: to be competitive enough to attract and retain foreign investment. And for developing countries such as India, this has meant rolling back environmental laws. Prohibitions against siting industrial facilities in ecologically sensitive areas have been removed and conservation zones stripped of their status so that cement plants, bauxite mines, prawn aquaculture and luxury hotels can be built. Forestry regulations have been relaxed for the pulp and paper industry, fisheries controls weakened for fishing transnationals, and mining laws watered down for mining corporations (Karliner, 1997, p146).

An increasing number of developing countries are going even further to sacrifice their natural environments on the altar of global competitiveness. They are creating hundreds of so-called 'free-trade zones', usually situated near key communications centres within their countries, and in which lax environmental enforcement is part of a package of measures designed to establish 'ideal' investment climates for foreign corporations. In the process, whole regions are being ecologically decimated. A particularly notorious free-trade zone is located on the Mexican side of the border with the US and is populated by more than 3400 factories known as *maquiladoras* (see Chapter 12). In China too, *maquiladora*-type zones have sprung up in the provinces of Guandong and Fujian, where low wages and lax environmental controls are attracting billions of dollars of investment.

The competitive pressures of the global economy also undermine ecological best practice in developing countries. Agriculture is a good example. Enormous volumes of staple crops – such as wheat, maize and rice – are grown for export in the North, in monocultures, with the aid of very high and unsustainable levels of chemical and mechanical inputs, as well as genetic engineering technology, and are benefitting from huge subsidies and economies of scale. With the dismantling of import barriers, these crops now flood markets in developing countries, fatally undercutting small-scale, low-input agriculture that is unable to compete. The more ecologically sustainable system of agriculture therefore goes to the wall. And the only way left for farmers in those countries to compete is to imitate the system of agriculture of their industrialized world competitors – with further devastating consequences for the natural environment. As Mexico's agriculture minister, Romarico Arroyo, recently said, with 25 per cent of Mexican corn imports now genetically modified, 'if we don't put genetic engineering to use, it will be difficult for us to compete', despite the damage to Mexican biodiversity that could result (cited in Tricks and Mandel-Campbell, 1999).

The forces of market competition undermine ecological best practice in developing nations in another way. Many such countries have slashed budgets dedicated to protecting the environment, since reducing non-commercial expenditure to lower the tax burden and increase competitiveness is often a condition of receiving an IMF–World Bank SAL. To cite two examples: the budget for the Mexican environmental protection agency was cut by 60 per cent in real terms between 1986 and 1989 (cited by Bello in Mander and Goldsmith, 1996, p283); and in 1998, Brazil's environment budget was cut by 66 per cent, and funds dedicated to protecting the Amazon rainforest were reduced from US$61.1 million to US$6.4 million (Steven Schwartzman, Environmental Defence Fund, Washington, DC).

If that were not enough, some industrializing countries will go even further to placate the gods of competitiveness and foreign investment. As an advertisement placed in *Fortune* magazine by the Philippine government has said: 'To attract companies like yours. . . we have felled mountains, razed jungles, filled swamps, moved rivers, relocated towns. . . all to make it easier for you and your business to do business here' (cited by Korten, 1995, p159).

To compete, as industrialized nations must in the global economy, with such countries and, which is still more often the case, with states at similar levels of economic development, they too have pursued deregulation programmes with serious consequences for environmental protection. The Reagan administration, for example, set up a taskforce on regulatory relief, headed by Vice-President George Bush, that was heavily involved in weakening, rolling back and obstructing environmental, consumer and worker safety protections. In 1989, during the Bush administration, Vice-President Quayle's council on competitiveness undertook the same work. The council was active in opening up half of American protected wetlands for development, and tabling over 100 obstructive amendments to the EPA's implementation proposals for the 1990 Clean Air Act (according to Public Citizen's Congress Watch). In the mid 1990s, another frenzy of environmental deregulation began, undertaken this time by the Republican-controlled US Congress led by House Speaker Newt Gingrich. It took place, in part at least, as a result of pressure from corporations using powerful new weapons available to them in the global economy.

In 1995, for example, transnational timber corporation Boise Cascade used the threat of relocating some of its operations to Mexico to try to water down US environmental standards. Its threat was credible because earlier that year it had closed mills in Oregon and Idaho and set up production in Guerrero, Mexico, to exploit lax environmental regulations and other new investment 'opportunities' fostered there by NAFTA. 'How many more mills will be closed,' Boise Cascade spokesman Doug Bertels told the *Idaho Statesman*, 'depends on what Congress does' (case and quote cited by Karliner, 1997, p154). It can be no coincidence that that same year, Congress passed the Timber Salvage Rider, designed to make US timber producers more competitive by opening up US national forests to deregulated logging at subsidized prices.

The drive to maintain economic competitiveness in industrialized countries extends beyond the overturning of existing regulations. It is also preventing governments from raising sufficient taxation from business and channelling that revenue into environmental programmes. If direct or indirect taxation is hiked, either industrial competitiveness is reduced, or corporations use their new-found global mobility in the world economy to relocate to tax havens or lower-tax countries. Either way, government revenues, that urgently need to be invested in renewable energy and energy efficiency technologies, public transport, forest regeneration or environmental cleanup operations, are significantly reduced.

THE IMPACT OF THE HARD RULES OF THE GLOBAL ECONOMY

If any environmental protections survive the onslaught of competitive deregulation, many are now vulnerable to being struck down by the WTO and the 'hard' rules of the global economy that the WTO is primarily responsible for enforcing. The principal purpose of these rules and of the WTO is to eliminate barriers to trade. Because many national and international environmental laws and agreements often restrict trade in some way, the WTO has the power to override, weaken, eliminate or prevent them from ever being drawn up. Under the rules, when there is a conflict, free trade effectively takes precedence over all other considerations – including that of protecting the natural environment.

Officially, global trade rules do allow for the adoption or enforcement of measures 'necessary to protect human, animal or plant life or health' and those 'relating to the conservation of exhaustible natural resources' (Article XX of GATT). But such measures must run the gauntlet of impossible legal hurdles created by a host of trade rules and rulings before these provisions can apply, rendering them virtually meaningless.

For example, no environmental measure is allowed if it is 'applied in a manner which would constitute a means of arbitrary or unjustifiable discrimination between countries where the same conditions prevail' or if it represents 'a disguised restriction on international trade' (Article XX of GATT). The same rule also states that no measures designed to conserve exhaustible natural resources are permissible unless they 'are made effective in conjunction with restrictions on domestic production or consumption' (cited by Shrybman, 1999, p22). No measure can, in fact, discriminate among foreign producers, or between foreign and domestic producers of a 'like' product (Articles I and III of GATT). In addition, no environmental measure affecting trade will be judged legitimate unless it is proved to be both 'necessary' and 'the least trade restrictive' way to achieve the conservation or environmental goal it is seeking (Article 2.2 of the WTO Agreement on Technical Barriers to Trade) (cited by Shrybman, 1999, p82). Moreover, no standards on food safety, biotechnology, pesticides, and plants and animals generally that affect trade are allowable unless an international scientific consensus is reached that such standards are scientifically justified, according to risk assessment (as stated by various articles of the WTO Agreement on the Application of Sanitary and Phytosanitary Measures).

All of these highly restrictive conditions provide enormous scope for subjective interpretation – scope that the biased nature of the WTO dispute resolution process has ensured is exploited fully in the interests of asserting the primacy of free trade over all environmental considerations (see Chapter 16).

In every case to date, WTO rules which restrict the ability of governments to implement policies that might even indirectly interfere with trade have been given expansive interpretation by WTO tribunals. Extremely narrow interpretation, meanwhile, has been given to provisions that might create space for environmental exceptions to free trade. That explains why every environmental or conservation measure that has been ruled upon so far by the WTO, and GATT before it, has been shot down. It also explains why the mere threat or possibility of WTO action has been sufficient to persuade many countries to change their laws voluntarily to be 'WTO compliant'. Under this so-called 'chilling effect', countless existing or prospective measures that are vital to environmental protection are either under threat or are no longer even considered by governments.

Among a whole raft of environmental controls that are now at risk because of world trade rules are those that apply to exports. Exports controls can be an important tool for conserving and protecting important and scarce natural resources, such as forests, fish and water, particularly when larger and larger volumes of these 'resources' are being exploited for global export. When governments have imposed export bans on raw materials to promote conservation and local employment in the past, such as the Canadian ban on the export of raw logs and unprocessed fish, they have had an immediate and obvious impact on the rate of resource exploitation (Shrybman, 1999, p60).

Such policies, however, are illegal under GATT–WTO rules, and tribunal rulings have confirmed that. The 1908 Canadian Fisheries Act prohibiting the export of unprocessed salmon and herring, for example, was struck down by a GATT panel, following a US challenge in 1986 designed to secure a larger share of Canada's valuable fisheries resources for its own domestic canning industry.

GATT–WTO rules also prevent the adoption of effective controls on imports, with serious implications for environmental laws and regulations. Quotas or bans on imports are forbidden, as is any discrimination among foreign producers and between foreign and domestic producers of a 'like' product – including through tariff policy. That means that no distinction can be made between products that look alike, even if the methods used to manufacture or produce them differ. Given that many goods and commodities are produced, grown, harvested and extracted in ways that seriously harm the natural environment, outlawing the ability to discriminate against goods that are produced in such ways removes an essential tool for achieving ecological sustainability (see Chapter 16).

We thus have a lose–lose situation for environmental protection. If governments only allow products to enter domestic markets on condition that they conform to domestic environmental production standards, such behaviour can be found in breach of GATT rules and banned by the WTO. That is exactly what has happened to key clauses of the US Marine Mammal Act that blocked imports of tuna caught in ways that kill dolphins, and to key clauses of the US Endangered Species Act restricting imports of shrimp caught without devices that reduce sea turtle deaths. If, on the other hand, governments allow imports of products that do not meet domestic environmental production standards, as is now the case with regard to tuna and shrimp in the US, those standards will clearly be undermined and domestic producers who abide by them (and whose goods are consequently often more costly) undercut and potentially forced out of business.

Given that the laws involved in both the tuna–dolphin and shrimp–turtle cases could be considered as part of attempts to fulfil the goals of multilateral environment agreements (MEAs) to protect endangered species, such as CITES, each ruling and the logic that lay behind it has serious ramifications for MEAs. Most MEAs contain trade instruments that can require other countries to change their policies and practices in pursuit of global environmental goals. Most, for example, either discriminate against 'like' products according to how they are made or where they are from, or generally restrict imports or exports in some way. Under GATT–WTO rules, most MEAs could thus be challenged.

As Steven Shrybman, director of the West Coast Environmental Law Foundation, explains, MEAs such as CITES, the Montreal Protocol and the Basel Convention violate GATT rules banning the use of quantitative trade controls, since each of these MEAs seeks to control or ban trade in endangered species, ozone-depleting chemicals and hazardous wastes respectively. By allowing different rules to be applied to foreign and domestic producers, these MEAs also violate the GATT requirement for 'national treatment'. The Basel Convention and CITES, for instance, seek respectively to restrict international trade in waste and endangered species, but do not regulate domestic trade or consumption. CITES and the Montreal Protocol also violate GATT rules by discriminating between 'like' products, according, respectively, to whether or not a product comes from a country where a particular species is threatened or is a full party to the protocol (Shrybman, 1999, pp20–21).

At least seven other MEAs, including the UN's Convention on Climate Change and the Kyoto Protocol, contravene GATT and WTO rules and are hence at risk, according to the World Wide Fund for Nature (WWF) (WWF press release, 4 October 1999). The threat posed is serious, especially since a proposal by the European Union that MEAs should override WTO rules was rejected by the WTO's committee on trade and the environment.

The only standards the WTO is keen to recognize are those international ones shaped by industry that it can use to overturn or lower national environmental standards. The harmonizing down of environmental and food standards in that way is the purpose of two WTO agreements – one on technical barriers to trade (TBT) and the other on the application of sanitary and phytosanitary measures (SPS).

Under the TBT agreement, national environmental laws are defined as 'technical barriers to trade' (also referred to as 'non-tariff barriers') and must be replaced with international standards where such standards have been established. Rather than harmonizing upward and thus improving protection everywhere, a lowering of standards usually results, since the process of reaching a consensus among governments subject to heavy industry lobbying often results in adopting the lowest common denominator. Worse, under the TBT agreement, such standards place a ceiling on environmental regulation, but no floor. Already, TBT provisions have been used to undermine or threaten a number of environmental regulations (see Chapter 16).

The WTO's SPS agreement – governing standards on food safety, biotechnology, pesticides and plants and animals generally – sets even stricter conditions for governments seeking to maintain or introduce any national standards that surpass weak, industry-shaped international ones recognized by the WTO. Governments must, in effect, demonstrate that an international scientific consensus has been reached in support of the proposition that their higher standards are scientifically justified, according to risk assessments. Absence of such a consensus constitutes proof that the protection is not justified and that it therefore constitutes an illegal barrier to trade. This rule is in fundamental contradiction to the precautionary principle – based on the premise that it is safer not to wait for complete scientific justification to take action to prevent potentially harmful effects, because scientific proof and complete scientific consensus can take years to establish, if at all.

The precautionary principle lies behind the EU's ban on the sale and import of beef from cattle treated with artificial growth hormones, which EU studies show increase both the risk of illness in treated animals and in humans who consume them. Even though the ban applies to domestic and foreign products alike, following a complaint from the US and Canada – the principal exporters of hormone-treated beef – two WTO panels ruled that the ban is illegal because it has been taken in advance of scientific certainty (which is forbidden under WTO provisions).

The panel would only accept the standard for artificial hormones in meat adopted by the Codex Alimentarius Commission in 1995, which stated that such meat was safe. The Codex standard, however, is highly controversial. It was set under undue industry influence (140 of the world's largest multinational food and agrochemical companies participated in Codex meetings held between 1989 and 1991 alone), and instead of being arrived at through consensus, it resulted from a vote of a bare majority of 33 countries in favour, 29 against and 7 abstentions (Greenpeace US study cited by Korten, 1995, p179). In these circumstances, the adoption of the European ban seems all the more legitimate. But for the WTO, the EU lacked sufficient scientific proof and it ruled that the ban would consequently have to be eliminated, or else the imposition of trade sanctions would follow. (To date, the EU has refused to comply with the WTO ruling and the ban thus remains in place, although the US and Canada – the two countries most affected by the ban – have been authorized by the WTO to impose tariffs on imports of European produce to the sum of US$128 million.)

The implications of that ruling for other regional or national health or environmental standards around the world are extremely serious. The EU ban on imports of certain genetically modified foods and crops could yet be threatened. Further conflict and further environmental damage are likely.

The prospects for national environmental protections will only become worse if, as proposed, during the next round of world trade talks, the WTO adopts the investment measures that featured in the proposed multilateral agreement on investment (MAI) that was defeated at the OECD in 1998. Under MAI-type investment rules, for example, national regulations preventing corporations with bad environmental track records from investing domestically could be forbidden. Laws requiring new investors to meet certain environmental conditions, such as having to transfer environmentally sound technology, could be banned. And foreign corporations could be given the power to sue national governments directly for monetary compensation if they believed government policies, including environmental or public health laws, 'expropriated' or undercut their future profits.

A clear indication of the devastating consequences such rules would have for regional, national and local environmental regulations can by gauged from the application of identical rules under NAFTA. A recent case is particularly illustrative. In 1996, the Canadian government introduced legislation banning the import and interprovincial transport of MMT – a neurotoxin used as a fuel additive that causes irreparable damage to vehicle pollution control systems, thereby increasing emissions of harmful gases such as carbon monoxide, carbon dioxide and hydrocarbons. As soon as the law was proclaimed, the only North American manufacturer of MMT, the US multinational Ethyl Corporation, sued the Canadian government for US$350 million in damages. It argued that the Canadian law violated national treatment rules of NAFTA and constituted an expropriation of Ethyl's Canadian investments. It even claimed that merely by introducing and debating the bill, the Canadian government harmed Ethyl's international reputation, thereby 'expropriating' part of its future profits. Lawyers advised the government that it would lose under NAFTA rules, and so the ban on MMT was repealed and millions of dollars and an apology were provided in compensation.

That outcome has set a terrifying precedent. According to Steven Shrybman, in its wake, 'More than one trade lawyer from the corporate sector has warned that there will be many more such suits as their clients make more frequent use of their rights under these investment treaties to "harass" governments contemplating regulatory initiatives the corporations oppose' (Shrybman, 1999, p134). The adoption of NAFTA-style investment rules by the WTO would therefore have disastrous consequences.

The logic that underlies such rules is nothing less than suicidal. Unless their adoption by the WTO is fully rejected, and unless the *current* rules of the WTO are changed, we can fully expect the list of essential environmental laws struck down in the name of free trade to grow ever longer – further emasculating democracy and crippling the ability of societies everywhere to address effectively the environmental and social crises of modern times.

CONCLUSION

At the core of the problem that economic globalization poses for the environment is the issue of scale: the transformation of economic activity from the small and local to the large and global, a change that underlies nearly all definitions of globalization. It is often referred to as *delocalization*: the uprooting and displacement of activities and relationships that until recently were local, into networks of activities and relationships whose reach is distant or worldwide (Gray, 1998, p57; Giddens, 1990, p64). The fundamental problem with that transformation when it is applied to economic activity is that it ends up violating the basic rules of environmental sustainability *and* sound economics.

Environmental sustainability requires economic accountability, which is best ensured at a local level. In a local economy, when a locally owned investment damages the environment, the investor and his or her local community are more likely to be immediately aware and directly affected by it. And as the local community is more likely to know or have access to that investor, it has a strong incentive and capacity to force the investor to address the problem rapidly. In a global economy, in contrast, power is detached from responsibility and those who take decisions are separated from those who are affected by them, thus ensuring that environmental problems continue unabated.

Economic globalization, moreover, increases the scale of environmental damage to a global level by extending the industrial market model throughout the world to vast swathes of the planet where it had never previously existed. Yet the global economy cannot expand indefinitely if the ecosystems on which it depends continue to deteriorate. If it attempts to do so, the planet will become uninhabitable. In the words of the United Nations *Global Environmental Outlook* report for the year 2000, 'The present course is unsustainable and postponing action is no longer an option' (UNEP, 1999).

Ultimately, we cannot live, and our economies cannot function, without a healthy natural environment. So if we are serious about giving our children a future, more of the same is not an option: fundamental reform is our only alternative.

Chapter 18

The World Trade Organization and Developing World Agriculture

Vandana Shiva

In this chapter, Vandana Shiva describes how the transformation of peasant agriculture in India to a globally industrialized model has reduced food security, threatened local businesses and biodiversity, driven farmers off their lands, and opened the door for global corporations to take over the nation's food processing. Shiva then examines the forces driving the globalization of agriculture, including the agribusiness giants and two of the WTO agreements these firms have promoted: the agreements on agriculture and intellectual property rights.

Vandana Shiva is a physicist, founder and president of the Research Foundation for Science Technology and Ecology, and one of India's leading activists. She played a key role in the famous Chipko movement to save the Himalayan forests and now works on behalf of Indian farmers, trying to resist the introduction of globalized industrial agriculture and biotechnology into Indian food production. She is a member of the board of directors of the International Forum on Globalization, and was a recipient of the Right Livelihood Award (also known as the alternative Nobel Peace Prize). Her most recent book is Biopiracy: The Plunder of Nature and Knowledge *(Boston: South End Press, 1997).*

Supporters of globalization often claim that this process is natural, inevitable and evolutionary and one that is bringing prosperity and growth, embracing us all and knitting us into a global village. Only by participating in global markets, they say, can developing world people get access to jobs and better lives. In reality, globalization is not a natural process of inclusion. It is a planned project of exclusion that siphons the resources and knowledge of the poor of the South into the global marketplace, stripping people of their life-support systems, livelihoods and lifestyles.

Global trade rules, as enshrined in the WTO Agreement on Agriculture (AOA) and in the TRIPs agreement, are primarily rules of robbery, camouflaged by arithmetic and legalese. In this economic hijack, the corporations gain, and people and nature lose.

The WTO's overall goal of promoting 'market competition' serves two functions. Firstly, it transforms all aspects of life into commodities for sale. Culture, biodiversity, food, water, livelihoods, needs and rights are all transformed and reduced to markets. Secondly, the destruction of nature, culture and livelihoods is then justified on the basis of the rules of competition. Policy-makers attack ethical and ecological rules that sustain and maintain life, claiming that they are 'protectionist' barriers to trade. In reality, the WTO does not reduce protectionism – it merely replaces protections for people and nature with protections for corporations.

The global reach of corporations to take over the resources of the poor of the developing world is made possible not just by the reduction and removal of tariffs, one of the goals of the WTO. It is facilitated by the removal of ethical and ecological limits on what can be owned as private property and what can be traded. In this way, globalization is completing the project of colonization that led to the conquest and ownership of land and territory. Biological resources and water, the very basis of life's processes, are being colonized, privatized and commodified.

Agriculture, which is still the primary livelihood for three-quarters of humanity, and which is as much a cultural activity as an economic one, is also threatened by 'trade liberalization', driven both by the structural adjustment programmes of the World Bank and the IMF, and by the WTO's Agreement on Agriculture. The globalization of food and agriculture systems, in effect, means the corporate take-over of the food chain, the erosion of food rights, the destruction of the cultural diversity of food and the biological diversity of crops, and the displacement of millions from land-based, rural livelihoods. Global free trade in food and agriculture is the biggest refugee creation programme in the world, far exceeding the impact of Kosovo. It is equivalent to the ethnic cleansing of the poor, the peasantry, and small farmers of the developing world.

GLOBALIZATION OF INDIA'S AGRICULTURE

Trade and investment liberalization have led to a dramatic transformation of agriculture in India that has had a devastating impact on peasant farmers. These policies have brought about:

- a shift in production from food to export crops that has reduced food security;
- a flood of imports that have wiped out local businesses and diversity; and
- an opening for global corporations to take over the control of food processing.

The shift to export crops

Cotton: seeds of suicide

Economic globalization is leading to a concentration of the seed industry, the entry of global corporations into agriculture, the increased use of pesticides, and, finally, increased debt, despair and sometimes suicide among small farmers. Capital-intensive, corporate-controlled agriculture is being spread into regions where peasants are poor but, until now, have been self-sufficient in food. In the regions where industrial agriculture has been introduced through globalization, higher costs are making it virtually impossible for small farmers to survive.

The new export-oriented policies that are part of agricultural globalization have led to a shift in India from the production of food crops to commodities for exports, such as cotton. Cotton cultivation has expanded even into semi-arid areas such as Warangal in Andhra Pradesh, where farmers traditionally grew paddy, pulses, millets, oilseeds and vegetable crops. Enticed by promises that cotton would be like 'white gold', yielding high profits, farmers in Warangal have nearly tripled the amount of land used for cotton production in the past decade, while slashing production of traditional food grains such as *jawar* and *bajra*.

However, what these farmers have learned is that while cash crops such as cotton may fetch higher prices, they also demand a higher level of expenditure. Under corporate pressure, farmers have largely switched from planting open-pollinated seeds, which can be saved by farmers, to hybrids that need to be purchased every year at a high cost. Because hybrids are very vulnerable to pest attacks, pesticide use has also increased. Expenditures on pesticides in the district went up from US$2.5 million for the entire decade of the 1980s to US$50 million in 1997 – a 2000 per cent increase. For poor peasants, this cost could be borne only through debts.

Because trade liberalization had also led to budget cutbacks on extension and withdrawal of low-interest credit from cooperatives and public-sector banks, peasants have had to take high-interest loans from the same companies that sell them hybrid seeds and pesticides. Thus, the corporations have become money lenders, extension agents, seed suppliers and pesticide salesmen rolled into one. As a result, peasants have become buried under the weight of unpayable debt. This financial stress is blamed for an epidemic of suicides in Warangal district. More than 500 farmers took their own lives in 1998, and the suicides have continued in 1999.

In the regions where high costs of industrial agriculture introduced through globalization are already pushing farmers to suicide, Monsanto has tried to introduce genetically engineered cotton seeds. While the argument used to promote these crops in the less-developed world is that they will increase yields, actually trials have shown a decrease in yields and an increase in the use of pesticides. In protest, farmers in Andhra Pradesh and Karnataka have uprooted the genetically engineered cotton, and the Research Foundation for Science, Technology and Ecology has filed a case in the Indian Supreme Court to stop the introduction of these genetically engineered crops in Indian agriculture. The case is based on the belief that genetic engineering would introduce new ecological and economic risks that developing world peasants cannot afford.

Shrimp factories

The shift from a 'food first' to an 'export first' policy is justified on grounds of food security, because export earnings are supposed to pay for food imports. In fact, export-oriented agriculture has reduced food security by encouraging a shift from small-scale, sustainable production to large-scale, non-sustainable industrial production. It also brings changes in ownership over natural resources and means of production, from small autonomous producer–owners to large corporate and commercial interests. Peasants are displaced from farming, while commercial interests take over land for industrial-scale production of export commodities such as shrimp, flowers, vegetables and meat. These enterprises often have negative environmental impacts, creating further hardship for local communities.

The transformation of shrimp farming in India is a prime example of the social and environmental costs of industrial agriculture. While small-scale, indigenous shrimp farming has been sustainable over centuries, shrimp exports require the establishment of factory farms for shrimp production. Each hectare of a shrimp farm needs 80 'shadow hectares' for absorbing the ecological costs of factory farming of shrimp. 'Shadow hectares' are the units required to supply resources to, and absorb the waste from, a particular economic activity.

Shrimp farming is so damaging because it requires enormous quantities of fish to be caught at sea for shrimp feed, most of which is converted to waste that is poured into the sea, polluting the water and damaging mangroves. Shrimp farming also destroys coastal agriculture because the shrimp factories require the pumping of seawater into the ponds for shrimp production. This causes salinization, reducing drinkingwater supplies and destroying trees and crops near the factories.

These costs undermine the claims that shrimp exports are a major source of economic growth. For each US$1 earned by corporations through exports of shrimp to consumers in the US, Europe and Japan, an estimated US$10 worth of damage is done to India's natural resources and local economic income. This includes the destruction of mangroves, water, agriculture and fisheries.

Shrimp factories have met with stiff resistance in India. In December 1996, local communities and environmental groups won a case in the Indian Supreme Court to ban industrial shrimp farming. However, the shrimp industry received a stay order and continues to operate. On 29 May 1999, four fishermen were killed when they protested against the commercial shrimp operators called the 'shrimp mafia' in the Chilka Lake in Orissa.

This tragedy illustrates how the inequalities aggravated or generated by export-oriented agriculture can also lead to violations of human rights and subversion of law and order. Trade can only be increased by taking resources away from people's subsistence and survival. When people attempt to defend their human right to work and live, commercial interests that gain from exports often work with the state apparatus to crush people's movements. Many people lose what little they have. In the most extreme cases, such as that of the Orissa fishermen, they pay for exports with their lives.

Other export crops: costs exceed earnings

Like shrimp exports, flower, meat and vegetable exports have costs that often far exceed the earnings generated. Large-scale meat exports, for example, have an external 'shadow' cost that is ten times higher than export earnings. This is due to the former ecological contribution of livestock in small-scale agriculture, now on the wane.

Particularly in developing countries, livestock are not just meat on legs. Animals are the primary source of fertilizer in the form of organic manure. They also generate energy for farm operations by ploughing and by helping with agroprocessing – for example, with edible oil extraction via animal-driven *ghanis*. Livestock in India help produce US$17 million worth of milk, and US$1.5 billion worth of food grain; they also provide US$17 million worth of energy. If the animals are slaughtered, all of these benefits are lost. In the case of one export-oriented slaughterhouse alone, meat exports earned US$45 million, whereas the estimated contribution of the slaughtered animals to the economy if they had been allowed to live was $230 million.

Under the pressure of so-called 'liberalization' policies, food prices have doubled and the poor have had to cut their consumption in half. Prices have increased because food has been exported, creating domestic scarcity, at the same time that food subsidies have been withdrawn. As a housewife in Bombay stated: 'We are eating half of what we used to after food prices doubled in the last year. Even *dhal* is a luxury now. After milk prices increased, I stopped buying milk as well.'

Export-oriented agriculture is also creating an agricultural apartheid, with the developing world being asked to stop growing food staples and instead to grow luxury products for the rich North. Production of food staples is now concentrated in the US and in the hands of a few multinational seed companies and grain trading companies.

Imports: diversity destroyed

As countries are forced to destroy their agricultural systems to grow and export commodities, both cultural diversity and biological diversity disappear. Diverse cereals, oilseeds and legumes are displaced by soybeans from the US. While exports destroy local food systems by diverting resources and changing ownership patterns, imports also destroy food systems by hijacking markets.

In August 1999, there was a case of mustard oil adulteration that was restricted to the city of Delhi, but affected all local brands of oil. In response, the government banned mustard oil, the main cooking oil in North India, and removed all restrictions on edible oil imports. Soybean and soy oil imports were liberalized or deregulated. Within one growing season, millions of oilseed-producing farmers growing mustard, groundnut, sesame and niger had lost the market for their diverse oil seed crops. Liberalized imports of soybeans have destroyed the entire edible oil production and processing in India. Millions of small mills have closed down. Prices of oilseeds have collapsed and farmers cannot even recover what they have spent on cultivation. Sesame, linseed and mustard have started to disappear from the fields as cheap, subsidized imports of soybeans are dumped on the Indian market. These imports totalled three million tons in one year (a 60 per cent rise compared to earlier years) and cost nearly US$1 billion, thus worsening the country's balance of payments situation.

US soybeans are cheap not because of cheap production but because of subsidies. The price of soybeans is US$155 a ton, and this low price is possible because the US government pays US$193 a ton to US soybean farmers, who would not otherwise be able to stay in production given the low commodity prices. This government support is not really a farmer subsidy; it is an indirect corporate subsidy. As heavily subsidized soybeans flooded India's domestic market, prices crashed by more than two-thirds. The local oil-processing industry, from the small-scale *ghanis* to larger mills, started to close down. Domestic oilseed production declined, and domestic edible oil prices crashed. Groundnut prices went down by 3 per cent from 48 rupees per kilogramme to 37 rupees per kilogramme. Meanwhile, some farmers protesting against the collapse of their markets were shot and killed.

Corporate control of processing and packaging

Global agribusiness is now attempting to take over food processing by making fresh, locally produced food appear backward, and stale food clothed in aluminium and plastic appear 'modern'. Industrial processing and packaging was first applied to edible oils, destroying the livelihoods of millions of oil mill operators and small farmers because of imported soybeans. An attempt is now being made to take over the wheat economy.

Wheat is called *kanak,* the word for gold in North India. The Indian wheat economy is based on decentralized, small-scale local production, processing and distribution systems. Wheat and flour *(atta)* provide livelihoods and nutrition to millions of farmers, traders *(artis),* and local mill operators *(chakki wallas).*

The decentralized, small-scale, household-based economy of food production and processing is huge in aggregate. It generates millions of livelihoods while ensuring that fresh and wholesome food at accessible prices is available to people. Moreover, such production and processing has no negative environmental impacts.

Millions of Indian farmers grow 6050 million tons of wheat every year. Most of this is bought as wheat by consumers from the local corner store *(kirana)* and taken to the local *chakki walla*. A chain of *artis,* or traders, brings the wheat from the farm to the local shops.

It is estimated that more than 3.5 million family-run *kirana* shops supply wheat to Indian consumers. More than two million small neighbourhood mills produce fresh flour. In addition, flour is also produced by millions of women working at the household level. The rolling pin *(belan)* used for making *rotis* has always been a symbol of women's power. It is often mistakenly said that only 2 per cent of food is processed in India. This is because officials ignore women's work in the home and the contribution of this work to the national economy.

While 40 million tons of wheat is traded, only 15 million tons is purchased directly as *atta* because Indians love freshness and quality in food. Less than 1 per cent of the consumed *atta* carries a brandname because Indian consumers trust their own supervision of quality at the local *chakki* better than a brandname attached to stale, packaged flour.

This decentralized, small-scale economy based on millions of producers, processors and traders works with very little capital and very little infrastructure. People are the substitute for capital and infrastructure. However, such a people-centred economy impedes large-scale profits for big agribusiness. They are therefore eyeing the Indian wheat economy to transform it into a source of profits.

In an industry report entitled *Faida* (profit), the hijack of the wheat and *atta* supply by global agribusiness is described as the 'wheat opportunity in India'. The plan is based on making farmers directly dependent on agribusiness corporations for the purchase of inputs such as seeds, destroying local seed supply and displacing the local *artis* or traders and destroying the local *chakki wallas*.

The destruction of millions of livelihoods, of the local decentralized economy, and of people's access to fresh and cheap *atta,* is described as 'modernization of the food chain'. In the developing world, packaged food is described as the food of the rich, even though the rich in industrialized countries, in fact, eat fresh food, while the poor are forced to eat heavily processed and packaged food.

India's wheat and *atta* economy is complex and highly developed, but global agribusiness defines it as underdeveloped because the big players such as Cargill and Archer Daniels Midland (ADM) do not control it. As the *Faida* report states, 'The Indian wheat sector is currently at a nascent stage of development. Despite its importance, the industry is at a very early stage of improvement.'

The main criterion used to declare India's wheat economy as underdeveloped is that the global corporations are missing from the scene. Underdevelopment is the absence of corporate control. 'Development' is then defined as equivalent to the corporate hijack of the economy.

A decentralized, locally controlled and small-scale system is defined as 'nascent' and 'underdeveloped', while monopolized food systems are defined as 'developed'. The hijack of the food system is thus made to appear as the 'natural evolution' from small to big. Freshness and wholesomeness are defined as 'low technology'. Impure, stale flour with a brandname is defined as 'high quality'. This distorted attitude is reflected in a section of the *Faida* report that states, 'As a result of the inadequate technology used by the millers, the shelf life of flour in India is typically 15 to 20 days. This is very short when compared to the six months to a year achieved in the United States.' What the report fails to recognize is that the brandname players have no choice but to ensure a longer shelf life, given the huge distances between the factory and the markets.

The highest level of Orwellian doublespeak is being used to accomplish the hijack of wheat from Indian farmers and processors. Decentralization is defined as *fragmentation*. But *centralization* is defined as *integration,* even though decentralized, locally controlled systems are highly integrated while centrally controlled systems are based on the disintegration of ecosystems and local economic communities.

Agribusiness has already begun to get Indian consumers to doubt their own quality-control systems and to trust the brandnames. They see a potential corporate-controlled market that would generate 3000 *crore* or 30 billion rupees of profits through the sale of packaged brandname wheat. The corporate agenda for India is to introduce monopolies in wheat such as those of Cargill and ADM, and in seed such as those of Monsanto, Novartis, DuPont and Zeneca. These seed corporations demand monopolistic intellectual property rights to seed, forcing farmers to pay royalties while also controlling other inputs. This trend is moving the country toward an agricultural economy in which only a small number of people are involved – and only as tractor drivers and pesticide sprayers. All other functions of farmers – as maintainers of biodiversity, stewards of soil and water and seed breeders – are destroyed.

The *Faida* report claims that five million jobs will be 'created' by the take-over of the food chain by global corporations. However, it is well known that giant firms often invest in technology that displaces people. For example, ADM owns 200 grain elevators, 1900 barges, 800 trucks and tens of thousands of railcars to transport and store wheat. The number of jobs generated by ADM is not significant, however, because the company uses pneumatic blowers to load and unload grain and other technologies to lower labour costs.

Moreover, if one takes into account the 20–30 million farmers, 5 million *chakki wallas,* 5 million *artis,* 3.5 million *kirana* shops and the households dependent on them, at least 100 million people's livelihoods and sustenance will be destroyed by the industrialization of the wheat economy alone.

THE DRIVING FORCES BEHIND GLOBALIZATION OF AGRICULTURE

The agribusiness giants

Agribusiness giants such as Monsanto and Cargill have driven the process of globalization in their efforts to gain control over the world's agricultural economy, from selling seeds and other inputs, to trading commodities, to processing food.

One of the most ominous developments in the past decade has been the merger of chemical, pharmaceutical, biotechnology and seed companies to create what they call 'life sciences' corporations. A more accurate name would be 'death sciences' corporations because they produce genetically engineered, herbicide-tolerant seeds that lock farmers into dependence on chemical inputs, destroy biodiversity and render agriculture more vulnerable. These corporations are also genetically engineering sterile seed, through what is called 'Terminator technology', so that farmers cannot save seed and are forced to buy seed every year.

The WTO agreement on agriculture

All over the world, structural adjustment and trade liberalization have already driven millions of farmers off the land because of rising costs of production and collapsing prices of commodities. Instead of supporting policies that help farmers survive, WTO rules are driving small farmers to extinction and ensuring that agriculture is controlled by global corporations.

The WTO Agreement on Agriculture is a rule-based system for trade liberalization of agriculture that was pushed by the US in the Uruguay Round of the GATT. However, these rules are the wrong rules for protecting food security, nature and culture. Instead, they are perfectly shaped for the objective of corporate rule over our food and agriculture systems.

The AOA rules apply to countries, even though it is not countries or their farmers who engage in global trade in agriculture but global corporations such as Cargill. These firms gain from every rule that marginalizes farmers by removing support from agriculture. They gain from every rule that deregulates international trade, liberalizes exports and imports, and makes restrictions of export and imports illegal. Market openings through the AOA are therefore market openings for the Cargills and Monsantos.

The outcome of negotiations for the AOA should not be surprising, because global agribusiness corporations held tremendous influence over the negotiations. In fact, the US delegation was led by Clayton Yeutter, a former Cargill employee.

There are three components to the AOA:

- domestic support;
- market access;
- export competition.

Domestic support

The WTO clauses on 'domestic support' demand commitment to reduce domestic 'support' to producers by 20 per cent of the country's 1986–1988 level by 1999. For developing countries, this has been reduced to 13 per cent to be implemented over ten years.

Support is defined by a formula called the aggregate measure of support (AMS). The AMS calculates all domestic support policies that are considered to have a significant effect on the volume of production. The AMS is nothing more than a device to anaesthetize the public so that no one senses the hijack of food systems by corporate power. Through an extremely complicated and confusing system of 'amber box', 'green box' and 'blue box' labelling, the WTO regime makes it difficult for citizens, policy-makers and governments to figure out what is really happening.

Trade liberalization has, therefore, left India with an additional burden just for subsidies for chemical fertilizers. The politics of subsidies in the WTO is therefore clearly weighted in favour of industry and Northern agribusiness and against farmers, especially those of the developing world.

Market access

The WTO agreement on the import of food is entitled 'market access' and is covered by part III, articles 4 and 5 and annexure 3. All signatory countries must convert quantitative restrictions and other non-tariff measures into ordinary customs duties. This is referred to as 'tariffication'. Countries have to provide minimum market access, beginning with 1 per cent of the domestic consumption in the first year of the implementation period, to be increased in equal annual instalments to 2 per cent at the beginning of the fifth year. After that, it has to be increased to 4 per cent. 'Market access opportunities' are defined as 'imports as a percentage of the corresponding domestic consumption'.

Customs and other duties on imports are to be reduced by 36 per cent (24 per cent for developing countries) to facilitate imports at cheaper prices. Customs and other duties will not exceed one-third of the level of the customs duties – that is, these duties will be calculated on the basis of the difference between the import price and the trigger price. (The trigger price is the average of 1986 to 1988 prices.) Removal of quantitative restrictions on imports of agricultural commodities is a major goal of trade liberalization.

According to the UN's FAO, as a result of trade liberalization measures, Africa's food import bill will go up from US$8.4 billion to US$14.9 billion by the year 2000. For Latin America and the Caribbean, the value of increased imports is US$0.9 billion. For the Far East, the import bill will increase by US$4.1 billion. For the Near East, the import bill will increase to US$27 billion and the trade gap will widen from US$11 to US$19 billion by the year 2000.

Export competition

Articles 8–11 of the AOA deal with exports under the title 'export competition'. The official justification for the AOA is the removal of export subsidies that have facilitated the sale of large EU and US surpluses on the world market. The main elements of the export subsidy commitments are as follows:

- Export subsidies, measured in terms of both the volume of subsidized exports and in terms of budgetary expenditure on subsidies, have been capped.
- Developed countries are committed to reducing the volume of subsidized exports by 21 per cent and the expenditure on subsidies by 36 per cent, both over a six-year period (1995–2000).
- For developing countries, the reduction commitments are 14 per cent and 24 per cent for volume and expenditure respectively, while the implementation period (1995–2004) lasts ten years rather than six. However, governments of developing countries can continue to subsidize the cost of marketing exports of agricultural products including handling, upgrading and other processing costs and the costs of internal and international transport and freight.
- The agreement precludes export bans even in years of domestic shortages.

While the liberalization of exports was justified by the argument that Northern agricultural markets would open up to India, India's exports to Europe have actually declined from 13 per cent to 6 per cent. One of the reasons for this is because high subsidies and protectionist barriers are still largely maintained in the North. Thus, trade liberalization is a unidirectional phenomenon that opens markets in the South for Northern business and corporations but closes markets in the North for trade from the South.

Direct export subsidies of US$14.5 billion will still be allowed under the AOA. The export subsidies that developing countries are allowed are not subsidies to developing world farmers or the poor, because farmers do not export, companies do. Developing world governments are, therefore, allowed to support global corporations but not their farmers and the poor, since they can continue to subsidize transport, processing and marketing.

Transnational corporations therefore gain both from Northern subsidies and southern subsidies under WTO rules. Further Northern subsidies to agribusiness have not been touched. Since the WTO was established, the US has expanded export credit and marketing promotion programmes. Even IMF loans to developing world countries have been used for export subsidies to US agribusiness.

Dan Glickman, US secretary of agriculture, has stated, 'The main reason we have not lost more exports to Asia is because the [US Department of Agriculture] extended US US$2.1 billion in export credit guarantees. Without IMF actions another US$2 billion in agricultural exports would have been at great risk in the short term and far larger amounts in the long term.'

The 1996 US farm bill mandated US$5.5 billion for export promotion. An additional US$1 billion was granted for promoting sales to 'emerging markets'. Another US$90 million has been allocated for market access programmes which go to food and agriculture corporations for product promotion abroad.

WTO rules are for preserving and enhancing corporate subsidies and withdrawing support to farmers and rural communities whether they refer to domestic support, market access or export competition. Protection of farmers' livelihoods, food security and sustainable agriculture requires major changes in the AOA.

Need for a new paradigm

For these proposals to be realized, we need to build a movement around a new paradigm for food and agriculture that identifies trade liberalization itself as the cause of environmental degradation and loss of livelihoods for the poor in the South. Even where exports are possible, they are often at heavy social and ecological cost to commodities from the South. Therefore, the rules of the WTO must change: imports and exports should not be forced, and food and agriculture must be removed and exempted from the 'discipline' of free trade so that they can serve the objectives of food security and environmental protection.

Trade cannot, and must not, be made the highest objective to govern food systems because this implies the rule of trading interests – that is, the rule of global corporations. Corporations view food as a source of profits, not a source of life and livelihoods. Because their profits can grow only by destroying livelihoods and self-provisioning systems of seed production and food production, globalization of trade in agriculture implies genocide. Revising free trade logic is necessary if the life of humans and other species is to be protected.

Protection of domestic agriculture needs to be recognized as a food security imperative, and WTO rules should not undermine food security by destroying local agriculture and food systems through subsidized dumping. Putting up tariff barriers to genocide is a moral imperative.

Developing world countries are now locked into growing export crops because of debt and balance of payment crises. Their exports should be facilitated through fair trade arrangements – trade that is not based on environmental destruction, the displacement of small peasants and the destruction of local food economies. Fair trade will not be ensured by the free trade rules of market access of WTO, which can be forced on the South but not on the North. It needs a spirit of solidarity and rules of cooperation. Genocidal market competition needs to be replaced by ethical trading, fair trade and new rules of North–South cooperation. We need to build a movement to allow countries to exclude food and agriculture from free trade arrangements, so that ecological and social justice concerns can be the basis of how food is produced, distributed and consumed.

TRIPS and biopiracy

In addition to the AOA, the WTO threatens developing world food and agriculture through the TRIPs agreement, which was introduced during the Uruguay Round of GATT. This agreement sets enforceable global rules on patents, copyrights and trademarks. TRIPs rules extend to living resources, so that genes, cells, seeds, plants and animals can now be patented and 'owned' as intellectual property. As a result, developing countries are being forced to reorganize their production and consumption patterns to allow monopolies by a handful of so-called 'Life Sciences' corporations that are, in reality, pedlars of death.

Over time, the consequences of TRIPs for the South's biodiversity and Southern people's rights to their diversity will be severe. No one will be able to produce or reproduce patented agricultural, medicinal, or animal products freely, thus eroding livelihoods of small producers and preventing the poor from using their own resources and knowledge to meet their basic needs of health and nutrition. Royalties for their use will have to be paid to the patentees and unauthorized production will be penalized, thus increasing the debt burden. Indian farmers, traditional practitioners and traders will lose their market share in local, national and global markets.

Neither TRIPs nor the US patent law recognize knowledge as a commons, nor do they recognize the collective, cumulative innovation embodied in indigenous knowledge systems. Thus, if indigenous knowledge is to be protected, then TRIPs and US patent laws must change. Nothing less than an overhaul of Western-style intellectual property rights (IPR) systems with their intrinsic weaknesses will stop the epidemic of biopiracy. And if biopiracy is not stopped, the everyday survival of ordinary Indians will be threatened, as, over time, our indigenous knowledge and resources will be used to make patented commodities for global trade. Global corporate profits will grow at the cost of the food rights, health rights and knowledge rights of one billion Indians, two-thirds of whom are too poor to meet their needs through the global marketplace.

Patents on indigenous knowledge and the use of plants are an 'enclosure' of the intellectual and biological commons on which the poor depend. Robbed of their rights and entitlements to freely use nature's capital – because that is the only capital they have access to – the poor in the developing world will be pushed to extinction. Like the diverse species on which they depend, they too are a threatened species.

CONCLUSION

The real millennium round for the WTO is the beginning of a new democratic debate about the future of the Earth and the future of its people. The centralized, undemocratic rules and structures of the WTO that are establishing global-corporate rule based on monopolies and monocultures must give way to an Earth democracy supported by decentralization and diversity. The rights of all species and the rights of all peoples must come before the rights of corporations to make limitless profits through limitless destruction.

Free trade is not leading to freedom. It is leading to slavery. Diverse life forms are being enslaved through patents on life, farmers are being enslaved into high-tech slavery, and countries are being enslaved into debt and dependence, and destruction of their domestic economies.

We want a new millennium based on economic democracy, not economic totalitarianism. The future is possible for humans and other species only if the principles of competition, organized greed, commodification of all life, mono-cultures and monopolies, and centralized global corporate control of our daily lives enshrined in the WTO are replaced by the principles of protection of people and nature, the obligation of giving and sharing diversity, and the decentralization and self-organization enshrined in our diverse cultures and national constitutions.

The WTO rules violate principles of human rights and ecological survival. They violate rules of justice and sustainability. They are rules of warfare against the people and the planet. Changing these rules is the most important democratic and human rights struggle of our time. It is a matter of survival.

Chapter 19

The World Trade Organization and the Liberalization of Trade in Healthcare and Services

Agnès Bertrand and Laurence Kalafatides

Under the General Agreement on Trade in Services, passed during the GATT Uruguay round and taken up by the World Trade Organization, nearly all the services that have so far been the prerogative of governments and whose fulfilment has provided much of the legitimacy in the eyes of the public have been opened up to competition from TNCs. These include health and education, which together provide a market worth something like US$5 trillion – a bonanza for the transnational corporations. It includes too – horrifying as it may seem – environmental services. It goes without saying that once they are privatized most of them will cease to be within the reach of the poor, especially the poor of developing countries. The authors show how this applies particularly to health services.

Agnès Bertrand graduated in philosophy from Nanterre University in France. She was general secretary of Ecoropa, a European network of ecological researchers and activists. The French branch of Ecoropa campaigned against GATT at a very early stage and launched the Farmers–consumers–ecologist Alliance. She is a member of the International Forum on Globalization and founder of the French think-tank Observatoire de la Mondialisation, one of the leading NGOs in France fighting the global economy.

Laurence Kalafatides is a freelance researcher and has become a specialist on GATS. She is vice-president of the Institute for the Relocalisation of the Economy based in Gard in France.

After World War II, public health became a major government concern, and access to healthcare for all came to be regarded as a fundamental human right in almost all the countries of the industrial West, and even some countries in the South. In line with these developments, the WHO formulated policies to promote these priorities. However, since the early 1990s, a major shift has occurred. Rather than being seen as a service that the state is morally obliged to provide to all its citizens, healthcare is increasingly considered a new field for commercial activity. Former director of the WHO Hirochi Nakajima approves of this development. For him, healthcare must take its rightful place in the market system, and thereby become the latest object of consumption (he is quoted in *Le Monde Diplomatique*, April 1999).

How can this turnabout be explained? The answer is that the medico–pharmaceutical industry has now overtaken the arms industry to become the world's leading business sector and is seen to have the greatest potential for growth and profits in the coming century. For this to be possible, however, governments must fully cooperate with industry, and state policies must refrain from holding back commercial developments. The major players in the sector, of course, tell us that the privatization and globalization of healthcare is, in any case, inevitable. But if this is so it is because powerful lobbying groups are at work worldwide to accelerate the process as imperceptibly and with the maximum efficiency as possible.

As it happens, an extraordinarily timely opportunity presented itself in Seattle at the end of November 1999 at the World Trade Organization. In this beautiful city, the 136 trade ministers of the WTO member states met to launch yet another wave of global trade liberalization under the grandiose title of the Millennium Round. On the agenda of the new round was the revision of past agreements on agriculture, on services and on intellectual propriety, which were written into the final act establishing the WTO.* Each of these agreements contains provisions for further 'roll backs' – that is, further deregulation of any national legislation which is seen to be inimical to trade. This, in the jargon of the WTO, is referred to as the 'built-in agenda'. Besides, fresh negotiations are tabled for agreements on investment, on public procurement, on competition policy and on trade facilitation.†

GATS

Top of the list for the millennium round was the revision of the General Agreement on Trade in Services (GATS). Needless to say, industrial interests played an unprecedented part in setting the agenda for this GATS revision, foremost among them the US Coalition of Service Industries (CSI), which sees

---

* The negotiators signed the final act concluding the Uruguay Round of GATT and establishing the WTO in Geneva in December 1993.

† Even before the multilateral agreement on investment negotiated at the OECD was officially declared dead (3 December 1998), French Prime Minister Lionel Jospin declared that the WTO was a better forum for an agreement on investment.

it as providing great potential advantages; in their own words, 'an opportunity for a quantum leap'.*

The service sector, in which healthcare is included, is as vast as it is undefined. It covers everything from telecommunications to transport, distribution, postal services, insurance, the construction industry, environment and real estate, as well as the tourism and entertainment industries of all sorts, from McDonald's of Moscow to the brothels of Bangkok. According to the WTO, the services that fall within the scope of GATS cover no less than 160 separate sectors. Though there is no common view on what should be included as service industries, the WTO took care from the start to ensure that healthcare would be in the jumbled list of sectors earmarked for commercialization and liberalization. This, astonishingly enough, gave rise to no debate whatsoever, not even to an article anywhere in the mainstream press.

While the issue of agriculture attracted a lot of attention when it became a battleground between the US and Europe, the GATS agreement, as a whole, passed by almost unnoticed. The Uruguay Round of GATT, coupled with the setting up of the WTO, was signed under tremendous pressure from the leading industrial countries.† When hurriedly ratified by the parliaments of the member states, very few MPs had the vaguest idea of the far-reaching implications of the GATS (or, indeed, of GATT–WTO agreements in general). One of the reasons for that, as incredible as it might seem, is that the list of sectors affected by the agreement was never made available to them! Nevertheless, the then French foreign minister, Alain Juppé, an adept of everything that smacked of free trade, had to admit that 'the GATS agreement applies to all services in all sectors, with the exception of those provided by the state'. Of course, this is not strictly correct. He should have added that this applies only if the state is not in competition in a particular sector with more than one service provider and, in addition, so long as the service is provided for free. Significantly, this is not the case with health services in France as only 70 per cent of their costs are at present covered by the state.

The aims are clear. After the liberalization of telecommunications and financial services, and that of postal services and air transport currently underway, it is the turn of the health sector to be opened up to competition and eventual take-over by major corporations. This, we are assured, will enable it to benefit from the 'economies of scale' and thereby become even more 'efficient'. All

---

* Stated by Robert Vastine, president of the Coalition of Service Industries, oral testimony before the Interagency Trade Policy Staff Committee, 19 May 1999.
† On 15 April in Marrakech, prime ministers or trade ministers of GATT member countries officially signed the final act establishing the World Trade Organization. By the end of that year, ratification had been rushed through the national parliaments of member countries whose constitution required it, which is not the case of the UK.

affiliated sectors are targeted: hospital care and other care services, ambulance services, care for the aged, social benefits, 'tele-medicine', without forgetting the highly lucrative area of plastic surgery. Patients will become customers, and hospitals healthcare supermarkets. One wonders when the first cut-price sale will be held?

One must bear in mind certain obvious realities. First of all, in terms of the logic of modern economics, it is not human needs that are taken into account but 'effective demand': needs backed by hard cash. Private companies catering for the market can, indeed, provide expensive high-technology care for wealthy customers; but everyone else will have to do with a considerably cheaper form of healthcare, provided by hospital services operating under tight budgetary constraints. This will mean longer waiting lists, shortage of equipment and, of course, the exploitation of the work force, working longer hours for less pay. Indeed, to subject healthcare to the laws of the market can only lead to increased inequity and tensions. In England, a large number of hospitals in the Greater London area have been closed over the last years. In France, hospitals, like that of Ales in the Gard, have seen some of their services closed down as a result of budget cuts. Meanwhile the huge tentacular company Vivendi has already acquired holdings in two clinics in the same area and the same thing is repeated in other regions.* Recently the French paper *Le Monde* announced that, with the hospital reform, no less than 100 hospitals in the Paris region would be closed within the next five years.

In addition, we must realize that it is not health which makes money but ill health. That is why there is practically no move on the part of the medico–pharmaceutical industry to take prevention seriously. On the contrary, governments, egged on by industry, have declared war on alternative medicine. In France homeopathy is under attack. Twenty-seven medical preparations that are essential to the practice of homeopathic medicine have recently been banned under the ludicrous pretext that their sale should be discontinued pending their screening for content of residual animal products. The homeopaths, like the herbalists, are competitors, which a totalitarian medico–pharmaceutical industry cannot tolerate and must destroy.

Significantly, the term 'disease' itself is being redefined. Even old age, which affects a class of customers with relatively high average purchasing power, is now referred to as a disease, as is obesity. Furthermore, once medical care is taken over by the market, the pressure to maximize sales and profits becomes such that rather than addressing the root causes of any problem, the tendency becomes instead to prescribe profitable commercial products that can only mask the symptoms.

With a little imagination, one can foresee the fate of medical research. The press is full of promotional articles stressing the progress of science leading to the development of future high-tech therapies, with genetic engineering at the

---

* It is interesting to note that the health department of Vivendi is headed by the former director of the Sécurité Sociale, the French National Health.

top of the list. State and European funding for research programmes in 'genomics' and gene-therapy is massive, though it is the private sector that captures the bulk of it, leaving the taxpayers to foot the bill without any say over how the funding is to be used. Needless to say, scientific research also happens to be a service sector that the GATS has been careful to earmark for revision.

SERVICES 2000

For the revision of GATS, the WTO has adopted the slogan 'Services 2000', as proposed by the service lobbies, as its own. The main services lobbies, the US Coalition of Service Industries (CSI), the Transatlantic Business Dialogue (TABD), which groups together the 100 largest firms both sides of the Atlantic, and the recently formed European Services Network (ESN), especially created for the event, are fully ready for action.* While the business sector has been preparing the ground for some time, Sir Leon Brittan decided to give businesses his full backing, as became clear in the 1988 conference entitled 'Towards GATS 2000' (speech by Leon Brittan, 2 June 1998).

But the benefits corporations expect to derive from this revision are by no means 'in the bag'. There are concerns that the fiasco of the multilateral agreement on investment (MAI) – which was torpedoed by public opposition – may be repeated. For this reason, the corporations regard it as important that neither national parliaments nor the public should be allowed to know what exactly is being negotiated. Hence the opaqueness of the preliminary confidential document prepared by the WTO Council on Trade in Services. The issues are clouded in a maze of interwoven and largely incomprehensible clauses designed to confuse the reader. The document is, of course, very comprehensive, not one issue having been overlooked. Also, to ensure that the outcome is as planned, they have been careful not to put all their eggs in one basket.

Furthermore, the Coalition of Service Industries persuaded the WTO to adopt, among other things, a 'flexible' and 'innovative' negotiating strategy. In particular, it has advised on how to classify the different services sectors, explaining that they 'need flexibility to include some services which may not be captured by (existing) definitions' (Vastine, 1999). The Council on Trade in Services, which endorsed these negotiating positions, is ready to deal with any opposition that might arise regarding the commercialization of any aspect of healthcare.

In contrast to the US, health for European voters is a sensitive issue. It was therefore essential to maintain the maximum secrecy regarding the true nature of the millennium round negotiations that were to be approved at the ministerial

---

* For readers who wish to enquire further about these lobbies, their websites are: CSI: www.uscsi.org; TABD: www.tabd.org; ESN: www.globalservicesnetwork.com

meeting in Seattle in November, and especially all details of the GATS revision, which started as early as 1 January 2000. Some of the measures proposed seemed limited in their scope, but in reality this was only true in the short term. Admittedly, governments had placed restrictions on the liberalization of some activities, but this meant registering them for liberalization in the longer term. In other words, by seeking to protect hospitals from corporate encroachment, governments by the same token had, in effect, issued corporations with a licence to take them over in the long term! The WTO's Council on Trade in Services had already developed a method to achieve this. As a result, under article 1.3.C of GATS, if a service is to be considered under 'governmental authority' and hence 'exempt' from liberalization, it is now argued that it 'should be provided entirely free'. However, 'since hospitals and clinics charge the patient or his insurance for the treatment provided, it seems unrealistic in such cases to argue for continued application of article 1.3.C'. In other words, if a treatment is free for the patient, but paid for by 'subsidies or other similar forms of financial advantages', then not only must the sector be opened to competition, but the same 'subsidies' should be offered to competing commercial suppliers! * This must be the case with regard to the infamous national treatment clause (article 7). It is, of course, significant that the WTO regards national health schemes as subsidies.

To make matters worse, there is a proposal to adopt what is referred to as the 'horizontal approach', which means that if a particular measure is agreed in one sector, say telecommunication, *it is also automatically applied to all other sectors, including health*. In the case of the sub-sector of 'tele-medicine', for instance – which involves patient customers consulting distant doctors and receiving prescriptions via video-phone – it will forcibly have to be liberalized, since member countries have already signed on to the agreement on telecommunications!

Even if this arsenal of provisions proved insufficient to ensure the liberalization of healthcare, other devices for doing so have been anticipated. For instance, the agreement on government procurement, itself backed up by another proposed agreement on competition policy which the US and the EU intend to table for negotiation in the millennium round, could perfectly well serve the same purpose.

It is essential not to be intimidated by the technicality of these issues. In reality, the situation is quite simple. The world's health budgets are massive, amounting to billions and billions of dollars. Why not then classify the health sector as a service industry as well as public procurement? As we have seen, one of the favourite methods used by the WTO to liberalize any sector is to reclassify it in a different category. In numerous countries, the CSI complains: 'contracts are awarded by the state following closed procedures which run contrary to the

---

* 'In scheduled sectors this suggests that subsidies and any similar economic benefits conferred on one group would be subject to the national treatment obligation under article XVII.' See Council of Trade in WTO RESTRICTED, S/C/W/50, 18 September (98-3558) in *Towards a Successful WTO Ministerial Meeting* by the TABD, May 1999.

interests of foreign suppliers'. Clear rules are therefore essential to ensure that all public procurement contracts, whether for road construction or, as they hope, for health, are always awarded to the most 'competent companies'. Redefining healthcare as public procurement offers a huge advantage. The funds spent – or rather redistributed – by governments, in this case social security contributions, can be tapped by private companies, whether national or foreign. In France, the AXA group has already bid for the management of health insurance in at least one region. The day this company obtains official consent, a precedent will have been set. Under the obligation to treat foreign companies and local firms alike (national treatment), the same conditions will have to be granted to whatever foreign corporation makes a similar bid. Similar trends are arising in the pension sector.

As for the agreement on competition policy, it does not involve reclassifying activities as in the GATS, but in establishing 'constraining principles' and 'disciplines'. As Robert Vastine, President of the CSI, explained in a recent speech in Tokyo: 'The WTO members will be asked to consider making reforms to their regulatory regimes.' National regulations, he tells us, should have four central attributes: 'adequacy, impartiality, least intrusiveness and transparency'. Needless to say, he is not demanding transparency of corporate practices, or non-intrusiveness of transnational companies over people's life. What he means, and what the agreement on competition policy is about, is that parliaments, whatever legislation is under consideration, will have to issue regulations that are 'adequate' and 'impartial' towards business interests. Robert Vastine further recommends that with the millennium round, the Dispute Settlement Body of the WTO will be strengthened. 'Compensation is not enough,' he declares. 'The Dispute Settlement Body must insist on members conforming to WTO rules.' Clearly, this means that when a WTO panel ruling condemns the European prohibition of American beef treated with hormones, the raising of tariff barriers by the US on European exports by US$114 million is not enough. The next time the EU refuses to import an American product of this sort, it will be made to open its market without any further delay and to impose the product on the people living within the community, whether they like it or not.

However, in Europe people are no more willing to hand over the protection of their health to the uncaring forces of the market than they are to be force-fed with hormone-treated meat. The economic globalization that has already occurred under the auspices of the WTO is impoverishing and rendering destitute hundreds of millions of people, especially in the developing world. The corporations are simply going too far and no efforts must be spared to prevent them from going any further.

The WTO's cynical, indeed Machiavellian, machinations to commodify, privatize and globalize the world's critical healthcare sector must and will undoubtedly be exposed. World public opinion must surely turn against it, demanding from national governments the rolling back of the whole body of trade legislation that has been passed since the setting up of the WTO.

Chapter 20

Fuelling Climate Change

Ladan Sobhani and Simon Retallack

The destabilization of the planet's climate is among the most destructive phenomena that man has ever unleashed. While governments slowly begin to accept the need to engage with the problem, they have yet to understand that their support for economic globalization is making it worse. By vastly increasing energy-intensive activities while strengthening the hand of the vested interests defending the status quo, economic globalization is placing us on a collision course with climatic disaster.

Ladan Sobhani took a degree in international relations at the University of California at Davis, where she focused her studies on environmental economics. She has worked on research at the International Forum on Globalization and has helped to organize teach-ins on the WTO, the World Bank and the IMF.

For biographical details on Simon Retallack see Chapter 17, The Environmental Cost of Economic Globalization.

Human-induced climate change is probably the most serious problem facing humankind. By burning more and more oil, coal and other fossil fuels, we are emitting ever more heat-trapping gases – principally carbon dioxide – just as we are destroying forests that normally absorb them. The result is greenhouse gas overload in the atmosphere – trapping solar heat and causing surface temperatures to rise. And that is no mere theory. As the Intergovernmental Panel on Climate Change (IPCC) – the official scientific body established by the UN to investigate climate change – stated in 1995 in its *Second Assessment Report*, written and reviewed by 2000 scientists: 'the balance of evidence suggests there is a discernible human influence on global climate' (IPCC, 1995).

Already, according to the IPCC, global average temperatures have risen 0.6 degrees Celsius above the pre-industrial average. Twelve of the hottest years in recorded history have occurred since 1980. With higher temperatures, there has also been more energy driving the Earth's climatic systems, which in turn has been causing more violent weather events, such as Hurricane Mitch which killed

10,000 people and destroyed the infrastructure and economies of two Central American countries in 1998. Rising temperatures have also caused polar ice sheets to begin to melt and disease-carrying mosquitoes to move north – even to New York City.

And that is only the beginning. Scientists expect average world temperatures to rise between 2.5 degrees Celsius and 10 degrees Celsius over the next 100 years (Watson et al, 1997, p4; see also Di Fazio, 1999, p75). As a result, if current trends persist, ever more frequent and severe storms, floods, droughts, dust storms, sea surges, crumbling coastlines, salt water intrusion of groundwater, failing crops, dying forests (including the Amazon rainforest), the inundation of low-lying land and islands, and the spread of endemic diseases such as malaria and dengue fever are all on the cards. Agriculture worldwide could face severe disruption and economies could collapse. There could also be millions upon millions of environmental refugees – people fleeing from the intruding sea or from the deserts they have left in their wake. Scientists are advising governments that millions will die worldwide because of the changes in global climate that we have unleashed.

Economic globalization is accelerating this highly dangerous phenomenon by expanding industrial activity and universalizing the carbon-intensive model of development worldwide. The distancing of producers from consumers and the massive boom in trade precipitated by economic globalization have required a vast increase in greenhouse gas-emitting transport. Liberalization of trade and investment around the world has also facilitated the global expansion of industrial agriculture and related food processing industries, which are highly energy intensive and generate vast quantities of greenhouse gases. It has also stimulated greater consumption of energy-intensive products, such as cars and electric appliances, and the construction of vast fossil fuel-based energy infrastructures.

At the same time, governments are prevented from taking adequate mitigating action by powerful obstacles spawned by economic globalization, including the spectacular growth of fossil fuel-related corporations and their consequent leverage over governments, as well as the increase in competitive pressures on domestic industry. New world trade rules, meanwhile, pose a threat to national legislation aimed at reducing greenhouse gas emissions. As a result, the climate will continue to change with very serious implications for us all.

INCREASING TRADE TRANSPORT

The modern global economy and the philosophy that inspired its creation by definition necessitate trade over long distances. The central policy prescription of *neo-liberalism* is that of free trade based on international specialization and comparative advantage. Accordingly, all countries should specialize in and export what they do or produce best, and import everything else. The consequence of adopting that philosophy by most governments around the world (principally by removing barriers to foreign trade) is that diverse local economies which supply their local populations with most of the things that they need are supplanted by economies that produce principally for export abroad and *import* most of their requirements. With economic globalization, products that we used to be able to produce ourselves, or foods that were simply unavailable for climatic or seasonal reasons, are now imported year round. The geographic distance between producers and consumers is thus increased dramatically and goods are transported far greater distances before they reach consumers. The average distance that goods travelled from producer to consumer in the US, for example, was 1000 kilometres in 1982 (Pimental and Pimental, 1996, p201). Now that even more local economies have been displaced by regional and global ones, that figure is likely to be even higher.

Similar changes have taken place in the process of production. With the liberalization of investment and trade policy, corporations engaged in manufacturing or food processing are able to locate or farm out the various phases of production at, or to, different sites around the world. Components are thus shipped back and forth tens of thousands of kilometres before the product is finally assembled or completed. Hence, as David Korten points out, when Otis Elevator set about creating an advanced elevator system, it contracted out the design of the motor drives to Japan, the door systems to France, the electronics to Germany, and small gear components to Spain. All of these components were then shipped to the US where they were finally assembled, before being exported around the world – travelling thousands of kilometres in the process (Korten, 1995, p125). Similarly, as a study by the German Wuppertal Institute on the distance travelled by various food products revealed, the components of a 150-gram strawberry yoghurt travelled a total of 1005 kilometres before being put together. The strawberries were imported from Poland, corn and wheat flour from the Netherlands, jam from West Germany, sugar beet from East Germany and the yoghurt itself from north Germany. Aluminium used for the cover travelled 300 kilometres (Lang, 1998).

In this way, economic globalization has stimulated massive growth in the leading modes of international transport for goods, all of which contribute to climate change. As global trade has expanded, world shipping has grown approximately tenfold by weight since 1950 (French, 1999). Shipping carries 90 per cent of the world's trade in goods and the energy demands of the industry are phenomenal: 140 million tons of fuel are consumed each year by ships worldwide – more than the annual consumption of the entire Middle East (International Bunker Industry Association, 1998). Moreover, shipping is set to increase by about 85 per cent between 1997 and 2010 because of the expected expansion in global trade (MergeGlobal Inc, 1998). Ports such as that of Los Angeles predict a doubling of cargo throughput over the next 25 years (Port of Los Angeles, 1998). Such growth can only lead to a rise in greenhouse gas emissions.

Similarly, world air cargo traffic nearly tripled from 44 billion revenue ton-kilometres (RTK – the distance each ton travels) in 1985 to 123 billion RTKs in 1997: a 280 per cent increase (Boeing Company, 1998). Boeing forecasts another tripling in air cargo traffic by 2017. Freight service is expected to continue growing at a rate 2 per cent faster than passenger traffic (Air Transportation Association of America, 1998). The problem with this boom is that transport by air is by far the most energy-intensive mode of transportation: each ton of freight moved by plane uses 49 times as much energy per kilometre than when it is moved by ship (French, 1999). This is particularly damaging because aircraft emissions are high in the troposphere, where the air is thinner and greenhouse gases are much more effective at absorbing outgoing infra-red radiation. Water vapour emitted from aircraft, which forms cirrus clouds or con trails high in the troposphere, may also have a considerably greater impact on climate as high clouds seem particularly effective at trapping heat.

Freight transport over land has increased, too, as a result of economic globalization. Europe, for example, has witnessed a tripling of transborder truck traffic from 400 billion ton-kilometres in 1970 to 1200 billion ton-kilometres in 1997, according to EU estimates. That growth is primarily the result of the liberalization of trade, which has made trading over longer distances much more viable, and not just the outcome of greater production and consumption. Hence, from 1986–1991, the distance over which food was transported in Europe increased by 19 per cent, while it only increased 8 per cent by volume (*Lost in Concrete*, 1996). Similarly, in the US, the ton-miles of freight accounted for by rail since 1960 has more than doubled – reaching 1.2 trillion ton-miles in 1994 alone, a year in which the average length of haul was over 800 miles (1300 kilometres) (Gorelick, 1998). Truck traffic has experienced even greater growth, especially since NAFTA, to the point where trucks travelled a total of 182 billion miles (293 billion kilometres) on US interstate highways in 1994 (Public Citizen, 1996).

The cumulative environmental costs of all such long-distance transport are extremely heavy and, were they accounted for in the final price of products, would make freight transport on this scale economically unviable. The fifteenfold increase in world trade that has resulted from the opening of markets around the world to free trade and investment since 1950 has clearly stimulated significant growth in global demand for fossil fuels (*World Economic Outlook October 1997*, 1997; see also *Financial Statistics Yearbook*, 1997; *International Financial Statistics*, 1998). As more and more goods have had to be carried over longer and longer distances, trade transportation has become responsible for the consumption of over one-eighth of world oil production (Lang and Hines, 1993). As that oil is burned and greenhouse gases are emitted, our climate is being dangerously destabilized.

GLOBALIZING INDUSTRIAL AGRICULTURE

Industrial agriculture has made the productivity of farmland almost entirely dependent on massive infusions of energy derived from fossil fuels. It is therefore a major contributor to climate change. Already widely adopted in much of the industrialized world, with economic globalization, industrial agriculture is spreading globally to countries such as China, India and Mexico which, until recently, have practised far less energy-intensive systems of farming. Their rapid transition to fossil fuel-intensive models of production will therefore dramatically increase global greenhouse gas emissions.

Of all human-created emissions of carbon dioxide, methane and nitrous oxide – the principal greenhouse gases contributing to climate change – industrial agriculture is responsible for 25 per cent, 60 per cent, and 80 per cent respectively (Bunyard, 1996). If that is so, it is essentially because industrial agriculture replaces the energy inputs of humans and animals with huge amounts of fossil fuel-derived energy, of which it consumes more than any other industry. Direct energy, mostly refined petroleum products, is used on farms to power machines for ploughing, planting and harvesting, fertilizer and pesticide application, and transportation, while electricity is used for irrigation and other purposes. Hence, US consumption of fuels for farm use, for example, in 1993 amounted to 1.4 million gallons of petrol (6.4 million litres) and 3.5 million gallons of diesel (16 million litres): 11 per cent and 29 per cent respectively of the national total (Gill, 1997).

Striking as these figures may be, they do not include the even larger amounts of energy consumed off the farm for manufacturing machines, fertilizers and pesticides, and for processing, packaging (almost 50 per cent of all consumer packaging in the US is used for food products), and transporting the food after it leaves the farm (Gill, 1997). Manufacturing each ton of nitrogen, phosphorous and potassium fertilizer, for example, requires between 10 and 72 megajoules (MJ) of primarily fossil fuel-derived energy, and manufacturing and processing food consumed 4.7 per cent of total energy in the US in 1991 (Gill, 1997). Industrial agriculture thus produces a particularly perverse outcome: it is estimated that it causes us to expend many times as much energy to produce food as we actually derive from eating it. And almost all of that energy is derived from burning fossil fuels – emitting large quantities of greenhouse gases in the process.

Industrial agriculture is responsible for even more greenhouse gas emissions when we include the consequences of applying 70 million tons of nitrogen fertilizer every year on soils – a process which generates at least 10 per cent of total nitrous oxide emissions (Rosenzweig and Hillel, 1998). In addition, industrial farming methods lead to soil erosion, which, in the US alone, is estimated to cause the release of 16 million tons of carbon into the atmosphere each year (USDA-ARS News Service, 1998). Intensive industrial practices also lead to higher methane emissions in rice and livestock production. Rice fields that are flooded rather than rain-fed produce much more methane, since flooding cuts off the oxygen supply to soil, causing organic matter to decompose into the gas (Rosenzweig and Hillel, 1998). In livestock production, meanwhile, when large numbers of animals are confined in one area, manure is usually stored in huge piles, releasing methane as it decomposes (*IPCC Guidelines for National Greenhouse Gas Inventories*, 1996). Emissions are also higher due to the high-protein diet of cattle in feed lots, compared to livestock who eat grass in pastures. It is estimated that intensive livestock production is responsible for 15 per cent of global methane emissions (Rosenzweig and Hillel, 1998).

Conversion from small-scale traditional farming to large-scale industrial agriculture has another important ecological impact: the displacement of people from their land and into cities. Today, most of the world's population still live in rural communities, where they can provide for at least part of their own food needs. But as small farmers throughout the world are increasingly undermined by imports of industrially produced, subsidized food, the mechanization and corporatization of agriculture, and the focus on producing export crops, millions are being displaced from their land to urban areas. In China, for example, agricultural industrialization recently caused 10 million peasants to leave their farms in just one year, while 440 million more are expected to migrate from the land to China's urban areas in the next few decades (Rosenzweig and Hillel, 1998, pp10–11). The implications for global climate are significant because the more cities grow, the more energy is consumed since food and water, building materials and energy must all be transported great distances via vast energy-consuming infrastructures, and since concentrated wastes must be hauled away in fossil fuel-consuming trucks and barges.

Industrialized agriculture has clearly proven to be a highly energy-intensive and unsustainable model. To export it to the rest of the world is a recipe for worsening climatic dislocation, yet that is precisely what is taking place. Because of economic globalization, industrial farming is being practised in more and more countries around the world. With fewer barriers to trade in food – as a result of regional and international trade agreements, such as NAFTA and the WTO's Agreement on Agriculture – cheap, subsidized, large-scale industrially produced food has flooded world markets, making it very difficult for farmers employing traditional, small-scale, less energy-intensive and less subsidized systems of agriculture to compete. As a result, the latter are forced to adopt industrial methods or go bust, as millions have done – in which case, if they do not starve, they are often reduced to buying imported industrial food and selling their land to wealthier farmers who use it to expand industrial production.

Governments are increasingly powerless to protect small farmers from such a fate because the WTO's Agreement on Agriculture and other trade agreements have removed their ability to control domestic agricultural policies. Tools that were once used to secure stable prices for domestic farmers are no longer allowed under WTO rules. Import controls to prevent the flooding of domestic markets; farmer marketing boards to give producers the ability to negotiate collective prices with domestic and foreign buyers; and family farm support programmes are all either forbidden or restricted under WTO rules. Thus, the world's remaining small, low-energy-consuming agricultural producers are rapidly being replaced with large agribusinesses using industrial practices. Transnational agribusinesses which produce on an industrial scale, such as Cargill and Pepsico, now control 70 per cent of world food trade. Cargill alone controls 60 per cent of the world trade in cereals (United Nations Centre on Transnational Corporations, cited by Lang, 1998).

Furthermore, the reorientation of economic activity towards production for exports that takes place when a country becomes part of the global economy, often following the adoption of an IMF–World Bank structural adjustment programme, leads to a vast increase in the production of exportable cash crops – such as coffee, sugar cane and cocoa – grown in monocultures, which require far more high-energy inputs than other varieties. Increased production of cash crops also results from investment liberalization and privatization, which open up national economies to foreign agrochemical companies. These companies are able to buy up farming conglomerates and vast tracts of fertile land around the world for that purpose.

The resulting global expansion of industrial agriculture is the cause of growing energy use in the agricultural sector of most countries throughout the world and a consequent increase in greenhouse gas emissions. In Canada, for example, on-farm energy use alone grew by 9.3 per cent between 1990 and 1996, and agriculture's share of CO_2 emissions rose by 8 per cent over the same period. In developing countries, energy used for agricultural production as a percentage of total commercial energy grew approximately 30 per cent from 1972 to 1982 – driven by the first 'green revolution' which brought industrial and energy-intensive agricultural production to many developing countries (Stout, 1990, p52). Since then, energy use in agriculture has increased still further, together with emissions of carbon dioxide, methane and nitrous oxide, with severe consequences for global climate.

DISSEMINATING FOSSIL FUEL-INTENSIVE TECHNOLOGY

As consumer markets in industrialized countries have become saturated, manufacturing corporations have turned to the developing world in search of new consumers. Those corporations have been instrumental in shaping inter-national agreements that remove barriers to trade, which, in the absence of an adequate international environmental regulatory framework, facilitate and promote the consumption of carbon-emitting products worldwide.

With trade and investment liberalization, environmentally destructive technologies such as the automobile and other energy-intensive appliances spread to cultures not yet dependent on such goods. Since the opening of markets to foreign imports, South Korea and Thailand, for example, witnessed annual car growth rates of 25 and 40 per cent respectively in the early 1990s (Matthews and Rowell, 1992, p6). Similarly, the number of cars in Mexico City grew a massive 60 per cent between just 1990 and 1993 (Calvillo Unna, 1993). Such proliferation is significantly increasing the threat of global climate change since motor vehicles are responsible for a major share of world carbon dioxide emissions. These are only set to increase as transnational auto companies increase sales to countries who are rapidly liberalizing their markets, such as the states of the former USSR who currently have only one car per 21 people; India who has one car per 455 people; and China – one car per 1000 people. Already, as a result of investment liberalization in China, where people have relied primarily on bicycles, public transportation and other low-input means of transportation, General Motors (GM) recently signed a US$1 billion contract to produce 100,000 mid-sized cars annually (Cable News Network, 1997). GM has also set up production in Russia, where it hopes to profit not only by producing cheap cars for export, but by gaining a larger share of the domestic market. The company is not the only one expanding in this new market – in 1995, over one million foreign cars and trucks were sold in Russia and the Ukraine (Cable News Network, 1996).

The climatic consequences of the global proliferation of the car through economic globalization are disastrous. And the car is but one of a vast array of modern home and office products and appliances, such as washing machines, clothes dryers, TVs, VCRs, computers and photocopiers, that require large inputs of climate-changing fossil fuels and that are now being exported and produced around the world.

BUILDING THE GLOBAL ECONOMY'S ENERGY INFRASTRUCTURE

International financial institutions – linchpins of the global economy – have directly promoted and financed fossil fuel-intensive energy projects throughout the developing world. Their principal goals are to create the energy infrastructure necessary to integrate developing countries within the global economy; to generate large quantities of cheap energy to fuel expanding manufacturing processes to enable household consumption to rise; and to support the vast cities that the globalization of industrial development is creating.

According to the US-based Institute for Policy Studies, the World Bank has financed US$13.6 billion worth of energy projects since the Rio Earth Summit in 1992, including 51 coal-, oil- and gas-fired power plants and 26 coal mines. These projects will emit 38 billion tons of carbon dioxide over their lifetimes, nearly double what was emitted in 1996 by all countries combined (Wysham, 1999). Meanwhile, less than 3 per cent of the World Bank's energy budget is devoted to renewable energy. Between 1992 and 1998, the bank spent 25 times more on fossil fuel projects than on renewable energy (Institute for Policy Studies, 1997; Wysham, 1999). Moreover, the immediate beneficiaries of the World Bank's projects are G7-based corporations, which have been granted 95 per cent of the contracts (explaining why for every dollar the US pays the World Bank, US$1.30 returns in the form of investments for US transnationals) and which are the primary consumers of the energy these projects produce (Institute for Policy Studies, 1998).

The Overseas Private Investment Corporation (OPIC) and the Export–Import Bank (Ex–Im) – US export–credit agencies (ECAs) which use taxpayers' money to subsidize US commercial interests in developing nations – have also devoted billions of dollars to huge fossil fuel-based energy projects. According to the Institute for Policy Studies, the cumulative support for coal, oil and gas projects by Ex–Im and OPIC between 1992 and 1998 totalled US$23.2 billion. These projects will release 29.3 billion tons of carbon dioxide over their lifetimes – more than all global emissions for 1996 (Institute for Policy Studies, 1998). European citizens fund a similar 'corporate welfare' programme through their national ECAs. The British Export Credit Guarantee Department, for example, is backing the construction of the Liaocheng, Heze II, Shiheng II and Huaneng coal-fired power plants in China, as well as an enormous coal-fired plant in Visakhapatnum, India. The massive Paiton coal plant complex in Java, Indonesia, meanwhile, has been backed with US$3.9 billion in guarantees and loans from the Japanese, US and German ECAs. The European Bank for Reconstruction and Development (ERBD) funds similar projects. Shell, Amoco, Mitsubishi and Texaco are among the corporations whose overseas investments in energy resources have been subsidized by the EBRD (Institute for Policy Studies and International Trade Information Service, 1997).

In the vast majority of cases, multilateral development banks ignore renewable energy projects and undermine localized systems of production and consumption that would significantly reduce overall energy consumption. By building fossil fuel-based infrastructures so mindlessly throughout the world to meet the ever growing energy-intensive needs of economic globalization and the development model it promotes, the World Bank and the other multilateral development agencies are playing a leading role in fuelling climate change.

THE REACTIONARY INFLUENCE OF TRANSNATIONAL CORPORATIONS

Despite the growing threat posed by climate change, governments are being prevented from taking adequate mitigating action by a number of obstacles created by economic globalization, including the increased power of large corporations – particularly those in the fossil-fuel industry. By opening new markets around the world to foreign trade and investment, economic globalization has greatly increased the opportunities for corporations to grow, increase their profits and eliminate or absorb competitors, often through mergers. The fossil-fuel sector and related industries have been no exception to this trend. The merger of the two oil giants Exxon and Mobil in 1998, for example, valued at US$250 billion, has created the world's third largest corporation and the largest oil company by far (Farrelly, 1998). Other recent mergers include that of BP with Amoco, and Total with Petrofina and Elf Aquitaine. These have been mirrored by countless other mergers in the auto, aircraft and utility industries.

The result of this corporate consolidation has been an unprecedented concentration of financial power in the hands of industries that profit from fossil fuels, to the point where many are now more economically powerful than a large number of nation states. The combined revenues, for example, of just General Motors and Ford – the two largest automobile corporations in the world – exceed the GDP of all sub-Saharan Africa (cited by Karliner, 1997, p5). This wealth has been used to great effect by fossil fuel-related companies to influence government policy in ways that have resulted in the defeat or watering down of many efforts to mitigate climate change.

It is no mere coincidence that the countries with the highest per-capita greenhouse gas emissions and who are the most recalcitrant in taking action to reduce those emissions – such as the US and Australia – are also home to corporations that have spent a fortune funding front groups, think-tanks, lobbyists, scientists, economists and, above all, politicians in order to obstruct political attempts to prevent climate change. In the US, for example, oil, gas, coal, utility, automobile and other fossil fuel-intensive corporations contributed US$63.4 million to both main US political parties between 1992 and 1998 (Centre for Responsive Politics website: www.crp.org). They also spent US$30 million lobbying politicians and government agencies in 1998 alone (Centre for Responsive Politics website) and US$13 million more on television, radio and newspaper advertising in the three months leading up to the Kyoto conference (designed to produce an international agreement to reduce greenhouse gas emissions) in order to promote political and public opposition to the resulting protocol (Beder, 1999). Millions more have been spent funding corporate front groups, or so-called 'Astroturf coalitions', such as the Coalition for Vehicle Choice and the Global Climate Coalition; think-tanks, such as the Competitive Enterprise Institute and the Heritage Foundation; and scientists such as Robert Balling – the recipient of US$700,000 from the fossil-fuel industry over the past five years (Beder, 1999).

The explicit goal of such funding – the extent of which citizens' groups could not possibly match – has been to discredit the science of climate change and prevent the changes necessary to prevent its worst effects. After years of effectively stalling global recognition of the problem, industry groups have successfully fought to limit countless measures to reduce emissions. For example, in the US – responsible for a quarter of global greenhouse gas emissions – the US Congress voted to bar the White House from requiring car-makers to build more efficient vehicles by increasing automobile fuel-economy standards, as a result of corporate influence. Indeed, Congress has tried to destroy what little fuel economy standards are in existence by successfully inserting an exemption for giant sport utility vehicles, which now account for one out of every two cars being purchased and which give as little as 14 miles to the gallon.

Congress has also prevented the Clinton administration from increasing the BTU, or energy, tax, as well as from increasing the 1999 budget for the development of renewable energy and energy-efficient technology to US$3.6 billion, as the White House requested. It has even rejected the president's policy that fossil fuels produced on public land should be subject to market-based royalty rates rather than the subsidized rate currently in existence. The most significant act of congressional subversion is the Byrd-Hagel Resolution, passed unanimously by the US Senate 95 votes to 0, in June 1997, which effectively prevents the ratification of the Kyoto Protocol that mandates the US to reduce its greenhouse gas emissions by 7 per cent below 1990 levels by 2012. If that were not enough, as the result of legislative efforts by the right-wing Republican Joe Knollenberg – whose constituency includes Detroit, the capital of the US car industry – and others, new programmes designed especially to fulfil US Kyoto commitments are now outlawed.

Such political behaviour defies all established scientific knowledge and the public interest, and can only have been taken to satisfy the short-term interests of corporations engaged in activities that are causing the climate to change. To varying degrees of success, the political power of fossil fuel-related corporations is being exercised in similar ways all over the world, including at regional levels such as the EU, and at all the international negotiations on climate change. Economic globalization has given these corporations the financial and political clout to have such influence, with devastating effects.

DEREGULATORY PRESSURES FROM GLOBAL COMPETITION

Another obstacle that governments face in attempting to mitigate climate change is the huge increase in competitive pressures on domestic industry generated by economic globalization. As opportunities for foreign investment increase, and as moving manufacturing overseas becomes easier with economic globalization, corporations can pick and choose the regulatory conditions under which they invest. Where local, national or regional environmental regulations are strict, companies complain that they are burdened with extra costs that make them uncompetitive in the global economy. Countries attempting to take serious measures to protect the environment are thus no longer deemed competitive locations for investment.

In such a climate, governments compete with each other to lower or freeze environmental standards in order to attract foreign investment or to prevent the flight of industries already based in their countries. In a globalized economy, even the threat of relocation is powerful enough to send policy-makers on a deregulatory frenzy or a policy freeze, and attempts to raise taxation or environmental standards become almost impossible. The EU's failed attempt at introducing a carbon tax in 1992 to reduce carbon dioxide emissions provides a clear example. Opponents of the tax argued that it would undermine the competitiveness of European companies abroad because the tax would not apply to their competitors, who would therefore gain a commercial advantage over them (Lang and Hines, 1993).

In refusing to ratify the Kyoto Protocol, the US Senate has cited similar reasons. The coauthors of the Senate resolution that has effectively blocked the ratification of this treaty, Senators Byrd and Hagel, argued that taking measures to reduce greenhouse gas emissions would damage the US economy, causing an exodus of manufacturing plants to developing countries who are not mandated to reduce emissions under Kyoto (Retallack, 1999). What opponents of the Kyoto Protocol fail to mention is that industrial relocation would not be possible were it not for the enhanced mobility corporations enjoy as a result of agreements which *they* ratified and that have reduced or eliminated barriers to trade and foreign investment.

Given the environmental threats that we face today, the solution to any loss of competitiveness cannot be the freezing, reduction or elimination of environmental protections. If the current global system of free trade and investment is impeding governments' abilities to set and enforce environmental protections, then the economic system itself, flawed as it is, needs to be changed.

THREATS FROM GLOBAL TRADE RULES

Global trade rules policed by the WTO also pose a significant threat to national and international efforts to address climate change. WTO rules could be used to challenge the Kyoto Protocol, for example, on a number of grounds.

Under the terms of the protocol, parties are encouraged to implement policies and measures aimed at 'enhancement of energy efficiency in relevant sectors of the economy' – a key goal of climate change mitigation. An important way in which that may be achieved is by setting energy efficiency standards for consumer products, such as motor vehicles. When this has been attempted by the EU, Japan and the US, however, global trade rules have been used to challenge their initiatives, and serious disputes have followed.

In January 1999, Japan announced its intention to introduce legally binding standards for energy efficiency for nine categories of cars on the basis of vehicle weight, in order to meet its commitment under the Kyoto Protocol to reduce its greenhouse gas emissions by 6 per cent below 1990 levels. The standards are based on the most energy-efficient vehicle currently commercially available within each weight category – 'the top runner' – which in each weight category happens to be a Japanese car. The EU, meanwhile, to meet *its* Kyoto commitment of reducing greenhouse gases by 8 per cent below 1990 levels, has forged a voluntary agreement to increase energy efficiency with the European Automobile Manufacturers' Association (ACEA). As a result, manufacturers agreed to reduce carbon dioxide emissions in new cars by 25 per cent by 2008 on the basis of fleet averaging rather than specific efficiency requirements on vehicles by category.

The EU and Japan have challenged each other's energy-efficiency requirements, arguing that they discriminate against imported vehicles – which is forbidden under world trade rules. Because European exports to Japan tend to be in the range of medium and luxury vehicles, they fall into the middle and heavier weight categories which are subject to the greatest percentage of improvements for fuel efficiency. The EU therefore claims that the effect will be to discriminate against *its* cars (a claim the US on behalf of its auto manufacturers, has now repeated) in violation of the WTO's Agreement on Technical Barriers to Trade, which prohibits standards that are discriminatory and more trade restrictive than necessary (Wallach and Sforza, 1999). Japan, meanwhile, claims that EU standards based on fleet averaging discriminate against *its* vehicle exports, which are primarily higher-end vehicles that would need substantial improvements in energy efficiency to meet EU standards.

It remains to be seen if the EU, the US or Japan will mount formal challenges at the WTO, but if they do, the chances of their respective energy-efficiency standards' survival are not good, especially given the fate under GATT of the US Corporate Average Fuel Economy (CAFE) standards. Designed to increase energy efficiency, the CAFE standards were challenged by the EU for discriminating *in effect* against EU auto-makers, citing almost identical arguments as the opponents of Japanese and European energy-efficiency standards today, even though the US average fuel economy standards were identical for domestic and foreign fleets. A GATT panel, however, agreed with the EU and, in 1994, overturned the US standards (Wallach and Sforza, 1999, pp32–33).

The application of carbon taxes – another important strand of any serious strategy for meeting national commitments under the Kyoto Protocol – could also fall foul of WTO rules. By internalizing the climate-related costs of using fossil fuels, carbon taxes create an incentive to use less fuel and to develop more fuel-efficient production processes. As we have seen, however, taxing commercial goods at a national level on the basis of how much those goods contribute to greenhouse gas emissions can place domestic industries at a competitive disadvantage in the global economy – because the tax would not apply to foreign competitors. One way around that problem would be to tax imports based on the energy used to produce them. But under GATT–WTO rules governing 'like products', this would be illegal. The rules prohibit internal taxes on imported products that are 'in excess of those. . . applied to like domestic products' (GATT article III) (Chambers et al, 1999). Any trade discrimination based on the way a product is produced – exactly what carbon taxes are designed to influence – is thus forbidden.

This represents a fundamental conflict between the WTO and the Kyoto Protocol. While, under WTO rules, 'like products' cannot be distinguished or discriminated against on the basis of how they were produced or where they came from, the Kyoto Protocol and all three of its main flexible mechanisms *mandate* discrimination between different manufacturing technologies and processes, between signatories and non-signatories and between higher-emitting developed countries and lower-emitting developing countries. Ultimately, without discrimination, the reduction of greenhouse gas emissions is all but impossible, since climate-changing technologies need to be discouraged.

CONCLUSION

Economic globalization clearly has significant implications for global climate change. Under this system, long-distance, high-emitting transport is increasing, energy-intensive industrial agriculture and carbon-intensive technologies are spreading, and fossil fuel-based energy infrastructures are being built – accelerating the rise in greenhouse gas concentrations. Furthermore, by tearing down barriers to trade in wood products and to corporate logging around the world, economic globalization is fuelling the destruction of the world's remaining forests, which play a vital role in absorbing greenhouse gases. To cap it all, nations and local communities are increasingly unable to reduce their contribution to climate change because of the growth in power and influence of transnational corporations, the generation of fierce competitive pressures, and international trade rules that undermine the democratic process – all of which are products of economic globalization.

Given these findings, and given the monumental threat that climate change poses, the resubordination of global trade rules to environmental imperatives which, among other things, must involve the relocalization of trade, is absolutely essential for reducing overall energy demand and for cutting greenhouse gas emissions. The energy-intensive model of economic globalization must be rejected if we are to stand a chance of preventing severe climate change.

Part 3

Steps Towards Relocalization

Chapter 21

Shifting Direction:
From Global Dependence to
Local Interdependence

Helena Norberg-Hodge

The arguments for changing direction – that is, for abandoning the emerging global economy in favour of community-based, localized, highly diversified economies – may be compelling, but such a change is clearly not in the interests of transnational corporations or the governments they put into power. New political alignments may eventually prove effective, but meanwhile, citizens can already undertake a host of local activities that contribute toward the creation of new community-based economies. Some are well underway. Helena Norberg-Hodge lists and describes some of those initiatives and suggests what their contributions might be.

For biographical details on Helena Norberg-Hodge see Chapter 14, The Pressure to Modernize and Globalize.

Around the world – from North to South, from far left to far right – recognition of the destructive effects of economic globalization is growing. However, the conviction that the solutions lie with localizing economic activity is far less widespread. Many people seem to find it difficult even to imagine a shift toward a more local economy. 'Time has moved on,' one hears. 'We live in a globalized world.'

On the surface, this is a perfectly reasonable point of view. How, after all, can we expect to tackle today's global ecosocial crises except on a global level? But it's not that simple. We need to distinguish between efforts merely to counter further globalization and efforts that can bring real solutions. The best way to halt the runaway global economy would undoubtedly be through multilateral treaties that would enable governments to protect people and the environment from the excesses of free trade. But such international steps would not in themselves restore health to economies and communities. Long-term solutions to today's social and environmental problems require a range of small, local initiatives that are as diverse as the cultures and environments in which they take place. When seen as going hand in hand with policy shifts away from globalization, these small-scale efforts take on a different significance. Most importantly, rather than thinking in terms of isolated, scattered efforts, it is helpful to think of institutions that will *promote small scale on a large scale*.

CONCEPTUAL RESISTANCE TO LOCALIZATION

Moving toward the local can still seem impractical or Utopian. One reason is the belief that an emphasis on the local economy means total self-reliance on a village level, without any trade at all. The most urgent issue today, however, isn't whether people have oranges in cold climates but whether their wheat, eggs or milk should travel thousands of kilometres when they could all be produced within a an 80-kilometre radius. In Mongolia, a country that has survived on local milk products for thousands of years and that today has 25 million milk-producing animals, one finds mainly German butter in the shops. In Kenya, butter from Holland is half the price of local butter; in England, butter from New Zealand costs far less than the local product; and in Spain, dairy products are mainly Danish. In this absurd situation, individuals are becoming dependent for their everyday needs on products that have been transported thousands of kilometres, often unnecessarily. The goal of localization would not be to eliminate all trade but to reduce unnecessary transport while encouraging changes that would strengthen and diversify economies at both the community and national levels. The degree of diversification, the goods produced and the amount of trade would naturally vary from region to region.

Another stumbling block is the belief that a greater degree of self-reliance in the North would undermine the economies of the developing world, where people supposedly need Northern markets to lift themselves out of poverty. The truth of the matter, however, is that a shift toward smaller scale and more localized production would benefit both North and South – and allow for more meaningful work and fuller employment all around. Today, a large portion of the South's natural resources is delivered to the North, on increasingly unfavourable terms, in the form of raw materials. The South's best agricultural land is devoted to growing food, fibres, even flowers for the North. And a good deal of the South's labour is used to manufacture goods for Northern markets. Rather than further impoverishing the South, producing more ourselves would allow the South to keep more of its resources and labour for itself.

It is very important to understand the differences between the economics of the North and the South. A project that might work well in the North is not guaranteed to be beneficial in less industrialized economics. For instance, introducing microloans for small-scale enterprise may actually contribute to the destruction of local, non-monetized economies and create dependence on a highly volatile and inequitable global economy, where factors such as currency devaluation can prove disastrous. By the same token, we should recognize that pulling 1000 people away from sure subsistence in a land-based economy into an urban context where they compete for 100 new jobs is not a net gain in employment: 900 people have, in effect, become *un*employed.

The idea of localization also runs counter to the belief that fast-paced urban areas are the locus of 'real' culture and diversity, while small, local communities are invariably isolated backwaters where small-mindedness and prejudice are the norm. It isn't strange that this should seem so. The whole industrialization process has systematically removed political and economic power from rural areas and engendered a concomitant loss of self-respect in rural populations. In small communities today, people are often living on the periphery, while power – and even what we call *culture* – is centralized somewhere else.

Rural life in the West has been marginalized for many generations, and most Westerners thus have a highly distorted notion of what life in small communities can be like. And even though much of the developing world is made up of villages, colonialism and development have left an indelible mark. In order to see what communities are like when people retain real economic power at the local level, we would have to look back – in some cases hundreds of years – to a time before these changes occurred. As I pointed out in Chapter 14, I have seen with my own eyes how the largely self-reliant, community-based culture of Ladakh was transformed by economic development. Only a decade ago, the traditional culture was suffused with vibrancy, joy and a tolerance of others that was clearly connected with people's sense of self-esteem and control over their own lives. Economic development, however, dismantled the local economy; decision-making power was shifted almost overnight from the household and village to bureaucracies in distant urban centres; the media educated children for a 'glamorous' urban lifestyle completely unrelated to the local context and alien to that of their elders. If economic trends continue to undermine cultural vibrancy and self-esteem, future impressions of village life in Ladakh may soon be little different from Western stereotypes of small-town life.

An equally common myth that clouds thinking about more human-scale rural economics is that 'there are too many people to go back to the land'. It is noteworthy that a similar skepticism does not accompany the notion of urbanizing the world's population. What is too easily forgotten is that the majority of the world's people today – mostly in the developing world – already *are* on the land. To ignore them and speak as if people are urbanized as part of the human condition is a very dangerous misconception that helps to fuel the whole urbanization process. It is considered 'Utopian' to suggest a ruralization of America's or Europe's population; but China's plans to move 440 million people into the cities during the next few decades hardly raises eyebrows. This 'modernization' of China's economy is part of the same process that has led to unmanageable urban explosions all over the South – from Bangkok and Mexico City to Bombay, Jakarta and Lagos. In these cities, unemployment is rampant, millions are homeless or live in slums and the social fabric is unravelling.

Even in the North, urbanization continues. Rural communities are being steadily dismantled, their populations pushed into spreading suburbanized megacities. In the US, where only 2 per cent of the population lives on the land, farms are still disappearing at the rate of 35,000 per year. It is impossible to offer that model to the rest of the world, where the majority of people earn their living as farmers. But where are the people saying, 'We are too many to move to the city'?

Instead, we hear that urbanization is necessary because of overpopulation. The implicit assumption is that centralization is somehow more efficient, that urbanized populations use fewer resources. When we take a close look at the real costs of urbanization in the global economy, however, we can see how far this is from the truth. Urban centres around the world are extremely resource intensive. The large-scale, centralized systems they require are almost without exception more stressful to the environment than small-scale, diversified, locally adapted production. Food and water, building materials and energy must all be transported great distances via vast energy-consuming infrastructures; their concentrated wastes must be hauled away in trucks and barges or incinerated at great cost to the environment. In their identical glass-and-steel towers with windows that never open, even air to breathe must be provided by fans, pumps and non-renewable energy. From the most affluent sections of Paris to the slums of Calcutta, urban populations depend on transport for their food, so that every pound of food consumed is accompanied by several pounds of petroleum consumption and significant amounts of pollution and waste.

What's more, these Westernized urban centres – whether in tropical Brazil, arid Egypt or subarctic Scandinavia – all use the same narrow range of resources while displacing more locally adapted methods that made use of local resources, knowledge and biological diversity. Children in Norwegian fishing villages enjoy eating cod, while people on the Tibetan plateau prefer their staple barley. Yet they are increasingly encouraged to eat the same food that is eaten in the industrial world. Around the world people are being pulled into a monoculture, which is levelling both cultural and biological diversity. The urbanizing global economy is thus creating artificial scarcity by ignoring local systems of knowledge and educating children to become dependent on a highly centralized economy. The end result is disastrously high levels of unemployment, increased competition and heightened ethnic conflict.

It is precisely because there *are* so many people that we must abandon the globalized economic model, which can only feed, house and clothe a small minority. It is becoming essential to support knowledge systems and economic models that are based on an intimate understanding of diverse regions and their unique climates, soils and resources.

In the North, where we have for the most part long been separated from the land and from each other, we have large steps to take. But even in regions that are highly urbanized, we can nurture a new connection to place. By reweaving the fabric of smaller communities within large cities and by redirecting economic activity toward the natural resources around such communities, cities can regain their regional character, become more liveable, and lighten their burden on the environment. Our task will be made easier if we support our remaining rural communities and small farmers. They are the key to rebuilding a healthy agricultural base for stronger, more diversified economies.

SHIFTING DIRECTION

Many individuals and organizations are already working from the grass roots to strengthen their communities and local economies. Yet, for these efforts to succeed, they need to be accompanied by policy changes at the national and international levels. How, for example, can grassroots participatory democracy be strengthened unless limits are placed on the political power of huge corporations? How can local support alone enable small producers and locally owned shops to flourish if corporate welfare and free trade policies heavily promote the interests of large-scale producers and marketers? How can we return to a local context in education if monocultural media images continue to bombard children in every corner of the planet? How can local efforts to promote the use of locally available renewable energy sources compete against massive subsidies for huge dams and nuclear power plants?

The policy changes that would allow space for more community-based economies to flourish will certainly elicit objections. Some will claim that the promotion of decentralization is 'social engineering' that would seriously dislocate the lives of many people. While it is true that some disruption would inevitably accompany a shift toward the local, it would be far *less* than that caused by the current rush toward globalization. It is, in fact, today's 'jobless growth' society that entails social and environmental engineering on an unprecedented scale, as vast stretches of the planet and whole societies are reconfigured to conform to the needs of global growth – encouraged to abandon their languages, their foods and their architectural styles for a standardized monoculture.

Others will interpret financial incentives for more localized production as 'subsidies'. However, these incentives should be seen as alternatives to current subsidies for globalization – that is, for transport, communications, energy infrastructures, education, and research and development (R&D) in the technologies of large-scale centralized production. Moving in the direction of the local will actually cost *less* than we are now spending to move toward the global.

Rethinking our direction means looking at the entire range of public expenditures.

- The money currently spent on long-distance road transport alone offers an idea of how heavily subsidized the global economy is. In the US in 1996, where there were already about four million kilometres of paved roads, another US$80 billion was earmarked for building yet more highways and plans are even being considered for a road link between Alaska and Siberia. The European Community, meanwhile, planned to spend US$120 billion to add an additional 12,000 kilometres of superhighways across Western Europe by 2002 and is considering a tunnel to connect Europe with Africa. Throughout the South, scarce resources are similarly being spent. In New Guinea, for example, US$48 million was spent on 37 kilometres of roads that allow timber interests to harvest and bring logs to the export market.

    Shifting this support toward a range of transport options that favour smaller, more local enterprises would have enormous benefits, from the creation of jobs, to a healthier environment, to a more equitable distribution of resources. Depending on the local situation, transport money could be spent on building bike paths, foot paths, paths for animal transport, boat and shipping facilities, or rail service. Even in the highly industrialized world, where dependence on centralizing infrastructures is deeply entrenched, a move in this direction can be made. In Amsterdam, for example, steps are being taken to ban cars from the heart of the city, thus allowing sidewalks to be widened and more bicycle lanes to be built.

- Large-scale energy installations are today heavily subsidized. Phasing out these multibillion-dollar investments, while offering real support for locally available renewable energy supplies, would result in lower pollution levels, reduced pressure on wilderness areas and oceans, and less dependence on dwindling petroleum supplies and dangerous nuclear technologies. It would also help to keep money from leaking out of local economies.

- Agricultural subsidies now favour large-scale industrial agribusinesses. Subsidies include not only direct payments to farmers but funding for research and education in biotechnology and chemical- and energy-intensive monoculture. Shifting these expenditures toward those that encourage smaller-scale, diversified agriculture would help small family farmers and rural economies while promoting biodiversity, healthier soils and fresher food. Urbanized consumers may not be aware that most agricultural subsidies benefit huge corporations such as Cargill and other middlemen, not small farmers.

- Government expenditures for highway building promote the growth of corporate 'superstores' and sprawling malls. Spending money instead to build public markets – such as those that were once found in virtually every European town and village – would enable local merchants and artisans with limited capital to sell their wares. This would enliven town centres and cut down on fossil-fuel use and pollution. Similarly, support for farmers' markets would help to revitalize both the cities and the agricultural economy of the surrounding region while reducing money spent to process, package, transport and advertise food.

- Television and other mass telecommunications have been the recipients of massive subsidies in the form of R&D, infrastructure development, educational training, and other direct and indirect support. They are now rapidly homogenizing diverse traditions around the world. Shifting support toward building facilities for local entertainment – from music and drama to puppet shows and festivals – would offer a healthy alternative.

- At present, investments in healthcare favour huge, centralized hospitals meant to serve urban populations. Spending the same money instead on a greater number of smaller clinics that relied less on high technology and more on health practitioners would bring healthcare to more people and boost local economies.

- Creating and improving spaces for public meetings, from town halls to village squares, would encourage face-to-face exchanges between decision-makers and the public, serving both to enliven communities and to strengthen participatory democracy. In Vermont, for example – where participatory democracy is still alive and well – people attend town meetings for lively debates and votes on local issues.

In addition to the direct and indirect subsidies given them, large-scale corporate businesses also benefit from a range of government regulations – and, in many cases, a lack of regulations – at the expense of smaller, more localized enterprises. Although big business complains about red tape and inefficient bureaucracy, the fact is that much of it could be dispensed with if production were smaller in scale and based more locally. In today's climate of unfettered 'free' trade, some government regulation is clearly necessary, and citizens need to insist that governments be allowed to protect their interests. This could best come about through international treaties in which governments agree to change the 'rules of the game' to encourage real diversification and decentralization in the business world. There are many areas that need to be looked at in this regard.

- The *free flow of capital* has been a necessary ingredient in the growth of transnational corporations. Their ability to shift profits, operating costs and investment capital to and from all of their far-flung operations enables them to operate anywhere in the world and to hold sovereign nations hostage by threatening to pack up, leave and take their jobs with them. Governments are thus forced into competition with one another for the favours of these corporate vagabonds and try to lure them with low labour costs, lax environmental regulations and substantial subsidies. Small local businesses, given no such subsidies, cannot hope to survive this unfair competition.

- Today, governments of every stripe are embracing *free trade policies* in the belief that opening themselves up to economic globalization will cure their ailing economies. Instead, a careful policy of using tariffs to regulate the import of goods that could be produced locally would be in the best interests of the majority. Such 'protectionism' is not aimed at fellow citizens in other countries; rather, it is a way of safeguarding the local culture, jobs and resources against the excessive power of the transnationals.

- In almost every country, *tax regulations* discriminate against small businesses. Small-scale production is usually more labour intensive, and heavy taxes are levied on labour through income taxes, social welfare taxes, value-added taxes and so on. Meanwhile, tax breaks (such as accelerated depreciation and investment tax credits) are handed out on the capital- and energy-intensive technologies used by large corporate producers. Reversing this bias in the tax system would not only help local economics but would create more jobs by favouring people instead of machines. Similarly, taxes on the energy used in production would encourage businesses that are less dependent on high levels of technological input – which, again, means smaller, more labour-intensive enterprises. And if petrol and diesel fuel were taxed so that prices reflected real costs – including some measure of the environmental damage their consumption causes – there would be a reduction in transport, an increase in regional production for local consumption and a healthy diversification of the economy.

- Small businesses are discriminated against through the *lending policies of banks*, which charge them significantly higher interest rates for loans than they charge big firms. They also often require that small business owners personally guarantee their loans – a guarantee not sought from the directors of large businesses.

- An unfair burden often falls on small-scale enterprises through *regulations aimed at problems caused by large-scale production*. Battery-style chicken farms, for example, clearly need significant environmental and health regulations. Their millions of closely kept fowl are highly prone to disease; their tons of concentrated effluent need to be safely disposed of; and their long-distance transport entails the risk of spoilage. Yet a small producer, such as a farmer with a few hundred free-range chickens, is subject to essentially the same regulations, often raising costs to levels that can make it impossible to remain in business. Large-scale producers can spread the cost of compliance over a greater volume, making it appear that they enjoy economies of scale over smaller producers. Such discriminatory regulations are widespread. For example, a local entrepreneur wanting to bake cakes at home to sell at a local market would in most cases need to install an industrial kitchen to meet health regulations. Such a regulation makes it economically impossible to succeed.

- Local and regional *land-use regulations* can be amended to protect wild areas, open space and farmland from development. Political and financial support could be given to the various forms of land trusts that have been designed with this in mind. In the US, there are now over 900 such trusts protecting more than 1.1 million hectares of land. In some cases, local governments have used public money to buy the development rights to farmland, thereby simultaneously protecting the land from suburban sprawl while reducing the financial pressure on farmers. Studies have also shown that developed land costs local governments significantly more in services than the extra tax revenues generated – meaning that when land is developed, taxpayers not only lose the benefits of open space but also lose money.

- In urban areas, *zoning regulations* usually segregate residential, business and manufacturing areas – a restriction necessitated by the needs and hazards of large-scale production and marketing. These could be changed to enable an integration of homes, small shops and artisan or other small-scale production sites, as was traditional in the world's great cities. A rethinking of restrictions on community-based ways of living would also be beneficial. Zoning and other regulations aimed at limiting high-density developments often end up prohibiting environmentally sound living arrangements such as cohousing and ecovillages.

In the developing world, the majority are still living in small towns and rural communities and are largely dependent on a local economy. In this era of rapid globalization, the most urgent challenge is to stop the tide of urbanization and globalization by strengthening these local economies. A number of policy-level changes could help to do so.

- Large dams, fossil-fuel plants and other large-scale energy and transport infrastructures are geared toward the needs of urban areas and export-driven production. Shifting support toward a decentralized, renewable-energy infrastructure would help to stem the urban tide by strengthening villages and small towns. Since the energy infrastructure in the South is not yet very developed, this could be realistically implemented in the near future if there were sufficient pressure from activists lobbying Northern banks and funding agencies.
- Colonialism, development and now free trade and globalization have meant that the best land in the South is used to grow crops for Northern markets. Shifting the emphasis to diversified production for local consumption would not only improve the economies of rural communities but also lessen the gap between rich and poor, while eliminating much of the hunger that is now so endemic in the so-called developing parts of the world.
- Countries in the South are also being hit hard by free trade agreements such as GATT and NAFTA. They would be far better off if, contrary to the aim of such treaties, they were allowed to protect and conserve their natural resources, nurture national and local business enterprises, and limit the impact of foreign media and advertising on their culture. Since free trade can pull people away from a relatively secure local economy and put them on the

bottom rung of the global economic ladder, even 'fair trade' may not always be in the long-term interest of the majority in the South.

- The South would benefit enormously from an end to the promotion of Western-style monocultural education. Instead, efforts are needed that would give preeminence to the local language and values while promoting more location-specific knowledge adapted to the bioregion and the culture.
- Local economies and communities in the South would also benefit if support for capital- and energy-intensive centralized healthcare based on a Western model were shifted toward more localized and indigenous alternatives.
- It is also of critical importance to elevate the status of primary producers (especially farmers) and rural life in general. In the South today, the message being transmitted by the media, advertising and tourism is that rural life is, in effect, a lower evolutionary stage. This message puts intense psychological pressure on people to become modern, urban consumers. This indoctrination process can be countered through the use of a variety of media, from comic books to theatre and films, and through exchange programmes that expose people in the South to the realities of life in the North. I have termed efforts of this sort *counterdevelopment*, since they are conscious attempts to counter the forces that are promoting an unsustainable, highly polluting consumer lifestyle around the world.

In the South, the majority of people still get their spiritual, cultural and economic strength from their connection to the place where they live. We need to keep in mind how our assumptions about human nature and about the 'efficiency' and 'superiority' of Western industrial culture are helping to destroy the existing fabric of local economy and community. Before the incursion of the West, people enjoyed singing their own songs, speaking their own language, eating the food from their own region. Even today, most adults would prefer to be able to maintain their culture and remain in their communities. Rather than pulling people into Westernized urban centres where they are robbed of their cultural and personal identity and made dependent on a global economy, we need to allow people to stay where they are and be who they are.

GRASSROOTS INITIATIVES

Economic localization should entail an adaptation to cultural and biological diversity; therefore, no single blueprint would be appropriate everywhere. The range of possibilities for local grassroots efforts is as diverse as the locales in which they would take place. The following survey is by no means exhaustive but illustrates the sorts of steps being taken today.

- In a number of places, community banks and loan funds have been established to increase the capital available to local residents and businesses and allow people to invest in their neighbours and their community, rather than in distant corporations.

- 'Buy-local' campaigns help local businesses survive even when pitted against heavily subsidized corporate competitors. The campaigns not only help keep money from leaking out of the local economy, but also help educate people about the hidden costs to the environment and to the community in purchasing less expensive but distantly produced products. Across the US, Canada and Europe, grassroots organizations have sprung up in response to the intrusion of huge corporate marketing chains into rural and small-town economies. For example, the McDonald's corporation – which added 900 restaurants worldwide in 1993 and plans to add a new restaurant every nine hours in the coming years – has met with grassroots resistance in at least two dozen countries. Polish activists, for instance, succeeded in blocking the construction of a McDonald's in an old section of Cracow, and activists in India are working to keep McDonald's from entering that market. In the US and Canada, the rapid expansion of Wal-Mart, the world's largest retailer, has spawned a whole network of activists working to protect jobs and the fabric of their communities from these sprawling superstores.

- An effective way of guaranteeing that money stays within the local economy is through the creation of local currencies. Local exchange trading systems (LETS) schemes have sprung up in the UK (where there are over 250 in operation) and in Ireland, Canada, France, Argentina, the US, Australia and New Zealand. These initiatives have psychological benefits that are just as important as the economic benefits. A large number of people who were once merely 'unemployed' and therefore 'useless' are becoming valued for their skills and knowledge.

- Another idea is the creation of local 'tool-lending libraries', where people can share tools on a community level. By reducing the need for everyone to have their own agricultural or forestry equipment, gardening implements or home repair tools, people can keep money within the local economy while simultaneously fostering the sense of neighbourly cooperation that is a central feature of real community.

- One of the most exciting grassroots efforts in the US is the community supported agriculture (CSA) movement, in which consumers link up directly with a nearby farmer. Significantly, in a country where small farmers linked to the industrial system continue to fail every year at an alarming rate, not a single CSA has failed for economic reasons.

- By connecting farmers directly with urban consumers, farmers' markets similarly benefit local economies and the environment. In New York City, there are now over two dozen farmers' markets, which add several million dollars annually to the incomes of farmers in nearby counties. Cornell

University's 'New Farmers New Markets' programme aims to add to these numbers by recruiting and training a new generation of farmers to sell at the city's markets. The project is particularly interested in attracting unemployed immigrants who have extensive farming skills.

- The movement to create ecovillages is perhaps the most complete antidote to dependence on the global economy. Around the world, people are building communities that attempt to get away from the waste, pollution, competition and violence of contemporary life. Many communities rely on renewable energy and are seeking to develop more cooperative local economies. The Global Ecovillage Network links several of these communities worldwide.

- Creating local economies means *rethinking education* – examining the connection between ever greater specialization and increasing dependence on an ever larger economic arena. Today, modern education is training children around the world for the centralized global economy. Essentially, the same curriculum is taught in every environment, no matter what the cultural traditions or local resources. Promoting regional and local adaptation in the schools would be an essential part of the revitalization of local economies. Training in locally adapted agriculture, architecture, artisan production (pottery, weaving and so on), and appropriate technologies suited to the specifics of climate and local resources would further a real decentralization of production for basic needs. Rather than educating the young for ever greater specialization in a competitive, 'jobless growth' economy, children would be equipped for diverse economic systems that depended primarily – but not exclusively – on local resources. This, of course, would not mean that information about the rest of the world would be excluded; on the contrary, knowledge about other cultures and cultural exchange programmes would be an important part of the educational process.

RECONNECTING TO COMMUNITY AND PLACE

The economic changes just described will inevitably require shifts at the personal level. In part, these involve rediscovering the deep psychological benefits – the joy – of being embedded in community. Children, mothers and old people all know the importance of being able to feel they can depend on others. The values that are the hallmarks of today's fast-paced, atomized industrial society, on the other hand, are those of a 'teenage boy culture'. It is a culture that demands mobility, flexibility and independence. It induces a fear of growing old, of being vulnerable and dependent.

Another fundamental shift involves reinstilling a sense of connection with the place where we live. The globalization of culture and information has led to a way of life in which the nearby is treated with contempt. We get news from China but not next door, and at the touch of a television button we have access to all the wildlife of Africa. As a consequence, our immediate surroundings seem dull and uninteresting by comparison. A sense of place means helping ourselves and our children to see the *living environment around us*: reconnecting with the sources of our food (perhaps even growing some of our own) and learning to recognize the cycles of the seasons, the characteristics of the flora and fauna.

Ultimately, we are talking about a spiritual awakening that comes from making a connection to others and to nature. This requires us to see the world within us, to experience more consciously the great interdependent web of life, of which we ourselves are among the strands.

Chapter 22

Conserving Communities

Wendell Berry

This chapter provides a passionate denunciation of the global economy our governments are bringing into being. Among other things, it paints a picture of what the world would be like once this process is completed. Wendell Berry sees it above all as 'a world in which the cultures that preserve natural and rural life will be simply disallowed'; it will be post-democratic, 'post-religious' and 'post-natural', and hence 'post-human'. However, there is some hope. A new political opportunity now exists. Berry foresees a novel political realignment with 'a party of community' that may well grow faster than we think, and provide an effective opposition to the 'parties of globalization'.

Wendell Berry is a poet, a teacher (at the University of Kentucky), an ecological thinker (with a huge following) and a prophet par excellence of traditional rural society. He is also a small farmer in Port Royal, Kentucky, where his father farmed before him. This chapter is a passionate plea for a return to community, but also an argument that a new political opportunity now exists. Berry foresees a novel political realignment that represents 'the party of community' against the 'parties of globalization'.

Berry is the author of numerous books of poetry and fiction and ten books of nonfiction, including the celebrated bestseller The Unsettling of America *(1977), described by the* Los Angeles Times *as 'the missing link between the crisis of the spirit and the crisis of the mass machine culture we live in'. Berry's most recent book is* Another Turn of the Crank *(1995).*

In October 1993, the *New York Times* announced that the United States Census Bureau would 'no longer count the number of Americans who live on farms'. In explaining the decision, the *Times* provided some figures as troubling as they were unsurprising. Between 1910 and 1920, we had 32 million farmers living on farms – about one-third of our population. By 1950, the number had declined, but our farm population was still 23 million. By 1991, the number was only 4.6 million, less than 2 per cent of the national population. That is, our farm population had declined by an average of almost a half million people a year for

41 years. In addition, by 1991, 32 per cent of our farm managers and 86 per cent of our farm workers did not live on the land they farmed.

These figures describe a catastrophe that is now virtually complete. They announce that we no longer have an agricultural class that is, or that can require itself to be, recognized by the government; we no longer have a 'farm vote' that is going to be of much concern to politicians. US farmers, who over the years have wondered whether or not they counted, may now put their minds at rest: They do not count. They have become statistically insignificant.

We must not hesitate to recognize and to say that this statistical insignificance of farmers is the successful outcome of a national purpose and a national programme. It is the result of great effort and of principles vigorously applied. It has been achieved with the help of expensive advice from university and government experts, by the tireless agitation and exertion of the agribusiness corporations, and by the renowned advantages of competition – among our farmers themselves and with farmers of other countries. As a result, millions of country people have been liberated from farming, land ownership, self-employment and the other alleged 'idiocies' of rural life.

The disintegration of our agricultural communities is not exceptional any more than it is accidental. This is simply the way a large, exploitative, absentee economy works. For another example, here is a *New York Times* news service report on 'rape-and-run' logging in Montana:

> '*Throughout the 1980s, the Champion International Corp. went on a tree-cutting binge in Montana, levelling entire forests at a rate that had not been seen since the cut-and-run logging days of the last century. Now the hangover has arrived. After liquidating much of its valuable timber in the Big Sky country, Champion is quitting Montana, leaving behind hundreds of unemployed mill workers, towns staggered by despair and more than 1000 square miles of heavily logged land.*'

The article goes on to speak of the revival of 'a century-old complaint about large, distant corporations exploiting Montana for its natural resources and then leaving after the land is exhausted'. It quotes a Champion spokesperson, Tucker Hill, who said, 'We are very sympathetic to those people and very sad. But I don't think you can hold a company's feet to the fire for everything they did over the last 20 years.'

If you doubt that exhaustion is the calculated result of such economic enterprise, you might consider the example of the mountain counties of eastern Kentucky from which, over the last three-quarters of a century, enormous wealth has been extracted by coal companies that have left the land wrecked and the people poor.

The same kind of thing is now happening in banking. In the county next to mine, an independent local bank was recently taken over by a large out-of-state bank. Suddenly some of the local farmers and the small business people, who had been borrowing money from that bank for 20 years and whose credit records were good, were refused credit because they did not meet the requirements of a computer in a distant city. Old and valued customers now find that they are known by category rather than character. The directors and officers of the large bank clearly have reduced their economic thinking to one very simple question: 'Would we rather make one big loan or many small ones?' Or to put it only a little differently: 'Would we rather support one large enterprise or many small ones?' And they have chosen the large over the small.

This economic prejudice against the small has, of course, done immense damage for a long time to small or family-sized businesses in city and country alike. But that prejudice has often overlapped with an industrial prejudice against anything rural and against the land itself, and this prejudice has resulted in damages that are not only extensive but also long lasting or permanent.

As we all know, we have much to answer for in our use of this continent from the beginning, but in the last half century we have added to our desecrations of nature a virtually deliberate destruction of our rural communities. The statistics I cited at the beginning are incontrovertible evidence of this; but so is the condition of our farms and forests and rural towns. If you have eyes to see, you can see that there is a limit beyond which machines and chemicals cannot replace people; there is a limit beyond which mechanical or economic efficiency cannot replace care.

What I have been describing is not, I repeat, exceptional or anomalous. I am talking about the common experience, the common fate, of rural communities in our country for a long time. It has also been, and it will increasingly be, the common fate of rural communities in other countries. The message is plain enough, and we have ignored it for too long: the great, centralized economic entities of our time do not come into rural places in order to improve them by 'creating jobs'. They come to take as much of value as they can take, as cheaply and as quickly as they can take it. They are interested in 'job creation' only so long as the jobs can be done more cheaply by humans than machines. They are not interested in the good health – economic, natural or human – of any place on this Earth. If you should undertake to appeal or complain to one of these great corporations on behalf of your community, you would discover something most remarkable. These organizations are organized expressly for the evasion of responsibility. They are structures in which, as my brother says, 'the buck never stops'. The buck is processed up the hierarchy until finally it is passed to 'the shareholders', who characteristically are too widely dispersed, too poorly informed and too unconcerned to be responsible for anything. The ideal of the modern corporation is to be anywhere (in terms of its own advantage) and nowhere (in terms of local accountability). The message to country people, in other words, is: don't expect favours from your enemies.

That message has a corollary that is just as plain and just as much ignored: the governmental and educational institutions, from which rural people should by right have received help, have not helped. Rather than striving to preserve the rural communities and economies and an adequate rural population, these institutions have consistently aided, abetted, and justified the destruction of every part of rural life. They have eagerly served the superstition that all technological innovation is good. They have said repeatedly that the failure of farm families, rural businesses and rural communities is merely the result of progress, and such efficiency is good for everybody.

We now obviously face a world that supranational corporations and the governments and educational systems that serve them may well control entirely for their own convenience – and, inescapably, for the inconvenience of all the rest of us. This world will be a world in which the cultures that preserve nature and rural life will be simply disallowed. It will be, as our experience already suggests, a postagricultural world. But as we now begin to see, you cannot have a postagricultural world that is not also postdemocratic, postreligious, and postnatural – in other words it will be post-human, contrary to the best that we have meant by *humanity*.

In their dealings with the countryside and its people, the promoters of the so-called global economy are following a set of principles that can be stated as follows. They believe that a farm or a forest is, or ought to be, the same as a factory; that care is only minimally involved in the use of the land; that affection is not involved at all; that for all practical purposes a machine is as good as (or better than) a human; that the industrial standards of production, efficiency and profitability are the only standards that are necessary; that the topsoil is lifeless and inert; that soil biology is safely replaceable by soil chemistry; that the nature of the ecology of any given place is irrelevant to the use of it; that there is no value in human community or neighbourhood; and that technological innovation will produce only benign results.

These people see nothing odd or difficult in the idea of unlimited economic growth or unlimited consumption in a limited world. They believe that knowledge is, and ought to be, property and power. They believe that education is job-training. They think that the summit of human achievement is a high-paying job that involves no work. Their public claim is that they are making a society in which everybody will be a winner, but their private aim has been to reduce radically the number of people who, by the measure of our historical ideals, might be thought successful: the self-employed, the owners of small businesses or small usable properties, those who work at home.

The argument for joining the new international trade agreements has been that there is going to be a one-world economy, and we must participate or be left behind – though, obviously, the existence of a one-world economy depends on the willingness of all the world to join. The theory is that under the rule of international, supposedly free trade, products will naturally flow from the places where they can be best produced to the places where they are most needed. This theory assumes the long-term safety and sustainability of massive international transport, for which there are no guarantees – just as there are no guarantees that products will be produced in the best way or to the advantage of the workers who produce them, or that they will reach or can be afforded by the people who need them.

There are other unanswered questions about the global economy, two of which are paramount:

1   How can any nation or region justify the destruction of a local productive capacity for the sake of foreign trade?
2   How can people who have demonstrated their inability to run national economies without inflation, usury, unemployment and ecological devastation now claim that they can do a better job in running a global economy?

US agriculture has demonstrated by its own ruination that we cannot solve economic problems just by increasing scale – moreover, that increasing scale is almost certain to cause other problems: ecological, social and cultural.

We can't go too much further, maybe, without considering the likelihood that humans are not intelligent enough to work on the scale to which our technological abilities tempt us. Some such recognition is undoubtedly implicit in US conservatives' long-standing objection to a big central government; so it has been odd to see many of these same conservatives pushing for the establishment of a supranational economy that would inevitably function as a government far bigger and more centralized than any dreamed of before. Long experience has made it clear – as we might say to the liberals – that to be free we must limit the size of government and we must have some sort of home rule. But it is just as clear – as we might say to the conservatives – that it is foolish to complain about big government if we do not do everything we can to support strong local communities and strong community economies.

But in helping us to confront, understand and oppose the principles of the global economy, the old political alignments have become virtually useless. Communists and capitalists are alike in their contempt for country people, country life and country places. They have exploited the countryside with equal greed and disregard. They are alike even in their plea that damaging the present environment is justified in order to make 'a better future'.

The dialogue of Democrats and Republicans or of liberals and conservatives is likewise useless to us. Neither party is interested in farmers or farming, in the good care of the land or in the quality of food. Nor are they interested in taking the best care of our forests. Leaders of both parties are equally subservient to the supranational corporations. NAFTA and the new GATT revisions are the proof.

Moreover, the old opposition of country and city, which was never useful, is now more useless than ever. It is, in fact, damaging to everybody involved, as is the opposition of producers and consumers. These are not differences but divisions that ought not to exist because they are to a considerable extent artificial. The so-called urban economy has been just as hard on urban communities as it has been on rural ones.

All these conventional affiliations are now meaningless, useful only to those in a position to profit from public bewilderment. A new political scheme of opposed parties, however, is beginning to take form. This is essentially a two-party system, and it divides over the fundamental issue of community. One of these parties holds that community has no value; the other holds that it does. One is the party of the global economy; the other I would call simply the party of local community. The global party is large, though not populous, immensely powerful and wealthy, self-aware, purposeful, and tightly organized. The community party is only now becoming aware of itself; it is widely scattered, highly diverse, small though potentially numerous, weak though latently powerful, and poor though by no means without resources.

We know pretty well the makeup of the party of the global economy, but who are the members of the party of local community? They are people who take a generous and neighbourly view of self-preservation; they do not believe that they can survive and flourish by the rule of dog-eat-dog; they do not believe that they can succeed by defeating or destroying or selling or using up everything but themselves. They want to preserve the precious things of nature and of human culture and pass them on to their children. They want the world's fields and forests to be productive; they do not want them to be destroyed for the sake of production. They know you cannot be a democrat (small *d*) or a conservationist and at the same time a proponent of the supranational corporate economy. They know from their experience that the neighbourhood, the local community, is the proper place and frame of reference for responsible work. They see that no commonwealth or community of interest can be defined by greed. They know that things connect – that farming, for example, is connected to nature, and food to farming, and health to food – and they want to preserve the connections. They know that a healthy local community cannot be replaced by a market or an information highway. They know that, contrary to all the unmeaning and unmeant political talk about 'job creation', work ought not to be merely a bone thrown to the otherwise unemployed. They know that work ought to be necessary; it ought to be good; it ought to be satisfying and dignifying to the people who do it and genuinely useful and pleasing to those for whom it is done.

The party of local community, then, is a real party with a real platform and an agenda of real and doable work. It has, I might add, a respectable history in the hundreds of efforts, over several decades, to preserve local nature and local health or to sell local products to local consumers. Such efforts now appear to be coming into their own, attracting interest and energy in a way they have not done before. People are seeing more clearly all the time the connections between conservation and economics. They are seeing that a community's health is largely determined by the way it makes its living.

The natural membership of the community party consists of small farmers, ranchers and market gardeners; worried consumers; owners and employees of small businesses; self-employed people; religious people; and conservationists. The aims of this party really are only two: the preservation of ecological diversity and integrity and the renewal, on sound cultural and ecological principles, of local economies and local communities.

So now we must ask how a sustainable local community (which is to say a sustainable local economy) might function. I am going to suggest a set of rules that I think such a community would have to follow. I do not consider these rules to be predictions; I am not interested in foretelling the future. If these rules have any validity, that is because they apply now.

If the members of a local community wanted their community to cohere, to flourish and to last, these are some of the things they would do.

- Always ask of any proposed change or innovation: what will this do to our community? How will this affect our common wealth?
- Always include local nature – the land, the water, the air, the native creatures – within the membership of the community.
- Always ask how local needs might be supplied from local sources, including the mutual help of neighbours.
- Always supply local needs first (and only then think of exporting products – first to nearby cities, then to others).
- Understand the ultimate unsoundness of the industrial doctrine of 'labour saving' if that implies poor work, unemployment or any kind of pollution or contamination.
- Develop properly scaled value-adding industries for local products to ensure that the community does not become merely a colony of the national or global economy.
- Develop small-scale industries and businesses to support the local farm and/ or forest economy.
- Strive to produce as much of the community's own energy as possible.
- Strive to increase earnings (in whatever form) within the community for as long as possible before they are paid out.
- Make sure that money paid into the local economy circulates within the community and decrease expenditures outside the community.
- Make the community able to invest in itself by maintaining its properties, keeping itself clean (without dirtying some other place), caring for its old people and teaching its children.
- See that the old and the young take care of one another. The young must learn from the old, not necessarily and not always in school. There must be no institutionalized childcare and no homes for the aged. The community knows and remembers itself by the association of old and young.

- Account for costs now conventionally hidden or externalized. Whenever possible, these must be debited against monetary income.
- Look into the possible uses of local currency, community-funded loan programmes, systems of barter and the like.
- Always be aware of the economic value of neighbourly acts. In our time, the costs of living are greatly increased by the loss of neighbourhood, which leaves people to face their calamities alone.
- A rural community should always be acquainted and interconnected with community-minded people in nearby towns and cities.
- A sustainable rural economy will depend on urban consumers loyal to local products. Therefore, we are talking about an economy that will always be more cooperative that competitive.

These rules are derived from Western political and religious traditions, from the prompting of ecologists and certain agriculturalists, and from common sense. They may seem radical, but only because the modern national and global economies have been formed in almost perfect disregard of community and ecological interests. A community economy is not an economy in which well-placed persons can make a 'killing'. It is an economy whose aim is generosity and a well-distributed and safeguarded abundance. If it seems unusual to work for such an economy, then we must remember that putting the community ahead of profit is hardly unprecedented among community business people and local banks.

How might we begin to build a decentralized system of durable local economies? Gradually, I hope. We have had enough of violent or sudden changes imposed by predatory external interests. In many places, the obvious way to begin the work I am talking about is with the development of a local food economy. Such a start is attractive because it does not have to be big or costly; it requires nobody's permission; and it can ultimately involve everybody. It does not require us to beg for mercy from our exploiters or to look for help where consistently we have failed to find it. By *local food economy* I mean simply an economy in which local consumers buy as much of their food as possible from local producers and in which local producers produce as much as they can for the local market.

Several conditions now favour the growth of local food economies. On the one hand, the costs associated with our present highly centralized food system are going to increase. Growers in central California, for example, can no longer depend on an unlimited supply of cheap water for irrigation. Transportation costs can only go up. Biotechnology, variety patenting, and other agribusiness innovations, intended to extend corporate control of the food economy, will increase the cost of food, both economically and ecologically.

On the other hand, consumers are increasingly worried about the quality and purity of their food, and so they would like to buy from responsible growers close to home. They would like to know where their food comes from and how it is produced. They are increasingly aware that the larger and more centralized the food economy becomes, the more vulnerable it will be to natural or economic catastrophe, to political or military disruption and to bad agricultural practices.

For all these reasons and others, we need urgently to develop local food economies wherever they are possible. Local food economies would improve the quality of the food. They would increase consumer influence over production and allow consumers to become participatory members in their own food economy. They would help to ensure a sustainable, dependable supply of food. By reducing some of the costs associated with long supply lines and large corporate suppliers (packaging, transportation, advertising and so on), local food economies would reduce the cost of food at the same time that they would increase income to growers. They would tend to improve farming practices and increase employment in agriculture.

Of course, no food economy can or ought to be *only* local. But the orientation of agriculture to local needs, local possibilities and local limits is simply indispensable to the health of both land and people and undoubtedly to the health of democratic liberties as well.

For many of the same reasons, we need also to develop local forest economies, of which the aim would be the survival and enduring good health of both our forests and their independent local communities. We need to preserve the native diversity of our forests as we use them. As in agriculture, we need local, small-scale, non-polluting industries to add value to local forest products. We also need local supporting industries (saw mills, woodworking shops and so on) for the local forest economy.

As support for sustainable agriculture should come most logically from consumers who consciously wish to keep eating, so support for sustainable forestry might logically come from loggers, mill workers and other employees of the forest economy who consciously wish to keep working. But many people have a direct interest in the good use of our forests: farmers and ranchers with woodlots; all who depend for pure water on the good health of forested watersheds; the makers of wood products; conservationists; and so on.

What we have before us, if we want our communities to survive, is the building of an adversary internal economy to protect against the would-be global economy. To do this, we must somehow learn to reverse the flow of the siphon that has for so long drawn resources, money, talent and people out of our countryside, often with a return only of pollution, impoverishment and ruin. We must figure out new ways to affordably fund the development of healthy local economies. We must find ways to suggest economically – for no other suggestion will be ultimately effective – that the work, the talents and the interest of our young people are needed at home.

Our whole society has much to gain from the development of local land-based economies. They would carry us far toward the ecological and cultural ideal of local adaptation. They would encourage the formation of adequate local cultures (and this would be authentic multiculturalism). They would introduce into agriculture and forestry a spontaneous and natural quality control, for neither consumers nor workers would want to see the local economy destroy itself by abusing or exhausting its resources. And they would complete at last the task of freedom from colonial economics begun by our ancestors more than 200 years ago.

Chapter 23

Local Money: A Currency for Every Community

Perry Walker and Edward Goldsmith

To reconstitute local economies is an imperative if we are to prevent misery and chaos when the global economy collapses. We need them in any case to reduce our environmental impact and to render possible local cooperation and solidarity that can alone assure our livelihood and welfare on a sustainable basis. LETS and Time Dollar schemes – both based on local currencies – provide a valuable tool for doing this.

Perry Walker directs the Centre for Participation at the New Economics Foundation. The centre's activities include: alternative currencies such as LETS and time banks; innovative methods of participation such as Imagine; *helping communities measure their 'social energy'; and measuring local money flows. At NEF he has edited* Participation Works! 21 techniques of community participation for the 21st century *and* Prove It! Measuring the effect of neighbourhood renewal on local people. *Perry read economics at Cambridge. He spent 12 years in the Civil Service in the United Kingdom, latterly in the Treasury. He then joined the John Lewis Partnership and spent five years there as assistant finance director.*

For biographical details on Edward Goldsmith see Chapter 1, Development as Colonialism.

It is by now clear that the global economy must inevitably marginalize and render largely destitute a very large section of the population of both the industrial world and the so-called developing countries. For this reason alone, everything must be done to fight any new versions of the multilateral agreement on investment and to prevent the further implementation of the NAFTA, Maastricht, GATT and other agreements that are now under the aegis of the WTO and that are designed to advance the globalization of the world's economy.

At the same time, we must revitalize local economies on which the vast bulk of humanity depends for its livelihood. There are a number of strategies for achieving this goal. In this article we shall examine two of them: the setting up of LETS and of Time Dollar schemes.*

LETS stands for local exchange (sometimes 'employment') trading systems. The role of a LETS scheme is to revitalize a local economy and therefore a local community by providing an alternative method of supplying people with the goods and services that they can no longer obtain via the formal (globalized) economy. The principle involved is very simple. If the formal economy no longer provides people with the goods and services that they require, then people must provide them for each other, with payment made in an informal local currency that is only valid within the local area. The second strategy consists of creating Time Dollar schemes which are basically alternative 'welfare' systems.

Industrial countries who have developed elaborate and very costly welfare services are now systematically dismantling them – as part of a strategy for reducing costs – so that their corporations may hope to compete with those operating in countries where labour costs are 20 to 40 times lower. Once again, if the state can no longer provide these services, then people must provide them for each other. Under a Time Dollar scheme, they do so without payment in the national currency; instead, they earn credits in a local currency to obtain similar services which can be used when they, in their turn, are old or sick.

These are not fantasies. There are already, for instance, over 350 LETS in the UK, with about 30,000 people involved, as well as a considerable number in Australia, Canada, New Zealand and, more recently, in France, where some 20,000 people are now involved; there are also a few in the US. Time Dollar schemes are confined to the US; 150 of them, with a membership of a few dozen to several thousand individuals, are now operating throughout 30 states.

Both LETS and Time Dollar schemes do more than merely deputize for the formal economy once it ceases to be capable of catering for people's more obvious needs. Access to the goods and services provided via the formal economy is via money, but Edgar Cahn and Jonathan Rowe, co-authors of an excellent book entitled *Time Dollars* (1992), point out that people need a lot of things that money cannot buy – in particular, the benefits provided by what Cahn and Rowe refer to as 'the kitchen table world' – the world of the family and its close friends

---

* For more information, or to get involved, write to:

LETS Link UK: Quinnell Centre, 2 Kent Street, Portsmouth, Hampshire, P01 3BS; Tel: 01705 730639; Fax: 01705 730629; E-mail: 1 04047.2250@compuserve.com; Website: http://www.communities.org.uk/lets

Time Dollars: David Boyle, New Economics Foundation, Cinnamon House, 6–8 Street, London, SE1 4YH, UK; Tel: 020 7377 5696; Fax: 020 7377 5720; Website: http://www.timedollar.org (US), http://www.timebanks.co.uk (UK)

See *The Ecologist*, vol 28, no 4, July/August 1998

to whom we once belonged and where everybody helped each other and cared for each other without any thought of remuneration. However, the functions that were once fulfilled by families and communities for free have been 'taken apart, function by function, and sold back to people, who missed the things that these once provided'. As a result, for most people in the industrial world the kitchen table world is no more and the things it represented – 'companionship, entertainment, security, intimacy, even gossip, must now be bought for money'. Increasingly, it is the TV and the computer and now the Internet that are rapidly replacing the 'kitchen table world'. Very much the same thing has happened to the benefits that were once provided free by the local community. As a result, security from crime 'no longer means the watchfulness of neighbours. Rather, it means insurance policies, burglar alarms and other devices, as well as greater demands for police'.

Inevitably 'massive social problems ensued, as the glue that held people together no longer seemed to be there' and governments 'have been forced to try and patch up the damage with programmes and services bought for money'. People have 'become purchasers of community and care, rather than participants in it' – and inevitably they are rapidly losing the capacity to produce the goods and fulfil the functions they once did. 'When lawyers settle all the disputes, teachers do all the teaching, doctors do all the curing,' as Ivan Illich puts it, 'then people lose their capacity to do these things, and the result is an ever enlarging circle of dependency and need' (Illich, 1999). This is not a mere side-effect of the process of economic development but its very essence. Indeed, the monetization of functions previously fulfilled for free by the now largely defunct family and community accounts for much of the economic growth that we identify with progress.

As Cahn and Rowe put it, the economy grows 'by eating the flesh and sinews that hold society together'. Of course, as this 'cannibalizing process takes place, ever more money is required to buy the services that the family and the community used to provide for nothing. Eventually, as is increasingly the case today, to earn their keep now requires a two-worker family sometimes holding down three or more jobs between them. But this, in itself, increases the requirement for more money, among other things, to pay the cost of the daycare centres where the children of working mothers will be looked after, and the old people's homes to which the grandparents will be consigned.

It is not surprising that government expenditure on social services has escalated in the last decades in an obviously unsustainable way. By creating a global economy, however, matters have now been brought to a head. If industrial countries are to compete with developing world countries, which now have almost equal access to capital, technology and management, while benefiting from incomparably cheaper labour costs, they can no longer afford a welfare state; not surprisingly, it is being systematically dismantled.

This creates a state of emergency, with the corporations providing ever fewer jobs and therefore producing goods and services that fewer and fewer people can afford. The state, furthermore, is incapable of caring for the growing number of individuals whose basic needs are not particularly the market.

The most obvious contribution that LETS and Time Dollar schemes can make is to give people access to a local currency in order to acquire the goods, services and care that they require. The local currency can take the form either of special banknotes, entries in a book or blips on a computer, as is usually the case. If this is possible, it is because the people who use this local currency for buying goods, services and care are at the same time those who provide them. What, in fact, we are seeing is the development of a local economy based on an emerging community of people who are willing to cooperate with each other in order to provide benefits that, in recent decades, have been provided (less satisfactorily) by the state and the market.

One of the advantages of LETS and Time Dollar schemes is that there can be no shortage of the local currency, as is the case with national currency in poor communities. There are two reasons for this. Firstly, people actually create their own currency themselves by the simple expedient of providing goods and services for other members. Secondly, there is no incentive to hoard money, as occurred with the national currency during the depression years: as local solidarity builds up, a new and more reliable form of security comes to replace that provided by money. Also, no interest is paid on credit balances, just as no interest is charged on debit balances.

Equally important is that the local 'currency' is not convertible into any other local currency, let alone the national one, and can only be spent on goods and services provided by other members. This means that rather than fund the production of, for instance, cash crops that are exported to satisfy the needs of distant populations – often at the price of creating local shortages – the currency is far more likely to fund the production of food for local consumption. This also provides a means of ensuring that purchasing power stays within the community. This is in sharp contrast to the situation today where money is sucked out of poor communities into the rich urban areas – where, among other things, the headquarters of the large corporations that control most of today's commerce are situated.

Thus, in the case of a predominantly black district in Baltimore, where the inhabitants are largely unemployed as a result of the closure of a steel works and the local railway station, the shops, according to Cahn and Rowe, have closed down so that there is now almost nowhere to spend the money locally. Shopping is almost entirely in an out-of-town supermarket. This means that all the money that flows into the area, mainly in the form of social security payments, almost immediately flows out again. In the case of Indian reservations, it has been calculated that it takes only 48 hours for 75 per cent of every dollar the federal government provides to flow out to border towns.

PRICING DIFFERENT SERVICES

Some LETS have a standard hourly rate for whatever the services rendered might be, but most LETS attribute a different value to different services, and in our view this certainly seems preferable.

We feel that one of the reasons why Robert Owen's Equitable Labour Exchange of 1832 to 1834 foundered was that people were paid a standard rate of UK sixpence an hour, regardless of what particular function they fulfilled; as a result, those who were earning more on the open market tended to stay away.

Most LETS seem to have adopted this view. The price of the different goods and services provided by members, however, is evaluated by the local community rather than being determined by the market. As a result, the price differential tends to be much lower than it would be within the formal economy. To take an example, a dentist in a Vancouver Island LETS started off by charging his normal fees, and then expected to hire other members to do unskilled work for him at a minute fraction of his own hourly rate. They refused. The differential still exists, but it has been drastically reduced. This change of attitude can be attributed to the ability of LETS to bring people together and negotiate as members of a community rather than as complete strangers. With Time Dollar schemes the situation is different. Payment for services provided in these schemes is not that important. Members see themselves as volunteers who are acquiring Time Dollars for doing work which many of them would be quite willing to do for free. Cahn considers that 'people who ask for help will get it even if they don't have any Time Dollars to pay for it'. Yet, the fact that they receive something for their efforts is important too, because it validates their contribution and encourages people to do things which they would never do for cash. 'A retired bank president would never mow a sick person's yard for money, but he'll do it for Time Dollars,' Cahn says. Price is not the issue, it is status. To accept money for such a task implies one has accepted the market status defined by the wage. 'Not entirely surprisingly, only 15 per cent of dollars are ever spent, and no one is refused care because of a shortfall in their account.'

BUILDING UP COMMUNITY

Perhaps the most important functions of LETS and Time Dollar schemes is their role in building up the local community. This occurs because the people involved rapidly get to know each other by working, and above all by caring for each other. As a participant in an early Canadian scheme put it, 'Just about every time I trade through the LETS system, I get to meet someone personally. I have got to know an extra 100–150 people in this way. To me, that wealth of relationships is synonymous with economic well-being' (Dauncey, 1988).

As you build up a community, people learn to trust each other. We are used to a central bank having the responsibility for maintaining confidence in the national currency – which is an increasingly difficult task – since the value of a currency is essentially determined by giant international banks and even more so by currency dealers such as George Soros. But it is not only a central bank that can create trust. Until the Scottish Bank Act of 1845, banks in Scotland were free to issue their own notes and there was no central bank. An authority on the subject, Laurence H White, concludes that bad money did not drive out good; banks did not tend to issue too many notes; and that loss of confidence in banks was not an endemic problem (White, 1987).

LETS is clearly even more decentralized, and so far there have been remarkably few defaults. This is mainly because members of the system trust and develop a sense of responsibility towards each other. It is also due to the openness of the system. One party to a prospective transaction can always ask to know the balance of the other party's accounts, and he may decline to trade if the latter's debit balance is too great. Finally, some systems also have limits on how far people can get into debt or 'in commitment' – to use the language of LETS.

THE LETS EXPERIENCE SO FAR

The first LETS was started by Michael Linton in January 1993 in the Comox Valley, British Columbia, Canada. The unit of currency was the green dollar, tied to the Canadian dollar. In its first 20 months, about 250,000 green dollars' worth of trade was carried out.

LETS was introduced to the UK in 1985, after Michael Linton described it at TOES (the other economic summit) (Linton, 1988). There are now around 400 systems with membership varying from 14 to 500. Today, roughly one-fifth of these are growing and developing dynamically.

The largest UK LETS have a turnover that equates to approximately UK£70,000 a year. The biggest, and arguably the most successful LETS, is in Australia – in the Blue Mountains of New South Wales, centred on the town of Katoomba, about one hour east of Sydney. The Blue Mountains LETS was started in February 1991 with the help of a committee of five people. Since then it has grown to be the world's biggest LETS with a current membership of about 1800 people, who between them have 1100 household accounts. In all, locally provided goods and services worth an equivalent of US$270,000 are traded every year. Among the more interesting services so far provided has been the organization of a wedding. This involved arranging for the design and production of the bridal gown, the food and the entertainment and, when it was over, the cleaning up of the mess. It has also dealt with the extension of another member's home, all the building work being paid for in the local LETS currency.

EXPERIENCE OF TIME DOLLAR SCHEMES

Time Dollars is the brainchild of Edgar and Jean Cahn. They met when students at Yale Law School and started their first Time Dollar scheme in Miami, Florida, providing services for the elderly, which is still today the main focus of many Time Dollar schemes. Tragically, Jean Cahn has since died and Edgar Cahn has moved to Washington, where he works up to 80 hours a week with students and volunteers to spread the Time Dollar idea as a memorial to her.

The Miami Time Dollar scheme remains one of the most successful. It had 900 participants in 1996, most of them elderly retired people with time on their hands. Today they are putting in more than 8000 hours of work a month at 32 different sites in different parts of the city. The scheme can be seen as a community welfare scheme and also as a vernacular insurance system. Retired people provide help for other retired people, as do younger volunteers. They are known as 'respite workers' and they are paid in Time Dollars, which they can use to obtain help for themselves or for their elderly relatives.

Similar schemes have been set up in Boston, St Louis, Brooklyn and San Francisco. In Michigan and Missouri, Time Dollar programmes have been launched with the help of the local state authorities. Several are already evolving into mini-economies, linking together people from different generations. Young people are mowing lawns and painting houses for elderly neighbours. Some members, rather than keeping the credits they have earned for themselves, actually contribute them to other elderly people who need them more. In several programmes, Time Dollars have been 'woven' into conventional medical care systems that provide services that normal dollars alone cannot buy. In this way, as Cahn and Rowe note, the elderly – among others – are becoming providers rather than simply consumers of care.

A particularly impressive Time Dollar scheme is in El Paso, a very poor town known as the poverty capital of the US, where almost two out of every four residents live below the poverty line and 80 per cent of children are born to teenage mothers. Lower Valley, directly outside the city, is even more poverty stricken. There are few jobs and hence no tax base to finance public schemes such as schools, water and medical care. Recently, Phylis Armijo of the Daughters of Charity started a Time Dollar service based on the San Vincente Health Clinic run by members of her religious order. Her idea was that under the Time Dollar scheme, people would themselves participate in the provision of health services. Although they obviously could not replace doctors, they could provide other very important services, such as transport. People had to get to the hospital for treatment, so other patients could earn Time Dollars by driving them there. They could also provide counselling and prenatal care, and help mothers once their babies were born, which turned out to be very effective in reducing infant mortality. They could also provide babysitting for the sick children of working parents and companionship for the elderly, whom they could also help with their shopping. There seemed to be no end to the services that patients could fulfil for other patients, all of which would reduce their hospital bill and give them access to medical services otherwise unavailable to them. This is exactly what is happening; for instance, the Time Dollar scheme has reduced the charge for prenatal care from US$250 to US$75.

However, Phylis Armijo is even more ambitious. Conventional medicine is largely concerned with treating those who are already sick and little is done about prevention: reducing the incidence of disease, which in the long run must be a far more effective strategy than treating the victims, which is expensive and not always successful. So Armijo extended the services that could be paid for by Time Dollars to such things as digging wells, removing lead-based paint and undertaking a survey of all possible sources of water pollution in the area, of which she identified several thousand.

WILL LETS AND TIME DOLLARS BE TAXED?

Fiscal authorities are unlikely to be overly concerned about LETS and Time Dollar schemes while they are still small; but as they grow bigger they may well feel that, as fiscal authorities, they are being done out of a lot of tax revenue. What, then, can we expect? In the UK the general position seems to be that if LETS workers are doing the sort of work they would normally do to earn their living, their LETS earnings are taxable. If, on the other hand, people are using skills they do not use in their normal work, their transactions are classified as social favours and are not taxable. This seems to be a position with which LETS can live. There have been attempts, particularly in Australia, to secure agreement that taxes, at the state level if not the national level, are paid in LETS. So far it does not seem that the government has accepted this proposition.

In the US, the experience with Time Dollar schemes in the state of Missouri has been significant. In the mid 1980s, the state passed a law to provide tax relief for members of Time Dollar schemes who took care of elderly family members at home. If no Time Dollar member was available to help the person who earned a credit in the local currency, the state committed itself to providing this help at its own expense. In 1985, the state authorities went further and asked the Internal Revenue Service (IRS) to declare money earned in the form of Time Dollars to be exempt from federal income tax. To everyone's surprise, the IRS accepted this. However, since then, the IRS has enacted new regulations which expand the definition of barter, requiring full disclosure of all such transactions on people's annual tax returns. Credits received through a barter network are now deemed to be taxable when received rather than when spent.

Fortunately, Time Dollars were made an exception to this rule. In March 1985, as Cahn and Rowe note, the regional IRS office in St Louis ruled that volunteers in the state programme who earned service credits would not be taxed on their value.

The reason is that such transactions are deemed to be of a charitable nature, which serve the public purpose and would otherwise have been provided by the State. As a result, a Time Dollar transaction is seen as fundamentally different from a transaction based on commercial barter, which could easily have been undertaken for cash. In commercial barter, it is pointed out, the parties are bound by contract and credits earned are a 'cash substitute'. In Time Dollars schemes, on the other hand, members who receive a service have no contractual and hence no legal obligation to pay for it, while people who render a service acquire 'no contractual right to compensation, the credits merely providing a means of motivating the volunteers to continue their community service'.

What is seen to be particularly important is that Time Dollar members do not have access to the courts to settle their disputes. Resorting to the courts 'means you are asserting the rights of a stranger against strangers, and that you are operating in a context of monetary values'. The IRS, as Cahn and Rowe put it, see Time Dollars systems as being very similar to the sort of transactions that once occurred among members of traditional families and communities in the pre-industrial age. 'Families and communities,' they note, 'operate on a standard of reciprocity. That is, a moral norm, not a legal one; the mechanism of enforcement is not the courts, but the sanctions that operate naturally between people' – people, they should have specified, living in a real community – of the sort that Time Dollar schemes are helping to benefit.

FUTURE DEVELOPMENTS

How, then, are LETS and Time Dollar schemes likely to develop? Firstly, it seems but a question of time before people start regarding as a hindrance the restriction that a LETS currency can only be spent in a specific locality. For example, within Perry Walker's own small scheme in London, he has no access to organic vegetables, nor to much food of any sort. There will therefore be pressure to link systems so that they can trade with each other. There are two ways in which this can happen. A centralized register could handle the accounts for several different systems. The systems could then trade with each other either if they shared a currency or if their currency could be converted into the national currency.

However, this could destroy the essence of LETS because trading would no longer be local. Hence, proponents of this view are likely to favour setting up additional systems to cover larger geographic areas, each with their own non-convertible currency, with the original, highly localized systems left in place.

Outside LETS itself there are plenty of ways to extend the range of services available to the membership. For instance, Michael Linton has suggested a LETS fund. This is a sort of community bank that only deals in the local currency. Unlike an ordinary bank, it would not charge interest on loans or, for that matter, pay interest on deposits.

The final development, which is already starting to happen, is the greater involvement of business. LETS, at least in Britain, was set up with a slightly New Age ethos. It was thus not surprising that businesses were initially suspicious. Furthermore, many individuals use skills to earn LETS funds that they would not otherwise use to earn national currency, which means that the LETS currency they earn is additional to the money they earn in their normal occupation. Businesses, on the other hand, are likely to feel that the LETS currency they earn will be at the expense of earnings in the national currency. Nevertheless, in many areas small local businesses do join after a while. One reason may be that charging partly in LETS can bring them new customers who could not afford to pay entirely in the national currency. Furthermore, their ability to pay in LETS funds reduces their expenditure in the national currency.

Again, the Australian experience illustrates how business can become involved. Already, 21 businesses have joined the Blue Mountain LETS system, together with 25 self-employed traders. The businesses involved include cafés, healing and medical centres, schools, hardware and fresh fruit and vegetable stores, together with a legal partnership, a few accountants, a bookstore, a nursery, a food cooperative and a local community newspaper called *The Weekender* (Leislink, 1994).

As this happens, what appears to be little more than a relatively marginal self-help system becomes, in effect, an almost mainstream local economy, though one that is, partly at least, insulated from the global economy that would otherwise swallow it up. This partial insulation is critical. This is why LETS cannot be allowed to expand indefinitely by allowing supermarkets and other large enterprises that are integral parts of the global economy to join – which they may well want to do if these schemes continue to grow. The end result would be totally self-defeating, and LETS must be very vigilant to ensure that this is not allowed to occur.

Cahn and Rowe make a number of interesting suggestions regarding the future development of Time Dollar schemes. One is the creation of a new government tax to meet basic social needs, and that can be paid either in dollars or in Time Dollars.

Another suggestion is to introduce Time Dollar schemes into the field of education. A portion of the financial aid to students, whether it takes the form of guaranteed student loans, tuition grants, work-study money and other benefits, would be set aside for students working in Time Dollar schemes. Students would become participants in their own education by doing such things as maintaining their college buildings, tending the gardens, growing and cooking their own food, and looking after the library. Some of these schemes are already underway at Berea College in Kentucky and also at Schumacher College in Devon, England.

The question of state involvement in Time Dollar schemes is contentious. Clearly, it is in the interests of the authorities to stimulate both LETS and Time Dollar schemes. Both seek to ensure the livelihood of people who otherwise may receive unemployment benefits and other welfare payments that the State, operating under the constraints of the global economy, must be ever less capable of providing. For this reason, the state should welcome these initiatives, even if they marginally reduce tax receipts.

This has been one of the objections levelled against these schemes. It is argued that they are just providing benefits that the state and big corporations should themselves provide, and that, as a result, they are discouraged from doing so. There is a certain element of truth in that, but the objection is not entirely fair. By building up local economies, LETS and Time Dollar schemes reduce our dependence on the state and the corporations, making it far easier for citizens to oppose the latter's socially and environmentally destructive development policies.

Finally, it could be argued that the formal world economy is already extremely unstable, and in September 1998 was on the verge of collapse. Since a vast proportion of people depend for their sustenance on the functioning of the global economy, the outcome of such collapse would have been dire. However, the consequences would have been less severe for those who organize their own local community-based economies and who, partly at least, insulate themselves from such an eventuality.

In any case, as already noted, the formal economy, dominated by corporations and the state, cannot even in the most propitious conditions provide all the benefits that were once provided by the 'kitchen table world' that they have so effectively supplanted.

Ralph Nader, in the prologue to Cahn and Rowe's excellent book, notes how 'the serious problems our society faces today come from the erosion of. . . the economy of the family and the neighbourhood', and 'the Time Dollar is a currency designed to reward time spent on rebuilding that economy' – and so, of course, are the LETS (Nader in Cahn and Rowe, 1992). That is why both these schemes are a source of great hope to us all.

Chapter 24

Saving Our Small Farms and Rural Communities

Jules Pretty

In this chapter the author documents the growing problem facing small farmers whose share of the retail price of their produce has fallen dramatically with globalization and who are being forced to leave the land in increasing numbers – leading, among other things, to the destruction of rural society. The author also catalogues the various strategies that small farmers can resort to in order to survive in the ever-less-propitious conditions that governments are creating just about everywhere. In the final analysis, of course, what is really required is a fundamental change in government priorities. Above all, the immediate economic interests of large companies must be subordinated to the imperative of sustaining a sound farming community and hence a healthy rural society.

Jules Pretty is Director of the Centre for Environment and Society (CES) at the University of Essex. From 1989 to 1997, he was Director of the Sustainable Agriculture Programme at the International Institute for Environment and Development. He is a founding member of the Agricultural Reform Group and the Neighbourhood Think Tank, a trustee for the Farmers' World Network and the Pesticides Trust.

The food and drinks system is one of the largest industrial and commercial sectors in the world, with global production amounting to some US$1500 billion per year. Half a century ago, at least half of the pound, franc, mark or dollar spent on food found its way back to the farmer and rural community. The rest was spread amongst suppliers of various inputs (feeds, pesticides, fertilizers, seeds, machinery, labour and so on) and amongst manufacturers, processors and retailers. Since then, the balance of power has shifted increasingly away from the middle, with value captured on the input side by agrochemical, feed and seed companies, and on the output side by those who move, transform and sell the food.

But for farmers and rural communities, the effect has been largely negative. Farmers get a smaller share, no more than 10 to 20 per cent, and they also pass on less, spending less in rural communities and employing fewer local people. Tens of millions of jobs have been lost in farming throughout Western Europe and North America in the past 50 years. And farms continue to be abandoned and farm labour laid off. In the US, the farmers' share at the turn of the century was 44 per cent of every dollar spent by consumers. By the 1990s, this had changed dramatically, with the farmers' share now only 9 per cent (Centre for Rural Affairs, 1996; Douthwaite, 1996). What is more, this problem can only get worse with the present trend toward economic globalization.

Similar changes have occurred in Europe. Over time, more and more of the value is being captured by manufacturing, processing and retailing. In Britain, food prices in supermarkets rose by about half between 1982 and 1992, yet only one-third of this increase got back to farmers (Raven and Lang, 1995). The centralized distribution systems and associated transport costs are expensive, and this is partly where the value is going. In Germany, about one-fifth of the food mark goes to the farmer, down from some 75 per cent in the 1950s (Greenpeace, 1992). This process has gone hand in hand with trade liberalization.

Since 1970, especially following the 1994 Uruguay Round of the GATT, large trade agreements have sought to make trade 'free' of quotas, tariffs and other trade barriers. But liberalization has not just encouraged companies to race to the bottom with their social and environmental standards. It has also led to greater concentration. Just five corporations control some 77 per cent of the cereal trade; three have 83 per cent of cocoa; three have 80 per cent of the banana trade; and three have 85 per cent of the tea trade. But only very small proportions of the price paid for this produce reach the farmers. For bananas, about 2 per cent of the price we pay in the shops goes to the fieldworker; 5 per cent to the farmer; and 88 per cent to the intermediary importers, wholesalers, retailers and freight companies (Lang and Hines, 1993; Madden, 1992; Paxton, 1994).

TAKING BACK THE MIDDLE

Can anything be done about this falling share of the food pound that finds its way back to rural communities? Or are the farmers' and rural communities' shares doomed to fall yet more, with further diminishing of rural natural and social capital? Rural communities need to find new ways of adding value to the goods and services derived from available natural capital. The Kansas Rural Centre and the Centre for Rural Affairs in Nebraska call this 'taking back the middle'. There are four ways to take back the middle, helping to spread the benefits more evenly amongst stakeholders.

SELLING DIRECTLY TO CONSUMERS

The first option is for farmers to find ways of selling their produce directly to consumers. The number of farmers already selling direct varies from country to country. In the UK, about 5 per cent of farmers sell directly, accounting for about 9 per cent of fresh produce sales. In Germany and the US, this rises to 15 per cent; in France and Japan, it is 25 per cent. But in all these cases, the volume of produce sold by each farmer is small, owing to the greater proportion of small farmers engaged in direct sales – only 5 per cent in the US and 14 per cent in France (Festing, 1997). There is a variety of proven mechanisms, including farm shops and direct mailing, farmers' and produce markets, community-supported agriculture and box schemes.

Farmers' shops and pick-your-own (PYO) operations have long been an important means for farmers to sell directly to consumers. When successful, they can make a very significant contribution to individual farm income. There are estimated to be some 1500 to 2000 farm shops and several hundred PYO enterprises in the UK (Chris Emerson, pers comm, 1997).

In France, there are some 200 collective farm shops located in cities and rural towns. These are run by small groups of farmers, each supplying a different product, such as vegetables, wine, cheese and sausages. The shops operate under a voluntary charter and seek to inform consumers about farm operations too (Festing, 1995).

Produce markets, in which growers sell directly to customers, are another option for taking back more of the food pound. Produce markets also offer the opportunity for consumers to buy organic or sustainably produced food without paying a premium. There is a long history of markets in rural towns and centres. Weekly or twice weekly markets are a part of the vitality of many small towns in Europe. In France, there are some 6000 weekly street markets involving 70,000 people. In the UK there are about 800. These markets are almost entirely dominated by traders selling wholesale produce. Very few farmers are directly involved, and so there are few direct links with the public (Festing, 1995).

In Britain, save for a recent experiment in Bath, the nearest equivalent is the Women's Institutes (WI) cooperative markets. These were started in 1919 as a way to help WI members, unemployed people, pensioners and ex-servicemen to sell surplus garden produce. They comprise a weekly market for the direct sale of homegrown and homemade produce from gardens and kitchens to the public. There are now 538 markets in England, Wales and the Channel Islands, with a further 74 in Ireland. A conservative estimate suggests that these markets reach at least 30,000 customers each week and involve a further 9000 households in production.

Turnover in the British markets has grown from UK£1 million in 1972 to UK£10 million in the early 1990s – an average of UK18,600 per market. This represents a substantial cash injection directly from consumers into local communities since all the income goes back to the shareholders of the market groups. Richard Douthwaite describes their value to consumers, who like them for the 'quality of the produce, its freshness and presentation'. But these markets have a vital social as well as an economic function since they help local people develop skills, market their produce by working together and provide a friendly meeting place.

Community-supported agriculture (CSA) is a partnership arrangement between producers and consumers designed, again, to take back more value and also to provide a guaranteed quality of food. The basic model is simple: consumers provide support for growers by agreeing to pay for a share of the total produce, and growers provide a weekly share of food of a guaranteed quality and quantity. CSAs help to reconnect people to farming. Members know where their food has come from, and farmers receive payment at the beginning of the season rather than when the harvest is in. In this way, a community shares the risks and responsibilities of farming (Clunies-Ross and Hildyard, 1992).

In most instances, a detailed annual budget for the farm is drawn up and the costs are shared by the community. Farmers start to receive payment when the crops are planted, and this income is guaranteed. Since they are growing for people, rather than an abstract market, they tend to produce a greater variety of crop. Most offer a mix of 8 to 12 vegetables, fruits and herbs per week; some link up with other CSAs to keep up diversity; and others offer value-added products such as cheese, honey and bread. The central principle is that they produce what people want, instead of concentrating on crops that could give the greatest returns. Farmers are, therefore, more likely to use resource-conserving technologies and practices.

In addition to receiving a weekly share of produce, CSA members often take part in life on the farm. Many CSA farms give out newsletters with the weekly food share, so that members stay in touch and know what crops are expected.

There are some 600 CSA operations in the US, involving 100,000 consumers and a turnover of US$10–20 million per year (this assumes an average share of US$550, an average number of 50 members and 600 CSAs). In Britain, however, there are fewer than ten subscription farms operating. Most of the growth of indirect marketing has been through box schemes.

These box schemes have several important attributes. Firstly, they ensure the good quality of the produce. Food is fresh, often picked the same day, and some 8 to 12 varieties of vegetables and fruit are put in each box each week. Farmers contract to supply the basics, such as potatoes, carrots, onions and one green vegetable, and add other produce depending on the season. Over time, box schemes also increase on-farm biodiversity. In response to consumer demand, many farmers have increased the diversity of crops grown from 20 to 50 varieties. Greater diversity satisfies demand and reduces the risk of complete failure in the face of climatic and market uncertainties.

Prices are comparable to supermarket prices for conventional vegetables, so consumers do not end up paying premiums. Box schemes also help to develop trust and understanding. Newsletters, farm visits and personal contacts increase the contact between farmers, consumers and local communities; by promoting local employment and care for the environment, they also foster community regeneration.

One rationale for these schemes is that they emphasize that payment is not just for food, but for support of the farm as a whole. It is the link between farmer and consumer that guarantees the quality of the food. This encourages social responsibility, increases the understanding of farming issues amongst consumers and increases the diversity of crops grown over time. These schemes have brought back trust, human scale and a local identity to the food we eat.

ENHANCING LINKS WITH URBAN COMMUNITIES

The second main route to taking back the middle is to enhance links with urban communities through community cooperatives and community gardens and farms. This can enable communities to take back more of the control of the food system from dominant institutions. Poverty is usually associated with ill health and poor diets. When money is tight, the cheapest way to get sufficient calories is to purchase sugary, fatty and processed foods. But these usually lack many vital ingredients, such as proteins, vitamins and minerals. Locally grown food can enhance diets as well as contribute to social capital.

Food cooperatives are an important way to get good food to urban groups with no direct access to farms and the countryside. The Cooperative Society was established over a century ago to do exactly this and has grown to be one of the largest wholesale and retailing companies in Britain. Community cooperatives are still having a significant effect. The Glasgow Healthy Castlemill project has a cooperative serving more than 3000 tenants in estates with high unemployment and high levels of heart disease. The coop buys wholesale and sells to local people with just a 1 per cent markup.

The Birmingham Organic Roundabout was set up in 1992 to supply organic foods to urban customers. It has grown rapidly, now sourcing from a group of 36 Herefordshire organic farmers, supplying 3000 regular customers and employing 15 full-time workers.

Direct links between consumers and farmers have had a spectacular success in Japan, with the rapid growth of the consumer cooperatives, *sanchoku* groups (direct from the place of production) and *teikei* schemes (tie-up or mutual compromise between consumers and producers) (Furusawa, 1994). This extraordinary movement has been driven by consumers rather than farmers, and mainly by women. There are now some 800 to 1000 groups in Japan, with a total membership of 11 million people and an annual turnover of more than US$15 billion. These consumer producer groups are based on relations of trust, and put a high value on face-to-face contact. Some of these have had a remarkable effect on farming, as well as on other environmental matters.

In countries of the South, it is common for very large numbers of urban dwellers to be directly engaged in food production. It has been estimated that 100 to 200 million urban dwellers are now urban farmers, providing food for some 700 million people (Schwarz and Schwarz, 1998; Cook and Rodgers, 1996; Smit and Ratta, 1995). In Latin American and African cities, up to one-third of vegetable demand is met by urban production; in Hong Kong and Karachi it is about half and in Shanghai it is over 80 per cent. But in the industrialized countries, far fewer people grow their own food.

Homegardens and allotments have long been important for home food production. During World War II, when the Dig for Victory campaign encouraged greater home production, half of all manual workers in Britain kept an allotment or vegetable garden; domestic hen keepers produced one-quarter of the national egg production; and pig clubs were promoted. In 1944, some 120,000 hectares of allotments and gardens produced about 1.3 million tons of food, about half of the nation's fruit and vegetable needs (Garnett, 1996). The National Society of Allotment and Leisure Gardeners' figures put the current number of allotments in England, Wales and Scotland at about 300,000, covering some 12,150 hectares, just one-tenth of the extent during the war. Nonetheless, these yield some 215,000 tons of fresh produce every year (G W Stokes, pers comm, 1997).

The US National Gardeners Association (NGA) estimates that some 35 million people are engaged in growing their own food in back gardens and allotments. Their contribution to the informal economy is huge. The so-called gross national home garden product, a measure of the value of the food grown, is estimated to be about US$12–14 billion per year. According to the NGA, private gardeners cultivate mostly to produce better tasting and more nutritious food, but also to save money, and for exercise and therapy. It makes them feel better. This is particularly true of community gardens and farms which, by contrast, seek to enhance both food production and social benefits. In New York, 87 per cent of community gardeners invest their time in gardening in order to improve the neighbourhood; 75 per cent for fresh vegetable production; 62 per cent for fun; and 42 per cent to save money (Weissman, 1995; 1996).

There are now several hundred city farms or community gardens in the UK. The 1996 report *Growing Food in Cities* by Tara Garnett for the National Food Alliance and the SAFE Alliance describes 38 examples of community schemes. They provide food, especially vegetables and fruit, for poorer urban groups and a range of other natural products such as wood, flowers and herbs. They add local value to produce before sale. They sometimes encourage derelict or vacant land to be transformed into desirable areas for local people to visit and enjoy, resulting in the creation of quiet, tranquil places for the community that can support wildlife. The involvement of schoolchildren can mean a reduction in vandalism, as well providing local children with an educational opportunity to learn about farming and animals. City farms also provide the opportunity for mental health patients to engage in work that builds self-esteem and confidence, and for unemployed people to use their time productively in their own community.

INCREASING COOPERATION BETWEEN FARMERS

The third option for taking back the middle is to increase collaboration between farmers' groups, cooperatives and alliances, in order to create social capital by learning and working together. Examples include participatory research and experimenting groups, machinery rings, comarketing groups and community food cooperatives. Sustainable agriculture is knowledge and management intensive and therefore needs timely and relevant information to produce value. Yet, farmers commonly lack this vital knowledge. By experimenting themselves, they are able to increase their own awareness of what does and what does not work. Few farmers can engage in new methods alone, and so collective efforts are vital.

These may be formal or informal groups, such as traditional leadership structures, water management committees, water-user groups, neighbourhood groups, youth or women's groups, housing societies, informal beer-brewing groups, farmer experimentation groups, burial societies, church groups, mothers' groups, pastoral and grazing-management groups, tree-growing associations, labour-exchange societies, and so on. They have been effective in many ecosystems and cultures, including collective water management in the irrigation systems of Egypt, Mesopotamia and Indonesia; collective herding in the Andes and pastoral systems of Africa; water harvesting and management societies in Roman North Africa, India and south-west North America; and forest management in shifting agricultural systems. Many of these societies were sustainable over hundreds to thousands of years.

During the agricultural revolution of the 18th and 19th centuries, farmers' groups played a vital role in spreading knowledge about new technologies (Pretty, 1991). At a time when there was no ministry of agriculture, no research or extension institutions, farmers organized their own experiments and extended the results to others through tours, open days, farmer groups and publications. Farmer groups and societies were central to the diffusion of new technologies. The first were established in the 1720s and increased in number to over 500 by 1840. These groups offered prizes for new or high-quality livestock, crops and machines; encouraged experimentation with new rotational patterns; held regular shows and open days; bought land for experimental farms run by the group; arranged tours to visit well-known innovators; and articulated farmers' needs to national agencies and government.

However, throughout the history of modern agricultural development, local groups and institutions have rarely been recognized. As a result, external institutions and governments have routinely suffocated local institutions during agricultural modernization. Local management has been substituted with state control, leading to increased dependence of local people on formal state institutions. Local information networks have been replaced by research and extension activities; banks and cooperatives have substituted for local credit arrangements; and cooperatives and marketing boards have been replaced by input and product markets. When traditional social institutions collapse or disappear, it is common for natural capital to degrade.

As indicated in earlier chapters of this book, the fundamental challenge for sustainable agriculture is to create and support processes that foster learning. When farmers and other rural people are well linked and trust each other, then it is possible for learning mechanisms to be established. Sustainability needs perpetual novelty and adaptive performance. These are best delivered by local people working together in groups. And the more that information and knowledge is locally generated and locally applied, the more that value is taken back into local systems.

PARTICIPATORY RESEARCH BY FARMERS

The normal mode of modern agricultural research has been to conduct experiments under controlled conditions on research stations, with the results and technologies passed on to farmers. In this process, farmers have no control over experimentation and technology adaptation. Farmers' organizations can, however, help research institutions to become more responsive to local needs, if scientists are willing to relinquish some of their control over the research process. But this implies new roles for both farmers and scientists, and it takes a deliberate effort to create the conditions for such research-oriented local groups. Nonetheless, there have been successes in both industrialized and developing countries.

Self-learning is vital for sustainable agriculture. By experimenting themselves, farmers can increase their own awareness of what does and does not work. But few farmers can engage in developing the new methods and principles alone, and so any kind of group activities that embody co-learning and study are vital. The transition to sustainable agriculture, therefore, needs networks of farmers who can jointly engage in learning and experimentation. In Norway, the first experimental farmers' groups, or *forsöksring*, were set up in 1937 (Gedde-Dahl, 1992). There are now more than 100, each employing an agronomist. Members contribute to costs, but only two-thirds of the funding comes from the state. The greatest impacts have been on mutual trust and respect, on farmers' changed knowledge and social learning, and on more rapid uptake of technologies developed by other farmers through on-farm research.

In the Netherlands, the 38 pilot farms that were part of the Integrated Arable Farming Systems (IAFS) network showed that it was possible to farm more sustainably without losing money. This was scaled up to involve 500 farmers as part of the Arable Farming 2000 Project. This, in turn, is beginning to have an impact on other organizations. The hitherto conservative Northern Agricultural Farmers' Organization, with 12,000 members, launched its own scheme to test and spread integrated farming amongst its members, even though it has, in recent years, been a vigorous supporter of only high-input farming. According to farmers, the IAFS network creates an opportunity to experiment with new practices; farmers feel there is greater use of their professional skills, and so they get increased pleasure from their work. And they know there is now a more positive contribution to the environment. This is a common feature of farmers working in groups. They feel less alone and more a part of a joint effort for agricultural improvement that they themselves can influence and control (van Weperen and Raling, 1995).

Recent work in Devon as part of the wider Sustainable Agriculture Partnership has also illustrated the critical role of farmer involvement in experimentation. Designed Visions has been helping farmers to develop regenerative technologies in the Blackdown Hills, a remote and predominantly livestock area. Soil reconditioning has been an important innovation for the rejuvenation of permanent pastures. The process involves machines that cut into the surface of grassland to leave parallel furrows 10 centimetres or more deep. These substantially increase the waterholding capacity, growing season, number of earthworms and soil organic matter. It also means that farmers do not need to engage in the destruction of traditional grasslands by reseeding or adding large amounts of fertilizer. According to Andy Langford, 'farmers' willingness to experiment and innovate has been crucial – without this the technologies would not have been fitted to highly site-specific conditions'.

ECOLABELLING, ASSURANCE SCHEMES AND TRACEABILITY

The fourth option is to enhance labelling and traceability of foodstuffs in order to increase consumers' confidence about both the source and quality of foods. This can be done through ecolabelling and other assurance schemes, organic standards and fair trade schemes. Although organic products have long been clearly labelled for consumers, it is only recently that there has been an expansion in the range of ecolabels. These have been given greater urgency by recent food scares about BSE, *E-coli* and pesticide residues. The question consumers are increasingly asking is: can the food on the shelves be trusted? Ecolabels are important since they tell consumers something about the way that the food was produced. They help to create a bond between consumer and producer. They allow growers and processors to be rewarded for using environmentally friendly production processes. They also permit consumers to express their values while making purchases. And, if they work, they help to push the food and agriculture industry towards more sustainable practices (Lang, 1995b; MacRae, 1997).

In Britain, the UK Register of Organic Food Standards sets strict standards for organic farmers; people buying products labelled with the Soil Association standard can be confident that they are getting what they expect. Recently, however, a range of 'assurance' schemes have emerged. These are not organic but do seek to assure consumers about the conditions under which livestock and crops are raised or grown. Interestingly, farmers' views of these schemes are changing from perceiving them as constraints to viewing them as vital in holding onto market share. One response has been to say that farmers should not subject themselves to tighter production rules than foreign competitors have, since they would lose market share. One farmer from Yorkshire, Peter Hepworrh, put it like this in July 1997: 'the NFU wishes to saddle future farmer generations with restrictions and straitjackets under the banner of cereal assurance schemes. . . The idea is totally mad. . . Only when our main cereal competitors seek to impose such rubbish should we even consider following suit' (*Farmers' Weekly*, 4 July 1997).

However, most now see traceability as an increasingly vital part of the industry. The intention is that any food product can be traced back to the individual farmer. Not only will this provide a link when food scares do happen, but it is also hoped that consumers' confidence will rise as the information with which they are provided also increases. The Farm Assured British Beef and Lamb (FABBL) scheme was the first to be launched by farmers in 1992. By 1997, it had some 20,000 members. In 1996, Farm Assured British Pigs (FABPIG) was also launched. Like the beef scheme, it covers animals from birth to slaughter and includes strict standards of cleanliness and welfare for farmers, transporters and abattoirs. Quarterly farm inspections by local vets will provide independent auditing of farm practices. Other schemes include the Scottish Quality Beef and Lamb Assurance, with 8000 members by 1997. This scheme provides independent audits of all members, whether feed markets, farmers, auction markets, hauliers, meat-processing plants or retail shops. The Assured Combinable Crops Scheme was launched at the end of 1996 to ensure that grain is produced with due regard to codes of practice and the quality of the environment.

Some of these new schemes have been criticized. One problem is that there are now so many that it is difficult to be sure what each guarantees. Some argue that all schemes need to be brought under one national umbrella that has strong teeth and is enforceable. Others say that they are not as well defined as organic standards. These have been tested and refined over many years and are widely accepted by growers, retailers and consumers alike. But some new labels give the impression that food is wholesome and produced in a sustainable fashion: these may simply be no more than hollow labels. 'Farm fresh' and 'environmentally friendly' may look good but have no effect whatsoever on food production methods. It has been alleged, for example, that intensively produced cattle in Britain are sometimes put out to graze on pastures for only very short periods, in order that the meat may receive a 'farm fresh' label. In Germany, 'Black Forest ham' is intended to conjure up images of environmentally sensitive pig rearing in a forest, perhaps where consumers once spent their holidays. Yet, according to Rainer Luick, '90 per cent of the pigs are fattened in pig units in the Netherlands, Denmark and Poland' (Luick, 1996). Nonetheless, new forms of labelling are vital since they let consumers know about the mode and place of production. It also lets them know more about the contribution that agriculture can make to social and natural capital. Real Foods of Ireland, for example, is a recent initiative intended to add value to food that is produced in an independent and responsible fashion. It has 45 members and, as Giana Ferguson of Cork put it, 'sees food culture at the centre of creating and building community' (Giana Ferguson, pers comm, 1997).

A good example of local labelling comes from Devon, where the Taw Torridge Estuary Project is bringing farmers together to make the best of distinctive local saltmarsh resources (Bell, 1996). Sheep grazed on saltmarshes can increase plant biodiversity if managed properly. They have fewer diseases and the lamb meat has a distinctive flavour, although management is more demanding owing to the uncertainties of tides and irregular inundation. Taking the success of the *pré salé* lamb raised on the saltmarshes of Normandy and Brittany as an example, Andy Bell and colleagues have been developing ways to market this lamb more effectively in order to increase returns to farmers.

A new Dutch green-label certification scheme is called Milieukeur. This has been established with the backing of the Dutch Ministry of Agriculture, Nature and Fisheries (de Vries, 1996). The Milieukeur label is applied to cereals, onions and field vegetables. This system is seen as a way of gradually raising standards without forcing farmers to change overnight, but it does rely on consumers being willing and able to pay premiums for the 'better-quality' food. It contains tough conditions for pesticide use, including a commitment to reduce by 50 per cent the amounts applied compared with 1980 levels.

The potato label is the most advanced. In 1995, 100 growers produced 20,000 tons of Milieukeur potatoes. Some 3 to 4 per cent of apples and pears are also marketed this way. As Milieukeur producers meet the conditions set out in the government's Multi-Year Crop Protection Plan (which sought to reduce total pesticide use by 50 per cent by the year 2000), Pat Matteson and colleagues have predicted that Milieukeur will market, by 2000, some 60 per cent of all sugar beet, 30 per cent of apples and pears, 25 per cent of cooking apples and 10 per cent of arable, vegetables, pork and dairy products (Proost and Matteson, 1997a, b).

In Canada, many organizations are developing 'locally produced' symbols that allow consumers to identify foods from their own region. Ontario has four such labels. Says Rod MacRae of the Toronto Food Policy Council: 'such labels allow consumers to make purchases based on their feelings about a particular place'. But not all are in favour: 'for transnationals, this is a direct contradiction to the type of food system they are trying to develop – one where consumers have no allegiance to place, but only to price and perceived quality, as expressed through brand allegiance' (MacRae, 1997).

Labelling, therefore, exposes some vital contradictions. Foods must contain details of all the additives and preservatives incorporated during processing, but no such rules exist for details of pesticide residues. Some countries label foods that contain genetically modified organisms (GMOs); others do not, giving consumers no choice. Many commentators are very concerned about how the international food standards bodies, the Codex Alimentarius Commission of the UN and the International Standards Organization (responsible for the ISO 14000 environmental protocols), are interpreting the new rules of the WTO. The Codex, for example, has 105 countries participating in its committees that deliberate and arbitrate on a wide range of food issues, yet it also has representatives from 140 multinational companies. One study of the 1988–1991 committee cycle found that there were 26 representatives from public interest groups and 662 from industry (Avery et al, 1993).

COMPANIES AHEAD OF LEGISLATION?

Despite this confusion, some European and US companies are adopting rules for their growers that are stricter than required by legislation. Some are now encouraging all their growers to use integrated crop management (ICM) technologies, not in order to acquire a label that leads to increased food prices, but to guarantee a market share. Birds Eye Walls has stipulated that all contract growers of peas (on 50,000 hectares) will be required to register with the linking environment and farming (LEAF) scheme in 1998.

In the US, the companies Gerber and Campbell have strict quality-control systems on farms and in processing. Yet neither company markets its products in a differentiated way (North West Food Alliance, 1995). The companies say it would provide no obvious market advantage; but it may well be that they simply do not wish to draw the public's attention to the fact that pesticides were used in the past, even though amounts have been reduced now. Alistair Leake of Cooperative Wholesale Society (CWS) Agriculture in the UK put it this way: 'Produce grown under an integrated regime will not, indeed should not, command a price premium. It is a standard to which every grower should aspire. . . The economic imperative will be the difference between selling and not selling their production, rather than any niche market "green" premiums' (Leake, 1996).

Other changes are being made ahead of legislation. In the US, the North West Food Alliance has brought together a wide range of stakeholder groups, including farmers, food producers, distributors, environmentalists and consumer groups, to encourage the transition towards sustainable agriculture (North West Food Alliance, 1995–1996). The major concern is to support maximum farmer innovation in order to produce better-quality food for consumers. The impact on farming practice has been significant: apple growers, for example, have found that by reducing nitrogen applications to 28 kilogrammes per hectare they can sustain yields since there is less aphid damage, earlier leaf drop and reduced pruning needs. Others have dramatically cut pesticide and fungicide use in vegetable cultivation.

This is surely good for consumers and for farmers; it widens choice and increases the number of farmers engaged in more sustainable practices. It does not, however, guarantee the complete transition towards sustainability.

CONSUMERS MAKE A DIFFERENCE WITH FAIR TRADE

Trade is enormously important to the global economy. Since 1970, it has more than tripled in value to US$4000 billion and is now outpacing the expansion of the world economy by a factor of three (Scenario 2010 Working Group). The EU is now the world's largest trading bloc, making up 21.5 per cent of world trade, compared with 18 per cent for the US and 10 per cent for Japan.

Trade has become progressively more liberal since 1970, especially following the Uruguay Round of the GATT, completed in 1994, and the setting up of the WTO. Now there are large trade agreements that seek to make trade 'free' of quotas, tariffs and other trade barriers. But there are many criticisms of the trend to globalization and free trade. As we have seen, increasing global trade has led to a race to the bottom in terms of environmental and social standards, as well as the concentration of trade into the hands of a few global players.

However, there are alternatives in the form of 'fair trade' products. These try to guarantee a better deal for producers of the South and ensure that consumers receive good-quality produce. Consumers can make a big difference to this market: the EU imports three times as much food from developing countries than does the US, and twice as much as the other G8 partners put together. The Fairtrade Foundation is an example. It licenses and promotes the fair trade mark as an indicator to consumers that their products are giving a 'better deal to producers in developing countries' (Fairtrade Foundation, 1995–1996). The basic assumption is that the conditions of poverty in which people live are due, at least in part, to the manner by which industrialized countries trade with them.

The products most commonly subject to fair trade marketing are chocolate, coffee and tea. Producers are paid a higher than world price and are guaranteed a market price for at least three years ahead. In 1995, it was estimated that UK£150,000 extra was paid to producers of Fairtrade-marked products over and above what they would have received. There are considerable social as well as economic benefits for local people. It is now estimated that there are some 100,000 Mexican farmers producing fair trade coffee by organic methods (Geier, 1996).

Other examples of successful fair trade products include organic cotton for textiles from Uganda, Senegal, Turkey and India; tagua nuts for buttons from Ecuador; bananas from the Caribbean; soft fruit from Chile; and tea from Sri Lanka (Robins and Roberts, 1997). All of these have resulted in greater returns to rural people, much of which goes towards improving the conditions of whole communities. Cafédirect is a brand of blended fair trade coffee now sold in 1700 supermarkets in the UK. Fourteen producer organizations in Mexico, Costa Rica, Peru, Nicaragua, the Dominican Republic, Uganda and Tanzania supply the coffee. In five years, it has captured 3 per cent of the share of the British market – which means that some 460,000 families in these countries are benefiting.

Ultimately, the long term fate of our farming community must hinge on a change in government priorities. Governments need to be reminded that a thriving farming community provides the backbone of a healthy rural society. To replace our small- and medium-sized farms with large-scale monocultures can only lead to further losses in both rural society and the quality of the rural environment. All governments must be persuaded that we can no longer afford to think in purely economic terms – we must also take into account social, ecological and purely human considerations.

Chapter 25

The New Protectionism of 'Localization'

Colin Hines and Tim Lang

Protectionism has received a bad name, due to the constant charge that any attempt to preserve regional or community values, traditional economies or local jobs is an assault against the higher cause of the global economy. But the global economy is little more than a protectionist tactic used by TNCs and banks against any ability of communities to preserve their own sustainability or that of nature. In this chapter, the authors turn the table on critics of protectionism. They argue that the preservation and rebuilding of communities and livelihoods is itself the higher goal. This 'localization' is far more urgent than preserving the globalization that is already failing.

Colin Hines is the coordinator of Protect the Local, Globally, an anti-free trade, pro-localist think-tank. He is also an associate of the IFG. Before that he was the coordinator of Greenpeace International's Economic Unit, having worked for the organization for ten years. His latest book, Localization – A Global Manifesto, *was published in 2000 by Earthscan. He is also coauthor with Tim Lang of* The New Protectionism – Protecting our Future Against Free Trade, *also published by Earthscan.*

Tim Lang is professor of food policy at Thames Valley University's Centre for Food Policy. He has worked as an academic, in NGOs and as a consultant to local, national and international bodies. He was director of the London Food Commission from 1984 to 1990 and director of Parents for Safe Food from 1990 to 1994. He is chair of Sustain, the UK's 105 food NGO alliance, and a member of the IFG. He works on food policy and the public interest, linking public and environmental health with consumers and social justice. He appears frequently in UK and international media.

The 1999 'Battle of Seattle' stopped the WTO in its tracks and was symptomatic of the growing worldwide opposition to globalization. It is now time for a coherent alternative to emerge to take its place, and this is what we term the new protectionism of localization.

We feel it crucial to move the debate about globalization beyond issue-specific horror stories such as banana and beef hormone wars, GM food, leg-hold traps and so on. Instead, we must focus on what should be the new goal of world trade and how radical change might be achieved. There is a need for a blatant and heretical call for the rejection of the worldwide theology of globalization and international competitiveness. Unless this occurs, social, community, environmental and developing world campaigners, trades unions and small businesses will win the odd skirmish, but continue to lose the war.

It is imperative to play the globalizers at their own game. They have a clear end goal: maximum trade and money flows for maximum profit. From this end goal comes a clear set of policies and trade rules supporting this approach. Those seeking a more just, secure, environmentally sustainable future need to have their own clear end goal and policies for achieving it. We are certain that what is required is nothing less than a 'mind wrench' away from simply opposing globalization towards the policies that will deliver its alternative – *localization*.

Localization reverses the trend of globalization by discriminating in favour of the local. Depending on context, the 'local' may be part of a nation state, the state itself or even a regional grouping of states. At the heart of localization is a rejection of today's environmentally and socially damaging subservience to the shibboleth of 'international competitiveness'. In its place we must prioritize *local* production and the protection and diversification of *local* economies. What can sensibly be produced within a nation or a region should be. Long-distance trade should supply only what cannot be produced within the local economy. Localizing policies will increase control of the economy by communities and nations, creating greater social cohesion, reduced poverty and inequality, improved livelihoods, social infrastructure and environmental protection, and with these a marked enhancement of the all-important sense of security.

Localization is *not* about restricting the flows of that sort of information, technology, trade, investment, management and legal structures that themselves further localization. These would be encouraged by the new localist emphasis in global aid and trade rules, and such transfers would play a crucial role in the transition from globalization to localization. The rules for this diminished international sector would be those of the 'fair trade' movement, giving preference to goods supplied in a way that is of benefit to workers, the local community and the environment. Beggar-your-neighbour globalization would give way to better-your-neighbour localization. We must stress that this is not a return to overpowering state control, or an attempt to put the clock back, but the provision of a policy and economic framework which allows people, community groups and businesses to rediversify their own local economies.

ACHIEVING LOCALIZATION

The first step to localization is the 'mind wrench' away from passive acceptance that globalization is as inevitable as gravity and towards a set of self-reinforcing measures that will bring about a 'protect the local, globally' end goal for the international economic system. Protective safeguards such as import and export controls, quotas and subsidies will need to be introduced over a clearly agreed transition period. These will not be introduced as old-style protectionism which seeks to protect a home market whilst expecting others to remain open. Any residual long-distance global trade will instead be geared to funding the diversification of local economies. Such a dramatic, radical change will need to be introduced firstly at the level of regional groupings of countries, especially the most powerful – Europe and/or North America.

LOCALIZING PRODUCTION AND CONTROLLING TRANSNATIONAL CORPORATIONS (TNCs)

Industry will be localized by 'site here to sell here' policies, to ensure localized production. Threats by TNCs to relocate thus become less plausible as the market is lost to existing, or government-encouraged, new local competitors. Once TNCs are thus grounded, then their domestic activities and the levels of taxation paid are back under democratic control. Campaigners' demands for social, labour and environmental standards also become feasible. Adequate company taxation can help compensate the poor for any increases in prices.

LOCALIZING MONEY

The disastrous effects of the unfettered international flow of money have led to global calls for some controls to be reintroduced. What is required is a regrounding of money to remain predominantly in the locality or country of origin in order to fund the rebuilding of diverse, sustainable local economies. Measures include controls on capital flows, Tobin-type taxes on speculation, control of tax evasion, including off-shore banking centres, and the rejuvenation of locally orientated banks, credit unions and LETS schemes. Public and private flows of money to other countries must also be directed to strengthen the local economies of the countries concerned.

A LOCALIST COMPETITION POLICY

Local competition policies will ensure that high-quality goods and services are provided as a result of a more level, but more local, playing field. Free of the 'race to the bottom' competitive pressures from foreign competition, business can be carried out within the framework of ever improving labour, social and environmental regulations, enhanced by the best ideas and technologies from around the world. Government competition policy will cover the structure and market share of businesses, as well as regulate the behaviour of firms through, for example, an 'open book' policy to tackle tax avoidance.

Taxes For Localization

To pay for the transition to localization and to improve the environment, the bulk of taxation will come from gradually increasing resource taxes, such as on non-renewable energy use and pollution. To promote a more equitable society, the increased barriers to imports, and the removal of the option of relocation or the availability of foreign tax havens, will make it possible for companies and individuals to be taxed according to their wealth and income, on their spending through value-added tax and on their land. Part of this taxation will be used to compensate the poorer sections of society from any resulting price rises and by shifting taxes away from those on employment to encourage more jobs.

Democratic Localism

A diverse local economy requires the active democracy of everyday involvement in producing the maximum range of goods and services close to the point of consumption. To ensure the broadest distribution of the ensuing benefits will require wider political, democratic and economic control at a local level. A citizen's income will allow involvement in the economy as a matter of right. Political funding will be strictly constrained and power will pass from the corporations to the citizens. This will involve the encouragement of maximum participation in defining priorities and planning local economic, social and environmental initiatives. It will also require a balance of involvement of the state, community networks and organizations and citizens' movements.

Trade and Aid for Localization

The GATT rules at present administered by the World Trade Organization should be revised fundamentally to become a General Agreement for Sustainable Trade (GAST), administered by a democratic World Localization Organization (WLO). Their remit would be to ensure that regional trade and international aid policies and flows, information and technological transfer, as well as residual international investment and trade, should incorporate rules geared to the building up of sustainable local economies. The goal should be to foster maximum employment through a substantial increase in sustainable, regional self-reliance.

THE 'NEW PROTECTIONISM' OF LOCALIZATION: A CRITIQUE

A number of arguments are often put forward against our approach.

The world lives by international trade and countries will suffer without it

This argument fudges the greater question: what sort of trade? Today, international trade pressures are causing a loss of jobs, driving the deregulation of wages and social and environmental conditions, reducing elected governments' control over their economy, and thus undermining the value of democracy. Of course, the transition from the present economic emphasis on competitive exports to one where trade takes place as locally as possible to rebuild sustainable local economies will occur over a number of years. This will allow those involved with long-distance trade to focus on markets closer to home. There will continue to be some sectors involved in long-distance trade, because their output is not available in many parts of the world. Examples are likely to include some cash crops and minerals and certain location-specific luxury items such as whisky.

Lack of competition is inefficient

This argues that consumers lose if countries and domestic companies are protected. Who wants expensive and shoddy goods and services? The scourge of inefficiency is competition. The assumption is that giant corporations compete for purchasers' favours, but their power frequently results in their monopoly of the market. By delineating markets more locally, localization policies promote the positive aspects of competition; the impetus to be cost competitive, utilize better design, make more efficient use of resources and so on will be maintained. Lack of competition from those countries where wages, conditions and environmental laws are laxer will allow standards to be increased. Although there will be constraints on long-distance trade of goods and services, it is crucial that there are no impediments to the international flow of new information and relevant technology where it contributes to the localization end goals.

No one country can go it alone

Since the retreat from the exchange rate mechanism, all European governments know the power of the global financial markets only too well. The turmoil in the

Asian Tiger economies has made this realization global. 'Localization' policies cannot be achieved through autarky (or go-it-alone) policies. They will only emerge if the countries of the most powerful blocs in the world, such as the EU or North America, promote them. They alone are big and powerful enough markets to be able to dictate conditions to international capital and TNCs. Other regions would follow suit very quickly. In any case, established trade blocs as well as newer regional trading blocks (ASEAN, Mercosur, SADEC, etc) are increasing intraregional trade which could make such a transition easier.

Why reduce long-distance trade, when most trade already occurs within regions anyway, and relocation from North to South is not that significant?

It is true that trade between nations in regional blocs is already on the increase, which could make this basic localization approach easier. It requires an acceleration of this trend, but with one crucial difference – the end goal of protecting, rebuilding and rediversifying the local economy. Today, such intraregional trade is highly competitive, involves relocation, or the threat of it, and so reduces the potential for maximum employment and environmental protection. Enough companies are moving from North to South, ranging from low-tech to hi-tech, from sandals to software, to make the challenge to workers and governments effective should they threaten the competitiveness and profit levels of business and capital by 'excessive' improvements in wages, conditions, tax rises and environmental protection.

A fortress economy in Europe or North America would be unfair to the poor of the developing world who depend on trade to escape poverty

A handful of developing countries, mostly in Asia, dominate trade with, and receive most of the foreign direct investment from, the OECD. They could substitute this trade over the five- to ten-year transition period to localization by increasing their interregional trade. For the rest of the developing countries, and indeed for most of Eastern Europe, the present system forces such countries to distort their economies to produce the cheapest exports, usually in competition with other poor countries. Competition is not just setting poor against richer workers, but poor against poor. This drains resources from meeting the basic needs of the poor majority in these countries. The key challenge is not to encourage further spirals of ruthless competition, but for aid and trade rules to be drastically rewritten so that they facilitate the building up and diversification of local economies globally. Only then will the needs of the poor majority be met. Transfer of information, skills and appropriate technology will be actively encouraged to further the end goal of rebuilding local economies.

Localization will pander to right-wing nationalism

At present, the adverse effects of the globalization process on the majority's sense of security is leading to the spread of what could be termed 'free market fascism'. In Europe, for example, the increased insecurity heightened by the public-sector job losses and expenditure cut-backs needed to meet the convergence criteria of the single currency have resulted in mass demonstrations greater than anything seen since the 1930s. Ominously, the conditions created by the single currency and other effects of globalization have led to the rise of the extreme right in Austria, France, Germany and Italy. The Asian crisis has led to increased racial tensions towards migrant labour and ethic minorities, and the Russian upheavals have seen an increase in anti-Jewish and anti-foreigner sentiment.

The hope and security offered by localization can help reverse the very conditions of insecurity which are fostering the rise of this ugly nationalist right.

Chapter 26

The Last Word

A Personal Commentary by Edward Goldsmith

There are no cosmetic solutions to the problems that confront us. They are the inevitable consequences of economic growth or development and in particular its globalization, which is the logical extension of this process to the world as a whole. Its main feature is that it involves the systematic takeover, partly by the state but increasingly by ever-more-powerful corporations, of all those functions that throughout our tenancy of this planet have been fulfilled at a family and community level. The author tries to show that it is unfortunately only at these levels, that is, within the context of the 'social economy', that these functions can be effectively fulfilled. This, particularly, is true of democratic government and this is one of the main reasons why the economy must be localized: for only in this way can it provide the necessary economic infrastructure for the resurgence of healthy families and communities. For the author, there is no other means of recreating a just and sustainable world, or even of assuring human survival on an increasingly beleaguered planet.

The development of the global economy, which has been institutionalized with the signing of the GATT Uruguay Round and the setting up of the WTO will, we were assured, usher in an era of unprecedented prosperity for all. However, as the contributors to this book have sought to show, this assertion is based on no serious considerations of any kind. On the contrary, it can only lead for most of humanity to an unprecedented increase in general insecurity, unemployment, poverty, disease, malnutrition and environmental disruption.

It is difficult for those who have had a modern education to understand why this must be so. We have all been taught that economic development, measured by an ever increasing GNP, is the key to world prosperity and human well-being. Hence, all possible efforts must be made to maximize GNP, which means investing as much as possible in scientific and technological innovation, and making sure that the whole development enterprise is managed by ever larger and more 'efficient' corporations that cater for an ever bigger and 'freer' market.

However, this is precisely what we have been doing in the last 50 years, during which time development has been the overriding goal of governments throughout the world. Trillions of dollars have already been poured into development schemes by multinational development banks, bilateral aid agencies and private enterprises. Revolutionary new technologies have transformed agriculture, industry and services alike. Tariffs have been drastically reduced, and small companies, catering for the domestic economy, have been systematically replaced by vast transnational corporations catering for an ever expanding world market. World GNP, as a result, has increased by sixfold and world trade by twelvefold. If conventional wisdom were right, then the world should have been transformed into a veritable paradise. Poverty, unemployment, malnutrition, homelessness, disease and environmental disruption should be but vague memories of our barbaric and underdeveloped past. Needless to say, the opposite is true. Never have these problems become more serious and more widespread.

By setting up the WTO, of course, governments are further accelerating the process of global economic development by removing all conceivable constraints on trade, and indeed on just about all the activities of the TNCs that control it, regardless of social, ecological and moral implications. In other words, instead of accepting the incontrovertible empirical evidence that this policy can only increase the problems we face today, governments, under pressure from the transnational corporations, insist in pursuing it still further.

If we are really to solve these problems, as in their hearts, most people must clearly realize, society must follow the very opposite path. Instead of seeking to create a single global economy, controlled by vast and ever less controllable transnational corporations, we should create a diversity of loosely linked, community-based economies, managed by much smaller companies that cater above all (though clearly not exclusively) for local or regional markets. In other words, it is not economic globalization that we should aim for but *economic localization*.

In saying this, I am, in effect, calling for a reversal of economic globalization and indeed of the very process of economic development, of which globalization is but the logical conclusion. But this does not mean reconstituting the past. We have been indelibly marked by the experience of the industrial era, and the local economies that we will seek to create cannot be slavish imitations of those that previously existed. However, since, until recently, economies have always been largely localized, their experience must clearly be seriously considered.

To understand why economic development, leading as it must eventually do to economic globalization, must be reversed, means looking very much more carefully at what it really involves and what are its inevitable implications.

For perhaps as much as 95 per cent of our tenancy of this planet, all those functions that today are fulfilled by the state and the corporations were once fulfilled by the family, or perhaps more precisely by the household and the community. The household produced most of its food, though the more demanding tasks involved cooperation between households and sometimes by the community as a whole. The household made most of its own clothes and other artefacts, and acquired those that it did not make itself from within the community. It brought up the young and looked after the old and the sick. The community administered justice, maintained social order and ensured that the traditional religious ceremonies were properly performed. It was thus largely self-sufficient and, indeed, self-governing.

Jeremy Rifkin refers to Labour historian Harry Braverman, who tells us that in the US as late as 1890, even those families living in highly industrialized regions, such as the coal and steel communities of Pennsylvania, were still producing virtually all of their food at home – over half the families raised their own poultry, livestock and vegetables, purchasing only potatoes at the market.

Of course, communities in New England were originally self-governing as well, as is amply testified by Alexis de Tocqueville in his *Democracy in America*; in parts of eastern France and in Switzerland, communities to a large extent still are self-governing today (Layton, 1995).

David Korten refers to the largely non-monetized economy of the household and the community as 'the social economy'. For him, 'social economies are by nature local, non-waged, non-monetized and non-market. Therefore, they are not counted in national income statistics, do not contribute to measured economic growth and are undervalued by policy-makers, who count only activities in the market economy as productive contributions to national output.' But their function was more important than this. As Korten says, 'the very conduct of these activities serves to maintain the social bonds of trust and obligation, the "social capital" of the community' (Korten, 1994).

Korten also notes that 'a considerable proportion of economic growth in recent decades is simply a result of shifting functions from the social economy, where they are not counted in GNP, to the market economy, where they are'. He might have added that this is what economic growth or development is all about. Thus, as it proceeds, food and clothes now have to be bought, the young are brought up in creches, schools and universities, and which under the new regulations of the GATS are now to be privatized; the old and the sick are looked after in special homes and hospitals which are also now to be privatized; and so on. In this way, all these and other critical functions are disembedded from their natural social context, commodified and increasingly privatized, and hence ever less available to the poor and the needy. In addition, in such conditions, the family and the community, stripped of their natural functions, can only atrophy and we get an atomized society made up of socially deprived and increasingly alienated people whose only remaining functions are to produce and consume.

If, until very recently, human families and communities were quite capable of looking after themselves without the intervention of any outside agencies, such as state institutions and corporations, so were the highly diverse ecosystems that make up the natural world, and it is largely on the inestimable benefits provided by their normal functioning, and on those of the natural world as a whole, that human life and indeed the lives of all other living things have always depended.

As development proceeds, however, these critical functions are also taken over by the state and the corporations. Thus, the nitrogen used to fertilize our land is increasingly produced at great cost in factories rather than fixed by nitrogen-fixing bacteria on the roots of leguminous plants; and the water we use, instead of being stored for free in the aquifers beneath the forest floor, is increasingly stored in large, man-made reservoirs.

It is now even proposed by economists (and tame scientists concur) that, rather than cut down on emissions of greenhouse gases which are now on such a scale that the stability of world climate is overwhelmingly threatened, the Earth's natural functions should be undertaken by vast geo-engineering schemes. Foremost among these schemes is a plan to site 50,000 100 square kilometre mirrors in space in order to reflect away the heat of the sun and keep the planet cool. In other words, economic development is therefore not only the systematic shift to the formal monetized economy of the functions that were previously fulfilled for free by 'the social economy', but also a shift away from 'the great economy', as Wendell Berry refers to the economy of the natural world as a whole.

The consequences of such an enterprise are, of course, dramatic. It can only cause the demise of the social economy as the household and the community – its basic building blocks – are condemned to atrophy from want of use. It also signals the demise of the 'great economy', which must become ever less capable of fulfilling its natural functions, which, as I shall argue, they alone are capable of fulfilling effectively and sustainably.

COMMUNITY DISINTEGRATION AND ITS CONSEQUENCES

The family has, until recently, always been the basic unit of social life, but it has also been the extended family and included people who lived in the same household, though not necessarily blood relations. This is in contrast to the truncated nuclear family of the type we have today. What is more, the family of the past formed an integral part of the community within which all its members lived and worked – and into which it practically merged, rather than existing as an island of solidarity in a vast indifferent non-society, as it does today. For this and similar reasons we should overcome our present prejudice against this irreplaceable institution, which we tend to see as tyrannical and claustrophobic, and whose virtues are only vaunted by heartless right-wing politicians, whose overriding policies – ironical as it may seem – can only lead to further social disintegration.

Much the same can be said for the community, which has also now fallen into disfavour. It is a basic, one might say natural, unit of social organization –

which it clearly must be since we have lived in extended families and communities during the whole course of our biological, psychological and cognitive evolution. Alexis de Tocqueville, that great student of town democracy in New England, saw the community as natural, indeed God-given. 'Man may create kingdoms,' he wrote, 'but the community seems to have sprung from the hand of God' (de Tocqueville, 1981).

Significantly, it seems to be only at the levels of the household and the community that most of the key social and economic functions can be effectively fulfilled – though, of course, to be able to do so these key social units must be sufficiently cohesive, imbued with the appropriate worldview, and in possession of the resources they require for fulfilling them.

Let us take an obvious example. One of the most serious problems our society faces today is a massive increase in all sorts of social aberrations, such as crime, delinquency, drug addiction, alcoholism and general violence. These problems are conspicuous by their absence in societies that have not been fully atomized. For instance, a visitor could walk in the poorest slums of Calcutta, where large numbers of people are homeless and sleep out on the pavement, in almost total security. If this is so, it is largely that such people do not suffer from the terrible social deprivation that they do in an atomized society. They may be very poor and even hungry, but the lives they lead within their family groups have meaning to them – which is ever less the case of the lives led by most people in the cities of the industrial world today.

In a traditional community, social order is also effectively maintained by an extremely powerful force: that of public opinion, reflecting traditional values – and crime and other social aberrations are reduced to a minimum.

We have been taught to regard the pressure of public opinion as an intolerable intrusion into our lives. One of the great advantages of becoming an anonymous inhabitant of a big modern city is that it 'liberates' us from the 'tyranny of public opinion' which imposes on us all sorts of obligations to our family, community, society and ecosystem.

But, no one has yet devised an alternative strategy for controlling crime and other aberrations, and hence for maintaining social order. The state can engage more and more policemen, spend billions on an ever more elaborate judicial system and build more and more prisons, but all this has very little effect – and, in any case, it is but a means of masking the symptoms of a social disease, which by rendering a little more tolerable such expedients can only serve to perpetuate. Today, needless to say, as the global economy marginalizes more and more people, this disease can only worsen and spread to those areas of the world that have succeeded, until now, in remaining relatively unaffected by it. Much the same can be said for the other serious problems that confront our modern society such as poverty, malnutrition, the annihilation of our natural resources, the population explosion and so on.

THE COMMUNITY AND DEMOCRACY

If crime and other social aberrations can only be dealt with at a communal level, the same must be true of democratic government. If democracy is 'government by the people for the people', it is difficult to regard as truly democratic the sort of political system under which we live, in which individuals limit their contribution to governing themselves by voting only every five years for a candidate over whose political conduct, until the next election, they have absolutely no control. This is particularly the case today, when the corporate world has mastered the art of influencing the outcome of elections by massive and increasingly sophisticated public-relations campaigns, and whose interests, rather than those of the people who elected them, governments everywhere have now come to represent.

If government is to be really 'by the people', then the people must themselves participate in the daily business of government, and it is clearly not at the national, let alone at the global level, that they can possibly do so, but only at the local level among people who know each other, see each other regularly and see themselves as members of the same community.

Jefferson also always insisted that face-to-face participation in municipal government alone enables citizens to subordinate what they take to be their immediate personal interests to the public good. He advocated that states should be broken up into local wards of such a size as to enable the full interaction and, participation of citizens in their own government (Coleman, 1994). De Tocqueville, like the ancient Greeks, 'identified freedom with self-determination, and saw democracy as fostering freedom, precisely because it enabled people to participate in municipal government' (Boesche, 1987, quoted by Hultgren, 1994). He also noted how, in the New England town democracies where such conditions were largely met, 'each person's cooperation in its affairs assures his attachment to its interests; the well-being it affords him secures his affection; and its welfare is the aim of his ambitions and his future exertions' (Herith, 1986, quoted by Hultgren, 1994).

The Swiss system of government may also provide a model. It has always been based on the commune or *gemeinde*, which is largely autonomous and self-governing. Traditionally, it decides what taxes should be paid and how the community should spend the money allocated to it. It also actively oversees the communal administration, whose proposals and expenditures it can reject, and deals with such issues as public service, primary education, local police and welfare for the poor and the sick. Really important decisions are made by a free assembly of the citizens.

Significantly, the commune existed long before the cantons into which the confederation is now divided. Communes located in a particular valley did occasionally join together to form loose organizations or alliances. However, it was only with the Napoleonic conquests at the beginning of the 19th century that they were raised to the rank of cantons, and even later that they were linked together to form the Swiss confederation. Even then, the central government has traditionally had relatively little power, partly because it is only elected for a year, and partly too because its political composition must reflect that of the parliament, which seriously limits the changes it can bring about.

Unfortunately, this system of government cannot survive economic development, which necessarily involves abandoning local self-sufficiency and turning what were once self-governing communes into dormitory towns no longer capable of running themselves. Indeed, in recent times there has been a steady fall in the number of people who take part in local assemblies, and whereas the power once resided with the communes, it is increasingly the confederate government and the large corporations that control the country's economic and social life.

Now that governments, by signing the GATT Uruguay Round and setting up the WTO, have delegated the task of running their economic affairs to what is, in effect, a world government, decisions will be taken by a body of people who remain distanced from those affected, who are indifferent to the real interests of the common people and who are subservient to the interests of transnational corporations. In other words, we will have moved still further away from 'true democracy'.

For this reason alone, and there are many others, true democracy – in the form of government by a loose association of largely self-governing communities – is only possible if the economy is structured in the same way. Political localization requires *economic localization* (the corollary, of course, also being true), and the conduct of the economy is yet another function that has to be fulfilled primarily at the community level.

SELF-SUFFICIENCY

Relative self-sufficiency is another prerequisite of true democracy. Not surprisingly, Thomas Jefferson considered that self-governing communities should be largely self-sufficient, and that they should at least produce their own food, shelter and clothes. This was essential in order to foster the honesty, industry and perseverance on which democracy must be built (Kemmis, 1990). Mahatma Gandhi fully agreed. The principle of *swadeshi*, which was critical to his philosophy, meant deriving one's resources from one's own area, rather than importing them from elsewhere.

Professor Ray Dasmann of the University of California at Santa Cruz says the same thing in a different way. He contrasts 'ecosystem man' – who lives off his local ecosystem – with 'biosphere man' – who lives off the whole biosphere. For him it is only when we learn once more to become ecosystem people that our society is truly sustainable.

Traditional communities are well capable of living off the resources of their ecosystems in a highly sustainable manner. Unlike export-oriented corporations that overtax the land and move elsewhere when it ceases to be productive, traditional communities have no other land available to them. Furthermore, they have developed cultural patterns that enable them to do so. It should be obvious that people who have lived in the same place for hundreds of years must have developed food-producing practices which enable them to make the optimum use of their resources, and also to make sure that these are applied. In other words, they alone are in possession of the requisite knowledge and capacities for living there.

Open-minded people who have studied agriculture as practised by local communities in traditional societies have confirmed that this is so. This was certainly true of the agricultural experts sent out by the British government at the end of the 19th century to see how Indian farming methods could be improved. Both A O Hume and John Augustus Voelcker agreed that traditional Indian agriculture was perfectly adapted to local conditions and could not be improved upon (Hume, 1878; Voelcker, 1893). To the dismay of the British authorities, Voelcker even went so far as to say that it would be easier for him to suggest improvements to British than to Indian agriculture.

Even the World Bank, which has spearheaded the modernization of agriculture in the developing world, admitted in one of its more notorious reports that 'smallholders in Africa are outstanding managers of their own resources – their land and capital, fertilizer and water' (The World Bank, 1981). Why then modernize and push them into the slums? The answer is that it has to be, as the report fully admits, '[because] subsistence farming is incompatible with the development of the market', and the market, of course, has priority.

It is for this reason that the community is best seen – as it always has been among traditional societies – as comprising not only its human members but the ecosystem with all the living things of which it is part. Wendell Berry sees the community in just this way. 'If we speak of a healthy community,' he writes, 'we cannot be speaking of a community that is only human. We are talking about a neighbourhood of humans in a place, plus a place itself: the soil, the water, its air, and all the families and tribes of the non-human creatures that belong to it.' What is more, it is only if this whole community is healthy 'that its members can remain healthy and be healthy in body and mind and in a sustainable manner' (see Chapter 22). It follows that a human community should have exclusive access to the wealth provided by the ecosystem of which it is part; together, both constitute what Wendell Berry regards as a true community.

Once communities no longer have this largely exclusive use of their wealth, once they have been privatized and made available to all comers, in particular roving transnational corporations – a situation which superficially sounds highly desirable and very 'democratic' – then their exploitation and rapid destruction become inevitable. This is precisely what happens when we set up the global economy.

This brings us to what must, perhaps, be the most important argument of all for returning to the local community-based economy. If the world's environment is being degraded so rapidly, with a corresponding reduction in its capacity to sustain complex forms of life such as the human species, then it cannot sustain the present impact of our economic activities. To increase this impact still further, as we are doing by creating a global economy based on free trade, is both irresponsible and cynical. The only responsible policy must be to reduce drastically this impact. It is only in the sort of economy that most of the contributors to this book propose, one in which economic activities are carried out on a far smaller scale and cater for a largely local or regional market, that we can hope to do so.

The great take-over can clearly not proceed indefinitely. Already, the state and the corporations are rapidly becoming incapable of fulfilling the functions they have taken over from the family, the community and the ecosystem, except on an increasingly insignificant scale. This is also true of the take-over of the functions previously fulfilled by the Earth's ecosystems and biosphere, whose roles are to maintain the necessary conditions for life on this planet.

For instance, if world climate is to be stabilized, it will not be by the absurd geo-engineering works that some scientists have proposed, but by drastically reducing emissions of greenhouse gases and by equally drastically increasing the biosphere's capacity to absorb carbon dioxide, the main greenhouse gas. This means allowing the world's badly depleted forests, its eroded soils and the beleaguered phytoplankton of its oceans to recover, which is only feasible if the impact of our activities on our environment is sufficiently reduced. In other words, the global economy must be replaced by a localized economy with its vastly reduced energy and resource requirements.

Another essential function that the state, in particular, is no longer capable of assuming is the provision of welfare to those in need. Even before the global economy was formally institutionalized, the cost of monetized welfare was in many industrial countries growing faster than GNP, and quite clearly could not be sustained for long. Today, however, in order to maximize competitiveness, the welfare state is being systematically commodified, monetized and provided to the minority that can afford it via the market system, even though the need for it is dramatically increasing as economic globalization increases the number of those in need.

Yet another key function that the state and corporations are ever less capable of fulfilling is the provision of the means to satisfy people's food and material requirements, which in the modern world necessitates jobs. That the global economy will be able to function with but a small fraction of its present work force and a still smaller fraction of that incomparably greater mass of marginalized people who will be looking for jobs in a matter of years has been pointed out throughout this book. According to an article in *Le Monde Diplomatique,* the formal economy in the Ivory Coast will, within a few years, provide less than 6 per cent of the jobs required, and that country's lot is probably not unique.

What is more, largely as a result of successive structural adjustment programmes (see Chapter 10), the purchasing power of those individuals who still have jobs is being drastically reduced. This is increasingly the case in the industrial world, where salaries are being slashed, long-term contracts replaced by short-term contracts, full-time work replaced by part-time work, and men replaced by women who are willing to work for less money. It goes without saying that people who have no jobs, and who no longer have access to welfare benefits, or who are paid slave wages, cannot buy many goods and services, while the computers – with which many of them will be replaced – can buy none at all. What is more, as consumption falls, the formal economy will provide still less jobs, which will further reduce consumption and, in turn, further reduce the number of jobs it can provide. We will thus be caught up in a veritable chain reaction that must continue until the formal economy ceases to be a significant source of jobs, food and other goods and services for the bulk of humanity on this planet. In other words, by marginalizing so many people, *the formal economy will marginalize itself.*

All this implies that most people will be forced by necessity to learn to live outside the formal economy. In such a situation the LETS and Time Dollar schemes described in this book are not mere curiosities – initiatives that are on too small a scale to make any significant contribution to today's ever more daunting problems. On the contrary, they can provide the very foundations for reconstructing the local economies that alone can fill the void created by the growing irrelevance of the formal economy to people's lives.

In other words, as the corporations and the state become less capable of fulfilling the key functions that they originally took over from the largely non-monetized social economy, there will be no alternative but to allow the latter to reassume many of its original functions.

Unfortunately, our social economy is, at present, ill equipped to take on any new functions since the viable households and communities and ecosystems that previously fulfilled these functions have been seriously degraded under the impact of past economic development.

For this reason we should spare no effort in helping them. Furthermore, if most people are to be marginalized, and many of them rendered destitute by the global economy, they will not simply sit down quietly and starve. Many will undoubtedly revolt against the big corporations that use up their resources, pollute their land and rivers, produce food and consumer goods that only the elite can afford, and provide only a few high-technology jobs that are filled by specialists from abroad.

The humiliation of the WTO at Seattle in November 1999 is undoubtedly the most significant sign of the world's reaction to the horrors of corporate domination – followed by the demonstrations at Washington and the anti-globalization festival at Millau in March 2000, in which more than 50,000 people took part.

But many of those who have been marginalized are also bound to reorganize themselves and form local economies that, in turn, will provide the economic infrastructure for new local communities. These communities will resume the functions they have always fulfilled, functions that provide them with their very raison d'être. That this must necessarily occur is one of the bright lights on what is otherwise a dismally black horizon, but Wendell Berry sees another. For him the issue of global versus local economy is likely to be of major significance in the next decade, and it should provide the basis of a new political realignment. The party of community, as he sees it, will have little money and hence little power, but its adherents can only increase, and soon it may well become the party of the majority. If such a party were really to come to power, it would be in a position to develop and implement a coordinated strategy for ensuring a more painless transition to the sort of society and the sort of economy which alone can offer our children any future on this beleaguered planet.

References

Air Transportation Association of America (1998) website: www.air-transport.org

Allsopp, Michelle, Pat Costner and Paul Johnson (1995) *Body of Evidence: The Effects of Chlorine on Human Health*, University of Exeter, Greenpeace Research Laboratories

American Banker (1991) 'Benefits of Big Mergers Said to Vanish Quickly' (11 December)

Anderson, Sarah and John Cavanagh (1997) 'The Top 10 List', *The Nation* (8 December)

Arax, Mark and Jeanne Brokaw (1997) 'No Way Around Roundup', *Mother Jones* (January/February)

Avery, N, M Drake and T Lang (1993) *Cracking the Codex*, London, National Food Alliance

Baker, Randall (1984) 'Protecting the Environment Against the Poor', *The Ecologist*, vol 14(2)

Beder, Sharon (1999) 'Corporate Hijacking of the Greenhouse Debate', *The Ecologist*, vol 29(2) (March/April)

Bell, A (1996) *Saltmarsh Lamb Study*, Devon, Taw Torridge Estuary Project

Bello, Walden (1996) 'Structural Adjustment Programs: "Success" for Whom' in J Mander and E Goldsmith (Eds) *The Case Against the Global Economy and for a Turn Towards the Local*, San Francisco, Sierra Club Books

Bello, Walden with S Cunningham and B Rau (1994) *Dark Victory: the United States, Structural Adjustment and Global Poverty*, London, Pluto Press

Benson, Susan, Mark Arax and Rachel Burnstein (1997) 'A Growing Concern', *Mother Jones* (January/February)

Boeing Company (1998) *World Air Cargo Forecast*, Boeing Company

Barnet, Richard, and John Cavanagh (1994) *Global Dreams: Imperial Corporations and the New World Order*, New York, Simon and Schuster

Barnet, Richard and Ronald E Mueller (1974) *Global Reach: The Power of the Multinational Corporations*, New York, Simon and Schuster

Bassett, P (1995) 'Insecurity of Part-Time Jobs and Full-Time Mortgages', *Times* (11 April)

Beal, Dave (1993) 'A Piece of the Action', *St. Paul Pioneer Press* (14 June)

Beijing Ministerial Declaration on Environment and Development 19 June, 1991

Bello, Walden, with David Kinley and Elaine Elison (1982) *Development Debacle: The World Bank in the Philippines*, San Francisco, Institute for Food and Development Policy

Bello, Walden and Stephanie Rosenfeld (1990) *Dragons in Distress: Asia's Miracle Economies in Crisis*, San Francisco, Institute for Food and Development Policy

Berry, Wendell (1987) *Sex, Economy, Freedom and Community*, New York, Pantheon Books

Boesche, Roger (1987) 'The Strange Liberalism of Alexis de Tocqueville', Ithaca, NY, Cornell University Press. As quoted by Hultgren, John (1994) 'Democracy and Sustainability', unpublished

Bowers, C A (1993) *Education, Cultural Myths, and the Ecological Crisis: Toward Deep Changes*, Albany, NY, State University of New York Press

Borgstrom, Georg (1967) *The Hungry Planet*, New York, Collier

Brandt, Richard (1986) 'How Automation Could Save the Day', *Business Week*, 3 March

Breed, C (1998) 'Checking Out the Supermarkets: Competition in Retailing' (May)

Breverton, T D (1994) 'Rules Under Different Visions of Economy and Society: The Economic Vision', paper presented at conference The Evolution of Rules for a Single European Market, 8–11 September, at Exeter University

Brighton, Debbie (1990) 'Cow Safety, BGH and Burroughs', *Organic Farmer* (Spring)

Brown, Alex (1999) 'Appendix 2: GMOs Are Dead', *Ag Biotech: Thanks, But No Thanks?* Deutsche Bank (12 July)

Brown, L and C Flavin (1999) 'A New Economy for a New Century' in *State of the World 1999*, Washington, DC, Worldwatch

Brown, Lester R (1988) *State of the World*, Washington, DC, Worldwatch Institute

Brummer, A (1999) 'Uncle Sam Invades', *The Guardian* (15 June)

Brundtland, Gro Harlem (1987) *Our Common Future*, United Nations Commission on Environment and Development (April)

Bruno, Kenny (1997) 'Say It Ain't Soy, Monsanto', *Multinational Monitor*, vol 18(1–2) (January/February)

Bryant, D, D Nielsen and L Tangley (1997) *The Last Frontier Forests*, Washington, DC, World Resources Institute

Burrows, Beth (1997) 'Government Workers Go Biotech', Edmonds Institute (19 May)

Burton, Bob (1999) 'Advice on Making Nice', *PR Watch*, vol 6(1) (First Quarter)

Business World (1999) 15 November

Bunyard, Peter (1996) 'Industrial Agriculture – Driving Climate Change', *The Ecologist*, vol 26(6) (November/December)

Cable News Network (1996) 'GM Sets Up Shop in Russia' (29 November)

—— (1997) 'GM to Sign China Contract' (10 March)

Cahn, E and J Rowe (Eds) (1992) *Time Dollars*, Emmaus, Pennsylvania, Rodale Press

Cairns, J (1975) *Cancer: Science and Society*, San Francisco, W H Freeman

Calvert, John and Larry Kuehn (1993) *Pandora's Box*, Toronto, Our Schools/Ourselves Education Foundation

Calvillo Unna, A (1993) 'La Contribucion del Transporte a la Contaminacion Atmosferica' in *El Transporte y la Contaminacion*, Proceedings of the Atmosphere and Energy Campaign Seminar, Mexico City, Greenpeace Mexico

Canine, Craig (1991) 'Hear No Evil', *Eating Well* (July/August)

Carson, Rachel (1987) *Silent Spring*, Boston, Houghton Mifflin

Centre for Responsive Politics website: www.crp.org

Center for Rural Affairs (1996) *The Beginning Farmer*, Issue 19, June, Hartington, Nebraska

Chambers, W B et al (1999) *Global Climate Governance: Scenarios and Options on the Inter-Linkages Between the Kyoto Protocol and Other Multilateral Regimes*, Tokyo, United Nations University and the Institute for Advanced Studies, Global Environment Information Centre

Chemical and Engineering News (1998) 'Chemical Producers: Dow Chemical, DuPont, Monsanto and Union Carbide Have Ranked Among Top 10 Biggest Chemical Makers Since 1940', *Chemical and Engineering News* (12 January)

Chira, Susan (1993) 'Is Smaller Better? Educators Now Say Yes for High School', *New York Times* (14 July)

Christiansen, Andrew (1995) 'Recombinant Bovine Growth Hormone: Alarming Tests, Unfounded Approval', *Rural Vermont* (July)

Clark, William C (1989) 'Managing Planet Earth', *Scientific American*, vol 261 (September)

Clunies-Ross, T and N Hildyard (1992) *The Politics of Industrial Agriculture*, London, SAFE Alliance and Earthscan Publications Ltd

Colborn, Theo, Dianne Dumanoski and John Peterson Myers (1996) *Our Stolen Future*, New York, Penguin Books

Coleman, Dan (1994) 'Ecopolitics: Building a Green Society', New Brunswick, New Jersey, Rutgers University Press. As quoted by Hultgren, John (1994) 'Democracy and Sustainability', unpublished

Coleman, Eliot (1989) *The New Organic Grower: A Master's Manual of Tools and Techniques for the Home and Market Gardener*, Chelsea, Vermont, Chelsea Green

Colchester, Marcus (1993) 'Slave and Enclave: Towards a Political Ecology of Equatorial Africa', *The Ecologist*, vol 23(5)

Congressional Research Service (1993) *Biotechnology, Indigenous Peoples, and Intellectual Property Rights*, Washington, D C, Library of Congress

Cook, C D and J Rodgers (1996) 'Community Food Security: A Growing Movement', *Global Pesticide Campaigner*, vol 6(3), pp8–11

Cornia, Giovanni Andrea et al (Eds) (1992) *Africa's Recovery in the 1990s: From Stagnation and Adjustment to Human Development*, Mkandawire, Thandika, LC 92-18007

Correio Braziliense (1998) 'Investigation: Police Close Circle Around Illegal Cultivation of Soybeans', *Correio Braziliense* (31 January)

Cowe, R (1999) 'US Retail Giant Takes Over Asda', *The Guardian* (15 June)

—— (1999) 'Superstore Curbs To Be Lifted', *The Guardian* (16 June)

—— (1999) 'Wal-Mart Fuels European Mergers', *The Guardian* (28 June)

Cox, Carolyn (1991) 'Glyphosate Fact Sheet', *Journal of Pesticide Reform*, vol 11(2) (Spring)

—— (1995) 'Glyphosate, Part 2: Human Exposure and Ecological Effects', *Journal of Pesticide Reform*, vol 15(4) (Fall)

Cringely, Robert, (1992) 'Hollywood Goes Digital', *Forbes* (7 December)

Crook, Clive (1992) 'Fear of Finance', *The Economist* (September 19)

Cummins, Joseph E (1998) 'PCBs – Can the World's Sea Mammals Survive Them?', *The Ecologist*, vol 28(5) (September/October)

Daly, Herman (1994) 'Farewell Lecture to the World Bank', College Park, University of Maryland, School of Public Affairs (14 January)

Daly, Herman E and John B Cobb, Jr (1989) *For the Common Good: Redirecting the Economy Toward Community, the Environment, and a Sustainable Future*, Boston, Beacon Press

Daly, Herman E and Robert Goodland (1992), 'An Ecological–Economic Assessment of Deregulation of International Commerce under GATT', Washington, D C, World Bank (September)

Danaher, Kevin, with Frances Moore Lappe and Rachel Schurman (1988) *Betraying the National Interest*, San Francisco, Institute for Food and Development Policy

Dauncey, Guy (1988) *After the Crash: The Emergence of the Rainbow Economy*, London, Green Print Books

Davis, D L et al (1994) 'Decreasing Cardiovascular Disease and Increasing Cancer Among Whites in the United States from 1973 through 1987', *Journal of the American Medical Association*, vol 271(6) (9 February). As quoted in *Rachel's Hazardous Waste News*, Environmental Research Foundation, no 385 (14 April)

Dembo, David et al (1990) *The Abuse of Power: Social Performance of Multinational Corporations: The Case of Union Carbide*, New York, New Horizons Press

Department of the Environment, Transport and the Regions (1998) Press Release, London, DETR (25 September)

de Tocqueville, Alexis (1981) [1835] *Democracy in America*, New York, Random House
—— 'Threat to Freedom and Democracy', Durham: Duke University. As quoted in Hultgren, John (1994) 'Democracy and Sustainability', unpublished

de Vries, J (1996) 'Sustaining Farming in Holland – Green Labels and Environmental Yardsticks', *Pesticides News*, Issue 33, p6

Douthwaite, R (1996) *Short Circuit: Strengthening Local Economies for Security in an Unstable World*, Dartington, Devon, Green Books

Downs, Peter (1998) 'Is the Pentagon Involved?', *St Louis Journalism Review* (June)

Dumont, R (1988) *False Start in Africa*, London, Earthscan Publications Ltd

Dumont, R and N Cohen (1980) *The Growth of Hunger: A New Politics of Agriculture*, London, Marion Boyars

Durning, Alan B (1992) *How Much Is Enough?*, New York, W W Norton

The Ecologist (1993) Special issue, 'Whose Common Future?', vol 23(6)

The Ecologist (1998) vol 28(5) (September/October)

Ekins, Paul (1989) 'Trade and Self-Reliance', *Ecologist*, vol 19(5)

Environmental Board of the State of Vermont (1995) *Findings of Fact*, Vermont (27 June)

Epstein, Samuel S (1996) 'Unlabeled Milk from Cows Treated with Biosynthetic Growth Hormones: a Case of Regulatory Abdication', *International Journal of Health Services*, vol 26(1)

Fanelli, José María, with Roberto Frenkel and Lance Taylor (1992) 'The World Development Report 1991: A Critical Assessment', *International Monetary and Financial Issues for the 1990's*, New York, U N Conference on Trade and Development

Farrelly, Paul (1998) 'Oil Sisters Troop to Altar as Price Sinks', *The Observer* (12 June)

Farmers' Weekly (1997b) 'Cereal Farm Assurance Schemes Totally Mad', 4 July

Faux, Jeff. As quoted in Rothstein, R (1993) 'As the Good Jobs Go Rolling Away. . . Who Will Buy?', CEO/International Strategies (December)

Di Fazio, Alberto (1999) 'Misreading the Models: the Danger of Underestimating Climate Change', *The Ecologist*, vol 29(2) (March/April)

Feder, Barnaby J (1995) 'Some Producers are Scowling at Meatpackers' Process', *New York Times* (17 October)

Feder, Barnaby J (1999) 'Monsanto Says It Won't Market Infertile Seeds', *New York Times* (5 October)

Ferguson, Jock (1990) 'Chemical Company Accused of Hiding Presence of Dioxins', *Globe and Mail* (19 February)

Ferrara, Jennifer (1998) 'Revolving Doors: Monsanto and the Regulators', *The Ecologist*, vol 28(5) (September/October)

Festing, H (1995) 'Direct Marketing of Fresh Produce', MPhil thesis, Wye College, University of London

Festing, H (1997) 'The Potential for Direct Marketing by Small Firms in the UK', *Farm Management*, vol 9(8), pp409–421

Ffrench-Davis, Ricardo and Carlos Munoz (1992) 'Economic and Political Instability in Chile', in Simon Teitel (Ed) *Towards a New Development Strategy for Latin America*, Washington, D C, Inter-American Development Bank

Fieldhouse, D K (1984) *Economics and Empire, 1830 to 1914*, London, Macmillan

Financial Statistics Yearbook 1997 (1997) Washington, DC, International Monetary Fund (November)

Financial Statistics Yearbook 1998 (1998) Washington, DC, International Monetary Fund (January)

Financial Times (1994) 'Can Europe Compete?' (7 March)

Financial Times (1998) 'Monsanto to Pay Cotton Farmers', (25 February)

Finanial Times (1998) 'Network Guerillas' (30 April)

The Food and Allied Service Trades Department of the American Federation of Labour and Congress of Industrial Organizations, with the United Food and Commercial Workers International Union (1998) 'Wal-Mart's Buy America Programme – Using Patriotism to Deceive the American People' (July)

Ford, Henry. As quoted in Barnet, Richard and John Cavanagh (1994) *Global Dreams*, New York, Simon and Schuster

Franke, R and B Chasin (1981) 'Peasants, Peanuts, Profits and Pastoralists', *The Ecologist*, vol 11(4)

French, Hilary (1993) *Costly Tradeoffs: Reconciling Trade and the Environment*, Washington, DC, Worldwatch

—— (1999) 'World Trade Declines' in Lester R Brown et al (Eds) *Vital Signs 1999*, New York, W W Norton & Co

Friedman, Lawrence M (1973) *A History of American Law*, New York: Simon and Schuster

Furusawa, K (1994) 'Cooperative Alternatives in Japan' in P Conford (ed) *A Future for the Land: Organic Practice from a Global Perspective*, Bideford, Resurgence Books

The Futurist (1993) 'Robot Farming' (July–August)

Galbraith, John Kenneth (1992) *The Culture of Contentment*, Boston, Houghton Mifflin

Gardner, G and P Sampat (1999) 'Forging a Sustainable Materials Economy' in *State of the World 1999*, Washington, DC, Worldwatch

Garnett, T (1996) *Growing Food in Cities: A Report to Highlight and Promote the Benefits of Urban Agriculture in the UK*, London, SAFE Alliance and National Food Alliance

Gedde-Dhal, T (1992) 'Identifying Development Needs and Decisions with Local Experimentation: Experimental Groups in Norwegian Agriculture', *Journal of International Farm Management*, vol 1(3), pp74–80

Geier, B (1996) 'Organic Agriculture: Part of the Food Security Solution' in B Dinham (ed) *Growing Food Security: Challenging the Link Between Pesticides and Food Security*, London, PAN and Pesticides Trust

Genentech (1998) 'Genentech Names Moore New Head of Government Affairs Office Based in Washington, DC', Genentech company press release (13 April)

George, Susan and Fabrizio Sabelli (1994) *Faith and Credit: The World Bank's Secular Empire*, London, Penguin

Gepillard, A (1994) 'Germans Plan to Shift Production Abroad', *Financial Times* (31 May)

Gershon, Diane (1994) 'Monsanto Sues Over BST', *Nature*, vol 368 (31 March)

Gibbons, Ann (1993) 'Where are "New" Diseases Born?', *Science* (6 August)

Giddens, A (1990) *The Consequences of Modernity*, Cambridge, Polity Press

Glover, Paul (1984) *Los Angeles: A History of the Future*, Los Angeles, Citizen Planners of Los Angeles

Goldsmith, Edward and Nicholas Hildyard (1990) *The Earth Report No. 2*, London, Mitchell Beazley

Goodland, Robert (1984) 'Environmental Management in Tropical Agriculture', Boulder, Colorado, Westview Press

Gore, Al (1991) 'Planning a New Biotechnology Policy', *Harvard Journal of Law and Technology*, vol 5 (Fall)

Gorelick, Steven (1998) 'Small is Beautiful, Big is Subsidized', International Society of Ecology and Culture (October)

Gray, J (1998) *False Dawn: the Delusions of Global Capitalism*, London, Granta Books

Greco, Thomas, Jr (1994) *New Money for Healthy Communities*, Tucson, Arizona, T H Greco

Greenpeace (1992) *Green Fields, Green Future*, London, Greenpeace

—— (1997) *Roundup Ready Soybean: a Critique of Monsanto's Risk Evaluation*, Chicago, Greenpeace

—— (1999) Greenpeace business conference typescript, posted to electronic list: biotech_activists@iatp.org (7 October)

Greer, Jed and Kenny Bruno (1996) *Greenwash: The Reality Behind Corporate Environmentalism*, Penang, Malaysia, Third World Network

Grinde, Donald A, Jr (1977) *The Iroquois and the Founding of the American Nation*, San Francisco, The Indian Historian Press

Haavelmo, T (1991) 'The Big Dilemma: International Trade and the North–South Cooperation', in *Economic Policies for Sustainable Development*, Manila, Asian Development Bank

Hammond, Edward, Pat Mooney and Hope Shand (1998) 'Monsanto Takes Terminator', *Rural Advancement Foundation International* (14 May)

Harris, John (1991) 'Universities for Sale', *This Magazine* (September)

Hawken, Paul (1993) *The Ecology of Commerce: A Declaration of Sustainability*, New York, Harper Business

Herith, Michael (1986) *Alexis de Tocqueville: 'Threat to Freedom and Democracy'*, Durham, Duke University

Hillier Parker, C B (1998) *The Impact of Large Foodstores on Market Towns and District Centres*, London, Department of the Environment, Transport and the Regions, Stationery Office

Hobsbawm, Eric (1986) *Industry and Empire*, Harmondsworth, Pelican

Hollinger, P (1999) 'When the Price Is Not Right', *Financial Times* (15 June)

Holstein, William J (1986a) 'Japan, USA', *Business Week*, 14 July

Holstein, William J (1986b) 'Will Sake and Sour Mash Go Together?', *Business Week*, 14 July

Hueting, R 'The Brundtland Report: A Matter of Conflicting Goals', *Ecological Economics*, vol 2(2)

Hultgren, John (1994) 'Democracy and Sustainability', unpublished

—— (1995) 'International Political Economy and Sustainability', Oberlin College, unpublished

Hume, A O (1878) 'Agriculture Reform in India', London, W H Allen and Co

Iglesias, Enrique (1992) *Reflections on Economic Development: Toward a New Latin American Consensus*, Washington, D C, Inter-American Development Bank

Illich, Ivan (1999) *Deschooling Society*, London, Marion Boyars Publishers

Institute for Policy Studies (1997) 'The World Bank and the G-7: Changing the Earth's Climate for Business', version 1.1 (August)

—— (1998) 'The World Bank and the G-7: Changing the Earth's Climate for Business', version 1.0 (15 May)

Institute for Policy Studies and the International Trade Information Service (1997) 'The European Bank for Reconstruction and Development: Fueling Climate Change', version 1.0 (November)

Institute of Grocery Distribution (2000) *Grocery Retailing 2000*

Inter-American Development Bank (1992) *Economic and Social Progress in Latin America, 1992*, Washington, D C, International Development Bank

Intergovernmental Panel on Climate Change (1995) *Second Assessment Report: Summary for Policy-Makers*, Cambridge, Cambridge University Press

—— (1996) *Guidelines for National Greenhouse Gas Inventories: Reference Manual*

International Bunker Industry Association (1998) website: www.seanet.co.uk/classifi/marrosoc/ibia/ibia.htm

International Labour Organization (1995) *World Employment*, Geneva, ILO

Jacobs, Jane (1961) *The Death and Life of Great American Cities*, Harmondsworth, Middlesex, Penguin

Jacoby, E H (1961) 'Agrarian Unrest in Southeast Asia', as quoted in G L Beckford (1983) *Persistent Poverty*, London, Zed Books

Jenkins, Cate (1990) 'Criminal Investigation of Monsanto Corporation – Cover-up of Dioxin Contamination in Products: Falsification of Dioxin Health Studies', USEPA Regulatory Development Branch (November)

Johansen, Bruce (1988) 'Indian Thought Was Often in Their Minds', in *Indian Roots of American Democracy*, Ithaca, NY, Northeast Indian Quarterly, Cornell University

Karliner, J (1997) *The Corporate Planet: Ecology and Politics in the Age of Globalization*, San Francisco, Sierra Club Books

Kastel, Mark (1995) 'Down on the Farm: the Real BGH Story', *Rural Vermont* (Fall)

Kelly, Frank T (1994) 'Letter to the President of Guatemala' (16 June)

Kelly, Kevin (1994) *Out of Control: The Rise of Neo-Biological Civilizations*, New York: Addison-Wesley

Kemmis, Daniel (1990) 'Community and the Politics of Place', Norman, Oklahoma, University of Oklahoma Press. As quoted by Hultgren, John (1994) 'Democracy and Sustainability', unpublished

Kilman, Scott and Thomas M Burton (1999) 'Monsanto Feels Pressure from the Street', *Wall Street Journal* (21 October)

Kneen, Brewster (1998) *The Ram's Horn*, no 160 (June)

Knight, Sylvia (1996) 'Glyphosate, Roundup and Other Herbicides – an Annotated Bibliography', *Vermont Citizens' Forest Roundtable* (January)

Knox, Patricia (1995) 'A New Green Economy? LETS Do It', *Earth Island Journal* (Summer)

Koenig, Richard (1990) 'Rich in New Products, Monsanto Must Only Get Them on the Market', *Wall Street Journal* (18 May)

Korten, David C (1994) 'Sustainable Livelihoods: Redefining the Global Social Crisis' (10 May)

—— (1995) *When Corporations Rule the World*, London, Earthscan Publications Ltd

—— (1995) *When Corporations Rule the World*, New York, Kumarian Press

Kozol, Jonathan (1991) *Savage Inequalities: Children in America's Schools*, New York, Crown Publishers

Kronfeld, D S (1994) 'Health Management of Dairy Herds Treated with Bovine Somatotropin', *Journal of the American Veterinary Medical Association*, vol 204(1) (January)

Lang, Tim and Colin Hines (1993) *The New Protectionism: Protecting the Future Against Free Trade*, New York, New Press

Lang, T (1995b) 'The Contradictions of Food Labelling Policy', *Informational Design Journal*, vol 8(1), pp3–16

Lang, T and C Hines (1993) *The New Protectionism*, London, Earthscan Publications Ltd

Lang, Tim (1998) 'Dietary Impact of the Globalization of Food Trade', *IFG News*, Issue 3 (Summer)

Langreth, Robert and Nikhil Deogun (1999) 'Investors Cool to Pharmacia Merger Plan', *Wall Street Journal* (21 December)

Layton, Robert (1995) 'Functional and Historical Explanations of Village Social Organization in Northern Europe', *Journal of the Royal Anthropological Institute* (December)

Leake, A (1996) 'Setting New Standards', *Pesticides News*, vol 31, p17

Leonard, H J (1988) *Pollution and the Struggle for the World Product*, Cambridge, Cambridge University Press

Leontif, Wassily (1983) 'National Perspective: The Definition of Problems and Opportunities', paper presented at the National Academy of Engineering Symposium, 30 June

Leontif, Wassily and Faye Duchin (1983) *The Future Impact of Automation on Workers*, New York, Oxford University Press

Lewis, Michael (1989) *Liar's Poker: Rising Through the Wreckage on Wall Street*, New York, Norton

Lichteim, George (1971) *Imperialism*, London, Penguin

Linton, Michael (1988) 'Money and Community Economics', *Creation* (July/August)

Lohr, Steve (1993) 'Potboiler Springs from Computer's Loins', *New York Times* (2 July)

Lost in Concrete (1996) 'The Internal Market and Transport: Heading for Environmental Disaster'

Lucas, Brian. As quoted in Connor, Steve (1992) 'Breasts Provoke Patent Conflict', *The Independent* (19 February)

Luick, R (1996) 'The Demise of Cattle Farming in the Black Forest', *La Cañada*, pp4–5, Peterborough, JNCC

MacNeill, J (1989) 'Strategies for Sustainable Economic Development', *Scientific American*, vol 261(3)

MacRae, R (1997) *Eco-labelling: Too Great a Threat to the Food Industry*, mimeo, Toronto, Canada

Madden, P (1992) *Raw Deal*, London, Christian Aid

Magdoff, Harry (1978) *Imperialism: From the Colonial Age to the Present*, New York, Monthly Review Press

Mander, K and A Boston (1995) 'Wal-Mart Worldwide – the Making of a Global Retailer', *The Ecologist*, vol 25(6) (November/December)

Marshall, George (1990) 'The Political Economy of Logging: The Barnett Inquiry into Corruption in the Papua New Guinea Timber Industry', *The Ecologist*, vol 20(5)

Martino-Taylor, Lisa (1997) 'Legacy of Doubt', *Three River Confluence*, no 7/8 (Fall)

Matthews, D and A Rowell (1992) *The Environmental Impact of the Car*, Washington, DC, Greenpeace

McNamara, Robert (1995) *In Retrospect: The Tragedy and Lessons of Vietnam*, New York, Times Books

Meller, Patricio (1992) *Adjustment and Equity in Chile*, Paris: OECD

Mendelson, Joseph (1998) 'Roundup: The World's Biggest-Selling Herbicide', *The Ecologist*, vol 28(5) (September/October)

Menotti, Victor (1995) 'Free Trade and the Environment', unpublished

MergeGlobal Inc (1998) 'World Seaborne Trade by Aggregated Route'

Mihelick, Stanley J (1987) 'Employers Plan Smaller Raises', *New York Times*, 13 October

Miller, Morris (1991) *Debt and the Environment: Converging Crises*, New York, United Nations Publications

Miller, Tom (1979) *Economics of Size in US Field Crop Farming*, Washington, DC, United States Department of Agriculture

Millstone, Erik (1996) 'Increasing Brain Tumor Rates: Is There a Link to Aspartame?', University of Sussex Science Policy Research Unit (October)

Mohinder, Gill (1997) *Agricultural Resources and Environmental Indicators*, US Department of Agriculture, Economic Research Service

Monsanto Company (1997) *1997 Annual Report*, Monsanto Company

Monsanto website: www.monsanto.com/MonPub/NewMonsanto/Officers/BioShapiro.html

Montague, Peter (1996) 'Brain Cancer Update', *Rachel's Environment and Health Weekly* (14 November)

—— (1997) 'Genetic Engineering Error', *Rachel's Environment and Health Weekly* (5 June)

Montbiot, G (1999) 'The Wal-Mart Monster Hits Town', *The Guardian* (17 June)

Morgenson, Gretchen (1993) 'The Fall of the Mall', *Forbes* (24 May)

Morris, David (1990) 'Free Trade: The Great Destroyer', *The Ecologist* vol 20(5)

Muller, T and B Humstone (1993) *The Phase One Report – The Retail Sales Impact of the Proposed Wal-Mart of Franklin County, Vermont*

Multinational Monitor (1996) 'Corporate Vultures, Rich Companies, Poor Workers', *Multinational Monitor*, vol 17(4) (April)

Mussolini, Benito. As quoted in Palmer, R and J Calton (1971) *History of the Modern World Since 1815*, New York, Knopf

Myerson, Allen R (1998) 'Monsanto Paying Delta Farmers to Settle Genetic Seed Complaints', *New York Times* (24 February)

Nader, R (1992) 'Introduction' in E Cahn and J Rowe (Eds) *Time Dollars*, Emmaus, Pennsylvania, Rodale Press

Nash, Nathaniel C (1987) 'Treasury Now Favours Creation of Huge Banks', *New York Times*, 7 June

National Labour Committee website: www.nlcnet.org

New Scientist (1999) 'Splitting Headache: Monsanto's Modified Soya Beans Are Cracking Up in the Heat', *New Scientist* (20 November)

New York Times (1974) 'Death of Animals Laid to Chemical', *New York Times* (28 August)

Nijar, GS and Yoke Ling Chee (1992) 'Briefing Papers for CSD. Intellectual Property Rights: The Threat to Farmers and Biodiversity', Third World Resurgence, no 39

Norman, A (1999) *Slam-dunking Wal-Mart! How Can You Stop Superstore Sprawl in Your Hometown*, Atlantic City, Raphael Marketing

North West Food Alliance (1995–1996) *Strategic Plans and Research Plans*, Briefing Papers, Olympia, Washington State, NWFA

O'Brien, Richard (1992) *Global Financial Integration: The End of Geography*, New York, Council on Foreign Relations Press

Office of Technology Assessment (1991) *Energy in Developing Countries*, Washington, DC, US Congress, Office of Technology Assessment

Ortega, B (1999) *In Sam We Trust – The Untold Story of Sam Walton and How Wal-Mart is Devouring the World*, London, Kogan Page

Oswald, Ursula (1991) *Estrategias de Supervivencia en la Ciudad de México*, Cuernavaca, Mexico, Centro Regional de Investigaciones Multidisciplinarias

Owen, Roger and Bob Sutcliffe (1976) *Studies in the Theory of Imperialism*, London, Longman

Palast, G (1999) 'Praise Uncle Sam and Pass the 18p an Hour', *Observer*, Business Section (20 June)

Partant, Francois (1982) *La Fin du Développement*, Paris, François Maspero

Passell, Peter (1992) 'Fast Money', *New York Times Magazine* (18 October)

Paxton, A (1994) *The Food Miles Report: The Dangers of Long Distance Food Transport*, London, SAFE Alliance

Payer, Cheryl (1991) *Lent and Lost: Foreign Credit and Third World Development*, London, Zed Books

Peck, Pamela (1989) 'Vermont's Polystyrene (Styrofoam) Boycott', Barre, Vermont, Vermonters Organized for Cleanup

Pender, Kathleeen (1995) 'Greenspan Boosts Use of Technology: Fed Chief Says Software Aids Economy', *San Francisco Chronicle*

Pesticide Action Network North America (1997) 'Monsanto Agrees to Change Ads and EPA fines Northrup King' (10 January)

—— (1997) 'Problems with Herbicide Tolerant Cotton in US' (7 October)

Peterson, R Neal and Nora L Brooks (1993) 'The Changing Concentration of US Agricultural Production During the Twentieth Century', Fourteenth Annual Report to Congress on the Status of the Family Farm, AIB-67I, US Economic Research Service, USDA, no 27, July

Pimental, David and Marcia Pimental (1996) *Food, Energy and Society*, Niwot, Colorado, University Press of Colorado

Pimental, D et al (1987) 'World Agriculture and Soil Erosion', *BioScience*, vol 37(4)

Platt, D C M (1976) 'Economic Imperialism and the Businessman: Britain and Latin America Before 1914' in R Owen and B Sutcliffe (Eds) *Studies in the Theory of Imperialism*, London, Longman

Porter, S and P Raistrick (1998) 'The Impact of Out-of-Centre Food Superstores on Local Retail Employment', The National Retail Planning Forum (January)

Pretty, J N (1991) 'Farmer's Extension Practice and Technology Adaptation: Agricultural Revolution in 17th–19th Century Britain', *Agriculture and Human Values*, VIII (1 & 2), pp132–148

Prokesch, Steven (1987) 'Remaking the American CEO', *New York Times*, 25 January

Proost, J and P Matteson (1997a) 'Integrated Farming in the Netherlands: Flirtation or Solid Change?', *Outlook on Agriculture*, vol 26(2), pp87–94

Proost, J and P Matteson (1997b) 'Reducing Pesticides Use in the Netherlands with Stick and Carrot', *Journal of Pesticide Reform*, vol 17(3), pp2–8

Public Citizen (1996) *NAFTA's Broken Promises: the Border Betrayed*, Public Citizen (January)

RAFI Communiqué (1997) *The Life Industry 1997: the Global Enterprises that Dominate Commercial Agriculture, Food and Health*, Rural Advancement Foundation International (November/December)

—— (2000) 'Suicide Seeds on the Fast Track: Terminator 2 Years Later', Rural Advancement Foundation International (February/March) on www.rafi.org

Raven, H, T Lang and C Dumonteil (1995) *Off Our Trolley? Food Retailing and the Hypermarket Economy*, London, Institute for Public Policy Research

Reich, Robert (1991) *The Work of Nations: Preparing Ourselves for 21st Century Capitalism*, New York, Random House

Reifenberg, Anne and Rhonda L Rundle (1996) 'Buggy Cotton May Cast Doubt on New Seeds', *Wall Street Journal* (23 July)

Reisch, Mark S (1998) 'From Coal Tar to Crafting a Wealth of Diversity', *Chemical and Engineering News* (12 January)

Retallack, Simon (1999) 'How US Politics Is Letting the World Down', *The Ecologist*, vol 29(2) (March/April)

'Retrospective Technology Assessment' Studies (1977) National Science Foundation and Massachusetts Institute of Technology (Available from National Technical Information Service, Research Services Branch, 5285 Port Royal Road, Springfield, Virginia 22161)

Ricardo, David (1996) [1817] *On the Principles of Political Economy and Taxation*, Prometheus Books

Rich, B (1994a) *Mortgaging the Earth*, Boston, Beacon Press

—— (1994b) 'The Cuckoo in the Nest: 50 Years of Political Meddling by the World Bank', *The Ecologist*, vol 24(1) (January/February)

Richman, Louis (1992) 'When Will the Layoffs End?', *Fortune* (20 September)

Rifkin, Jeremy (1995) *The End of Work: The Decline of the Global Labor Force and the Dawn of the Post-Market Era*, New York, GP Putnam's Sons

Rigdon, Joan E (1991) 'Retooling Lives: Technological Gains are Cutting Costs and Jobs in Services', *Wall Street Journal* (24 February)

Robins, N and S Roberts (1997) *Unlocking the Trade Opportunities*, London, IIED and New York, UN Department of Policy Coordination and Sustainable Development

Robinson, E (1999) 'Mutual Admiration Society Bonds Together', *Financial Times* (15 June)

Rosenzweig, Cynthia and Daniel Hillel (1998) *Climate Change and the Global Harvest*, Oxford, Oxford University Press

Roy, J (1990) 'GE Is Assailed by US Judge in WPPSS Case', *Wall Street Journal*, (27 September)

Russ, Joel (1995) 'Local Energy, Electric Currency' in Susan Meeker-Lowry (1995) *Invested in the Common Good*, New Society

Sachs, Wolfgang (Ed) (1992) *The Development Dictionary: A Guide to Knowledge as Power*, London, Zed Books

Sampson, Anthony (1989) *The Midas Touch: Money, People and Power from West to East*, London, BBC Books, Hodder and Stoughton

Sanches, Adérito Alain (1993) 'Explosif Mélange de la Croissance Urbaine et da la Régression des Services Publicques', *Le Monde Diplomatique* (May)

Scenario 2010 Working Group (1996) *Vision 2020: Scenarios for a Sustainable Europe*, Brussels, Scenario 2020 Working Group of the General Consultative Forum to DG XI, European Commission

Schmitz, Sonia (forthcoming) 'Cloning Profits: The Revolution in Agricultural Biotechnology', University of Vermont

Scott, Mary (1996) 'Interview: Robert Shapiro – Can We Trust the Maker of Agent Orange to Genetically Engineer Our Food?', *Business Ethics* (January/February)

Schuck, Peter (1987) *Agent Orange on Trial: Mass Toxic Disasters in the Courts*, Cambridge, Massachusetts, Harvard University Press

Schumacher, EF (1989) *Small Is Beautiful: Economics as if the Earth Really Mattered*, New York, Harper and Row

Schwarz, D and W Schwarz (1998) *Living Lightly: Travels in Post-Consumer Society*, Bideford, Devon, Green Books

Sclove, Richard (1994) From a workshop at the International Forum on Globalization, San Francisco, publication forthcoming

—— (1995) *Democracy and Technology*, New York, The Guilford Press

Seabrook, Jeremy (1990) *The Myth of the Market: Promises and Illusions*, Bideford, Devon, Green Books

Shabecoff, P (1993) *A Fierce Green Fire: The American Environmental Movement*, New York, Hill and Wang

Shand, Hope (1989) '*Bacillus Thuringiensis*: Industry Frenzy and a Host of Issues', *Journal of Pesticide Reform*, vol 9(1) (Spring)

Sheahan, John (1992) 'Development Dichotomies and Economic Strategy', in Simon Teitel (Ed) (1992), *Towards a New Development Strategy for Latin America*, Washington, DC, Inter-American Development Bank

Shrybman, Steven (1990) 'International Trade and the Environment: An Environmental Assessment of the General Agreement on Tariffs and Trade', *The Ecologist*, vol 20(1)

Shrybman, S (1999) *A Citizen's Guide to the World Trade Organization*, Ottawa and Toronto, The Canadian Centre for Policy Alternatives and James Lorimer and Co

Shultz, Eugene (Ed) (1992) 'The Wonders of the Neem Tree – Revealed' *Science* (17 January)

Sklar, Holly (Ed) (1980) *Trilateralism: The Trilateral Commission and Elite Planning for World Management*, Boston, South End Press

Smit, J and A Ratta (1995) *Urban Agriculture: Neglected Resources for Food, Jobs and Sustainable Cities*, New York, UNDP

Smith, Adam (1978; original publication 1776) *The Wealth of Nations: Books I–III*, Harmondsworth, Middlesex, Penguin

Steinbrecher, Ricarda A (1996) 'From Green to Gene Revolution: the Environmental Risks of Genetically Engineered Crops', *The Ecologist*, vol 26(6) (November/December)

Stokes, G W (1997) Personal communication, National Society of Allotment and Leisure Gardeners, 15 May

Stone, K (1995) *Competing With the Discount Mass Merchandisers*

Stout, B A (1990) *Handbook of Energy for World Agriculture*, New York, Elsevier Applied Science

Summers, Larry, former US Treasury Secretary (1999a) 'The Right Kind of IMF for a Stable Global Financial System', remarks made to the London School of Business, 14 December

Summers, Larry, former US Treasury Secretary (1999b) Testimony before the US Senate Committee on Foreign Relations, Washington, DC, 5 November

Technological Change and Its Impact on Labor in Four Industries (1992) US Department of Labor, Bureau of Labor Statistics Bulletin Z409, October

Technology and Labor in Five Industries (1979) Washington, DC, US Department of Labor, Bureau of Labor Statistics Bulletin 2033

Thurow, Lester (1980) *The Zero Sum Society*, Basic Books

Times Beach Action Group (1995) 'Citizen Inquiry Uncovers Blatant Violation of Environmental Law Surrounding the Proposed Time Beach Incinerator', *St Louis Journalism Review* (November)

Tinbergen, J and R Hueting (1991) 'GNP and Market Prices: Wrong Signals for Sustainable Economic Development that Disguise Environmental Destruction', *Population and Environment*

Tokar, Brian (1992) 'The False Promise of Biotechnology', *Z Magazine* (February)

—— (1995) 'Biotechnology: the Debate Heats Up', *Z Magazine* (June)

—— (1996) 'Biotechnology vs Biodiversity', *Wild Earth*, vol 6(1) (Spring)

—— (1997) *Earth for Sale: Reclaiming Ecology in the Age of Corporate Greenwash*, Boston, South End Press

Tricks, H and A Mandel-Campbell (1999) 'Mexico's Farming Habits Under Pressure from Transgenics', *Financial Times* (12 October)

Union of Concerned Scientists (1995) 'Managing Resistance to Bt', *The Gene Exchange*, vol 6(2/3) (December)

—— (1996) 'Bt Cotton Fails to Control Bollworm', *The Gene Exchange*, vol 7(1) (December)

—— (1996) 'Expanding in New Dimensions: Monsanto and the Food System', *The Gene Exchange*, (December)

—— (1997) 'Unexpected Boll Drop in Glyphosate-Resistant Cotton', *The Gene Exchange* (Fall)

—— (1998) 'EPA Requires Large Refuges', *The Gene Exchange* (Summer)

—— (1998) 'Transgenic Insect-Resistant Crops Harm Beneficial Insects', *The Gene Exchange* (Summer)

—— (1998) 'Mississippi Seed Arbitration Council Rules Against Monsanto', *The Gene Exchange* (Summer)

United Nations Conference on Trade and Development (1992) 'International Monetary and Financial Issues of the Nineties', UNDP

United Nations Environment Programme (1999) *Global Environment Outlook 2000*, London, Earthscan

University of Nottingham Business School (1998) 'Neighbourhood Shopping in the Millennium', Nottingham, University of Nottingham

USDA (1973) *The One Man Farm*, Washington, DC, United States Department of Agriculture

USDA–ARS News Service (1998) 'Cropland Helps Control CO_2 and Ease Greenhouse Effect' (29 September)

US Department of Labor Bureau of Labor Statistics (1979) *Technology and Labor in Five Industries*, Bulletin 2033, Washington, DC

—— (1992) *Technological Change and Its Impact on Labor in Four Industries*, Bulletin Z409 (October), Washington, DC

—— (1994) 'Business Establishment Survey', provided from on-line search, 12 August

US General Accounting Office (1992) 'FDA's Review of Recombinant Bovine Growth Hormone', US GAO (6 August) (GAO/PEMD-92-96)

van Liemt, Gijsbert (1992) *Industry on the Move: Causes and Consequences of International Relocation in the Manufacturing Industry*, Geneva, International Labour Office

—— (1993) 'Labor–Management Bargaining in 1992', *Monthly Labor Review* (January)

van Weperen, W and N Röling (1995) 'Integrated Arable Farming in the Netherlands' in *Hetveranderingsproces* (The Change Process), Wageningen, The Netherlands

Vastine, J R (1999) 'Services 2000: Innovative Approaches to Services Trade Liberalization', Tokyo, USCI (13 May)

Vermont Forest Resources Advisory Council (1996) 'Testimony of Champion Paper Company', Island Pond, Vermont (26 June)

Vidal, John (1999) 'How Monsanto's Mind Was Changed', *The Guardian* (9 October)

Vitousek, PM et al (1986) 'Human Appropriation of the Products of Photosynthesis', *BioScience*, vol 37(4)

Voelcker, Augustus (1893) 'Report on the Improvement of Indian Agriculture', London, Eyre and Spottiswoode

Wallach, Lori and Michelle Sforza (1999) *Whose Trade Organization: Corporate Globalization and the Erosion of Democracy*, Washington, DC, Public Citizen

Wall Street Journal (1993) 'IBM is Overhauling Disk Drive Business, Cutting Jobs, Shifting Production to Asia' (August)

Wall Street Journal (1998) 'Case of Mislabeled Herbicide Results in $225,000 Penalty', *Wall Street Journal* (25 March)

Walton, Sam with John Huey (1992) *Saw Walton, Made in America: My Story*, New York, Doubleday

Warwick, Hugh (1998) 'Agent Orange: the Poisoning of Vietnam', *The Ecologist*, vol 28(5) (September/October)

Washington Post (1999) Reproduced in *Today (Manila)*, 15 November

Waters, John (1993) 'Sacrificing Aer Lingus Jobs on the Altar of Economic Viability', *The Irish Times*, 22 June

Watson, Robert T, Marufu C Zinyowera and Richard H Moss (Eds) (1997) 'Summary for Policymakers', *The Regional Impacts of Climate Change: an Assessment of Vulnerability*

Watzman, Nancy and Christine Triano (1991) *All the Vice President's Men*, Washington, DC, Public Citizen's Congress Watch

Weismann, J (ed) (1995) *City Farmers: Tales from the Field*, New York, Green Thumb

Weismann, J (ed) (1996) *Tales from the Field: Stories by Green Thumb Gardeners*, New York, Green Thumb

White, L H (1987) *Free Banking in Britain*, Cambridge, Cambridge University Press

Wilkerson, Isabel (1995) 'Paradox of '94: Gloomy Voters in Good Times', *New York Times* (31 October)

Wilkes, Alex (1995) 'Prawns, Profits and Protein: Aquaculture and Food Production', *The Ecologist*, vol 25(2–3)

Winner, Langdon (1986) *The Whale and the Reactor*, University of Chicago Press

Wood, A (1994) *North–South Trade, Employment and Inequality: Changing Fortunes in a Skill-Driven World*, Oxford, Oxford University Press

World Bank (1981) *Accelerated Development in Sub-Saharan Africa*, Washington, DC, World Bank

—— (1993) *Global Economic Prospects and the Developing Countries* (1993) Washington, DC, World Bank

—— (1990) 'Mexico: Basic Health Care Project', Staff Appraisal Report (8 November)

—— (1995) *Workers in an Integrating World*, Washington, DC, World Bank

World Development Report (1992) New York, Oxford University Press

World Economic Outlook, October 1997 (1997) Washington, DC, International Monetary Fund

World Health Organization (1980) *The Global Eradication of Small Pox, Final Report of the Global Commission for the Certification of Small Pox Eradication*, Geneva, WHO

World Investment Report 1994 (1994) Geneva, UNCTAD

World Investment Report 1996 (1996) Geneva, UNCTAD

World Investment Report 1998 (1998) Geneva, UNCTAD

World Wide Fund for Nature (1999) 'Environmental Agreements at Risk', WWF Press Release (4 October)

Wysham, Daphne (1999) 'The World Bank: Funding Climate Chaos', *The Ecologist*, vol 29(2), March/April

Ziegler, Bart (1994), 'IBM Is Overhauling Disk Drive Business, Cutting Jobs, Shifting Production to Asia', *Wall Street Journal* (5 August)

Index